WITCHCRAFT AND WELFARE

T0385465

Witchcraft and Welfare

SPIRITUAL CAPITAL

AND THE BUSINESS OF MAGIC

IN MODERN PUERTO RICO

RAQUEL ROMBERG

 University of Texas Press, Austin

Second paperback printing, 2004

Requests for permission to reproduce material from
this work should be sent to Permissions, University
of Texas Press, Box 7819, Austin, TX 78713-7819.
utpress.utexas.edu/index.php/rp-form

♾ The paper used in this book meets the minimum
requirements of ANSI/NISO Z39.48-1992 (R1997)
(Permanence of Paper).

Library of Congress Cataloging-in-Publication Data

Romberg, Raquel.
Witchcraft and welfare : spiritual capital and the
business of magic in modern Puerto Rico /
Raquel Romberg.
        p.   cm.
Includes bibliographical references and index.
ISBN 978-0-292-77126-0

1. Witchcraft—Puerto Rico.   2. Magic—Puerto
Rico.   I. Title.
BF1584.P9 R66   2003
133.4'3'097295—dc21   2002015171

In dear memory of
Andrés Freiman
Victor Freiman
Haydée Trinidad
Tonio Lacén

CONTENTS

As I began my research in Puerto Rico in May 1995, I immediately sensed a predicament: how was I to explain my research interests to people both in and outside academic circles? I found myself using all kinds of circumlocutions, as my topic is problematic in a predominantly Catholic society.[1] Neutral terms such as *religión popular* (popular religion) and *catolicismo popular* (folk Catholicism) soon became my linguistic saviors and, through trial and error, drove me to what seemed a more successful if yet ambiguous way to name my topic, *espiritismo* (Spiritism),[2] a word that gradually became a key that opened many doors. In the archives, in the streets, and at the Universidad de Puerto Rico, people would react immediately to my inquiries, directing me to written sources or volunteering their personal experiences and secondhand stories that involved their neighbors or family members. I noticed that sometimes when I mentioned religión popular it prompted people to recall some sensational or out-of-the-ordinary event usually related to Santería.[3] Santería is a religion based and heavily dependent on a hierarchical system of initiation, and—as part of its foundational belief in the reciprocal exchange of cosmological energies—it includes animal sacrifice. In the public domain Santería is construed as a foreign, often dangerous religion brought to Puerto Rico after Castro's revolution by Cuban exiles who were initiated in the religion as *santeros* and *babalawos* (high-ranking priests). For noninitiates, it was as if Puerto Ricans, by the mere fact of being Catholic—even in the most anticlerical ways—practice a form of religiosity that is "normal" or uneventful, certainly not "weird" or foreign enough to be the object of anthropological study.[4]

To my relief, these linguistic strategies—tiptoeing between religión popular and espiritismo—finally came to an end, thanks to Sara, one of my neighbors in Old San Juan. Because I passed by her open bay window every day on my way to and from the Archivo General, we began exchanging hellos. This is one of the advantages or disadvantages of living on the ground level of a rowhouse apartment in the colonial quarter of a tropical country such as Puerto Rico, where windows are kept open throughout the day and the sidewalks are so narrow that it is almost impossible for a passerby not to see what is going on inside. I soon found myself initiating conversations with Sara, who, having retired from the government several years earlier, would customarily sit by her partially shuttered window, enjoying the breeze and conversing casually with her neighbors. I found myself using these conversations to get closer to her window so I could peek inside her small apartment and see more of the four-foot-tall wooden figure of Archangel Michael hanging on the wall to the left. After my landlord told me that Sara was a well-known, rough, hot-tempered santera, I became even more curious about her unusual sculpture.

Every morning on my way to the archives and every evening returning, I would stop to chat with her for an hour or so, and on the occasions when I was invited in, we would have a cup of coffee or a snack together. I learned that she was not only a Catholic and a santera but an espiritista as well. Actually, she saw herself as an espiritista who had to undergo initiation in Santería as a result of a sacred message given to her in divination during a *bembé*, a drum and dance festival for the *orishas*, or deities, that asserted it was essential for her health to do so. Many espiritistas also undergo initiation in Santería, and even those who do not, incorporate some Santería elements in their worship and spiritual work—except, of course, animal sacrifice. Depending on who is speaking, the latter practice is labeled respectfully or half mockingly "santerismo." But Sara never used this term. After listening to my painfully lengthy explanations about my dissertation plans, Sara became my teacher, instructing me to recognize the nuances of Spiritist mediumship. "There are some [mediums] who learn to control their trances in Scientific Spiritism centers," she told me early on. "In these schools they learn to receive the spirits in more refined, less coarse ways. But there are others who enter a trance in more expressive 'uneducated' ways." Jokingly, I exclaimed, "Then I'm more interested in those 'uneducated' ways!" With relief, Sara responded, "Oh, so you are going to do a doctorate in *brujería*!"[5]

In retrospect, I realize that this was one of the most important lessons I learned at the beginning of my research, one that would enable me to feel like an insider from that moment on. What Sara was telling me was that brujos are espiritistas, powerful enough to have mastered communication not only with "enlightened" spirits but also with those "evil," "dissatisfied," "wild" ones.[6] I had been introduced into the lingo used by insiders. For them, *brujería* is a legitimate term that indexes not only their ability to heal and solve spiritual problems (as I would learn afterward) but also their pride—even arrogance—in their trade, a far cry from the dread and shame of the past.[7] Conscious that the negative stereotypes of brujería stem from a long history of persecution (paralleling that of European witchcraft), *brujos,* or witch-healers,[8] today seem to take pleasure in deliberately using the word *brujería*—a word that hitherto would have sent them to the stake—to label what they do. I have learned from Sara that openly mentioning brujería actually indexes the pride and empowerment of brujos now that alternative healing practices are "in" and the legacy of the Inquisition is "out." After all, their trade has survived centuries of public vilification. Surviving attacks for being rooted in so-called evil, primitive, and superstitious beliefs, their trade is still thriving in a postcapitalist[9] urban society.

For practitioners, that I—a Jewish-born Argentinean university woman—stated publicly my interest in studying brujería was a gesture that made clear my willingness to hear and write about what they had to say in the manner they chose to communicate it—without hiding behind euphemisms. I think it was my way of honoring their pride in what they do. What follows is inspired by this basic attitude, which enabled me to establish a personal relationship with several brujos, especially Haydée, a woman who from the outset defined herself as La Bruja de Villas de Loíza (the Witch-Healer of Villas de Loíza)[10] and with whom I formed an intimate, long-term friendship. As part of her mission—helping people with her "gifts," as she put it—she wanted to divulge what brujería really is. Curiously and contrary to classical anthropological fieldwork entry stories, I did not have to do much to enter into her life and work. She did it for me.

I remember the day I met Haydée, "La Bruja Número Uno de Villas de Loíza" (the Number One Witch-Healer of Villas de Loíza). Tonio, an old, well-known brujo I met by chance in Loíza Aldea, had sent me to her because "she's a positive medium—she has a beautiful, clean *cuadro* [spiritual power]." As he had only her address, no telephone number, I would have to go without first setting up an appointment if I wanted to meet her. I was quite apprehensive about doing this, but I felt the urge to meet her right away. Following his directions, I arrived by car without once having lost my way through highways, roads, and paths. It seemed to me that the house looked exactly like the others in the area, except for the yellow window trim and columns. Like the other houses, Haydée's had an iron fence in front of the garden and the driveway, but it also had an entirely enclosed, attached garage. There was no bell to ring. I felt intimidated and discouraged at finding all the entryways—the iron gate and the main and garage doors—closed and no way to communicate that I was there to see her. It was already midday, and the temperature had risen into the nineties. The street was deserted. I called out a timid "Hello?" No response. Seeing all the shades down, I ventured several more, less timid hellos, all unanswered. I was about to leave when a black woman opened the front door and, without approaching, asked me in a raised voice what I wanted. I uttered the first thing that came stumbling to mind, "I was sent by Tonio to see Haydée," unsure whether she in fact was Haydée. Without a word, she turned and went back inside. When she returned a few minutes later, she told me that Haydée was not working that day because she was ill and suggested that I come back "in a couple of days." I insisted that I had not come to consult with her but just to talk. "I am from Philadelphia," I said, "from the University of Pennsyl. . . ." Again, she left abruptly. When a few minutes later I heard the sound of keys turning, I was relieved. The woman finally opened the iron gate. When we were at the door she said simply, "Pase" (Come in), and silently steered me inside, to Haydée's bedroom.

In a comforting air-conditioned, dimly lit room, I distinguish a woman lying on a twin bed between white satin sheets and lace pillows, her lips painted bright red, her hair up in rollers and neatly covered by a net. She smiles at me. As I begin introducing myself and telling her about my interest in espiritismo, she takes over my explanation as if she already knows my intentions. I feel relieved. I will not have to struggle to articulate my reasons for doing research on such a topic, reasons I still had not figured out myself. Haydée conducts the content and pace of this, our first encounter.

"I'm not feeling well today, you know?" she says. "Spiritual work has its own risks. After days of work from dawn till dusk, this is what happens to me. I always feel ill afterward. So . . . Tonio, El Brujo Número Uno de Loíza, sent you to *me*—La Bruja Número Uno de Villas de Loíza? He's the greatest. He's my spiritual father. My own father used to come to his *veladas* [nighttime spiritual gatherings open to the public]; and I remember, as a kid, coming with my father at 5:00 A.M. to his *altar* [altar room], which was already packed with people who had come from every corner of the island.[11]

"But now Tonio's very old. He begged me to take over his altar, but I can't. I don't have enough time for *my* people. You see me now; I have to rest after so many consultations. They drain me—my matter, I mean. So then I come to my room, turn on my air conditioner, and tell Nina not to let anyone in. But I let you come see me because Tonio has sent you and you say that you want just to talk to me, to make an interview about me."

At this point I find myself asking that always dreaded question: "Would you mind if I use my tape recorder?"

"Sure, anything you want. I want people to know what espiritismo is, what brujería really is. You said you're from which university? I could come with you and tell them what espiritismo really is, as I practice it, nice and clean. But the life of a bruja is not easy, as you see. I suffer a lot. This is why I have my Bible here by my bed. I read, I pray, I cry; this is how I cleanse myself. But I'm happy. I don't have to eat, I just need my spiritual bread.

"Usted tiene un cuadro de Gitana" (You have the cuadro of a Gypsy woman), she tells me as I am about to leave and, without asking if I can, instructs me to come back tomorrow early in the morning to begin my work with her: "Nina will open the gates for you." My spiritual apprenticeship had begun.

Calling me "mi reportera" (my reporter), Haydée would make sure that I documented each and every aspect of her trade, and I recorded every prayer, divination session, and healing ritual. Haydée also allowed me to take unlimited, uncensored photographs of any part of her work and life. From the outset, my role as researcher had been redefined by Haydée as a two-way exchange, whereby she had as much to say as I did. Responding to her wish to record every aspect of her spiritual work, I followed her cues, shooting sometimes frame after frame as if not to lose any important detail. Whereas I initially planned to use these photographs mainly as mnemonic ethnographic devices, I realize now that it was as if she wished to leave a testimony to posterity, like "writing" her own ethnography in picture format. This resulted in two large collections of photographs and tapes: one for her and one for me. Every morning we would go over the new photographs and she would show me the new albums she filled with them.

As an anthropology student I knew how powerful photographs might be in magical manipulations, how people often avoided being photographed for fear that sorcerers would steal their images. But now I am also reminded by Michael Taussig's (1993b) masterful relational account of mimesis and alterity, of the fascination of the white man with the fascination of "natives" being photographed and recorded, and I cannot avoid reflecting on my own fascination with Haydée's fascination, not fear, of being photographed and recorded. Here I was not just allowed but encouraged to play a part in a "mimetological theatre" (Taussig 1993b:191) as a reportera, where I was entrusted with the image and voice of the main character played by Haydée because of her own mimetic self-awareness. She knew that being famous means being photographed. This mimetic excess—the result of "second contact," in Taussig's (1993b:247) words— engulfed me, as a reportera, in the magic of what may be a "third contact." Shooting more pictures than I could ever reproduce, I nonetheless took them. And as with any surplus, I am still puzzled by their secret power as I glance through them, pondering about which will be published and which not.

As I would later learn, Haydée's reputation as a bruja increased in direct proportion to, among other things, the thousand or so photographs I took of her and the nearly one-hundred-ninety-minute cassette recordings I made of her consultations right up to my last day on the island, December 20, 1996.

This book responds to the agenda of brujos who, like Haydée, see their work as socially positive and based on personal sacrifice and are eager to be recognized in the public sphere as legitimate healers and spiritual leaders.[12] Indeed, against the expectations of some readers, this book does not exoticize or ethnicize their work. Further, unlike in other parts of Latin America, in Puerto Rico these vernacular religious practices, as I like to call them, do not defy capitalism or the American way of life. Quite the contrary.

In my attempt to represent as nearly as possible the different faces of brujería in their complexity, I have drawn on several disciplines and scholarly traditions. I also ended up unintentionally producing—in the words of a friend—a work of quite baroque narrative style. I therefore ask the reader to go along with my layered, often discontinuous form of presentation and actively partake in reconnecting the past with the present as it is being laid out bit by bit in each chapter. I am aware that this is quite demanding. Not only do I combine very distinct perspectives—historical and ethnographic-experiential (each with its own disciplinary orders)—I also shift from extremely general depictions to painstakingly minute transcriptions of divination rituals (for example), in which every word and expression is meaningful and in which my emotional reactions might also be intertwined. Furthermore, I allow myself to drift into disparate theoretical ruminations on topics such as nationalism, consumerism, the welfare state, syncretism, magic, and authenticity. I can only promise that, like the topic I examine here—brujería under consumerism and the welfare state—even when not immediately evident, the connections are indeed there.

On March 21, 2000, Haydée died suddenly of a heart attack while on a personal pilgrimage to Santo Domingo—the land of powerful brujos, as she used to say. I now remember what she said to me the first time we met: "Yo nací bruja y bruja moriré; brujería es mi comida. En mi entierro que haya brujos como yo" (I was born a witch-healer, and as a witch-healer I'll die. Witch-healing is my food. At my burial I want witch-healers, as myself, to come). Inspired by Haydée's mission and pride in being a bruja in life and in keeping with her desire to let the world know what brujos really do, I dedicate this book to her and to those goals.

Elkins Park, Pennsylvania
January 31, 2002

ACKNOWLEDGMENTS

When I think of Puerto Rico, I think of the warmth with which people welcomed me and my inquiries. I was fortunate to find brujos and espiritistas who identified with my goals and opened their *altares* and homes, becoming my teachers, friends, and family. I am forever indebted to Tonio Lacén and Haydée Trinidad, both now deceased, for letting me share their lives and work so generously and intensely. My gratitude also goes to Reina Gómez, Lisi, Doris, Arnaldo, Noemí, John, Sara, Lucy, Bolina, Manolo, Marita, Nitza, and Tony, for enriching my understanding of the variety within the commonalities of spiritual work; Basilisa Rodríguez, who became my protector, hostess, mother, guardian angel, and confidante, always waiting to exchange notes with me over a delicious meal together with her lovely daughter and granddaughter; and my neighbor Madi in Old San Juan, for being such a good friend.

At the Centro de Estudios Avanzados de Puerto Rico y el Caribe, where I spent long hours learning about Puerto Rican research, I am indebted to Professor Ricardo Alegría for his warm welcome and guidance and Norma López de Victoria and Carmen Silva Arroyo for facilitating my bibliographic research. José (Chevo) Flores and Hilda Mercedes Chicón at the Archivo General de Puerto Rico were relentless in sorting out and directing me to various archival materials. Thanks also to Else Rodríguez of the Archivo Diocesano de Puerto Rico.

At the Universidad de Puerto Rico, Recinto Río Piedras, I profited greatly from conversations with Professors Ángel (Chuco) Quintero Rivera, Juan Carlos Quintero Rivera, and Jorge Duany, who also invited me to attend a seminar on revolving-door migration at Sagrado Corazón at the very beginning of my research, which was crucial for my conceptualization of the specificity of Puerto Rico; and from the zeal of librarians María Dolores and Josefina Maldonado of the Colección Puertorriqueña and Carmen Lazú and Rosalinda Irrizarry of the Law School.

Special thanks go to Calixta Vélez, a researcher who not only shared her knowledge with me but also drove with me on weekends through the mountains of Puerto Rico to visit remote Spiritist centers and healers; Ricardo Cobián, who graciously made the files of the Centro de Estudios Puertorriqueños available to me; Rafael López Valdés, for his illuminating conversations about Cuban Santería; Soraya Aracena, Rafael Nevárez Nieves, Luis Rivera, and Jorge Mercado, for adding to my knowledge of vernacular religions in Puerto Rico and the rest of the Caribbean; Miriam Ramos, Hanny Gallardo, and Jorge F. Serra of the municipality of San Juan and Norma Monrouzeau of the Departamento de Comercio de Puerto Rico, for going out of their way to answer my inquiries.

At the University of Pennsylvania, I benefited from the support of Ian Lustick and the comments of the participants in the Ford Workshop on States and Identities on my first predissertation fieldwork reports. Regina Bendix and Patricia Smith made excellent suggestions at the early stages of my work, and Greg Urban's incisive questions helped to sharpen my argument. Margaret Mills and Roger Abrahams are longtime inspirational teachers and researchers as well as enthusiastic mentors, whose insights and deconstructionist wit always remind me of my dear anthropology teacher and friend Haim Hazan of Tel Aviv University.

The summer Pre-dissertation Research Grant given by the Ford Workshop on States and Identities and the Penfield Fellowship funded my fieldwork in Puerto Rico and are deeply appreciated. Swarthmore College generously funded the production of the photographs published here. During my Mellon postdoctoral fellowship at the Institute for Global Studies in Culture, Power and History at Johns Hopkins University, my work was influenced considerably by debates on globalization, colonial encounters, and the Caribbean held at the seminars of the institute and the Departments of History and Anthropology. The work of Michel-Rolph Trouillot, Michael Taussig, George Brandon, and Karen McCarthy Brown has been inspiring as well. I also acknowledge warmly the friendship and support of Franklin Knight, the encouraging and helpful comments of Braulio Munoz, the suggestions of Raquel Higgins and Patricia Gherovici, and the vision of Theresa May. Jorge Duany and a reader who chose to remain anonymous made invaluable criticisms, which forced me to make that extra leap when I thought I was at the end of the path. Bernard F. Stehle tirelessly turned my Spanglish into readable English and suggested the subtitle. Thanks to Rita Roling and Sheila Berg for copyediting different stages of the manuscript.

Finally, I am grateful to my spouse, Osvaldo Romberg, for his friendship and unflagging support as well as his perceptive comments at each stage of my work; my children, Joanna, Noa, David, and Victoria, who passionately remind me of what really matters in my life; and my mother, Lily Freiman, for being there and filling in for me over the continents with her undefeatable positive energy and unconditional love.

WITCHCRAFT AND WELFARE

RITUAL ALCHEMY

After centuries of persecution by the Catholic Church in Europe and the Americas and against the predictions of the Enlightenment, brujería has not disappeared with modernity; it has just changed its face. Long defined by the Catholic Church in theological terms as evil and the result of the workings of the devil, brujería has been continuously under attack in the Americas in various degrees of severity since colonization, its practitioners often persecuted and even punished with death. A very different set of attacks was launched since the nineteenth century by a secular ideology that portrayed brujería as an anachronistic remnant of a premodern era. This secular ideology, adopted by most postemancipation Latin American states in the process of state building, advocated the creation of a new world guided by reason, not religion and "superstition" (Borges 2001; Ortiz 1906; Salvatore and Aguirre 2001). As formulated by seventeenth-century philosophers, it proposed to harness what they considered dangerous, negative "passions" through a new "interest"-driven world that would be steered by science, rationality, and technology (Hirschman 1977). Because witchcraft and magic were perceived to epitomize the dangers of "passions," erasing them symbolized, in great measure, one of the quests of modernity (see Foucault 1988).

Although unsuccessful in this endeavor, the Enlightenment has nonetheless left a still-pervasive legacy of an imagined modern world opposed to an equally imagined traditional world. Symbolizing a premodern world of irrationality and tradition, witchcraft and magic have been easily cast as the villains in narratives of progress and development, in particular, vis-à-vis rational moneymaking systems, since (as one of the Enlightenment plots goes) superstition was to fade into religion, and the latter was to be substituted by science in a universal movement away from "error" and toward a modern order of knowledge that would contribute to a more systematic, rational management of society (see Foucault [1966] 1973).

Present-day transformations in most so-called Western modern societies show that this scenario has not been a linear or a totalizing one, to say the least.[1] Instead of a remission of mysticism in favor of secularism and reason, there has been an increasing emergence of charismatic movements, spiritual healing, and transcendental practices in highly industrialized and technological environments (Giddens 1991:207).

Rather than *be* harnessed, Puerto Rican brujería *seems to have* harnessed any local vestiges of Enlightenment agendas to its own advantage, shifting its faces throughout the long history of repressive attacks during the period of colonial Catholicism and the following nation- and state-building periods. In its tortuous trajectory, brujería has continued to reshape its modus operandi—as if driven by a stubborn disregard of orthodoxy—selectively blending elements of such diverse religious worlds as folk Catholicism, African magic and healing, Kardecean Spiritism, and folk Protestantism. Freed under Puerto Rico's U.S. commonwealth status from the legal and religious constraints of Spanish Catholic rule, brujería has taken full advantage of a free material and religious market. Entering a new propitious unorthodox spiritual laissez-faire space, brujería has also commodified its practices in the last twenty years, becoming an emergent local force that works in conjunction with, rather than in opposition to, consumer capitalism and welfare values (see Miller 1995).

In the spirit of Max Weber's *The Protestant Ethic and the Spirit of Capitalism* (1958), brujería has elevated material acquisitiveness and desire for success to a higher moral and spiritual order of aspiration. Indeed, brujos and their followers see material and spiritual progress as well as the attainment of high social status as not only morally legitimate quests but also visible signs of being "blessed" by the spirits, in addition to being a spiritual "calling" and a godly duty. In this space Puerto Rican brujería has become a form of "spiritualized materialism," which does not imply that it has adapted to a capitalist-invested materialism but rather that profit and success (under capitalism) can become infused with an ultimate moral purpose, once spiritual forces are believed to have intervened in achieving these goals.[2]

This general orientation is not unique to Puerto Rico; it has also permeated the practices of other New World Afro-Latin vernacular forms of spiritual healing and magic, such as Haitian Vodou, Cuban Santería, and Brazilian Candomblé and Umbanda. Yet the combination of Afro-Latin forms of religiosity and a pervasively American-based postcapitalist welfare ethos since the late 1970s is what characterizes brujería as a unique Puerto Rican version of spiritualized materialism.

"I don't believe in brujería, but it works"

One might wonder at this point how it is possible for people who participate in and share the values of a modern consumer society to still believe in brujería. On learning that I was investigating brujería, people often asked, "Do *you* believe in it?" I would like to address these complex questions by drawing on words I overheard spoken by a woman while she was waiting for a consultation with a bruja: "I don't believe in brujería, but it works." It is telling that belief in brujería can be presented as if it were totally disconnected from brujería's efficacy—contrary to what brujos usually claim: Faith is the most important thing. Notably, the former position allows one to maintain contradictory justifications for one's choices, especially on the part of many physicians and churchgoers who secretly consult brujos. Objectifying subjective states is a complex if not impossible task, of course. And although skeptics and believers alike might disagree on the causal explanation of an extraordinary occurrence linked to brujería, they are likely to agree that the contested episode had at least occurred. This might explain another common expression: "I don't believe in brujería, but I respect it,"[3] which hints at the mixed wonder and awe such inexplicable events elicit among nonpractitioners, who might—just in case—avoid any contact with these events and recoil in the presence of brujos and people who consult them.

Indeed, the question of belief as it appears in the scholarship on witchcraft and magic and as it is experienced in practices of brujería is a tricky one not only for skeptics and for clients but, as Claude Lévi-Strauss has shown, for practitioners as well. Although brujos define themselves in ways that are not entirely the same as African sorcerers or Asian shamans, the argument Lévi-Strauss makes in "The Sorcerer and His Magic" (1963b) is relevant in more than one way to their practices. He relates cases in which sorcerers became famous and expert practitioners regardless of their belief in the system. Clients' satisfaction with their services was enough to build their fame and power. Focusing on the pragmatic aspects of shamanism, which I also recognize in brujería, Lévi-Strauss adds that a great shaman does not necessarily lose his critical faculties in the process of magical healing; he can even interpret his success in psychological terms: "My intervention was successful," he might think, "because [the sick person] *believed* strongly in his dream about me" (1963b:176; my emphasis); that is, in the shaman's power to intervene on his behalf. Is Lévi-Strauss suggesting that from the shaman's perspective the belief in shamanism might be partial, even nonexistent, and yet be effective? Shifting perspectives, Lévi-Strauss provocatively turns his previous suggestion on its head, arguing that a certain shaman "did not become a great shaman because he cured his patients; he cured his patients because he had become a great shaman" (p. 180). It seems that a client's belief in shamanism or in the shaman's power is sufficient for the magic to work. In comparing sorcerers and psychotherapists, Lévi-Strauss concludes that the former, very much like modern therapists, are able to effect their curing by enacting or performing the beliefs and trust of their clients.

Finding myself employing both of the above perspectives during my research, I often struggled to uphold contradictory types of explanations for my belief in brujería—a struggle often noticed and commented on by my brujo friends, who would say something like "Raquel, you constantly shift [your attitude]" or "Sometimes you analyze and ask too much, and then you just experience the spiritual work as it is." They were right. At times analytic, at times experiential, both modes of explanation alternated throughout my research. Initially during my fieldwork, I did not take belief in brujería as a precondition to studying it, as I could see its effects on others and thus could understand those who did believe in it. When I experienced it myself—albeit vicariously—I realized that there is another form of understanding, which is left out in most scholarly explanations. It is a form of understanding that Edith Turner (1992) and Paul Stoller (1997), among others, have explored and which can be described as a form of feeling, of knowing through the senses rather than through rational thought. Whenever, for instance, I would feel goosebumps, cry, or engage in some sort of "flow" experience (to use a symbolic interactionist term) along with the other participants, I "knew"—even if I could not account for it analytically—that I had "understood" *experientially* what was going on. The following vignette from my fieldnotes addresses my own very personal experience with the question of belief.

As usual, I arrive at Haydée's house at 8:00 A.M. Nina [the housekeeper] opens the gate for me without hesitation, since I have already become part of Haydée's inner circle. But Haydée is not in the house; she went to a doctor's appointment. Nina tells me she'll be back in a while. I see the waiting room full with clients. At about nine o'clock a controller of the local water company calls out from the sidewalk and asks to speak with the owner. He came to turn off the water, he says, because payments had not been made for a few months and warning notices had not been answered. Since Haydée was not home, I decide to go outside to speak to him. I plead with him to wait until Haydée comes home to clarify what seemed a bureaucratic mishandling and to give Haydée a chance to settle the problem. The temperature is over ninety degrees, and thus the prospect of not having water is devastating. I beg him not to cut off the water supply: "You can't leave us without water on such a scorching day." He refuses to leave and is already setting himself to open the street lid of the water meter. Very politely, though unwaveringly, he suggests we start collecting water in the bathtub. I implore him to wait a little longer til Haydée comes back. Seeing that my pleas are unsuccessful, I go to the kitchen and bring him a cold glass of water. As I offer him the glass of water, he looks at me puzzled, almost frightened and rejects it, as if suspecting my sudden hospitality. He refuses even to hold the glass. Smiling, I insist. He then seizes the courage to ask, "Why do you want me to drink *this*?" "It's a burning day," I respond naturally, "and I thought you might be thirsty." He insists, "What's *in* it?" As I am about to answer—"water"—I suddenly realize where this unusual question is coming from. He must have guessed, by peeping at the waiting room, that this was an unusual house, the house of a bruja, and thus must have feared that the glass of water I was offering him was tainted with some magical manipulations. An inexplicable pleasure takes me over as I see the fear on his face and his refusal to even touch the glass. When I get back to the house, Nina—who had heard Haydée on several occasions say that unless I too were a bruja, I would not be so attracted to her work—tells me, "Raquel, you really *are* a bruja! Look, he's folding his instruments and is about to leave. You did it, Raquel!"

Although I had not "believed" in brujería or done anything that would suggest I did, I saw its effect, the "respect" it elicits, contrived though it might have been. Realizing the tangential congruence with the effects of what "real" brujos do, I "felt" nonetheless *as if* I were a bruja, "empowered" by having "spooked" the controller, making him flee. Had I asked this state employee if he believed in brujería, he might have responded with a resounding "No!" and, feeling almost insulted, dismissed the legitimacy of the question. Early on I had learned never to ask this question. As we all know, an immediate answer to what we *believe in* is accessible through what we *say*, but what we actually *do*—and experience—often has little or no relation to what we say we believe in.

Aware of the analytic, methodological, and ethical traps of an inquiry into beliefs—those of the past and in particular those concerned with supernatural forces—I suggest a pragmatic and historical rephrasing of the problem as a viable (albeit partial) way out. Understanding brujería as a set of strategic choices in a particular time and space assumes, following Pierre Bourdieu's (1980) notion of "practice," that such choices are not only the result of individual, subjective perceptions of reality but also are constrained by specific social and institutional alternatives for action—already enmeshed in dynamics of power and inequality—that delimit the possible choices that can be made. In this light, agency is constrained by historically structured social relations and forms of feeling. As Michel de Certeau (1984:xiii) notes, subversion of Spanish religious laws and symbols in the colonial context was often accomplished by native peoples in the New World "not by rejecting or altering them, but by using them with respect to ends and references foreign to the system they had no choice but to accept." In problematizing the nature of beliefs as historically determined, the ambiguity that subverts from within the imposition of one culture on another arises as part of the problem under study. Brujería thus could be imagined, improving Raymond Williams's (1980:40) notion of "residual" culture, as a form of vernacular culture emerging out of the sum of strategic, individual defiant moves made through time in response to imposed official religious laws and symbols. Its intimate relation to official culture, then, would be almost its defining quality. In looking at the practices of brujería in the present, must we still relegate them to the primitive and exotic, or necessarily fear their effects as subversive?

Our Religion, Their Magic

The distinction between religion and magic has forever vexed anthropologists attempting cross-cultural definitions. Even if by now laypeople have become accustomed to purchasing diversity and students of culture have even relativized anthropological relativism, the term "religion" is still infused with legitimacy in opposition to "sect," "magic," "sorcery," "witchcraft," and "shamanism." Apparently vestiges of modernity theories persist in this linguistic usage, presupposing, among other things, the matter-of-fact break between traditional and modern societies in terms of a basic shift from particularistic-magical to universalistic-rational reasoning (just to mention two of these pairs).

If I wished to draw a distinction, it would be based on whether the beliefs and rituals are institutionalized, regardless of which kind of transcendental forces become the objects of worship or manipulation or the types of reasoning behind them. Weber's (1969a:416–417) distinction between religion and sorcery based on their relative systematization and organization is useful. Priests and sorcerers differ, he says, because the first depend for their legitimation on a "fixed doctrine," are equipped with "vocational qualifications," and belong to a hierarchical organization; they are full-time specialists and learn their trade through formal systems of instruction. Sorcerers, in contrast, exert their influence by virtue of often inherited "personal gifts (charisma) made manifest in miracle and revelation," might improve their trade through secret associations, and are self-employed more likely on a part-time basis.

Traditionally studied in relation to the evolution and function of the primitive mind and society (Malinowski 1948), witchcraft and magic also have been intimately tied to family relations and communal societies on the margins of the technological world (Douglas 1970; Evans-Pritchard 1937; Favret-Saada [1977] 1980; Gluckman 1959; Mauss [1950] 1972). For example, Evans-Pritchard's influential work on Azande witchcraft and magic answered the intriguing question for a Western reader about the logic underlying witchcraft, comparing it to the rationalist and empiricist logic of the West. He showed that witchcraft was invoked as a feasible explanation for sudden and random health, work, and family misfortunes—uncertainties the West has been trying to control by means of less than satisfactory statistical models of probability theories. "Certainty" is what witchcraft supplies to questions such as why me? why now?—after empirical explanations for mishaps have been carefully examined.

But besides showing the "rationality" behind witchcraft and magic, Evans-Pritchard—like other British anthropologists—has shown that their flexibility allows for a vast area of ambiguity in the process of determining who is a witch and when to find a certain witch guilty, for example, that is intimately connected to the tensions arising from Azande's social structure and as such are collective representations guiding everyday life actions. A major contribution of British anthropology to the study of witchcraft and magic rests on the assumption that witchcraft and magic are collective representations that relate to social institutions.

Jeanne Favret-Saada ([1977] 1980:9), adding a linguistic approach à la Roman Jakobson, claims that in the French peasant community of Bocage witchcraft actually boils down to "words," as it does not depend solely on the ability to cause evil to someone but on creating a "misunderstanding about who it is that desires the misfortune of the bewitched." Everyone in this community, even the researcher, becomes entangled, because "nobody talks about witchcraft to gain knowledge, but to gain power"; that is, in order to appear as a subject who is "able" (to bewitch or lift bewitchments) and not as "unable" (a potential victim or bewitched person) (p. 11). As part of the collective deception, people talked in front of the ethnographer about witchcraft as a "childish, preposterous and ridiculous set of beliefs," of course setting themselves "apart from it" (p. 16). Intimately related to any claim of bewitchment was the notion of "secrecy," automatically setting the victim apart from "official theories of misfortune" (of the school, the church, and the medical association) and in the realm of "superstition" and "backwardness" (p. 15).

These otherwise tenable propositions—that witchcraft is a collective representation, a social code intimately related to the social structure, and a form of exchange that mediates interpersonal conflicts that might arise from it—are hardly applicable to a modern urban context in their totality, in which individuals might share more than one set of collective representations and might be at the center of nonoverlapping social institutions. In fact, the limits of anthropological studies that have looked at witchcraft in relatively small face-to-face communities for the study of contemporary urban realities are evident. In stressing the functional role of witchcraft among small groups through the trope of the "pressure valve," for instance, these studies not only assert its homeostatic role, but also its disconnection—temporally and spatially—from modern Western realities and influences. Although synchronic explanations of witchcraft and magic in small groups have elucidated basic sociocultural mechanisms, they cannot account for more complex, heterogeneous social spaces, such as the ones discussed in this book.

In relating Puerto Rican Spiritism to large-scale urban societies, previous research (conducted mostly on the mainland) has presupposed the inherent marginality of mediums from mainstream society while portraying their (ethnically fashioned) practices as viable, positive parallels to mainstream psychiatry. Informed essentially by functionalist theories and advancing a mentalist and universalistic approach, most of this research has equated the therapeutic role of the modern psychiatrist with that of the Spiritist medium (Lewis-Fernández 1986; Núñez Molina 1987), insofar as both promote their clients' well-being and adaptive behavior. Yet most of it has portrayed the move of mediums from espiritismo to brujería as dysfunctional and doomed to disintegrate their social relations.[4] Although striking in their own ways, these frameworks cannot adequately encompass the complex world in which urban vernacular religions, in general (Orsi 1999) and unorthodox forms of Spiritism, *santerismo* and brujería, in particular, operate today. This is a world in which distant peoples, commodities, and desires circulate through new communication and technological systems. As Arjun Appadurai (1990, 1996) claims, social relations in today's urban settings are no longer confined to the nuclear or extended family or dominated solely by face-to-face encounters but rather are swayed by complex, long-distance networks of mediated relations and desires. Brujería practices are a part of this world.[5]

Recent anthropological studies of witchcraft and magic in Europe, Latin America, and Africa have suggested their linkage to modernity.[6] In this tradition, historical anthropologists studying contemporary decolonized societies reinsert witchcraft and magic in discourses of modernity, mainly as local practices that have arisen typically as forms of resistance to Western colonial and modernization processes.

In a relational account of terror and healing, Taussig (1987) challenges the view of witchcraft and magic as closed, timeless systems of belief, showing that they have emerged as a result of a joint venture tying the imaginings and fictions of the colonizers to those of the colonized. Indeed, for Taussig, Evans-Pritchard's attempt to offer Western ears a clear-cut rationalization of witchcraft as a closed system is comforting but misleading. "Doubtless this 'it' we call magic, like calling into an echoing abyss, existed in third-world countries before European colonization. But surely this 'it' from that point on contained as a constitutive force the power of colonial differentiation such that magic became a gathering point of Otherness in a series of racial and class differentiations embedded in the distinctions made between Church and magic, and science and magic" (Taussig 1987:465). In this line of inquiry, Joan Dayan (1995) and Sidney Mintz and Michel-Rolph Trouillot (1995) have examined the turbulence of Haitian political history as inseparable from the tribulations of Vodou, its wars, gods, and fictions. Some studies suggest that the feared Haitian "zombie" and West Indian Obeah-man are Creole creations that owe more to the nightmares of slavery than to the survival of African beliefs in the Caribbean (e.g., Fernández Olmos and Paravisini-Gebert 1996).

Indigenous forms of witchcraft and magic are depicted as Creole forms of empowerment that not only have emerged out of relations of inequality in colonial times (Mintz and Price 1976) but also have been mobilized in sustaining the elusive spirit-power of postindependence states (Taussig 1997). In other works, witchcraft appears as a cultural idiom intrinsically tied to colonial systems of inequality that has the potential to destabilize the political and economic orders of decolonized nations at the local and regional levels (e.g., Comaroff and Comaroff 1993). Peter Geschiere ([1995] 1997, 1998) has noted that on the African continent, for instance, economic and political powers under modernity are inherently connected to local witchcraft practices. "Witchcraft . . . continues to be a key element in discourses of power, despite modern processes of change (or perhaps because of them), thereby creating new forms of domination and resistance" (Geschiere [1995] 1997:7–8). Here witchcraft appears to be a form of political action—a predominantly subversive local idiom that engages in a contestation of colonial and postcolonial forces.[7] Also, Adeline Masquelier (1993) shows that witchcraft has become a local form of resistance to nonindigenous forms of trade relations in a community; and Mark Auslander (1993) argues that witchcraft accusations reflect the lack of equitable forms of integration of members of a community into a market economy.

Interestingly, historians of European witchcraft have traditionally related witchcraft and magic to the modern world in a diachronic mode, stressing the connection of witch-hunts to larger and more complex political and economic realities, such as the state and the church.[8] Yet, equipped with economic and political models, historians have portrayed witchcraft and magic as basically class- and gender-motivated practices that subvert the modern state. Thus, although asserting a temporal connection between modernity and the practices of witchcraft and magic rectified the otherwise misleading perception that the latter belonged exclusively to the world of the "primitive," it also diminished them by foregrounding mainly their subversive character. Witchcraft and magic were portrayed as antithetical to the social order.[9]

Is it possible, instead, to envision brujería not only as destabilizing or contesting modernity but also as boosting, albeit unexpectedly and inconspicuously, postcapitalist societies characterized—in the case of Puerto Rico—as modern colonies or by welfare, consumer, and transnational relations?[10] In this book I show that while spatial- and temporal-distancing assumptions are still directing much of today's scholarly and lay perceptions, witchcraft and magic are not as absent from modern economic circuits and political developments as assumed. The existence of plural modernities suggests that "interests" do not necessarily harness "passions" (cf. Hirschman 1977) and that interests and passions are not necessarily irreconcilable. The assumed rationality and homogenization necessary for the birth of modern systems of government and economic development has not hindered the formation of hybrid forms of political economy and culture. For instance, feudal societies might operate under capitalist systems, and preindustrial societies might be involved in late-modern urbanization processes. Likewise, rural-based vernacular religious practices such as Vodou might adapt their myths and rituals to fit the transnational urban lifestyles of Haitians living in megacities such as New York (see K. M. Brown 1991, 1995b, 1999).

Indeed, brujería as practiced in urban Puerto Rico shows the vernacular co-optation of discourses of interest and passions, of consumerism and spirituality, commodity fetishism and morality, and welfare capitalism and magic. Rather than contest the state or the social order, brujería practices help to reproduce it, not only through holistic and individualized types of intervention, but also by endorsing mainstream social values in redirecting their clients' actions. Further, brujería might even be helping to prevent social discontent, deviance, and unrest and be working as an off-the-record branch of the welfare system (see chaps. 7, 8).

Neither a purely surrogate psychological treatment nor a form of resistance, Puerto Rican brujería has become an invisible yet active partner of consumerism and welfare, speaking in their idiom as well as engaging with them. In response to interlacing global flows of ideas and commodities and by way of strategic and unorthodox elaborations, brujos articulate capitalist and welfare values with the ethos of the world of spirits in order to promote their clients' prosperity. In this sense, brujos, far from being an endangered species or subversive, are active participants in a postcapitalist world—a world guided not only by capitalist modes of production but also by the sensuous insatiable consumption of lifestyles and self-images.

Acquisitiveness and Self-Identity

How can brujería live and thrive in a consumer society that is mediated by globalization or social relations characterized by "time–space distanciation" (Giddens 1991:21)? The choices of lifestyle offered by consumerism in conditions of "high modernity" offer a more or less integral set of practices that an individual "is forced" to embrace, "not only because such practices fulfill utilitarian needs, but because they give material form to a particular narrative of self-identity" (Giddens 1991:81).

Acquisitiveness as an endless process of materialization satisfies at one and the same time the possibility of enhancing and renewing one's self according to ever-changing narratives of self-identity and lifestyles. The materiality of these lifestyles acquires yet an added value within brujería. If achieved, material success becomes a marker of one's *bendiciones*, or spiritual powers; and if it is yet to be achieved, it becomes an endless motivational force that guides personal and social choices. Taussig (1993a:217), reflecting on the materiality and ghostliness of state fetishism, suggests, "Fetishism elucidates a certain quality of ghostliness in objects in the modern world and an uncertain fluctuation between thinghood and spirit" (see also Taussig 1992). If both self and commodities become entangled in fetishist relations, one's personal power becomes materialized and desired objects become spiritualized. Having acquired and at the same time confounded their assumed qualities, the need to perceive one's personal power materialized in objects destabilizes both the self and the objects that are meant to embody it.

Brujería thereby operates in a murky ground, articulating the desires and frustrations akin to high modernity by foregrounding the centrality of material consumption simultaneously as proof, reflection, and anticipation of one's personal power. And yet bendiciones of the thinghood sort can be targeted and reached separate from the spiritual sort. For witch-healers are in an advantageous position: they are the masters of correspondences. Comaroff and Comaroff (1993:xxix) recognize this, arguing that "[w]itches . . . embody all the contradictions of the experience of modernity itself, of its inescapable enticements, its self-consuming passions, its discriminatory tactics, its devastating social costs."

This wedding of the rhetoric of commerce and magic makes sense. Occult magical and other wealth systems have accumulated around the "marketplace" over a long period.[11] Witches, like traders, prosper best not in the bush but in centers of commerce where the surplus of productive energies can be exchanged between people and the spirits. Just as the trader has by tradition maneuvered open and hidden agendas, so too have witches. Their trade partners include clients, followers, protective spirits, and the dead; and their forms of exchange resemble commercial transactions in which goods and information are paid for with propitiatory rituals and prayers.

But competition and desire for money and luxury items do not fully explain the belief in spirits or the elaborate rituals created to communicate and plead with them. Taussig's (1993a:232) convincing proposition of the fetish as "spiritually material" and "materialistically spiritual" fits well with the idea of bendiciones, since the double bind of bendiciones, their materiality and spirituality, allows for a form of "being blessed" that depends on concrete physicality and yet could well exist outside any concrete form as a potential force ready to be materialized at any time—like the Golem. But if the potential for materialization is forgotten in the frenzy of acquisitiveness, instead of being a manifestation of spiritual power, it can be mistaken for what it is supposed to index. When the representation of bendiciones or the materialization of bendiciones takes over that which it supposes to be a sign of, "[t]he representation acquires not just the power of the represented but power over it as well" (Taussig 1993a:235).

While consumerism is essential in giving material form to the particular narrative of self-identity defined in no small measure by the idea of bendiciones, the negative effects or vices of consumerism—as envisioned by critical theorists of consumerism and the culture of modernity—do not necessarily carry over to the practices of brujería. Strangely, against the tropes of loss and spiritual maelstrom projected by critics of the culture industry and capitalist consumption, brujería cannot be characterized by the "disembedding" of social relations and a disregard for social responsibility (Giddens 1991). Intimately associated with being blessed by the spirits, consumerism fits rather into a morally grounded personal and civil local ethos. As a result of specific circumstances that I examine later, this morally grounded consumerist ethos constitutes material and spiritual well-being as interdependent and as such does not create—in cultural critique lingo—an "alienated individuation." On the contrary, the ability to consume newer lifestyles in the present is perceived as a reward, as the fruit of having enjoyed propitious worldly and otherworldly relationships. Herein lies also the explanation for the lack of overt antiestablishment and apparently uncritical market ideology driving brujería practices.

I agree with Peter Beyer's (1990:373) view of the new role of religion in a globalizing society—that contrary to the secularization and privatization thesis inherent in theories of modernity, the privatization of religion can provide "a fertile ground for the renewed public influence of religion" and become a source for collective obligation. Beyer's thesis incorporates the idea that under globalization religion will eventually become more involved in the public sphere by gaining access to public and private services, as do individual health professionals, business experts, and political leaders.

Through a conflation of spiritual and social responsibility to others, Puerto Rican brujería does answer to this agenda, but it does so outside an institutional setting. Stemming from—what I will persistently argue—its unique, noninstitutional way of operating, it offers an unorthodox, individualistic form of spiritual guidance and religiosity in a plural society in which choices are strongly constrained by some form of organized system. Guided by the Spiritist ethos, which foregrounds personal civic responsibility, among other things, and the preeminence of spiritual laws and justice, brujos manage to muster—for a modest fee of $10 to $20 per consultation, compared to $60 to $120 charged by physicians, lawyers, and psychologists—diverse functions commonly held by public and private institutions in addressing their clients' practical and moral problems.

Extending the area of influence and control beyond the management of spirits and saints, brujos develop their expertise so as to encompass those areas of social life that hitherto had been under the control of state and commercial agents. Knowledge and control over the transcendental world is now complemented with knowledge and control of market and civic forces. As a result, brujos have become spiritual entrepreneurs, expanding their services to include those traditionally assigned not only to psychologists and social workers but also to officials of the labor, justice, and public health systems. Taking advantage of new economic opportunities and welfare regulations, brujos can answer the emotional, economic, and spiritual needs of their clients and at times even become adjudicators between man-made laws and Spiritist ethics. In essential ways they redefine the meaning of material acquisitiveness and success, reinterpret the written law, and co-opt bureaucratic systems. And yet brujos do not subvert these systems. Operating within and at the same time without, they irreverently poach the liberal and religious professions, state and commercial agencies, with their own visions and envisionings.

Taussig (1999:107) reminds us that "the labor of the negative" is essential to the "magical power that converts the negative into being." The power of negation, especially as it has shaped the practices of brujos in opposition to church and state, is still relevant today. But another important ever-mentioned aspect of their labor lies in positive action, when key mainstream values and the gestures of powerful agents of society are irreverently incorporated and adapted to their rituals and goals.

Ritual Alchemy, History, Mimesis, and Globalization

The idea that the defining quality of ritual stems from its fixed, structured, and repetitive nature has been challenged by scholars such as Stanley J. Tambiah (1970, 1985) and John D. Kelly and Martha Kaplan (1990), who stress its pragmatic and innovative qualities. Rather than ask what specific rituals mean for the observer, I propose to ask what they do, or, in Talal Asad's (1983) terms, to look at their instrumentality. In this book I examine brujería rituals as a set of ongoing processes of continuity and transformation, fusing official and vernacular forms of worship, the past and the present, economic and transcendental notions of success and progress, and so forth. Moreover, as unfolding social dramas, its rituals both reflect and index past and current processes in society—their structure, gestures, values, and contradictions.

Along this line, Comaroff and Comaroff (1993:xxii) portray ritual experts as creative figures who, along with prophets and poets, manipulate, change, and recombine signs through the positioning, contrast, redundancy, and figurative play of images, or draw on the "metaforces" of poetic forms—in Michael Silverstein's apt coinage (cited in Comaroff and Comaroff 1993:xxi). Looking more closely at the nature of the metaforces of ritual innovation, it is mainly through mimesis that this creativity comes to life. It is by means of the mechanism of imitation or "creative imitation" (Abrahams n.d.) that vernacular religious practices speak both to and within global discourses. In this context mimesis loses some of its commonly attributed negative aspects, such as lack of spontaneity, charisma, or sincerity, and acquires a magical effect. I argue in chapters 4 and 5, following James Frazer's well-known account of the technologies of magic, that brujos empower their rituals by imitating the symbols and gestures of powerful others (see also Romberg 1999a, 1999c). Essential to the dynamics of ritual change, then, is the recognition of powerful others and the appropriation of their symbols (Stoller 1997; Taussig 1987, 1993b, 1997).[12] Embedded in this view is a theory of identity and alterity that explores rituals "as expressions of relations between historically specific selves and others" (Kelly and Kaplan 1990:132).

It is through this framework that I tackle, for instance, an otherwise incongruous practice found in brujería rituals: brujos incorporate the liturgical symbols, words, and paraphernalia of Catholicism and adopt the role and demeanor of priests. This practice suggests, on the one hand, the continual pervasiveness of a Catholic ethos in Puerto Rico; and, on the other, the ambivalent attitude of brujos toward Catholicism. It would be historically naive to gloss over the long-term effect of Catholicism and Christianity in Puerto Rico, as they were used as folk synonyms for personhood and civility. After centuries of persecution by the church and in spite of an essentially antiecclesiastical attitude toward religion, Puerto Rican brujos still find the need to appropriate its symbols and gestures, albeit often for impious purposes. It seems that through the imitation of Catholic gestures and signs they can seize on the transcendental powers embodied in the church and transfer them by means of a "rupture and revenge of signification" (Taussig 1987:5) to their own practices. For example, slaves had not simply become Christians; rather, out of their experience of enslavement in the Americas they fashioned a "Christianity" to fit their own needs (Glazier 1996:422). Brujería has always managed to find ways to bypass the constraints of economic systems or the imposition of a disempowering social order by taking advantage of structural possibilities, such as demographic isolation or the ambiguity of laws or symbols, or by appropriating the very symbols that were meant to marginalize it.

Recent theories of global culture and society provide an array of outlooks and frames for the analysis of these issues. Some theories stress the uniqueness of globalization processes in terms of the pervasive spatial interconnectedness created by world economic systems, the technological revolution, or the creation of a global culture (Featherstone 1990; Featherstone, Lash, and Robertson 1995; Hinkson 1990). Other theories stress the temporal continuity and cumulative effects of globalization on local sociocultural structures as they were constituted by colonial encounters and deployed by postcolonial displacements (Bhabha 1990; Clifford 1994; Hall and du Gay 1996).

While academic and lay interest in globalization may seem novel, not so its effects since ancient times, as Eric Wolf has shown in his *Europe and the People without History* (1982). Taking this wide definition of globalization in temporal and spatial terms, I show how the practices of brujería in Puerto Rico have been affected not only by waves of globalizing discourses and ideas such as Catholicism and consumerism but also by actual global movements of people and goods from Africa, the Americas, the Caribbean, and Europe since colonial times.

Catholicism and slavery were the initial globalizing forces to affect the island. But the totalizing worlds that these institutions had aimed to create from the very beginning of colonization proved in the end to be failed projects. Instead, the island—a "sociedad cimarrona" (Quintero Rivera 1995)—produced its own forms of social and cultural maroonage that shaped indigenous versions of vernacular Catholicism and social systems of feeling and behaving. Ramón Grosfoguel, Frances Negrón-Muntaner, and Chloe Georas (1997:30-31) aptly use the folk term *jaibería* (astuteness) to denote a wide range of popular practices of resistance to and negotiation with colonialism, "of taking dominant discourse literally in order to subvert it for one's purpose, of doing whatever one sees fit not as a head-on collision . . . but a bit under the table." Demographic and ideational in nature, these local responses of jaibería to globalizing forces succeeded in hindering the formation of a homogeneous Catholic society and a passive, acculturated slave and free-labor peasantry (see chap. 1).

By the mid-nineteenth century a second wave of globalizing discourses made its appearance on the island. This time it was the Creole elite who chose to embrace these new cosmopolitan, nationalist discourses, appropriating and transforming them in a way that would fit their anti-Spanish, pro-independence agendas. In this context, Kardecean Spiritism was embraced by the elite in fashioning new progressive national and civic identities against Spanish hegemony (see chap. 2).[13] A third set of globalizing ideas that would resonate among the local, progressive elite was introduced with the U.S. invasion of Puerto Rico in 1898 (also discussed in chap. 2), transforming into what could be best characterized as the "megarhetoric of developmental modernization" (Appadurai 1996:10). Regardless of their differences in political affiliation, the prospect of rationalizing and democratizing the state apparatus was appealing to a group of Puerto Rican intellectuals and professionals who from the early 1920s took an active role in the "Americanization" process (see Flores 1993).

Yet Americanization, as a comprehensive transformation of Puerto Rican society and culture, which included in its initial phases the adoption of English as the sole language of instruction, failed. As Jan Nederveen Pieterse (1995) has suggested, globalization is in fact a process of hybridization. Indeed, American images of democracy, freedom, and welfare and capitalist forms of production and consumption were translated and reinterpreted by local institutions and interest groups. Appadurai (1996:10) aptly terms such processes "vernacular globalization." At one side of this process, brujería became a symbol of the past—a past this Creole profes-

sional elite as well as the U.S. colonial government had tried to erase—
and thus it became the locus for a more general attack against tradition.
At the other side, brujos reacted to American-based discourses indirectly,
by confronting the political elites' attack on their practices, and directly,
by incorporating, not before they "punctuated, interrogated, and domes-
ticated" (Appadurai 1996:10), the American ethos in their healing and
magic techniques.

A fourth global wave that shaped the practices of brujería began
roughly in the 1980s and was essentially economic (see chaps. 3, 6). Aided
by a global market, the circulation of ritual goods from the Caribbean,
Latin America, the United States, and Asia has increased considerably
what is available in *botánicas* (stores that sell religious paraphernalia, medicinal and magical herbs, and flowers) on the island.[14] Indeed, the intense
intra-Caribbean circulation of ritual specialists—especially from Castro's
Cuba in the 1960s and more recently from the Dominican Republic—
and the availability of ritual commodities by large mainland distribution
companies have contributed visibly to the internal dynamism of Puerto
Rican brujería, which has become more and more a form of transnational
vernacular religious practice.[15]

The practices of brujería have also been affected by an increasing flow
of Caribbean immigrants and a "commuter migration" between the island
and the U.S. mainland. Further, the influx of international immigrants
to major mainland cities has facilitated the encounter of Puerto Rican
ritual specialists with specialists from other parts of the world, yielding
incomparable opportunities for mutual learning and exchange (see Chambers 1994). The phenomenon of an increasing number of Haitian, Cuban,
Dominican, Puerto Rican, and other Caribbean immigrants living in New
York City, Miami, Los Angeles, and other urban centers in the United
States and Canada has given a more cosmopolitan, transethnic dimension
to Afro-Latin religions (Cornelius 1992; Laguerre 1987). In his work on
the adaptation of Haitians to life in the United States, Michel S. Laguerre
(1984) mentions the "cross-fertilization" and syncretism between Mesa
Blanca, Santería, and Vodou in New York City. He shows, on the one
hand, that Haitians in New York introduce Cuban, Puerto Rican, and
Dominican acquaintances to Vodou healers, and, on the other, that some
Haitians consult Spanish-speaking healers (1984:131).

The current transnational circulation of people and commodification
of religious goods has exponentially enlarged the already transnational
nature of Puerto Rico's Spanish colonial past and commonwealth status

since 1952. Specifically in regard to the development of brujería practices in the last century, especially since the early 1900s, the uncommon marriage between Spanish Catholicism and North American Protestantism has yielded a complex set of values and attitudes. Indeed, adding the Protestant and political individualist ethos to the equation widened, albeit unwillingly, the space for vernacular religious choice and creativity. A laissez-faire orientation—in particular, the value embedded in free choice, both in economic and in cultural terms—helped to legitimate in the eyes of some Puerto Ricans those vernacular practices that were hitherto marginalized by the Catholic and Protestant churches (see chap. 6). Apparently, the will to widen one's spiritual choices, in keeping with the high value attached to individualism, was greater than the residual fears that lingered from the Catholic past and those more recently instilled by Protestant churches.

Ritual Alchemy and a Baroque Ethnography

I'm in the altar of Haydée, who lives in a small town on the outskirts of San Juan. It is the first time I have ever entered her altar. She shows me around, pointing out and explaining, shelf by shelf, the various ritual objects and their significance, her way, I sense, of introducing herself and her trade to me.

"My rosary is the one of San Judas Tadeo, that one over there is San Aparicio el Beato, he helps find lost things; this is Papá Candelo—this saint deals with the dead, he's a *palero*. With his help, if you put your enemies in the cauldron he makes them disappear, but you have to do it outside the altar. Here is the Mano Poderosa; a santera [one who is initiated in Santería] gave it to me after I helped her with a magic work. She came to me although I told her I don't deal with Santería. She came to me because a *doctor* cannot cure herself. After she saw the results of my magic, on a Mother's Day she brought me the Mano Poderosa. Outside, in the niche, I have the Milagrosa, and these two are the Marta la Dominadora; they help dominate your enemies. That one is the Madama, she's a coquette like me. Then, the Buddha for good luck, San Lázaro, El Niño de Atocha, and this is my Papá Dios. On this side is La Virgen del Perpetuo Socorro, La Virgen Guadalupana [the Virgin of Guadalupe]. I found this one in a well—she is the saint of the Mexicans. This is the Cross, the one Papá Dios was nailed on."

The beeper on Haydée's dress interrupts this mini tour. Immediately she takes her cell phone and speaks with a client who is in need of urgent

help. I realize that the figurines on the shelves are not simply objects but her close companions, her spiritual entities; and the tour, a performance of her spiritual powers. We continue the tour, moving into the living room, where she has an additional shrine—a public one.

In her altar, African, Catholic, and Spiritist ritual objects stand side by side, erasing any hierarchical order in which their respective cosmologies might have been couched outside brujería. Haydée, a ritual expert, manifested her intimate, personal relationship with a host of Catholic saints, African orishas, Spiritist entities, and Asian deities. It seemed that in enacting the collapse of time and space distinctions between these iconically unrelated traditions, she had also collapsed, at a conceptual level, the historically constituted boundaries between sacred and evil, primitive and modern, religion and magic, and extraordinary and ordinary. In a concrete manner, this collapse is naturalized in the altar, confounding any neat distinctions we outsiders have learned to expect.

The transnational circulation of spiritual commodities offers yet another resource available for brujos and clients in achieving personal empowerment. Collapsing time and national boundaries, the array of ritual objects and procedures supplied by global markets considerably enlarges the choice of spirits, potions, and rituals. In Puerto Rico ritual innovation is enhanced further by the convergence of Asian ritual paraphernalia and

I.1
La Mano Poderosa

I.2
Haydée calling
a client on her
cell phone

Afro-Latin and indigenous forms of trance, exorcism, music, and dance. The unorthodox, syncretic, and transnational nature of these practices compel an essential shift in the perception of brujería—one that takes account of its affinity with mainstream forms of exchange and values. Indeed, novelty has become an ongoing tradition in brujería. Following the logic of capitalist consumer expansion and its intimate connection to narratives of self-identity, new products and rituals are welcomed signs of progress and improvement that help to increase one's bendiciones (see chaps. 3, 4, 6).

In looking at present practices of brujería in Puerto Rico, one can see an archaeology of these reelaborations come to life through its shifting histories, revealing nodal points of past reelaborations of faith. Ritual bits and pieces that had proved successful in attracting spiritual power during previous times of persecution resurface today in gestures or words with renewed meaning. Through the workings of ritual alchemy, some ritual elements merge into totally new forms while others remain as stubborn outgrowths appearing again and again through time. For instance, in looking at altares, listening to practitioners, and participating in brujería rituals, one senses both the merging and the disruption of past and present Catholic, African, and indigenous symbolic elements with contemporary mass-produced signs. The agglomeration of these distinct signs embodies an ongoing meaning-making force that engulfs the past in the present and transcends spatial boundaries.

By means of an unusual alchemy, brujos can at once be fervent Catholics, be possessed by African deities, use New Age lingo, follow the French Spiritist tradition of the dead, put on a pointed black witch hat during Halloween, and act as welfare state agents. In the pages that follow, this ritual alchemy is brought to life through an in-depth anthropological study that flashes back and forth in history, offering a heretofore never attempted account of the personal and intimate side of the workings of brujos in urban Puerto Rico. This book discloses the intricate ways in which trance, dance, magic, and healing practices are combined with expertise in the workings of the modern welfare state, and with the desires of a consumer society, to provide a holistic answer to the problems affecting modern urban dwellers. After being persecuted as heretics in colonial times and viewed as charlatans on the margins of society during the era of nation building, brujos have reinvented themselves as spiritual entrepreneurs. As such and infused by the power of Afro-Latin spirits and by personal knowledge about American corporate and federal systems, they are able to encourage their clients to take advantage of new economic opportunities as they may arise and to solve their personal and professional problems.

The irreverent collapse of categories that occurs when images and beliefs coalesce in ad hoc formations is almost the defining quality of vernacular religious practices in general and of brujería in particular. Helped by the lack of a theological center that would dogmatically institutionalize relations to the sacred, vernacular rituals involve innovative meaning-making processes that mediate quite unusual political, social, and economic negotiations with the transcendental.

The signs and gestures of world economic systems and globalizing discourses—such as Catholicism, nationalism, and modernity—have been incorporated along with their ideological baggages in various ways in the practices of brujería. Ritual practices thus offer a window into the workings of history. They provide a special space and time in which colonial—or nationalist—embodied memories can be enacted and the contradictions brought by globalizing discourses can be locally reelaborated. Yet beyond being repositories of past reactions to globalization processes, vernacular religions also articulate more current local responses to and qualms about global forces that affect the lives of individuals on a daily basis. In this respect, the rituals of vernacular religions are always *in the making*.

When I saw the ease with which people integrated historically opposed religions in their worship and how they shifted their religious memberships without necessarily changing their faith, I felt compelled to reexamine basic Western notions of the coherent self. It was as if the very idea of continuity at the level of religious identity and the assumed integrity of the self no longer seemed to hold real significance for brujería. This presented a methodological and analytic challenge: How can one study the processes of change in vernacular religions in their unpredictable temporal and spatial discontinuity and patchiness?

The structure of my book reflects this quandary in more than one way. In the process of conjoining a historical perspective with my ethnographic experiences, I recognized how much at odds they were, analytically and methodologically, but how exceedingly entwined they were empirically (see Roseberry 1989). I sought the past to better understand the present. This is why in Part One I explore three different histories of brujería and present each of its facets as emerging in response to broader political, religious, economic, and state discourses (see Asad 1983, 1988). Although presented separately for the sake of clarity, the periods or layers overlap.

Moreover, traces of each period appear as outgrowths in practices today, making history even more relevant as it relates to selected practices in the present. Part Two develops the entrepreneurial aspect of brujería, where the relevance of examining the histories of brujería becomes apparent as symbols and gestures of previous periods keep reappearing in the present. In trying to represent in writing these overlapping yet often discontinuous layers, my narrative has become, in the words of a good friend quoted earlier, "quite baroque." Recognizing the conceptual rather than the aesthetic aspects of this remark, I suggest the following road map as one possible way in which these layers may be uncovered or recovered.

The first layer of the history of brujería is developed in chapter 1. It covers the period of the Spanish Catholic state (1502–1860), when the administration of the state was legitimized by religion and brujos were persecuted as heretics. It was a period when a cosmic-based religioethical rhetoric, spoken as emanating directly from God, supplied the moral basis for their persecution and annihilation, effected by the Inquisition.

Chapter 2 traces the emergence of cosmopolitan and nationalist discourses during and after the 1860s, as well as the Americanization process that would be initiated with the 1898 invasion of the island and its subsequent annexation. These discourses are discussed vis-à-vis the belief in spirits as codified by Allan Kardec and their relation to the construction of a national and civil identity. With the end of Spanish rule and the subsequent decreasing influence of the church, science, rationality, and technology replaced religion and faith as the pillars on which the state apparatus would be erected. In this new space (1898–1970s) brujos were no longer heretics but began to be vilified by the medical and legal apparatuses as well as the media as social parasites or charlatans. The medical establishment, mainly its educational programs—guided by a rhetoric of progress—took over the "administration of the well-being of society" and launched a variety of "hygienic" programs to fight against "social ills." These included practices labeled in the public sphere as folklore, magic, and superstition and alleged to be, in the medicoeducational rhetoric of the state, "contagious" among the "less educated and less fortunate elements of society."

Chapter 3 discusses the transnational commodification of the spiritual world (1980s–present), which has been increasing exponentially as a result of the collusion of Puerto Rico in both Spanish Catholic and American neoliberal rule. Specifically, this chapter explores the extraordinary marriage between a Spanish Catholic and a Protestant–North American reli-

gious ethos with regard to the complex sets of values and institutionalized practices that it has yielded. Unlike previous periods, this new layer
is marked by a total lack of specific state provisions against brujería (unless practitioners violate tax regulations, civil rights, or private property).
In this economic and spiritual laissez-faire space, marked by the transnational circulation of spiritual commodities and people, brujos operate as
spiritual entrepreneurs.

The entrepreneurial aspect of brujería is the focus of Part Two. The
five chapters in this part, based on my close ethnographic work with a
number of brujos and their clients, show various ways in which brujería
fuses spiritual and worldly notions of success. I draw more heavily on the
daily practices of Haydée since it was she who allowed me to tape record
and photograph each aspect of her work and convinced her clients to let
me take part in their private consultation and rituals. The main argument
linking these chapters is that in the eyes of brujos and their clients, assets in the spiritual world are there to be acquired, accumulated, and exchanged for prosperity in this world: the more riches in the former, the
more success in the latter. Chapter 4 explores the legitimation basis for the
empowerment of brujos both in terms of their acquisitiveness and in terms
of their sense of godly mission — expressed in sacrifice and charity. Chapter 5 looks at the accumulation of spiritual assets more closely, pointing
to the paradoxes that might arise from being blessed. While they might
guarantee unlimited material progress, spiritual blessings can hardly guard
against envy — a major source of misfortune. Another side of the entrepreneurial aspect of brujería emerges in chapter 6, where I trace the interface
between different forms of healing, divination, and magic. I show that
innovation in ritual matters caters both to the desire of brujos to be experts in a competitive arena and to clients who search for the best services
available. In chapters 7 and 8 I examine the role of urban brujos in the
context of the commonwealth status of Puerto Rico and develop the argument that brujos in Puerto Rico should not be viewed, as in other parts of
the world, as contesting or subverting the forces of modernity but rather
as reproducing them. These chapters show that the most successful brujos are able to help their clients in a holistic manner by centralizing the
functions of various liberal professions and state agencies alike, as well as
by providing a moral charter for economic success. The latter illuminates
the claim that brujería is a form of spiritualized materialism, which blurs
the boundaries between material and spiritual worlds, blending them into
a holistic conception of progress.

The epilogue enlists this realization for a methodological and essentially reflexive discussion of the limitless nature of magic and the academic as well as lay enchantment with authenticity. The simultaneous seduction and fear of including consumer, manufacturing, technological, and tourist worlds in local brujería practices suggests that different criteria of authenticity might be operating. These are assessed from the point of view of practitioners, patients, and outsiders—nonpractitioners and researchers. To what degree is the entrepreneurial aspect of brujería accepted, welcomed, or rejected by these different groups? Coming full circle after this ethnographic exploration of brujería, might outsiders finally free themselves from ancestral dichotomies and recognize it as a legitimate if unexpected partner in a world guided by the desires and frustrations of high modernity?

Part I

SHIFTING FACES

CHAPTER
ONE

GATEKEEPERS AND HERETICS:
DISPUTING SACRED TERRITORIES

Catholic Brujos

"It's a perfect day," Haydée says as I arrive at her house in the morning. "Today I will show you the exact place where I had the revelation, when God spoke to me." Haydée, Reina, and I get into her car and drive to the seashore along Loíza, one of the most "African" towns in Puerto Rico. We pass by the village's narrow streets, singing to the sounds of merengue on the radio. As we pass an intersection, Haydée spots a patch of vines and shrubs and asks Reina, her assistant and driver, to stop the car. "Look! There's *brazo fuerte* here; let's take some." She opens the door and cuts some branches of brazo fuerte, which she needs for making a *trabajo*[1] for a client who will come that afternoon to her altar. We continue slowly through unpaved roads bordering the seashore of Loíza. "Stop here!" Haydée shouts. I take my camera and, following her advice, begin to tape-record, waiting for Haydée to direct me. "Come here," she says. "Under this palm tree I had the revelation. Here's where God talked to me." Carefully straightening her white dress, she sits under the tree in the exact spot where, some seven years ago, she had the revelation that would change her life. "I was very depressed at that time. After I had a knee operation and I kicked my husband out of the house, I came to this spot to think, pray, and cleanse myself by crying. I was suffering a lot. Suddenly, I heard a voice that told me 'I want you seated.' I replied, 'But I am already seated. You know that I work seated as an administrative secretary, working at the computer.' I heard God say again, 'I want you seated.' I then understood what it meant: he wanted me seated at an altar, helping people, doing the *trabajo espiritual* [spiritual work]."

As she talks into the microphone, I take several photographs of her reenactment of the mystical moment. As she dramatizes that moment for me, I record her verbal cues and explanations and take more photographs of the orchestrated gestures she makes. Aware that I intend to publish my dissertation, Haydée carefully constructs her poses for the pictures to accord with her own vision of the book. The commemoration of that vision has to be perfect. Wearing flashy white designer sunglasses, she smiles as she would for the cover of a famous magazine. I perform my part as diligently as possible, trying to fulfill her expectations. I try not to miss any angle, gesture, or expression. I shoot one of her with sunglasses, one without. It is crucial that the right image is documented and preserved for posterity. I think that both of us enjoy these sorts of make-believe roles: hers, spiritual diva; mine, photojournalist. My task is easy. She adroitly freezes a look or a hand at the exact arc of gesture she wishes me to capture — and our prospective readers to remember. It is a sacred moment, the commemoration of an extraordinary event. It is a reenactment of God's revelation. It is odd, I think, to see and hear a witch-healer talk like a saint. It is no less odd, however, to photograph a witch-healer as she displays herself very much like a movie star.

By what kind of awkward revenge does a witch-healer have a revelatory vision, à la Catholic saint, in an urban consumer society today? Perhaps the usurpation of Catholic signs, gestures, visions, and miracles has left its mark not only on priests and fervent churchgoers but also on witch-healers, so-called heretics. This odd complicity between persecutors and persecuted, originating in the distant past and surviving the Inquisition, seems to be resurfacing now in unexpected ways. Fame and pride replace destitution and shame.

Burned or Sanctified: The Politics of Divination

If the conquest of the Indies had been attained through the sword, colonization was carried out under the auspices of the Cross. Colonization of the native population thereby remained — at least from the point of view of Spaniards and Portuguese — not only unquestioned but also legitimized by God. Transcendental power was undifferentiated from and totally enmeshed with political power. Extending Spanish Christendom meant not only "civilizing" so-called savages, who were seen as biological extensions of the conquered environment,[2] but also sanctifying Spanish dominion over the newly conquered lands of the Indies. Since kings were divinely entrusted with the spiritual protection of the land and its inhabitants (plants and animals included) through "royal patronage," the religious dominion was indivisible from the political one. Only by acknowledging this bond between Spain and the Indies, between God and king and church and state, can one begin to grasp the motive behind the king's and the church's massive efforts to control the religious lives of the colonial population. Through their judicial and executive agents, epitomized by the Santo Oficio (Holy Office), a phenomenal energy was to be diverted from the economic to the religious sphere to recognize, persecute, and punish "heretics."[3] By examining in greater detail this partnership between the political and religious centers of power, it is possible to elucidate why it is that throughout subsequent centuries brujos have stubbornly persisted in co-opting the gestures and rituals of their persecutors.

A close reading of the cases that were persecuted by the Holy Office reveals that the divide between heretics and priests was based on the location, not the essence, of transcendental power. This spatiomoral exclusivity meant that any spiritual manipulation on this earth enacted within the confines of the church would belong to the realm of holy goodness. If, on the other hand, it was performed outside the church, it would pertain to the punishable province of evil. From the church's perspective, to contain the transcendental domain within its confines was more than a religious matter: it was a political necessity. Although this runs counter to most theological justifications for the condemnation of evil and the righteousness of the church in persecuting witch-healers, it is an alternative, viable explanation for the persistence of Puerto Rican vernacular religious practices through the centuries. More than violating Catholic beliefs, the practices of the accused appear to have been essentially similar to those of the accusers. "Colonizers carried their fears of *maleficia* and witches among other items in their cultural baggage. . . . The colonization of the Americas coincided with the major phase of European witch trials. The *Malleus Maleficarum* preceded Columbus's first voyage by just five years" (Monter 1983:101).

From the beginning of Spanish Catholic colonial rule, the church fought to keep the transcendental domain within its purview. It seems that legitimate priests shared with "heretics" or "witches" the ability and the will to communicate with the transcendental world through divination and propitiatory rituals.[4] Legitimate priests and heretics entered into competition for the management of the sacred and the interpretation of its signs—visions, miracles, and divining systems.[5] Throughout roughly three centuries, the Inquisition and numerous ecclesiastical and government decrees have sought to restrict the practices of individuals who had "illegally" appropriated the management of the sacred outside the church.[6] As reports on the work of the Inquisition suggest, the colonial meeting of three continents cannot be characterized as the result of "an organic synthesis or 'syncretism' of the three great streams of New World History— African, Christian, and Indian—but as a chamber of mirrors reflecting each stream's perception of the other. . . . [T]his chamber of mirrors was, from the colonizer's point of view, a chamber conflating sorcery with sedition, if not in reality at least as a metaphor" (Taussig 1987:218).

The Inquisition was effected in Puerto Rico and surrounding islands in 1511 with the appointment of the first bishop of the island, Don Alonzo Manzo. In 1519 he also held the title Inquisidor General de las Indias (Fernández Méndez 1976:131; Zeno n.d.:125–126). Because he was the first Inquisitor of the Indies, "delinquents" from other islands in the area were brought before him to be processed and burned. Unfortunately, archival or material evidence of these proceedings is not available today. The Dutch, during their invasion of the island in 1625, burned all the material evidence of the Inquisition together with the archival documents housed in the Cathedral (Zeno n.d.:128; Coll y Toste 1926:2; Miyares González [1775] 1954:29).

The first *quemadero* (place of burning) in the Americas was located on the outskirts of the ancient gate of the Castle of San Cristóbal, where the Lincoln School is located today in Old San Juan. Until the eighteenth century this place was called El Charco de las Brujas (the Puddle of the Witches) (Fernández Méndez 1976:188, 190; Miyares González [1775] 1954:29). The accused were made to walk to the pyre through the streets of Mondongo, now called San Sebastian (*El Mundo* 1962). The other material evidence appears in an account by the chronicler and prebendary of the Cathedral, Diego de Torres Vargas (quoted in Fernández Méndez 1976:188 and Zeno n.d.:128). He reports the existence of *estampas,* engravings that included the names of heretics as well as the kinds of punishments they received. He also mentions *sambenitos,* the penitential garments that were customarily hung on the wall behind the Cathedral choir. Colonial discursive misrecognitions seem to have contributed in no small measure to ecclesiastical persecutions of vernacular religious practices.[7] Misreading signs of religious worship, their referents were made to fit the terms by which boundaries between legitimate worship and those of heretics were drawn institutionally. Two Inquisition cases suggest an institutionally biased translation of both the confessions of heretics and the accusations made by the authorities to fit the ecclesiastical idiom of heresy. It is known today that the African worship of the deity Shango, brought to the colonies by enslaved Africans, includes the sacrifice of a goat. Notably, the archbishop of Santo Domingo and fifth bishop of Puerto Rico, Nicolás Ramos, wrote in 1594 to the Council of the Indies about a group of "black brujos [male and female] who engaged with the devil in the shape of a goat and, every night in front of this goat, cursed God, Santa María, and the sacraments of the Holy Church." Ramos writes, "[A]sserting that they did not have nor believe in a god other than that devil . . . they performed these rituals in some fields [apparently they were in a trance], . . . not in dreams since there were some people who saw them." These people, Ramos continues, "tried to make them [the sorcerers] refrain from their doings through chanting and holy gifts [*dádivas*], and with all this [information they] came to me." Ramos explains in this letter that he took proper judicial charge of this case and punished these brujos in a variety of ways (Coll y Toste 1916b:48).[8] Evidently the ritual elements of African worship were conflated with the imagery of the devil constructed by the church. Reference to the attempts made by neighbors to stop their rituals by means of prayers are notably reminiscent of exorcising procedures that are still practiced in Catholic and Protestant churches—as well as among Spiritists and witch-healers.

Another frequently mentioned case is that of a "black woman" who, during the time of Governor Gabriel Roxas (1608), claimed to "have a spirit in her stomach" that "talked" to her.[9] She was taken to the church to be exorcised, and in the process the spirit "said he was called Pedro Lorenzo." When induced to "speak" (the woman was in a trance), the spirit referred to "bygone and occult stories" (*cosas ausentes y ocultas*). Subsequently, the Inquisitor ordered no one to "talk to this spirit"; those who did "[would] be excommunicated." The investigators revealed that those "black women" who "had" spirits said that in their land people usually have spirits in their stomach, that these spirits take the shape of an animal or monster, and that they are passed on from one person to the other, becoming their *mayorazgo* (guardian spirits) (Fernández Méndez 1976:203). It can be seen that while sharing basic beliefs about the possibilities of spirit communication and possession, the paths of bishops and heretics were very different. Some historians claim that not all of the proceedings of the Inquisition concluded with an *auto de fé* (burning at the stake; lit., "act of faith"). In some cases, autos de fé were performed in the form of public flagellations conducted during a religious procession (Zeno n.d.:133). Occasionally slave owners appealed for this lesser form of punishment to protect their "investments." It was a possible solution only when a slave confessed his or her alleged crime *behementi* (i.e., voluntarily, without having to be first tortured) (Coll y Toste 1916b:48). Another document mentions the punishment of Martín García, from the island of Española (present-day Haiti and the Dominican Republic), who was brought to and sentenced by the Inquisitor Bishop Alonso in 1529; the victim was made to march on his knees, holding a lit candle in his hand, through the streets of his village, after which he was banished for two months (Coll y Toste 1916d:149). Similarly, Nuñez Carrasco, accused of conniving with the English invaders during Bishop Ramos's tenure, was sentenced by the civil judicial system to be flogged one hundred strokes; he was then punished by the Inquisition and made to wear the sambenito in public while holding a green candle. He was ultimately banished to Seville (Perea 1972:102).[10]

Accusations of heresy were not exclusive to the population outside the institutional church. Public officials in the ecclesiastical hierarchy sometimes accused each other of heresy. But when the accused was a member of the church hierarchy, the punishment was less severe. The historian Salvador Brau mentions the case of Doctor Carreras, a priest accused of practicing "medicine and surgery" outside the specifications of the church. Doctor Carreras was granted special consideration: instead of being subjected to the Inquisition, he was sent back to Spain to be judged there by the cardinal of the Supreme Court (cited in Zeno n.d.:132). His ultimate fate is unknown.

When the accused were found guilty by the Supreme Court, they were stripped of their priestly rank and estate. Such was the case of an Inquisition judge and interim governor of the island, the lawyer Sancho Velázquez, who was accused of "scandalous acts against the Faith and Holy Religion" by none other than the one who, after removing him from office, would take his place—the next Inquisition judge and interim governor, the lawyer Antonio de la Gama. Since the accuser would become the judge at the time of the prosecution, Velázquez's fate was decided by the Inquisitor General, Bishop Manso, himself, who—in accordance with the high rank of the accused—ordered the confiscation of all his property and wealth and his imprisonment, which—the new judge de la Gama established—was to be followed by deportation (Zeno n.d.:129). The persecution or elimination of heretics in cases such as this served other than purely religious purposes, reflecting rather the internal and external politics of the church as a kind of ecclesiastical coup d'état.

At high official levels, heresy accusations point to basic structural conflicts embedded in the joint secular-religious colonial government of the island. In fall 1719, just a few months after he became bishop, Don Fray Valdivia was convinced that he was the object of witchcraft. Fearing for his life, he wrote two letters to the king of Spain—on September 4 and November 15—about his chronic "indisposition," implicating his secular rival, Don José del Pozo Onesto, who controlled the civil *cabildo* (council) and the militia, as the primary cause of his suspiciously declining health. The bishop accused Onesto of using magic against him in order to put an end to his ecclesiastical activities (Murga and Huerga 1990:82). This request arose from the bishop's belief that his two recently deceased predecessors in the ecclesiastical cabildo, Don Fray Pedro Miguel de la Concepción de Urtiaga and Don Fray Raimundo Caballero—the latter dying only two months after taking over the diocese—had also been the victims of poisoning (p. 83).[11] In addition, the frightened bishop asked the king to immediately replace Onesto and the officials of the civil cabildo (whom he assumed to be in complicity with Onesto). It was not until 1721 that the Royal Council in Spain responded to his letters. The Royal Council asked the bishop to calm down, reminding him that even though his suspicions might be unfounded, the governor had assigned a special guard to his service. This noncommital response and the ongoing tensions with the civil officials drove the bishop into a deeper depression (pp. 83–85). Increasingly weakened and troubled by his fears of being poisoned and having lost his initial energy for managing the episcopal responsibilities of the diocese, the bishop finally died on November 25, 1725, just six years after arriving in Puerto Rico. It took his successor, Bishop Don Martín Calderón, one year and three months to inform the king—in a short, cold note—of Valdivia's death (p. 86).

These cases are indicators of the potential eruption of political conflict between civil and ecclesiastical cabildos, specifically, of the structural tension between governors and bishops in Puerto Rico. More generally, they point to the pervasiveness of the threat of heresy among all sectors of colonial society, including those of its persecutors. They illustrate in yet a profounder way the ambiguity and malleability of witchcraft accusations in legal and political terms as well as their economic impact on those in power.

A murky distinction between the "holy" versus "evil" manipulation of transcendental power had emerged since medieval times, in spite of attempts by the church to codify and sanction the legitimate means of exercising influence. By the middle of the thirteenth century, Alfonso X (the Wise) (1221–1284), king of Castile and Leon, had written his *Siete Partidas,* which established the laws that would regulate the sacred space of medieval Catholicism. In a comprehensive religious world it was imperative to establish the criteria by which transgressors would be defined. With this in mind, Alfonso X decreed that the practice of divination through games of chance, lottery, and the flight of birds was prohibited; on the other hand, he decreed that the "judgments made" through astrology had to be accepted because "they are based on the natural course of the planets and the stars, and are inspired by the books of Ptolemy" (read: science). He also proclaimed that "sorcerers" and "necromancers" should be punished with death; but "those who through charms extract demons out of bodies, 'untie' [*desligan*] those who are unsuitable to be man and wife, help either 'the snow to fall or stop it from falling to prevent the crops from spoiling' . . . or help kill plagues, should not be punished but praised and rewarded" (quoted in Ortiz 1906:377). What kind of line could divide the "despicable" practices of sorcerers from those that should be rewarded? Apparently the power to determine the proper goals of divination, not the procedures themselves, would determine their legality. If the church blessed the goal, the procedure itself was not to be questioned. It follows that those practices that would fall under the rubric of heresy were different not in kind but in purpose. Indeed, the arbitrary nature of these criteria seems to better suit the volatile area of whim than the unequivocal domain of legal practice.

The following case further illustrates that it was the dispute over the sacred domain that lay behind the social production of heresy. During a natural disaster that had struck the island, Bishop Manzo, General Inquisitor of the Indies, who had sent numerous heretics to the pit, resorted to divination. Through a *sorteo* (drawing of lots) he determined which saint could help to end a plague of termites in Loíza. The termites had eaten the yucca plants used to make *casaba,* the staple bread of the islanders. The first draw of the lots pointed to Señor San Saturnino as the patron saint or *abogado* (lawyer) of the plague. Indeed, this saint "miraculously solved" the problem. Later, another worm attacked the yucca plants. Additional draws of lots were made by the bishop, at the end of which the divination process pointed twice to San Patricio. Because the bishop considered this saint relatively "unknown," he ordered the lots to be drawn three more times. Each time the same saint was drawn, "giving sufficient signs of a manifest miracle." It is no wonder that this saint was installed as the patron saint of the casaba and that processions, masses, and festivities were subsequently dedicated in his honor in both the ecclesiastical and the civil cabildos (Fernández Méndez 1976:188; Miyares González [1775] 1954:92; Zeno n.d.:141). In line with Alfonso X's code of laws, Manzo's mediation between godly and worldly matters deserved to be praised and rewarded. The same transcendental practices if performed outside the confines of the church would have been read as signs of witchcraft and therefore punished.

This example shows how thin was the line dividing Catholicism and "superstition." Not as surprising as it may first appear, after centuries of allegations by the Catholic Church that deviant forms of worship were heretical and with the advent of European evolutionist theories in the nineteenth century, "superstitions" began to be cast as pertaining to certain human groups—"African" or "primitive"—and not others, even though in the early periods of colonization, deviant religious practices had never been ascribed to a specific ethnic group or geographic area. Legitimate versus illegitimate forms of spiritual endeavors were defined according to an institutional cosmological taxonomy that specified both who was entitled to contact the supernatural realm and which purposes were deemed acceptable for mediation.

The ideology of Spanish Christendom implied the sanctification of all that was Catholic on this earth. Politically and legally, royal patronage had entrusted the king with leadership of the church in all but doctrinal matters (Silva Gotay 1985:54). The legitimation of both the church and the king to govern on earth thus came directly from God. Under this premise, then, any individual or group apart from the church or the king that would claim direct access to this power was sure to be persecuted. Strict adherence was a matter of colonial survival. Godly inspired and kingly executed rule over the people and the environment of the newly acquired Indies depended on sustaining the church's demarcation between the holy and evil realms.

But it was not an easy task, especially on smaller islands such as Puerto Rico, whose rural population were left much on their own, because of the endemic lack of priests and geographic isolation from centers of Catholic worship. As reported by numerous envoys from the courts to the island and local church officials, the management of the population was always less desirable than expected.[12] The population's failure to partake of the

Catholic sacraments, especially those related to the life course—from birth to death—appears to have troubled the hierarchy, according to the bulk of official documentation produced on these matters. For example, while searching for documents related to vernacular religious practices I found instead numerous boxes full of ecclesiastical dispatches that discussed the troublesome fact that the great majority of the population did not fulfill the sacrament of marriage and thus lived "in sin." No less important—but less available for researchers today as a result of the mishandling or concealment of archival materials—are the accounts of constant devotional appropriations by the Creole population. In matters such as vernacular transgressions of Catholic liturgy or worship, there is a loud silence in the archives available to the public.[13] Thus the muffled voices of "brujos," also called *nigromantes* (conjurers), *agoreros* (diviners) or *hechiceros* (sorcerers), are available to researchers today only through the laws that were created to counter their practices. These are the only actual voices that can be heard through the centuries, whereas the voices of brujos themselves appear to us only as mere mirages, or reflections.[14] Assuming that positive laws emerge as a response to contraventions, church edicts and local police ordinances offer indirect though reliable traces through which the space of anti-institutional religious practices can be reconstructed. By backtracking through these ecclesiastical and governmental regulations, the story of brujos comes to life. Even if limited by the distorting lens of the state's perspective, one can see something of the nature of the infractions—their substance and details—and who was assumed to have made them.

Maroons, Slaves, and Hacendados

The constant socioeconomic and cultural lag between Spanish society and the colonies troubled colonial officials in Puerto Rico. After the initial centrality of the Caribbean islands as strategic outposts for the control of and access to its southern colonies, Spain shifted its colonial resources farther to the south and west, especially Peru and Mexico, where silver and gold mining promised greater revenues. Suffering from constant church and government underfunding, as well as from tardy shipment of supplies, the island was increasingly left on its own over the ensuing centuries—regaining support only when it was threatened with naval invasions by other European countries.[15] "A military outpost and provision station, Puerto Rico played a largely passive and defensive role for centuries" (Mintz [1974] 1989:85). Diminishing metropolitan investments in the island made it difficult if not impossible to attract wealthy Spaniards and priests to settle there.[16] Contributing to this political and economic lag were problems associated with the early colonists, most of whom came from Andalusia and later the Canary Islands (Knight 1990:34) and were from the lower and marginalized classes. These colonists settled in isolated areas of the island and engaged in subsistence agriculture and trading in contraband with nearby islands and passing pirate vessels.[17] They practiced a popular form of medieval Mediterranean Catholicism common to various sixteenth-century European societies. On the island, however, this form of popular Catholicism continued to flourish with little control by the official church (Vidal 1994:13).[18]

The geographic and economic marginality of the island of Puerto Rico fostered the creation of a *sociedad cimarrona* (maroon society), composed at different times of native Indian and Creole peoples, subsistence farmers, former convicts, freed people or *libertos,* and runaway slaves (from within Puerto Rico and from neighboring Caribbean islands) (Quintero Rivera 1995).[19] By and large it included what Mintz ([1974] 1989) defined as "squatters" and "runaway peasantries." The first were composed of "peasantries of mixed cultural and physical origins [which] seem to have come into being as a mode of escape from official power" (p. 147); the second were maroon communities formed "in defiance of slavery and the plantation system" (p. 152).

Demographic isolation, colonial scarcity of funds, and a basic antiofficial attitude created, in Mintz's terms ([1974] 1989), an "interstitial" resistance zone—from the very beginning of colonization—that promoted the creation and ongoing pervasiveness of an individualist, antiecclesiastical, popular form of Catholic worship. In view of the establishment of populations on the mountains outside colonial centers, far from churches and chapels, the church authorized and promoted Catholic worship in provisional spaces such as *ermitas* (small country chapels). In 1647 Archbishop López de Haro proclaimed that churchgoers who lived more than six *leguas* (approximately eighteen miles) from the nearest church were exempted from weekly mass, except during Los Días Santos (Holy Week, concluding on Easter Sunday) (Díaz Soler [1953] 1974:171). Further, because there were few priests on the island, services were conducted in these small countryside chapels by devotees who had proven in some way their faith or spiritual qualities.[20] The lack of economic resources on the island thus contributed to the dispersion of the population, mainly lower-class Spaniards, free colored groups, and Indian and slave runaways. This demographic and cultural displacement facilitated the creation of alternative worship spaces and practices and the burgeoning preeminence of surrogate priests—*rezadoras* and *mantenedoras* (female devotees in charge of conducting the liturgy and guarding ritual objects, respectively) (Vidal 1994:21; 213, n. 36).[21]

The system of slavery added to this state of affairs. Most slaves who were brought to the island from Spain in the sixteenth century had already been baptized. During subsequent centuries, especially the eighteenth and nineteenth, a large number of slaves were shipped directly from Africa, imposing on the church two important and intimately related tasks, namely, converting the slaves to Christianity and overseeing the slave-owning *hacendados* (landowners). Because fulfillment of the first task depended on the hacendados' commitment to assuring that the slaves learned the catechism and partook of the sacraments, it was also their responsibility to carry out this process in the form established by the church (Coll y Toste 1926:5). The church did not trust the hacendados to fulfill their religious duties.[22] Based on the numerous regulations created to define the scope and control the fulfillment of these duties, one can assume that although unquestionably Catholic, hacendados cared less for the Christian education or moral development of their slaves than for the economic benefits they could reap from their labor. Slaves were usually branded at the time of purchase as proof of ownership with a *carimbo* (branding iron) (see Coll y Toste 1920:147–150);[23] after a year of Christian instruction, they were to be baptized under the auspices of their owners— as established by the church.[24] Of all the sacraments, the baptism of slaves and especially their offspring was dutifully carried out by hacendados. One might assume that the purchase papers were enough proof of ownership, but it was not so for the offspring of slaves. Until they were baptized at the parish church, they were not registered as the property of the hacendados.

The required catechism needed for baptism was cut short, however, and the Christian instruction that was expected to follow baptism was never carried out. The mass of rules and regulations that deal with these issues are proof. During the first half of the nineteenth century, there was a huge increase in the number of slaves brought to the island. In 1779 there were 8,153 slaves in Puerto Rico, but by 1802 the number had tripled to 24,596 slaves. By 1846 the number of slaves reached its nineteenth-century peak of 51,265 (Baralt 1981; Coll y Toste [1969] 1972; Negrón Portillo and Mayo Santana 1992).[25] This increase explains the intervention of Governor Miguel de la Torre, who in 1826 issued the "Reglamento de Esclavos" (Slave Regulations), aimed at complementing the unsuccessful efforts of the church to force hacendados to have their slaves baptized.[26] De la Torre's decree contains detailed rules and regulations for the proper treatment of slaves, the types of labor, and the Christian education they should be given (Coll y Toste 1917:263; 1923:262–273).[27] Still, the neglect of baptism and Christian education was an ongoing worry even more than a quarter of a century later, as can be seen in an 1853 report of the Real Audiencia (Royal Tribunal) condemning the lack of action regarding the stipulations of 1826. The tribunal ordered that local judges make three annual visits to the haciendas to oversee compliance with the law (Coll y Toste 1925:56).[28]

Insurrection and Heresy

Puerto Rico, like the rest of the Caribbean, was significantly affected both directly and indirectly by the slave insurrections in Haiti. Begun in August 1791 with an animal sacrifice ritual conducted by a former slave (folk narratives tell), a mass slave insurrection lasting more than ten years ended successfully with the creation, in 1804, of the first black republic in the New World. The profound fear that similar occurrences might happen on other Caribbean islands fueled a renewed need to further restrict the lives of slaves, even during their few nonworking hours. Backed by slaveowner interests, the church and the governor in Puerto Rico joined efforts to control more forcefully all aspects of the slave's life. If previously hacendados had turned deaf ears to the church's exhortations to restrict the antiecclesiastical religious expressions of slaves and to see to their indoctrination, now under the threat of insurrection and massacre hacendados were more eager to take an active role in the totalizing control of their slaves' lives. In their eyes, the provisions decreed by the church had ceased to be concerned merely with religion; and compliance had become a more pressing need, tightly connected to the hacendados' own physical survival and the continuity of colonial rule.

Slaves often ran away during festivities, when the *bombas* (drumming and dances) that were performed provided a secret, coded communication system (Baralt 1981). In 1823 forty slaves escaped in this manner (Baralt 1981:67, 175). To preclude such escapes in the future, in 1824 the governor issued the "Bando de Policía y Buen Gobierno" (Edict of Police and Good Government) and in 1826 the "Reglamento de Esclavos"; each focused on restricting two of the most important leisure activities of slaves—games and dances. The latter were engaged in mostly on the Feast of Epiphany (Fiesta de Reyes)[29] and during Lent (Cuaresma), which offered legitimate opportunities for slaves to gather together and feast communally (Díaz Soler [1953] 1974:175). Prohibiting bomba drumming and dances thus functioned to repress any attempt at revolt.[30]

Church-state-hacendado interests were never more united than when trying to limit the mobility of slaves at public religious feasts and during their nonworking hours. Through their many laws and regulations the authorities aimed at controlling secret associations of slaves that might lead to conspiracies.[31] The 1790 slave insurrections in Haiti and the early emancipation of Martinique and Guadeloupe were perceived as warnings to all Caribbean colonial centers. Fearing the detrimental effects of these revolutions in the Spanish colonies of Cuba and Puerto Rico, the colonial administration became more alert to the dangers of managing angry, unsatisfied slaves and became more conscious of the precariousness of their power in the colonies. The 1829 "Bando contra Ratería" (Edict against Pilfering) (Coll y Toste 1916a:345) and the 1848 "Bando del General Prim contra la raza africana" (Edict of General Prim against the African Race) (Coll y Toste 1915:122–126) were particularly harsh in that they bestowed on hacendados almost total judicial power to control, torture, even kill their slaves under certain, broadly defined conditions, for example, if they were disrespectful to their owners, refused to follow orders, were suspected of sabotaging their work, were caught trying to escape, or were captured after having managed to escape.[32]

The Totalizing Aspects of Catholic Rule or the Micromechanisms of Gatekeeping

By means of institutions such as the Inquisition and of numerous royal and ecclesiastical decrees and edicts, the Puerto Rican Catholic colonial state had hoped to stop the intermittent transgressions of individuals who took sacred matters into their own hands. These general laws empowered ecclesiastical officials in the colonies to act as overseers of the colonization and evangelization enterprise. These officials were responsible for seeing to the fulfillment of the doctrinal precepts proclaimed by the church (Zeno n.d.:124). By way of metropolitan and local interventions in the private and public realms, the theoretical separation between ecclesiastical and civil spheres of social action was de facto undermined. Instead of a separation of functions, an intrinsic symbiosis was constituted in practice, perpetuating as a way of life the convergence of the sacred and the civil management of Puerto Rico. The sacred and secular spheres were so interconnected—at so many levels of existence—that a person's conviction of a crime in one realm automatically entailed conviction in the other.

To make overseeing the Creole population more feasible, parish priests were entrusted as the religious and civil bookkeepers of the population. They had to manage all aspects of the life cycle—recording all the births and baptisms, the attendance of mass at least once a year, weddings, and deaths of their parishioners. Apparently as a result of numerous contraventions in these areas, priests were explicitly forbidden to administer the sacrament of confession in "any place outside the parish church" (Constitution XXXI of the 1645 Synod of Fray Damián López de Haro, quoted in Coll y Toste 1926:5–6). Similarly, when a patient's fever persisted beyond three days, physicians, under threat of excommunication, had to report the fact immediately to the parish priest so that the patient could comply with the obligation to confess his or her sins and receive the sacrament of penance before dying (Constitution CXVII, in Murga and Huerga 1989:133).

The church allowed only priests to perform and supervise healing procedures leading to spiritual cures, which were carefully defined in a series of laws. Specific techniques and rituals that involved the invocation of supernatural powers were described in Constitution CXV (1645), in accordance with the Council of Trent (1545–1563). Constitution CXV prohibited the exhibition of *nóminas* (lists of saints used as amulets), the use of *ensalmos* (magic spells), and the use of objects of superstition (e.g., "unknown characters," "divination systems") unless they were first seen and approved by the church (Huerga 1989:132). As set out in Constitution CLVII, the ultimate right to "excommunicate" an individual was the privilege of church officials, who would determine whether a certain practice was to be punished as superstition, sorcery, bewitchment, divination, or enchantment through spells (Murga and Huerga 1989:480).

Saints, Devotees, Fraternities, and Miracles

Symbolizing the sacred nature of Catholic rule over the colonies, a calendar-based schedule of devotion to the saints was created at the beginning of colonization, one for the island in general and others for each town and village as it was founded. In addition to a special mass for patron saints, these public celebrations included games, singing, and dancing. Apparently these forms of religious merriment facilitated the inclusion of other than church-approved devotions (or, as often stated in ecclesiastical records, "less than purely Catholic forms of veneration") in the lives of the people. Interestingly, this concern still haunts the church today. Several *loiceños* (inhabitants of Loíza) told me that the local celebrations of Santiago Apóstol (Saint James the Apostle), which include *diablitos,* also called *vejigantes* (people masquerading as devils), have changed over the years due to restrictions imposed by the church.[33] In the words of a staff member at the community library of Loíza, "Today they go quietly, whereas before they used to go frolicking" (Hoy van calladitos, antes iban brincando). Three centuries ago vernacular forms of celebrating the feast days of Corpus Christi and Santiago Apóstol were also seen as dangerous. In 1686, for example, the bishop of Puerto Rico, Don Fray Francisco Padilla, prohibited on those two feast days what then was called "La danza de los mulatos" (the Dance of the Mulattoes) and ordered the priest not to give his sermon because he had failed to submit it to the censors ahead of time (Murga and Huerga 1989:202–203). Also, as a result of the liberties that were usually taken during the *autos sacramentales* (allegorical plays on the Eucharist),[34] Constitution LXXI (1645) stated that "profanities," "laughter," and "vanity" should be eliminated in temples of God and that "profane" representations or "masquerades" would not be tolerated during religious rites (Huerga 1989:96–97).

As part of the general goal of controlling every aspect of daily life and creating a secular arm that would assist ecclesiastical officials in managing the lives of their flocks, the church encouraged the formation of *cofradías* (secular fraternities).[35] These cofradías were created, following the model of fifteenth-century Spanish social clubs, to organize and promote the ritual activities of the parish church. As soon as they were created, however, fear arose that they would become ritually independent of the institutional church, a concern that occasioned the creation of detailed regulations for their operation. Constitutions CII–CIV, written between 1611 and 1695, reasserted the church's determination to control every aspect of the formation, organization, and daily activities of the cofradías and their *cófrades* (members) (Murga and Huerga 1989:432–434).

Inevitably, as occurred in other parts of the colony as well, the cofradías exceeded the purposes and forms preestablished by the church. Especially difficult to control were those cofradías that were in charge of the *mantenimiento del recuerdo de muertos* (commemoration of the dead). As a way to tackle what the ecclesiastical hierarchy saw as the un-Christian proceedings of the cofradías, a regulation was issued declaring that "commemorations of the dead" could not be used to sponsor the big festivities that would follow (Murga and Huerga 1989:433–434). Furthermore, fearing that the assumed magical power emanating from the ritual management of the dead during these commemorations would be used in un-Christian ways, the church prohibited the cófrades from conducting the ritual of watching over (*velar*) the open casket throughout the night. Oddly, in spite of the religious precept to conduct *vigilias* (vigils) for the dead throughout the night and against the typical custom of leaving churches open day and night, it was ordered that all churches be closed to devotees at night. This measure was rationalized as a means of preventing disorderly conduct. It explained that since the prescribed vigilias had been turned into mere occasions for feasting, singing, laughing, and dancing (instead of the prescribed fasting, silence, and then singing of *cánticos*), there was no longer any reason to leave the church open at night (Murga and Huerga 1989:433–434). The wish to protect the civility of these rituals actually marked the church's real fear: the potential misuse of the power emanating from the ritual manipulation of the dead.

Some two hundred years later, in 1862, the need to control the ritual management of the dead and the celebrations that accompanied and followed it reappears in the civil realm. Evidently the communal aspects of these celebrations were seen as threatening and potentially uncontrollable by both religious and public officials. The "Bando de Policía y Buen Gobierno" of 1862 (article 113) prohibited the dances performed during the *baquiné*, the Afro-Latin–based funerary rite for infants. Because it was believed young children died as *angelitos* (little angels), their death provided the occasion for merriment and feasting. Addressing as well the funerary practices of slaves, the civil ordinance also prohibited kin from "[the ritual] carrying of [deceased] blacks from house to house" and "singing for [the deceased] in the style of the nation to which they belong" (Díaz Soler [1953] 1974:172).[36]

The church also found it necessary to moderate the use of its liturgical objects. The images of saints (both sculpted and pictorial) located in churches, and the miraculous stories that legitimized their worship, were the most available sites for vernacular creativity on the part of slaves and peasants alike. The church not only had to contend with protecting existing images in chapels and churches from being changed or from having additions attached to them; it also had to prevent the more dangerous act of creating new images in private homes. Making sure the images of saints would be used only in accordance with the church's liturgy was a vital gatekeeping mechanism. Because the great majority of the population leaned toward creating unorthodox forms of worship around these saints, tempering and keeping popular devotions and symbolic expressions in the church's hands was of cardinal importance. Reading between the lines of these laws, we come to realize that besides the alarming profusion of "catholic devotions" (called *milagros,* or miracles) among the people, the church faced the ongoing threat of "corruption" (read: reproduction) of its symbols outside the church walls and the need to limit the kind of additional adornments to the images of the saints that it considered non-Catholic in nature.[37] Constitution CVIII dictated that "holy relics" be kept under lock and key in places constructed especially for this purpose—never to be exposed in the *sagrario* (sanctuary), where the Santísimo Sacramento (Sanctified Sacrament) is placed (Murga and Huerga 1989:436–437). This clearly shows that priests and nonpriests alike shared a belief in the spiritual power attached to religious objects, creating the institutional need to monitor any nonecclesiastical manipulations. Constitution CVII stated that images had to be protected from "indecent" additions and manipulations that were not in keeping with the institution's criteria. It referred specifically to "the composition of the images of Nuestra Señora with rites and other novelties that women without holy purposes had invented." This law also prohibited "dressing up altar images that were taken [by devotees] out of the church for these purposes," a provision aimed at preventing what the Church saw as devotees' "indecent actions upon them" (p. 436).

Ironically, by virtue of the very system of imitation that had been in place in accordance with the church's own devotional teachings, the gates to the realm of miraculous occurrences had been opened wide to an eagerly devout public ever since the earliest days of colonization. Indeed, the possibilities of vernacular reworkings of the ideology of sacred mimesis—which promoted the imitation of the life of Jesus—had become unlimited. Many of the faithful, following the official stories heard in their churches, claimed to have been involved in miraculous experiences—some in the form of apparitions, others in the form of wondrous encounters with sacred artifacts, which then often became the objects of popular devotions, outside the confines—and control—of the church.[38] With the aim of restricting the creation and propagation of unauthorized images, Constitution CIX reserved to the church alone the right to certify miracles and to incorporate into its liturgy new holy relics (*reliquias*) (Murga and Huerga 1989:437).

Clearly, the experience of miracles and the devotion to various saints had been central in Spanish Catholic life since colonization. The sanctity of—and popular devotion to—certain images were determined largely by the accounts detailing the "life" journeys of the images, mainly the events leading to a particular image's "miraculous" arrival on the island. The trajectory of their voyage from Spain to the colonies by sea was not infrequently interrupted by disastrous winds or rocks, often resulting in the temporary loss (if not complete disappearance) of the objects themselves. Of course, the subsequent "miraculous" recovery of these images when they washed up on the beaches of various Caribbean coasts became the source of their providential existence on earth. Materializing the transcendental energies that guided their recovery, the paintings and statues themselves became the site of this power. Fernández Méndez (1976:183) mentions the wondrous arrival in Puerto Rico of a wooden figurine of Nuestra Señora de La Candelaria from Seville and of Nuestra Señora de Bethelem [*sic*] from a Dominican convent on the island of Española (Hispaniola). About Nuestra Señora de Bethelem the chronicles report that "she was the first to appear in the Indies, and the angels, instead of the faithful, sung for her the divine psalms in the Dominican convent of Hispaniola" (Miyares González [1775] 1954:37-38). Among her numerous miracles, one in particular deserves to be mentioned: "the resurrection of a Doña Juana Guilarte who, after six hours of being dead and already shrouded in the coffin, suddenly sat up praising God and the blessed Virgin Saint [Santísima Virgen]" (p. 38).

The very location where images had been miraculously recovered became sacred too and formed in time a geographic map of the manifestations of God on earth. These places were also used to mark the site of a new convent or chapel and the dedication of the village or town to a patron saint, whose feast day was then added to the calendar-based veneration of saints. A wondrous image of Nuestra Señora de Monserrate was reported to have miraculously appeared in the ermita of Hormigueros (Fernández Méndez 1976:185), yet was never recognized by the church. The chronicles tell about the astounding experience of the *mayordomo* (sacristan, sexton) of the chapel at Hormigueros. Giraldo Gonzáles's eight-year-old daughter had disappeared into the *montes* (mountainous rain forest); fifteen days later she was found healthy and well, as "if a lady fed and took care of her." "Everybody knew" it was the Virgen de Monserrate, because the father of the girl was a devotee of that virgin and founder of the ermita that bore her name.

The chronicles report many other cases. For instance, in the city of San Felipe del Arecibo (present-day Arecibo) there was an ermita dedicated to Nuestra Señora del Rosario, which attracted processions and was sustained by "una renta y capellanía de Misas" (moneys that subsidize liturgical expenses) left by a villager named Juan Martín de Benavides (Fernández Méndez 1976:186). The crucial element, however, was that the church and its officials, not the faithful, were to be the arbiters and interpreters of such miraculous events. What the church could not foresee was that once it had certified the authenticity of an apparition, subsequent determinations of the legitimacy of other "miracles" related to that saint would be appropriated by the popular imagination, never again to be under ecclesiastical control.

During natural catastrophes such as hurricanes—which were, and still are, commonly experienced in the Caribbean region—special signs from the saints were usually expected. In these critical times the church, monopolizing the management of these signs also, reserved the right to authenticate the sacredness of reported uncanny events. Notwithstanding these limitations, vernacular experiences of sanctity continued largely to remain outside the scope of institutional control. One such experience, reported by Fernández Méndez (1976:187), concerns a little child who was thrown into the air between the village houses by a strong storm. Her fate was entrusted to the Virgen de Guadalupe, and she was found three days later, alive and well, under a tile roof.

Especially in times of natural disasters, people made promises and created blessings, prayers, and *rogativas* (rogations, litanies) for the well-being of the population. In Constitution CXV there is an express warning against those who make use of nóminas to achieve a desired outcome. They were to present nóminas first to church officials, who would then consider whether to recognize them as legitimate. Without formal approval, individuals were not allowed to publicly make use of nóminas or to practice any kind of "enchantments, charms, spells, soothsaying, divination, superstitions, or judicial astrology" that were meant either to seek out "matters of the future" or to "find lost or stolen things" (Murga and Huerga 1989:440).

Despite the prohibitions of the church, individuals who believed strongly in the stories of the church persisted in claiming to have experienced their own private miracles, wrought by prayer to a statue or picture of a saint, which then would eventually become the subject of public veneration. Such was the case of Francisca Lares, a woman from the village of Moca. She was accused by the parish priest on July 4, 1865, of claiming that her carved-stone image of Nuestra Señora del Rosario had "grown and developed miraculously" through time.[39] Amazingly, her case instigated a huge revolt, fueling the exchange of official letters (through the rest of July and August of that year) between the mayor, the parish priest of La Moca, the bishop, and the civil governor of the island. These letters discuss the charges brought against Francisca Lares for conducting "public religious services in her house." The bishop and the priest express their apprehension about this woman, adducing that she had managed illegally to assemble parishioners on Sundays and holidays. The priest writes that parishioners, falling for her charms, "erroneously believed that they were complying with the precept of going to mass by attending that place in order to hear readings and prayers presided by the above-mentioned Señora, and thereby had stopped going to the temple, even though to attend the temple is a precept of Nuestra Santa Madre la Iglesia [Our Holy Mother the Church]" (Archivo Nacional de Puerto Rico, Box 283). It becomes apparent that Francisca Lares was blamed not only for claiming to own a "miraculous image" and taking over the functions of the parish priest but also for "bringing a multitude of people to her home causing, naturally, public disorders."

It is at this point that the municipal police and the civil arms of the state took action. Beyond her religious transgressions, she was found guilty of contravening not only municipal ordinances but also taxation laws. That this case required the involvement of the governor becomes clear after examining the subsequent accusations made against her. She was also indicted for "taking large amounts of alms for the veneration of the image in her home, monies that were not declared since they had been allegedly invested in the maintenance [of the image]." Ostensibly to protect civilians from fraudulent exchanges and to prevent "the continuous abuse of the credulity of these simple neighbors," the civil authorities finally ruled that the image was to be confiscated and put under the protection of the priest. The woman appealed the decision, asking the bishop to have the confiscated image returned to her. The bishop declined her request, "based on information provided by [the accused woman herself] about a few occasions in which she had to reprimand two devotees for the informality and limited respect that were shown in their devotions." The bishop decreed that the priest should hold on to the image "until the enthusiasm which its owner helped beget in her neighbors would dwindle out."

"The Church Is within Ourselves"

For centuries the macro- and micromanagement of the sacred by the Catholic colonial state has left its mark in the popular imagination in quite unexpected ways. If by means of myriad disciplinary practices the church had aimed at creating a tangible world in its own image, the effects of these practices surely exceeded the intentions of their producers. Although instrumental in establishing and sustaining the God-driven state sovereignty in the colonies, the exclusive appropriation of all matters related to the sacred and the monopoly over divine signs, visions, miracles, and divining systems were systematically contested. In many instances there were individual appropriations of divine signs and their veneration that managed to escape the church's totalizing control of the sacred.

Much to the continued dismay of the church, traces as well as new attempts to pursue unmediated relationships with the sacred are still visible today. Although the church has never recognized them as holy, numerous old as well as new sites that mark purported Marian apparitions and miracles throughout Puerto Rico persist as objects of ongoing devotional fervor on the part of thousands of devotees. The "Miracle of Sabana Grande" in 1953, for example, was extensively debated in newspaper articles for years. Entirely funded by the donations of hundreds of devotees, however, a chapel was quickly constructed by the well in the neighborhood of Rincón where the apparition of the Virgen was reported to have occurred. With the dedication of the chapel on April 23, 1955, a procession of several of the faithful carrying candles for the Virgen del Pozo (Virgin of the Well) marked the anniversary of the apparition and the opening of the chapel for worship. The procession began at the public park in Rincón and ended at the newly constructed chapel (*El Mundo* 1955).

Other similarly private miracles and apparitions mark more ephemeral sites of procession in Puerto Rico. In the last days of September 1949, a mysterious religious image was reflected on the balcony of an apartment house on Calle Las Flores in Santurce, attracting thousands of curiosity seekers and ardent believers for weeks (*El Mundo* 1949). So long was the procession of believers and so loud the noise and frequent the number of public disturbances arising from this miracle that the occupants of the apartment house had to leave for their own peace of mind. Apparently the previous owner—a devout Catholic woman—had maintained a small chapel in the house dedicated to the Virgin of Miracles and other saints. She used to spend days praying to the Virgin in her homemade chapel, neighbors said. After a serious illness, she finally died at home, completely alone. Except for some furniture and an image of the Virgin, her belongings were thrown out as trash, and the house was rented to a family. According to popular opinion, the spirit of the dead woman—who had not been given a proper burial (i.e., with the proper prayers)—caused the miraculous image of the Virgin to appear on the side of the building. Following the lead of several fervent Catholic neighbors, a public recitation of the rosary on nine consecutive days (a *novenario*) was offered to honor the spirit of the woman. Her own godchild, who had been very distant for the previous ten years, wished to be forgiven and thus decided to preside over the prayers but not before asking the municipal police to grant him permission and protection for this public event.

Popular forms of Catholic veneration have permeated Puerto Rican society and persisted to this day. What the church labels as heretical or evil misappropriations of its signs and liturgy, practitioners of vernacular forms of spirituality perceive as not merely harmless but indeed legitimate forms of veneration. In this context, I remember once driving west in spring 1996 to visit some botánicas in Cabo Rojo with Lisi, a young woman who said she was a Catholic medium. She expressed at length her indignation at the church's excluding mediums from participating in ordinary Catholic services, even as she realized why the church has traditionally rejected them: "It's because the church is fearful that what we do doesn't match with God. But if our powers are not normal, they're still something that God himself gives us. It's a power that is *in* our psyche [*mente*]; it's not invented or learned from a book. We're born with our [spiritual] gifts. Like doctors, we help people on the material and spiritual plane, and then people succeed [in their endeavors]."

As I drive up and down the hilly highway along the beautiful northwest stretch of the island, my tape recorder is on and Lisi continues her self-administered interview, becoming very emotional as she tells me about her life experiences as a medium. "Since the time I was born I started having visions, and started helping people. I was born with this [spiritual power]. I saw visions with my own eyes. God is always there. Catholicism is always there in me." She then tells me she went to a Catholic school, where she got a very good education, and that is why she sends her teenage daughter to a Catholic school. Stressing her Catholic faith, she says (as if trying to convince not only me but the whole world): "I believe in God—there's no conflict in that, and there shouldn't be. If you're in communion with God, and you're not harming no one, then you're not against the law of God." Lisi received a Catholic school education, so she is very aware of why priests and nuns have a negative attitude toward people who, like herself, are gifted with special spiritual powers and visions: "They [priests and nuns] have closed minds; they think that this [mediumship] is something dark, that it is witchcraft, without knowing that we do good to our fellow humans." She once had a rich boyfriend who was a devout Catholic and whose socially prominent parents and siblings were fanatic churchgoers. Commenting on elite Catholic families such as her boyfriend's, she says:

> These super-Catholic families think that what we do is diabolical, that to light candles is shameful. Yet in the church candles are lit, incense is burned. . . . Priests do it since they think they are ordained to do it. But I think that your temple is your house, and you cleanse your house [of negative energies] like they cleanse the church with all its saints and candles. Now they even persecute the saints, because the very Santa Bárbara [Lisi's patron saint], they took her out of the Catholic church. Here [in Puerto Rico], you won't see Santa Bárbara in the church. You'll see San José, San Miguel, San Rafael, . . . but you won't see Santa Bárbara and La Caridad del Cobre [the Virgin of Charity, also called the Virgin of Copper].[40] Yet you'll see these Catholic families come to consult mediums in secret [and worship Santa Bárbara and La Caridad]. They think it's a shame to be seen because it's unusual, not normal.

Other mediums, espiritistas, and brujos voice similar opinions. Haydée, for example, in one of our first encounters, said, "We brujos and espiritistas pray and plead to God either in the church or here [at home, in our altar rooms]. You don't need to be kneeling in the church, with a black heart. You'd be better off here with a white heart and espiritismo. You are your church. The church is within ourselves."

Even after centuries of persecution and coercive gatekeeping mechanisms against witch-healers, the Catholic Church has not managed to convince them to stay away from its business. Instead, brujos keep reminding institutional religions and their followers that sacred power is also *their* business and that the world of God belongs to and can be approached by anyone who knows how to incorporate the transcendental world into their lives.[41]

NATION BUILDING AND THE
SECULARIZATION OF SPIRITUALITY

···

Spiritist Brujos

Tonight, as she does on the last Friday of every month, Haydée will hold a velada, a nighttime spiritual gathering open to the public, in her home. Her friends and regular clients help with the preparation of this event, either by bringing additional chairs, flowers, and candles or by setting out the table assigned to the mediums. This morning, Ángel, a client who works in the municipality, brings some thirty extra folding chairs from his job and arranges them in rows in the garage, the assigned place for the velada. The atmosphere is energetic: everyone is included in the excitement of the planning. Haydée and I drive to a nearby botánica to buy *alcoholados* (spiritual herbal solutions); Florida Water; yellow candles for her patron saint, La Caridad (Our Lady of Charity), and some flowers. "It's a fiesta espiritual," Haydée tells me as she sets her statue of La Caridad on the floor by the table and surrounds it with bouquets of flowers and a circle of yellow candles. Together with her regular clients, we cover with a white cloth the table assigned to the mediums—hence these types of veladas were called in the past Veladas de la Mesa Blanca (Veladas of the White Table)—and place on it a Bible, the Spiritist books by Kardec (the codifier of Spiritism), her personal rosary, and a number of white candles (signifying good energies).

It is now evening, and everyone dresses in their best clothes. All the lights in the house have been turned on and the gate and doors opened wide, and at seven o'clock people start arriving in cars from all parts of the island. The loud sounds of spiritual music can be heard in the neighborhood, announcing a fiesta espiritual, during which the *pan espiritual* (spiritual bread) will be eaten. Haydée and her guests dance joyfully and sing along to the tapes of sacred music. (This is the best way to summon the *espíritus de luz,* the spirits of light, I am told.) At about eight o'clock all the guests, about thirty, are asked to take their places in the chairs arranged in rows along two vertical columns in the now-converted chapel-like garage. With my tape recorder and microphone, I take a seat in the front row. The three mediums, headed by Haydée, who is the *presidente de mesa* (lit., "president of the table"; i.e., presiding medium), sit around the White Table.

These mediums are at various stages of spiritual development and through their participation in this velada, are hoping to advance in their mediumship. All the lights are turned off and candles lit, creating a distinctly spiritual ambience in the glowing silence. "I hereby open this fiesta espiritual where the pan espiritual will be eaten," Haydée announces. "Let's pray the Our Father all together in communion. Let's begin."

After the prayer, Haydée says, "Here [in this velada], we'll uncover the *causas* of the people gathered here. By *causa,* I mean that—as the president of this humble but sacred home and humble but sacred altar, as the daughter of the Caridad del Cobre—I state 'this person has this [problem]' and 'this person is bitter.'"[1] After these words about causas—explanations that seem directed less to the audience than to me, a first-time participant in a velada—Haydée shifts her tone and asks a man to stand up, saying, "You, that man there [pointing in his direction]—Sori's husband, is it or isn't it right?" (As I would learn later, this is common practice during veladas. Each time a medium has a vision and receives a message for someone, that person is addressed and asked to stand up. If the name of that person is not known to the medium, the medium will mention other identifying marks, like the color of the person's dress or the location where the person is seated.)

Addressing the standing man, Haydée says, "You live your life bitterly and I don't know why. Life is so beautiful. It's not worth getting bitter, my fellow Christian. This morning I woke up and felt that something was wrong, that some bad energy was taking hold of me. And then over an insignificant matter, my son and I exchanged very harsh words, something very unusual for us. . . . Realizing that it was not me who had motivated that [but a negative energy], I stopped myself and asked my son to forgive me, in order to purify myself. This is another proof that, as a bruja, I can't harbor bad feelings. I have to strive to be always humble."

Then, changing her tone again, Haydée says, "We'll begin," and addressing one of the most experienced mediums at the table she asks,

2.1 Haydée and mediums seated at the White Table

"Clara, read, in communion with our Celestial Father." Clara reads aloud from the small Spiritist prayer book she has opened at random (as is customary) to a prayer for making an offering to the Niño de Praga (the Infant of Prague, also called Niño de Atocha).

Chills run up and down my spine as I hear Haydée say, "Clara, this is for you and your son who is wearing you down with his many problems" (the Infant of Prague is the patron of children). Under the sign of this prayer, which is perceived as an omen, the velada proceeds. Mediums and the presidente de mesa, Haydée, start to receive messages from the spirits for each person seated in front of them. Individuals are addressed and invited to stand in front of the table. "You, in the red sweater, stand up." . . . "That man, sitting in the third row, come here!" . . . "That young woman who is hiding her face—don't be afraid, stand up." In some cases, a cleansing with the alcoholados and the Florida Water is done for a person who appears burdened by bad spirits. In other cases, a spiritual recipe might be dictated or a person invited for a private consultation for a problem needing further elucidation. That night we stayed well past midnight—adults,

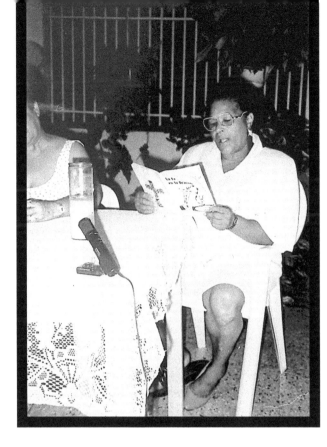

2.2
*Clara reading
aloud a Spiritist
prayer*

children, and babies—because, as the rules dictate, a velada cannot end until each person has received a message.

Veladas such as these have been extremely popular on the island since the late 1850s, when Kardec's books on Spiritism were first introduced. One historian writes that the "evocation of spirits was in great vogue at fashionable parties in Puerto Rico as early as 1856" (Cruz Monclova 1958:643). In the early years, however, and probably even as late as the first years of the 1900s, veladas seem to have been initiated or conducted not by members of the general public but by physicians, lawyers, journalists, and intellectuals identified with liberal and emancipation ideals who had access to these imported Kardecean texts.

Kardec's ideas about a secular form of spirituality met with instant acceptance in Puerto Rico as well as in other parts of the Caribbean and Latin America. A brief summary of the major Spiritist ideas, as codified by Kardec, explains their appeal among the liberal, anticlerical (though

Catholic), Creole elite. Born Catholic, Leon Hippolyte Denizard Rivail, better known as Allan Kardec (1804–1869), became a student of medicine and literature as well as a disciple of the humanist educator Johann Heinrich Pestalozzi (1746–1826). Kardec's views on Spiritism (which came to be called Scientific Spiritism) as an alternative to antiecclesiastical spirituality are codified in his *Book of Spirits* (1857), *Book of Mediums* (1861), and *Gospel According to Spiritism* (1864). According to his followers and interpreters in Puerto Rico, Kardec's views are based on the following principles: There is a superior infinite intelligence (God) that finite men cannot completely comprehend; spiritual life is eternal and the soul immortal; an enlightened spirit (Christ, for example) is a projection of God and should be emulated; evocation of and communication with spirits is possible under certain circumstances (and everyone can develop these abilities); humans have to live many material lives to evolve and reach perfection; the divine Law of Cause and Effect makes us pay for our wrongdoing in subsequent reincarnations; through good deeds and charity toward our fellow humans we can compensate for social debts (wrongdoings to fellow humans) acquired in previous existences; there is no hell or Satan, these being religious myths that contradict the essential goodness of God; and, finally, there are other inhabited worlds in the universe.[2]

The immediate, pervasive appeal of Scientific Spiritism was not coincidental. Risking oversimplification, two reasons can be ventured to explain its success in Puerto Rico. First, the general belief in the existence of spirits and the ability to communicate with them existed among the native Taíno Indians and African slaves in Puerto Rico more than three centuries before Kardec's Scientific Spiritism was introduced. Further, the personal worship of spirits had persisted in conjunction with the practices of medieval Mediterranean popular Catholicism introduced by the colonizers. Second, the anticlerical tenets of Spiritism found willing listeners among liberal, anticonservative, and emancipation- and independence-minded groups in the late nineteenth century. In response to similar needs, two organizations were established at the same time in Puerto Rico: the Freemasons and Scientific Spiritism, each attracting similar audiences among the liberal, progressive elites.[3]

Unlike the conservative elites who fought for the continuation of Spanish Catholic rule on the island, liberal elites stood for autonomy from Spain, the abolition of slavery, and freedom of worship. Some more radical individuals strove, as well, for total separation from Spain. Spiritism—defined by Kardec as a philosophy, not a religion—suited the political and moral agenda of these progressive *criollos* (Creoles). Spiritism, identified with modern cosmopolitan democracies and especially French Republicanism, enabled them to pursue some form of spiritual connection with the transcendental world that would be outside the church and hence not in conflict with their revolutionary ideologies. Spiritist gatherings, although initially facilitated by the Freedom of Worship Decree (1868), did not become an alternative form of religious worship (as attested by the insistence on excluding any religious icons in their gatherings) but rather tended to be framed as a "scientifically" based form of spirit communication. In the twentieth century both elite and lower-class Catholics ended up embracing Spiritism, albeit of a different kind. Even if the historically based bitterness of these groups toward the Spanish Catholic Church had been experienced differently, both groups embraced Spiritism as a way out of what they considered a repressive, dogmatic, classist, and often racist institutional church (see Vidal 1994:3, 22, 47–48).

Scientific Spiritism was incorporated first into emancipation and revolutionary agendas by the criollo elites and later into nationalist ideologies by the Puerto Rican people at large. The popularity of Kardec's books might be indicative of a major shift from a clerical to an anticlerical (i.e., secular-philosophical) relationship to the transcendental world in nineteenth-century Puerto Rican Creole society. Belief in spirits and reincarnation accompanied the process of liberalization and nation building in Puerto Rico. As in other Latin American independence movements, instead of serving just alternative channels of communication with the supernatural world, some mid-nineteenth-century intellectuals, separatist politicians, and Freemasons recruited these esoteric beliefs in the service of their political activities.[4]

Although the sanctity of Spanish colonial rule had already been shattered by *independentistas criollos* (Creole supporters of independence) throughout the Americas by the 1820s, Puerto Rico and Cuba remained colonies of Spain until the last years of the nineteenth century.[5] Furthermore, by the mid-1800s ties between the metropole and the island were as tightly secured as ever, probably because of the increasing success of the island in producing coffee and sugar. Puerto Rico took over the supply of sugar to the United States, substituting for Cuba's more refined and expensive product (Dietz 1986; Scarano 1984). Also, as a result of the *Cédula de Gracias,* loyalists escaping from newly independent Latin American colonies found on the island a haven for their business endeavors and political ideas. The comparatively late sugar boom and the interests of loyalists would make it impossible to sever ties with the metropole, much to the regret of revolutionary-minded Creoles. Loyalty to Spain, on the one hand, and fear of independence, on the other, although not necessarily parts of the same political position, were combined in the creation of unprecedented alliances among loyalists, autonomists, and separatists.

With the death of Fernando VII in 1833, a rocky process of secularization and democratization began in Spain, leading to the liberal revolution of 1868 and the formation of the first Spanish republic in 1873.[6] These events helped to foster the hopes of the criollo liberal elites—both the *autonomistas* (who envisioned Puerto Rico as a province of Spain) and the *separatistas* (who favored severing all ties with Spain)—to achieve, in the former case, a more equitable relationship with Spain; and in the latter, independence. Autonomy, independence, the emancipation of slaves, and the secularization of the state, however, were not always advocated jointly. Some participants in these liberal movements agreed with emancipation but opposed independence. Others agreed on the separation of church and state but did not advocate emancipation. Indeed, these conflicting agendas were resolved neither by metropolitan nor Creole liberals.[7]

One of the results of the Spanish liberal revolution was the Freedom of Worship Decree, issued on September 23, 1868. It entitled Puerto Ricans "publicly and privately to profess their faith," subject only to the limitations established by moral and civil law. It also freed public offices and civil and political rights from dependence on the religious creed of individuals and gave citizens "the right of parliamentary representation, amnesty of political prisoners, freedom of the press, and so on" (Silva Gotay 1985:60).

The other agenda, long desired by the autonomist party in Puerto Rico and supported by Spanish liberals, was to achieve autonomy for Puerto Rico. Under this status, Puerto Rico could become a Spanish province, and, as in the metropole, it could also attain the separation of church and state. Conservatives on the island, most of whom were wealthy hacendados and merchant *peninsulares* (born in Spain), were inclined to support the old colonial Catholic rule, not so much for religious as for economic reasons. Even though hacendados were not necessarily fervent Catholics, the old system legitimized by the church had assured their hegemony and profits by securing the continuity of slavery and the forced labor of landless poor whites. Bearing in mind that by the 1860s there were more sugar plantations than ever before, emancipation and autonomy were seen as real threats by conservative Creoles and peninsulares alike. The total separation of church and state in Puerto Rico was marked by conflicting attitudes largely because it simultaneously involved anticolonial feelings toward Spain and partnership with and support of Spanish liberalism. These two attitudes could not coexist without creating some dissension. Indeed, they were often substantially at odds. A poignant example of the inherent contradiction of Creole revolutionaries vis-à-vis the church can be seen in the event that followed the Grito de Lares rebellion. Occurring only a few months before the Spanish revolution of 1868, the Grito de Lares insurrection in the hills of Lares had been aimed at severing colonial rule and establishing a new Puerto Rican republic.[8] Interestingly, the revolutionaries, some of whom subscribed to liberal ideas such as freedom of religion, celebrated the short-lived capture of Lares "with a singing of the Te Deum in the Catholic church," the newly created flag of independence "draped over the main altar" (Silva Gotay 1985:60).[9]

Spiritism: Sacredness in a Secular World

Liberal rule in Spain facilitated the growth of Freemason societies, esoteric schools, and Spiritism in Spain as well as on the island. After 1868, particularly between 1870 and 1873, Freemasons, who had been active since 1820, created a system of lodges throughout the island and recruited a large number of young abolitionist liberals (Picó 1988:208). Indicative of these new forces in Puerto Rican society, by the 1880s Freemasonry was being publicly discussed in four newspapers, and four new books had been published and widely distributed (Cruz Monclova 1957:854–855). But greater than the success achieved by Masonry "was the prosperity that, by these times, Spiritism was continuously exhibiting" (p. 855). During the last quarter of the nineteenth century, while several Protestant churches were being founded in Puerto Rico in Ponce, Mayagüez, Aguada, Vieques, and other municipalities, "some elitist sectors began to search for systems of belief and ethical principles akin to Christianity, yet grounded on the esoteric debates prevalent at that time in France, Great Britain, and other industrialized countries. Theosophy, Rosicrucianism, and Spiritism, as well as other movements, began to be endorsed by and to lure members from the highest ranks of society" (Picó 1988:222), the very same people who were also the most vocal in the media and other important spheres of public life.[10]

Despite the increasing ideological pluralism and the newly established individual civil liberties, "as long as the church was bound to the state, freedom of thought in religious matters could be punished with imprisonment. Puerto Rican liberal leaders were therefore largely anticlerical" (Silva Gotay 1985:63). It was in this atmosphere that Spiritist centers were founded all over the island, especially in Mayagüez on the west coast, during the late nineteenth century.

For upper-class Puerto Ricans, adherence to Spiritism meant more than the belief in and the ability to communicate with spirits; it meant a radical change in the ways Puerto Ricans related to spirituality in general and to the role of Spiritism in the education system. Indeed, beyond circulating and publicizing Spiritist ideas in order to influence public opinion, Spiritist criollos aimed at institutionalizing their worldview. With this in mind, in 1873 the Puerto Rican delegate to the Spanish Cortes (House of Representatives), Don Manuel Corchado Juarbe, presented a motion aimed at replacing traditional metaphysics courses with courses in Spiritism in secondary schools and universities. By 1882 a Spiritist society was sending out flyers advertising the sale of eleven books by Allan Kardec and an additional nine titles by other Spiritist authors. In addition, six newspapers were publishing articles on Spiritism (Cruz Monclova 1957: 854–855).

The success of Spiritist centers in attracting Catholics was not uncontested by the church, which waged a public campaign against Spiritists of all kinds by publishing books on the lives of saints, news on religious matters, *novenarios* (prayer booklets), catechisms, and newspaper articles, and by delivering sermons denouncing Spiritists as heretics. In 1886 Benito Cantero, director and editor of the *Archbishop's Ecclesiastical Bulletin,* published a theological attack on Kardec's interpretation of the Gospels, striking an aggressive blow at the movement's major theorizer.

Starting in about the mid-nineteenth century, cemeteries became controversial sites, as can be seen in the 1857 Royal Decree prohibiting private eulogies in cemeteries. In the words of this document, "[T]his novelty, imported from countries that have different religious circumstances than ours, gives a profane, secular, rabble-rousing [*gentílico*] character" to funerary rites. Eulogistic practices of any kind—from speeches and poetic compositions to performances of secular rituals—were construed as "dangerous and unusual." They had to be banned not only because they were anticlerical but also because they disturbed the "public order" (Coll y Toste 1916e:139).

In 1870 the civil authorities prohibited, under the 1868 Freedom of Religion Act and pressure from church officials, the circulation and sale of imported books that were disparaging or offered alternatives to the

Catholic faith. When these measures proved ineffective, sanctions targeted against the private life of individuals were put into effect. Several cases were reported of priests refusing to perform Catholic marriages, baptisms, or funeral rites for suspected Spiritists, which served as a warning to others not to follow Spiritism lest they too be excluded from mainstream (Catholic) life-cycle rituals (Cruz Monclova 1957:856–864).[11]

The last quarter of the nineteenth century marks a period of damaging developments for the institutionalization of Spiritism, which naturally produced a more forceful mobilization of its followers in the political arena. After the emancipation of slaves had been proclaimed on March 23, 1873, and freedom of association decreed two months later, the hopes for a liberal society were shattered once again, just a year later.[12] The fall of the Spanish republic in 1874 came as abruptly as had its birth in 1873, dragging with it a wave of political persecution and public disorder (Picó 1988:209). The counterrevolution of 1874 (which became effective in Puerto Rico only in 1876) restored the church's status within the state. The charter of the counterrevolution stated that the "Roman Catholic and Apostolic faith is the State's religion." Privately, individuals would still enjoy freedom of worship, but "ceremonies or public manifestations other than those of the state religion [would] not be permitted" (quoted in Silva Gotay 1985:62).

In the aftermath of the counterrevolution, the church, the local government, and a number of individuals vigorously renewed their public attacks on Spiritism through various exclusionary tactics. Editorials by conservative Catholics show the unease produced by the proliferation of Spiritist ideas in Puerto Rican society. Lamenting the expansion of esoteric movements on the island, these editorials often portray the threats that belief in Spiritism presented to the well-being of society. In a letter to the editors of a respected newspaper, a reader named Don Alejandro Infiesta García argued that although it was clear that "Spiritism was invading the island," its detrimental effects were still to be seen in the near future. In the same vein, Don José Perez Moris, another reader, wrote: "Spiritism, that sect so anti-Catholic and socially corrosive, like Masonry, which has driven so many crazy and mad, has been gaining many adherents in Puerto Rico" (quoted in Cruz Monclova 1957:855).

A founding member of the first Spiritist center in Puerto Rico, Don Emeterio Bacón, recalled that between 1879 and 1889 the Spanish government became suspicious of veladas (which were being held in Spiritist centers all over the island) and therefore decreed that organizers had to request municipal permission for these gatherings. As if this provision were not enough, "a pair of civil guards were also assigned at the gates to watch over the centers" during veladas, because government authorities feared their potentially subversive nature (Yañez 1963:19–20).[13] Teresa Yañez's work on this subject does not state explicitly the reasons for these measures from the government's perspective, but one can infer that they were motivated in part by the rising sense of lack of control over the public sphere following the concessions granted by the 1876 articles on religious tolerance and the 1880 civil reforms. But perhaps the most concrete threats were the 1887 political rebellions of autonomistas, who were reorganizing themselves in municipalities following the ideas professed by separatistas. Fear that Spiritist centers would easily become sites of seditious activities — under the guise and protection of freedom of worship and association — was more likely the true motive for such measures.

The State, Progress, and Charlatans

By the early decades of the twentieth century Spiritism was flourishing, not only among the liberal elites — as had been the case in the mid-nineteenth century — but also among the general population. Arcadio Díaz Quiñones (1996) points out that by the 1920s Kardec's *Gospel According to Spiritism* was outselling the Bible in Puerto Rico, which I suppose must have gained popularity as a sacred, ritual object, given that the majority of Puerto Ricans were illiterate in that period (see Guerra 1998). Under Spanish rule, such books had had to be smuggled in because they promoted a secular form of spirituality that was a threat to the church's hegemony. Once American rule began in 1898, however, the state's overt intervention in matters of faith had become almost nil and books of this sort circulated freely.

In this new space, Spiritism was a local force that was recruited, along with the Protestant churches of America,[14] for carrying out the process of modernization and progress. Unlike Protestant teachings, however, Kardec's books on Spiritism and mediumship offered not only a scientific, antireligious explanation of the spiritual world,[15] but an alternative to the moral and social order of the old Spanish Catholic Church. Their aim was to guide society by means of reason and science toward modernity, economic and social progress, and nation building, ideas that suited the agenda of progressive Puerto Ricans. Indeed, Yañez (1963:29) mentions that the early Spiritist centers clearly state in their founding charters that their role in society is essentially moral and social in nature and that their goal is to establish and fund humanitarian institutions such as orphanages, hospitals for the poor, and various kinds of asylums.[16]

One of the booklets published by the Spiritist center Club Amor y Ciencia (Love and Science Club) of Arecibo in 1913 shows how Spiritism was construed as an alternative to the ethos of Catholicism. More than advance a morality that was concerned with a parochial solution for individual salvation, it promoted a more inclusive civic mode of consciousness. By means of transcribing messages given by spirits during mediumistic events, the publisher seems to have aimed at propagating among the followers of Spiritist centers ideas that encouraged the civic transformation of Puerto Ricans in a way that would be in line with the expressed Spiritist ethos—both moral and modern. A sample of such messages is as follows: "Intelligence without morals is like the dawn without the sun"; "The arrogant architect is reminded of foundations laid on sand"; "The work of humans that are not cemented on true principles of love and charity will be destroyed and no stone will be left on another"; "Those who spill lots of words without enriching them with science and virtue resemble those who throw pitchers full of water to the streets" (Club Amor y Ciencia 1913:75–79). Supernatural forms of advice such as these integrated political, moral, and social issues and portrayed the ideal modern human being according to European esoteric schools of thought and Spiritist values. In poetically evocative yet practical ways—through aphorisms and commonsense sayings—these supernatural messages addressed general social concerns in didactic ways. Writing in the 1990s and sharing his predecessors' envisionings of the role of Spiritism in modern Puerto Rican society, Rodríguez Escudero (1991:4), a Puerto Rican Spiritist-historian, succinctly characterized Spiritism as "a force that is called on to play an important role in the modern world and in our homeland."

Throughout the twentieth century and under the moral charter of the famous Spiritist dictum "Amor, Caridad y Esperanza" (Love, Charity, and Hope), new centers were founded, attracting a wide variety of participants: white, black, and mulatto middle- and lower-class people. *Curanderos* (popular healers)[17] and brujos formed new centers in their homes, in which private consultations and weekly gatherings were held on a regular basis. Their practices added to the previously more austere centers of Scientific Spiritism an array of ritual objects, such as *santos* (figurines of the saints),[18] candles, incense, and flowers; rituals such as *santiguos* (healing blessings),[19] *despojos* (spiritual cleansings), prayers, and spells; and an array of indigenous, medieval Catholic, and African offerings.[20]

In contrast to Scientific Spiritists, who kept striving to maintain the Kardecean, orthodox notion of a secular "modern" form of worship devoid of any signs of Catholicism, the new forms of "popular" Spiritism that developed in the twentieth century gradually included the idiom and functions of folk Catholicism.[21] Small altars modeled after those in churches; baptismal ceremonies; and santos, prayers, and group recitation of the Rosary were added to the practices of Scientific Spiritism and specifically to the velada of the White Table. Therefore, those "popular"[22] Spiritists who had previously practiced folk Catholicism (the dominant tradition in mountain areas for centuries) never ceased to see themselves as Catholics. Even after the more recent introduction of African deities into their pantheon, these popular Spiritists continued to define themselves as fervent Catholics.

With the American presence on the island in 1898, another set of changes was introduced to the practices of Spiritism. As part of the general quest for Americanization (ca. 1920) that guided the U.S. colonial period of the first half of the twentieth century, American Protestant churches and, to a lesser degree, the American Catholic Church began to participate programmatically in the civil arena. Under the flag of democratic capitalism, these Christian organizations invested their proselytizing efforts in reshaping the religious lives of Puerto Ricans.[23] Many families found themselves divided in terms of their religious affiliation. Within a single family, the father might be a Spiritist, the mother a convert to Protestantism, and their children converts to the recently established American form of Catholicism on the island, while the grandparents might still be following the old Spanish Catholic Church.

In this context the "Americanization" of Puerto Rico included more than economic arrangements. It also promoted the replacement of the European educational system by the American one, the introduction of English as the instructional language, and the participation of Protestant ministers and American Catholic priests in the reorganization of the education system and in the designing of welfare policies and legislation. Protestant hymns and songs were sung and the Bible read in public schools. Although these arrangements were hardly the best examples of the alleged separation of church and state, their aim was to transmit in practice the most cherished notions of the American ethos. Emphasis was put on concepts such as freedom of conscience, separation of church and state, and freedom of religion (Silva Gotay 1985:69). It is plausible that in the first two decades of the twentieth century the deep involvement of Americans in various areas of Puerto Rican social life—the construction of roads, the centralization of primary and secondary schools, military recruitment during the war, the founding of the first university (1903–1925)—promoted among a certain part of the population a strong disdain for traditional local values and respect for the superiority of American culture (see Morales Carrión 1983:173–199, 299–311). The unilateral granting of citizenship to all Puerto Ricans through the Jones Act of 1917 officially materialized the infamous tenets of Manifest Destiny.

At the same time, as a result of American policies during the 1930s and 1940s, especially those aimed at solving the social and economic problems of the island, fundamental changes in the social structure of the ruling elites were initiated. Although tracing the economic policies of the United States vis-à-vis Puerto Rico in detail is outside the scope of my work, I mention some that I consider milestones in the development of a new technocratic class. The importance of this class lies in its central though politically invisible role in sustaining a major popular reformist movement on the island by means of its scientific expertise. Indirectly, by stressing the need to develop and bring progress to the countryside (which by the 1940s included more than half of the population), this plan indirectly contributed to the condemnation of brujería for being opposed to modernity, development, and progress.

With the intent of preventing social unrest, the American state extended civil and labor rights to the local population by the 1930s, even if this contradicted the immediate interests of U.S. corporations that were investing in the island. This strengthened the connection of Puerto Rican labor movements to their American counterparts and also reinforced the U.S. government's idea that prosperity is the road to democracy (Morales Carrión 1983:200–211). Improving the living conditions of a poverty-stricken society was a priority, Theodore Roosevelt Jr., governor of Puerto Rico (1929–1932), wrote after seeing "farm after farm where lean, under-fed women and sickly men repeated again and again the same story—little food and no opportunity to get more" (quoted in Wagenheim and Wagenheim [1994] 1996:168). With the onset of the Great Depression, relief and public works projects were carried out on the island as a direct result of Franklin Delano Roosevelt's 1933 New Deal government, which supported the Chardón Plan, an industrialization program aimed at transforming a predominantly agrarian society into a modern one (Morales Carrión 1983:212–241). A crucial result of this change of policy was "the transfer of U.S. colonial administration in Puerto Rico from the Department of War to the Department of the Interior" (Grosfoguel 1997:64). Almost a decade later, in 1941, Rexford Guy Tugwell, who had been the first president of the newly founded University of Puerto Rico in 1925, became the governor of Puerto Rico. His liberal ideas resonated with the socioeconomic reform plans envisioned by the rising popular leader Muñoz Marín (later the first native governor), whose party had won the insular elections to the Senate in 1940 and remained in power until 1968 with a political agenda that stressed the connection between bread and progress and having a real *patria* (homeland) (Morales Carrión 1983:249–255). The object of this succinct chronology is to show that the populist reformist quest for the social and economic improvement of the island—which was a high priority before the colonial status question could even be addressed—propelled the creation and forceful intervention of a new class of Creole experts in various areas of public welfare and administration who would be instrumental in shaping Puerto Rican society and culture in the second half of the twentieth century.

By the mid-twentieth century the professional intelligentsia had already undergone socialization into the utilitarian and rationalist models of social theory taught in American universities. Guided by a general program of modernization and progress, these notions were being translated into public policy. In 1948 Puerto Rico was allowed to elect its first native governor and in 1952 was granted more self-rule under the commonwealth form of government, the Estado Libre Asociado (ELA). As a result of a new commonwealth politics, new programs were being sought to ameliorate the conditions of Puerto Ricans in all areas of life, and the newly created commonwealth state agencies took it upon themselves to pursue any such programs.[24] In this context, motivated by the quest for bureaucratic rationality, the Puerto Rican state apparatus launched, during the late 1940s and the 1950s, an attack on brujería and curanderismo via the medical, educational, and legal systems and the media. Unlike the justifications of the colonial church, however, this was an attack framed in terms of the newly adopted philosophy of social progress. Not coincidentally, it needs to be said, the Partido Popular Democrático (PPD) was in power at that time and sponsoring Operation Bootstrap, a major industrialization and development program devised after World War II by the United States to modernize Puerto Rico.

New and comprehensive federal and state development programs were designed to help "modernize" the Puerto Rican countryside. Launched in about 1947, Operation Bootstrap, or "industrialization by invitation," was seen by the then-ruling party and the United States as a major economic achievement, one that could be showcased as a success story of U.S. intervention in the Caribbean.[25] As part of the ideology of "welfare capitalism," the notion of development also entailed better education and health services. The medical establishment took responsibility for the latter, of course; but in trying to provide modern health services for the population, it overstepped its traditionally granted role of preventing and treating illness, engaging instead in a full-scale social battle against *supersticiones* (superstitions).

In the new hegemonic discourse of the state, "heretics" had thereby been transformed into "charlatans." With the expressed aim of "modernizing" and "developing" the countryside, the educational and medical bureaucrats had devised several educational programs, for example, the Division of Community Education (DIVEDCO), a grassroots education program established in 1949 (Dávila 1997:34). One of them proposed to eradicate "supersticiones," "magia," and "curanderismo" from Puerto Rican society.[26] The driving force behind such programs was not the clergy but the Puerto Rican intelligentsia and civil servants as well as some American consultants and aides. Unlike during Spanish Catholic colonial rule, vernacular "folkloric" healing and magical practices were not being condemned in these state programs as heretical or as threats to hegemony but as signs of national stagnation and as threats to the project of state building (a position that would change dramatically by the 1970s).[27] Portrayed by state health officials as anachronistic remnants of a premodern society, vernacular forms of healing had to be eradicated forever for a rationality-based government to be able to administer public health services (*El Mundo* 1948c). A series of journalistic reports and editorials published in *El Mundo* (the Puerto Rican equivalent of the *New York Times*) testify to the negative conflation of curanderismo and brujería, carefully crafted and referred to under the general rubric "supersticiones" in administrative discourses of the medical and judicial systems, in effect dismissing these vernacular practices as indistinguishable from the archenemies of modernity. These practices had already begun to merge spontaneously with Kardecean Spiritism in private altar rooms, but under the gaze of the state they appeared as counterforces to modernization and rationality. Following Greg Urban's (1993:215–218) distinction between "marked" and "unmarked" cultures, the aim of the state apparatus was to eliminate marked cultures from the public sphere. Any effort to modernize Puerto Rico would mean that specific traditional cultures had to be converted into the one general culture, identified as modern and rational. Paradoxically, when the Instituto de Cultura Puertorriqueña (ICP) was founded only a few years later, in 1955, under the rule of the PPD as part of Operation Serenity, it promoted in an idealized form the very rural lifestyle that was being eradicated by Operation Bootstrap, "images of a rural utopia that were said to represent the essence of Puerto Ricanness" (Dávila 1997:35). But before the modernist project could be joined with the strengthening of national cultural pride, as envisioned by the PPD, in separate articles between February and May 1948, the editors of *El Mundo* spoke of vernacular religious and healing practices as social ills that needed to be extirpated from Puerto Rican social life. Translating the ideologies of modernization into a medical idiom, one editorial claimed that "curanderos . . . contribute to maintaining the people in their ignorance, and, without curing the body, fill [their] minds with superstitions and fantasies, at the same time poisoning the soul and the body" (*El Mundo* 1948b). Editorials also urged the Asociación Médica de Puerto Rico (Medical Association of Puerto Rico) to provide accessible health services for the people who would agree to turn away from curanderos, if the proposed programs were to succeed. The president of the Asociación Médica, Dr. Manuel A. Astor, declared that one of the goals of his association was "to devise an educational program to eliminate curanderos, who are still tolerated and consulted by the great majority of the less-educated sectors of the population" (*El Mundo* 1948c). The Asociación de Salud Pública de Puerto Rico (Association of Public Health of Puerto Rico), having consulted with a commission of the U.S. Department of the Interior, also revealed its plan to conduct a "survey [the English word in the original] of the existing public health conditions." And a special committee of doctors and legislators announced that they were in the process of discussing how "to enlist the help of the legislative power in any corrective measures that might be needed" (*El Mundo* 1948c). In a front page article in *El Mundo* three months later, Dr. Astor publicly denounced the "harm caused by curanderos" and announced the initiation of a program that would "put an end to the role of curanderos in Puerto Rican society . . . and implement an intensive educational program to direct the population to medical centers of the Department of Public Health." Recruiting the media in this fight, the doctor ended his announcement by thanking the "printed communication services and the radio for their future cooperation" (1948a).

Several editorials, also in *El Mundo,* mocked brujos and curanderos. One skillfully vilified the practices of brujos, using academic, historical and ethnographic evidence of their "unsophisticated deceit." It alerted readers to the recent "invasion" of brujos and curanderos in urban centers and portrayed clients as "simpletons" who not only mistakenly referred to curanderos as *médicos* (medical doctors) but who also "mispronounce[d]" the Spanish word *doctor,* saying "dotol" (dō-tól, a dialect pronunciation attributed by the elite to peasants) (*El Mundo* 1949).

Joining in this phenomenon and in full agreement with the declarations of Dr. Astor, the Puerto Rican Department of Health and Education launched a public war of its own, also in print, against brujería and curanderismo. A booklet entitled "La ciencia contra la superstición" (Science against Superstition) was published by DIVEDCO in 1951. Three hundred thousand copies were distributed in rural areas to "lance primitive healing practices" (*El Mundo* 1951) and promote the newly formed public health centers.

The booklet tells the story of Juanita ("La historia de Juanita"), the young daughter of a poor family that consulted popular healers until they experienced a tragic event—the death of their son. Grafted onto a pseudo-folktale tragedy occurring in a rural area and accompanied by very simple, comic book–style illustrations, the booklet contained a general message against superstition, encompassing all the healing and spirit-related practices outside the medical profession, directed to the rural population.[28] In this fiction the medical establishment appears as the rational savior of a family that suffered the tragic consequences of consulting curanderos instead of doctores. Enlightened now about the effects of superstition, the eldest daughter, Juanita, decides to become a physician, embodying metaphorically the lesson that all Puerto Ricans are meant to draw from the tale: superstitious healing practices are dangerous, even fatal.[29]

In a 1954 monograph, *Males del medio ambiente* (Evils of the Social Environment), published by the Department of Public Instruction in a series disseminating scientific information, J. Rodríguez Pastor, M.D., attacked curanderos, superstition, chiropractors, astrologers, and Spiritist mediums. Writing from a physician's point of view, he stressed that these phenomena were survivals of irrational medieval beliefs and thus argued for their total elimination in modern times. He also denounced the "unfair profit" that some manufacturers of trademark magical concoctions were making with the help of physician-pharmacists who agreed to sell bogus products alongside bona fide ones in their pharmacies. Dr. Pastor warned that the claimed efficacy of the magical potions packaged in little bottles and sold in pharmacies, such as Amansa Guapo (Subduer of the Abusive Male), was based on "pure deceit" and "error"—clearly in violation of current consumer laws—and motivated only by profit. He ended with an exhortation to the medical profession in general—pharmacists and physicians alike—to be more involved in "eradicating the outrageous distribution, sale, and consumption of bogus magical potions" by engaging in a "collective educational mission" (Rodríguez Pastor 1954:147).

Three years later a program designed to create a regional system of medical centers in Puerto Rico, along the lines of a U.S. regional health program, continued this preoccupation with eradicating the spiritual healing practices of the rural population of Puerto Rico. In a series of questionnaires, investigators used only one category, "curanderos and espiritistas," to determine the extent to which people still consulted "popular healers and Spiritists" in cases of illness (*El Mundo* 1957). The distinctions between Scientific and "popular" Spiritism, seen as essential by Scientific Spiritists, were again not taken into account, the most important being that "true" Spiritism is devoid of any profit-oriented motivation as well as of any "superstitions," that is, additions from Catholic or African forms of worship.

On occasions such as the following, however, a distinction was made in the public sphere. Distinguishing between different forms of Spiritism, Senator Arturo Ortiz Toro resumed the war against popular healers in 1962 by proposing legislation aimed at "punishing the commerce in pain, desperation and human ignorance conducted by *curanderas, pitonisas, adivinadoras,* and *falsos consejeros*" (female popular healers, fortune-tellers, and soothsayers, and both male and female fake spiritual advisers). Only by assuming that this senator was a follower of Scientific Spiritism can we understand the caveat that then follows: "And yet in no way is [the proposed legislation] directed against people who, in good faith and without a profit-making motivation, practice Spiritism as a science or religion" (*El Mundo* 1962:17).

Unlike the previous three cases that conflated curanderismo, brujería, and espiritismo under one category—"supersticiones"—the senator differentiated popular misappropriations of espiritismo by *espiriteros* (a derogatory term for fake espiritistas) from "true" espiritismo. He based the difference on the essentially commercial aspects of the first and the wholly altruistic motivations of the second.[30] It should be noted that it has usually been lawyers, politicians, and physicians—that is, the more vocal and powerful members of Puerto Rican society—who have publicly admitted to practicing only the latter form of Spiritism, never the former.

The typical merging of curanderismo, brujería, and popular forms of Spiritism in terms of their alleged persistent negative effects in Puerto Rico resurfaced in the public sphere again in 1968, when a story titled "Witch-Healing and Spiritism" (Brujería y Espiritismo), illustrated with a witch holding a broom and a smoking bottle, appeared in *El Mundo* (1968a:7). The author of the editorial, Miguel A. Santín, relates (half cynically, half seriously) the accusations by the General Cigar Company, a Utuado-based factory, that one of the two competing employees' unions at the factory (the International Association of Machinists [IAM] and Aerospace Workers AFL-CIO) had won the election illegally through the workings of spirits, brujería, and magic. A well-known New York law firm represented the company and compiled a book-length document filled with evidence purportedly detailing how the IAM leaders had used the "spirits" at election time to "guide" the hands of workers—through charms, incense, and weather changes—to vote for them and not the others (*El Mundo* 1968c:7). One such piece of evidence tells of a female worker who brought to work a tiny bottle allegedly containing a magical potion, prepared by a woman in Ponce, which, when smelled by or sprayed over her coworkers made them vote for the IAM.

Although the formal charges filed by the General Cigar Company (asking to annul the election results) before the Council for Labor Relations were dropped, *El Mundo* subsequently published editorials with the responses of widely respected Scientific Spiritists, who were insulted by the arbitrary conflation of brujería and espiritismo as if they were one and the same thing, mistaking *fufús*[31] for "true" (i.e., their own) espiritismo. The public debate had shifted from the legal investigation of witchcraft accusations to "marking" local differences within espiritismo. A letter by José A. Suárez, president of the Casa de las Almas (a Spiritist center in Santurce), in response to Santín's column, states, "Of course, we [the members of the center] do not question the occurrence of the events that you describe in your column, but we deeply regret that the name of Spiritism is shuffled together with practices that this noble ideal fights against because of their immorality and the gross ignorance they reveal. . . . *Espiritismo* does not deal with *brujería* or with *brujos;* in fact, it repudiates these practices" (*El Mundo* 1968b:7). Other responses were also included in the editorial. One of them is by the children of the famous "good Samaritan" Doña Julia Vázquez Vda. de Fernández. In clarifying their position on Scientific Spiritism to *El Día,* a newspaper published in Ponce, they mention her miraculous, charitable deeds. Although she was uneducated, the children remark, she had a "natural" gift to heal people with the "guidance of supernatural forces." But, "unlike *embaucadores* [charlatans] who pretend to have these powers," Doña Julia never charged for her services; she did it "for *caridad* [charity]" (quoted in *El Mundo* 1968b:7).[32] It seems that the criteria for differentiating "true" from "false" Spiritists are based on the authenticity and purity of their motives, and on whether they charge for their services.

The need to define the boundaries of Scientific Spiritism and to distinguish its practices from other forms of Spiritism did not end in the late 1960s. More than thirty years later, in 1996, I could still recognize during my fieldwork this acute (maybe even greater) need among Scientific Spiritists. Perhaps what changed are the kinds of justifications for drawing boundaries and the ways in which differences are characterized. While visiting several Scientific Spiritism centers, I have noticed that when defining their own legitimacy, present-day members still disparage other forms of Spiritism, for example, by calling them "syncretic."

On one occasion, when I naively asked the director of one of these centers about the syncretic process within Spiritism, he referred me to the booklet *Africanismo y espiritismo* (1994), by the Brazilian Spiritist Deolindo Amorim (1908–1979). After reading it, I understood that the director was telling me that syncretism within Spiritism is detrimental and that its roots lay in the African elements introduced to the island by Santería practitioners. The Spanish translation of the booklet is sold at every center's bookstore. Amorim (1994:32–33) bluntly attacks some versions of Brazilian Spiritism that include African and popular Catholic practices, giving the example of Umbanda as a second level of syncretism of the already syncretic Afro-Catholic beliefs in Brazil. Therefore, he argues, Umbanda has nothing to do with Kardecean Spiritism. This assertion is obviously not shared by Umbanda practitioners, who argue that they have been equally influenced by Kardecean Spiritism, popular Catholicism, and African and indigenous beliefs (see Hess 1991). Unabashedly, Amorim suggests further that while these practices can legitimately be the focus of "folkloric" or "ethnological" studies because they deal with superstitions, mediumship, and animism, they should be excluded from the study of Spiritism, which should be investigated solely in accordance with its doctrine. The term *espiritismo folklórico* (Folkloric Spiritism) was used by Rodríguez Escudero (1991:328–330) to designate the practices "of people who did not study this philosophy from the books of its exegetes but who have learned somehow about Spiritism by going to centers and by listening to certain orators who had developed healing abilities that had become the object of popular admiration."

Rejecting Folkloric Spiritism and thereby monopolizing the social ownership of Spiritism, some centers have recently become more dedicated to teaching the tenets of Kardec than to conducting public veladas similar to those of the nineteenth century. They offer lectures on parapsychology, Kardec's books, extraterrestrial beings, and so forth. Also, the famous communal veladas of the past are now limited to individual private sessions held at the center, usually by a couple of mediums in the presence of a person who, the mediums feel, is in need of spiritual advice. To paraphrase a center director I met in Caguas, today Spiritist sessions are done in private to preclude espiriteros and ignorant people from learning the techniques of mediumship at a communal velada—techniques that might then be inappropriately used for communicating with *espíritus atrasados* (undeveloped spirits). According to Scientific Spiritists, the spirits worshiped by popular Spiritists are those that "drink rum and smoke tobacco" (indeed, these are their offerings). These undeveloped spirits have to be "raised" (*hay que levantarlos*) and "enlightened" (*darles luz*) because they operate at "lower levels of vibration."

One man stopped going to Spiritist centers, he told me, because he was hurt by the arrogance of the director, who scolded him for having "primitive" spirits. When his body contorted during a trance, the director told him that he must "educate these wild spirits." Of course, this man has been going ever since to private veladas (like those organized by Haydée), often as a member at the White Table, and has been giving consultations to clients in his own altar. But, he said, he will never go back to a Spiritist center again.

Similarly, during a class on *metafísica*[33] that I attended, an elderly woman was seriously hurt both physically and emotionally when the coordinator, very much like the above-mentioned director, instructed the students not to interfere when she showed the initial signs of a thrashing-about type of trance that sometimes occurs. The point of the instructor's admonition was to teach the students how to "educate" a spirit when it

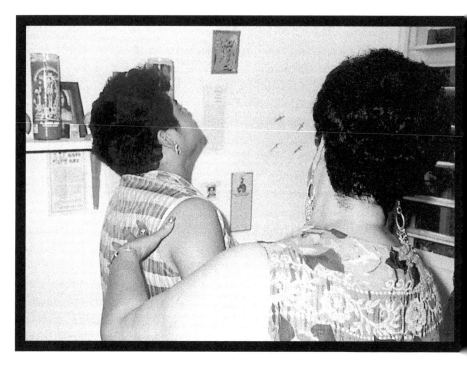

2.3 *Haydée assisting Reina in trance*

"violently descends on" or "takes possession" of their bodies. For this purpose, the instructor had the woman's husband conduct her carefully to the
front of the classroom, whereupon the instructor told the woman to "control the spirit" while the rest of the class was asked to pray aloud Hail
Marys and Our Fathers. Not able to control her body movements and with
no one to assist her, the woman suddenly fell down, the back of her head
hitting the tiled floor with a frightening thud. The teacher had clearly
contradicted the practices I had observed among brujos, espiritistas, and
santeros, which are meant to protect the "material" body from injuries
during trance.

The instructor, sensing the tension caused by the unfortunate accident, explained to the appalled class in quite apologetic terms (even as the
dazed woman returned to her seat), "Spiritual energies are like children,
you have to educate them. You know when they arrive, and you have to
stand up, control them, receive their energy, process it—and then deliver
the message."[34] In this way the woman was hurt emotionally: her way of
trance and even her spirits had been labeled "childish." In this context and

following current teachings of Scientific Spiritism (e.g., of Amorim and Rodríguez Escudero), "to educate" had meant to avoid letting the spirits dominate body movements, in a way reminiscent of Afro-Latin forms of possession. According to this perception, spirits need to be taught to communicate only via those forms accepted and institutionalized by *Scientific* Spiritism, even if clearly not acceptable in mainstream *science* (e.g., automatic writing, telekinesis, telepathy, clairvoyance, psychometry).

Popular forms of Spiritism have been perceived by Scientific Spiritism, as well as by the state apparatus, as operating outside the realm of rationality and modernity and therefore as needing to be eliminated. That all things African have been equated with primitivism is hardly a new concept. But remarkably, until quite recently very few in Puerto Rico have addressed this issue. In a pioneering book about the forgotten African roots of Puerto Rico, Isabelo Zenón Cruz (1974:207) notes that Puerto Rican vernacular religions had been studied by folklorists but not by comparative religionists, because of classist and racist assumptions. It is compelling to note, following Jürgen Habermas ([1962] 1992), that the media have also followed this trend; they have become active producers of stereotypes in their presentation and discussion of the nature and ownership of vernacular religious practices. Further, these publicly circulated stereotypes resurface in daily practices not only substantively but also judgmentally, reshaping rituals and their meaning in local spheres of identity politics.

For instance, people have been careful not to mention anything that would place them outside the acceptable or "progressive" forms of Spiritism. Therefore, expressions such as *hacer la obra espiritual* (to perform spiritual deeds) and *levantar causas* (to lift bewitchments) and even the word *espiritismo* itself have been used as generic, acceptable euphemisms in an attempt to hide from the public eye less acceptable practices such as brujería and curanderismo. The latter two have been viewed, in line with old-time perceptions of folklore studies, as part of a premodern world of superstition and error.

Reminiscent of early church claims for distinguishing between holy and unholy interventions, Scientific Spiritists have paradoxically claimed that practices such as divination and trance (with the help of Catholic saints, or Latin American, Asian, and African deities) are outside Spiritism. At the same time, they recognize as valid the messages spoken via mediums by the "enlightened spirits" of recent or past *muertos* (dead), or even by extraterrestrials. Also outside "true" espiritismo are reading the Spanish or Tarot cards and casting magical spells of any kind, as no "fully developed spirit" would ever be involved in such "primitive" practices (Machuca 1982). Scientific Spiritism does approve spiritual cleansing rituals for the body and the house, using herbs or candles, but only if "enlightened" spirits dictate their use; if African deities were to dictate these procedures, they would be prohibited.

As we have seen, the Department of Public Health, the lawyers for the Cigar Company, and scholars such as Zenón Cruz supply very different reasons for the erasure of differences between the "Scientific" and "popular" forms of Spiritism. Likewise, the perspectives of practitioners and those who consult popular healers are very different. One person's economic survival is another's greed. Further, what for academic purposes might be a proof of transnational globalizing processes (Hannerz 1996) becomes for practitioners a matter of identity politics and economic survival.

Indeed, brujos, curanderos, and espiritistas each define their own practices as intrinsically true and authentic, because, as each would claim, they emanate directly from appropriate spirits. Their knowledge, abilities, and power are gifts from God, revealed to them through visions, dreams, and other signs, but certainly not, as outsiders and scholars might believe, through a long history of cultural contact among European, indigenous, and African beliefs. They also ignore, or choose to disregard, the ways in which Scientific Spiritism and often the media, state agents, and historians have relegated them to the realm of the "syncretic," "primitive," or "folkloric."

For those who practice it, espiritismo is far from being perceived as the convergence of European, African, and indigenous beliefs and practices. For them, espiritismo is in practice a space for spiritual and social difference making and survival, in which each group defines itself by demarcating racial, national, and class differences. Although syncretic processes are admittedly involved, it is just as—if not more—important to look at the way "syncretism" is appropriated or rejected in local discourses of authenticity to construct strategically essential identities.[35] The social space in which this occurs, or its "regime of value"—to use Appadurai's (1986) term—explains the relative position of social groups and the exchange value of their symbols. Indeed, in recent public debates in Puerto Rico the "syncretic" aspects of brujería, curanderismo, and espiritismo have been recast in a completely new light—a positive one.

So far, I have shown how the development of the rational state apparatus and the rise of a new local technocratic elite under commonwealth status was engaged in defining the meaning and value of syncretic practices. In their edited volume, *Syncretism/Anti-Syncretism*, Charles Stewart and Rosalind Shaw (1994) show a variety of ways in which the controversial aspects of religious syncretism are played out in various nationalist discourses, an argument that I would like to extend in addressing the unique political status of Puerto Rico.

Following their lead, I want to suggest that since the 1980s the process of nation qua culture building can help us to understand how the shifts in the characterization of syncretism in Puerto Rico can be seen as positive. It is evident that in the case of Puerto Rico, syncretism had been constructed in the first fifty or so years after the American invasion as inauthentic. In constructing an "acultural" rationalist ecumene, "anti-syncretism" had been established as the measure of purity, authenticity, progress, and development. With the creation of the Instituto de Cultura Puertorriqueña, a change in the meaning of syncretism emerged — at least ideologically — in its emblem representing the three roots of the nation: Taíno, Spanish, and African. Similarly, in Greece syncretism has helped nationalists to reconstruct an authentic national identity that recaptured the continuity of modern with ancient Greece without contradicting the Orthodox Christian faith (Stewart 1995).

The recent mainstream revaluation of so-called alternative medicine and the "Africanization" of American culture seem to have opened in Puerto Rico a new venue for reinterpreting syncretic practices as authentic also in religious terms.[36] By labeling as "our own" the alternative popular medicine and wisdom of their ancestors, present-day intellectuals and politicians are able to make claims about a primordially ethnic Puerto Rican "marked" community.[37] With the ongoing political debate over the future of the island regarding statehood, independence, and commonwealth status, this shift in the public valuation of syncretism becomes not only apparent but indeed the essential representational attribute of Puerto Rican culture itself.

The praxis of syncretism also sheds light on the global effect of academic theories on local practices, such as when practitioners of vernacular religions refer to and interpret syncretism in their everyday practices following scholarly definitions. As with "creolization," the historical roots of syncretism are connected to colonial notions of pollution, which are then obliterated in nationalist discourses that sponsor national integration. Through an unintentional partnership, academic portrayals of syncretism can also become part of an "indigenous exegesis of the cultural process" (Aijmer 1995:7). Whether syncretism will be appropriated or excised will depend on the cultural value or ideology attributed to it. Stewart (1995:36) rightly asserts that when syncretism occurs, "a parallel discourse, which might be termed meta-syncretic," includes the "commentary . . . and registered perceptions of actors as to whether amalgamation has occurred and whether this is good or bad." The compelling questions are, What is the social status of competing definitions of syncretism, and how will people of different social positions and involvement with syncretism use these definitions? In the next chapter, these questions are readdressed within the new laissez-faire and multicultural social space of brujería, where profit and commercially based spiritual innovations cease to be regarded as signs of charlatanism.

CHAPTER THREE

SPIRITUAL LAISSEZ-FAIRE AND
THE COMMODIFICATION OF FAITH

Botánicas: Sites of Unorthodoxy

Hesitantly, as a strange sense of the unknown—both tempting and fright-ening—takes hold of me, I enter a botánica for the first time. Browsing over shelves and pretending to be at ease, I try to understand what I am experiencing—but to no avail. Imagine figurines of all shapes and sizes—busts of an African king and a Gypsy woman; statuettes of a seated old black man smoking a pipe and of a Catholic Virgin, surrounded by flowers—plates of sweets and coins, bottles of rum, fresh sugarcane stalks, and flickering candles. Seldom does one enter a store in which such a potpourri of objects and sensuous experiences coalesce. The whole space is crammed from top to bottom and side to side. Rows of multicolored bead necklaces and all kinds of amulets are hanging in the air above feathered American Indian warriors, Japanese-looking princesses, and Arab-looking priests of all sizes. An impressive colorful porcelain of a Chinese warrior, encircled by awe-inspiring dragons, catches my eye. The strong scent of fresh jas-mine mingled with musk incense allures me. I regain some composure near a collection of booklets on prayer and magic propped against the wall on a table, stacked next to New Age, Santería, "Voodoo," and Spiritist books from various places in Latin America. I pause to peruse them. On carefully arranged shelves on the other side of the wall stand hundreds of small colorful bottles and sprays labeled with tags that read "Arrasa con Todo" (Wipes Out Everything), "Amansa Guapo" (Subduer of the Abusive Male), and "Plata y Oro para Ti" (Silver and Gold for You). I am intoxicated by the sensuous colors, shapes, and perfumes surrounding me. The strong smell of incense burning with other exotic-looking herbs and the profusion of figurines of Catholic saints and faraway deities have transported me to a realm I have never experienced before.

Only in a world pervaded by the dynamic circulation of commodities does such an array of disparate religious icons and beliefs have the possibility of coming together in one place. Free-flowing international healing and magic beliefs found a fertile space here under laws protecting free trade and freedom of religion. Encouraged by the liberal consumer-capitalist state, practices previously marginalized enter a new phase within the free market enterprise of religious practice and alternative healing systems.

Ernesto Pichardo, a santero promoting the institutionalization of Santería as a religion in the United States, said to Russell Miller of the *New York Times* that he began "marketing" his church. Pichardo filed a lawsuit challenging a ban on ritual sacrifices that had been imposed on his church by the municipality of Hialeah, a suburb of Miami, after seeing that other nonmainstream religious groups had managed to become recognized and protected by the law.[1] Pichardo explained why it was important to debunk the stereotype of Santería as a sect, or even a satanic secret society, and to open the church to the public. "The long tradition of secrecy can be overcome," he said. "When our religious community starts to understand that there is the First Amendment and that this is a democracy, then we're in business" (Miller 1994). Although Pichardo's case arose in Florida, the same principles apply to the Commonwealth of Puerto Rico, where identical laws protecting nonmainstream religious practices have been passed.

However, recent controversies over "naturopathy," especially in regard to the lack of certification of folk healers, suggest that alternative healing systems—when they involve the commercial distribution and consumption of medicinal plants—are still not tolerated by the medical establishment. Nevertheless, the sacred, noncommercial space formerly inhabited exclusively by Western saints is flooded by a host of market-oriented deities and spirits from all over the world.

Botánicas in Puerto Rico, on the mainland, and even in Brazil are the most publicly visible sites of the commodification of faith and the quintessence of religious unorthodoxy. In a kind of transnational shrine, the saints and deities used in various degrees in the practices of brujería, Santería, santerismo, Vodou, and Catholicism, deriving from African, Chinese, Hindu, American Indian, Venezuelan, and Peruvian spiritual worlds, are there to be purchased, possessed, venerated, and summoned. Iconicity—or rather the excess of iconicity in Afro-Latin worship—has a long colonial history in Latin America, now being recharged by the global commodification and circulation of images. As I would learn, this does not suggest that people believe in the objects themselves. Brujos stress that images are only the material representations of spiritual entities and the mediating vehicles for their worship. Although icons enable devotees to venerate saints, for example, by adding their regalia and crowning them, as well as by placing offerings in front of them, the crucial issue is *la fé*, faith, in the power of the entities that inhabit these icons.

Botánicas exemplify the ongoing prevalence of pluralistic, vibrant, syncretic processes that transcend locality and nationality (see Appadurai 1990, 1996). In mainland barrios, botánicas offer their clients not only religious commodities but also the opportunity to consult espiritistas or santeros on their premises for about $10. In areas where Latino communities are few and far between—and small at that—other ethnic groups often cater to their needs. For instance, Korean-owned stores in North Carolina that sell Buddhist religious paraphernalia have also usually included the products desired by local followers of Afro-Caribbean religions.

Botánicas house a truly global spiritual world. Catholic saints, Hindu divinities, Chinese goddesses, Peruvian mythological heroes, and Venezuelan historical heroes coexist with New Age quartz crystals and books on meditation, the symbolism of dreams, Vodou, and extraterrestrial encounters. In this multinational space, people from various religious orientations meet to exchange vital information about their unique experiences. Botánicas can thus be characterized as "multireligious fields," to use Jonathan S. Walters's (1995) phrase depicting the social interactions on Sri Lanka's interregional pilgrimage–tour buses. For travelers, these "fields" become nonthreatening spaces for creative interaction with people from a variety of religious and social backgrounds.[2]

Before the late 1950s the role of botánicas had been filled by traditional *yerbateros* (peddlers of herbs and amulets) and *boticas* (traditional pharmacies). Yerbateros gathered medicinal and magical herbs in the mountains of the island and then, moving their carts from street to street, sold them still fresh in the villages and cities. Neighborhood *boticarios* (traditional pharmacists) prepared medicinal potions for their patients with the same substances brujos, curanderos, and espiritistas would buy in boticas for concocting their own spiritual and healing potions. José A. Toro-Sugrañes (1991), a researcher and grandson of one of the early boticarios, provides an unprecedented insight into their customs for contemporary readers. He (1991:46) describes, in his grandfather's words, the significant

3.1
*Haydée visiting a
well-supplied,
"good" botánica*

role of boticarios in filling the prescriptions ordered by espiritistas during the last years of the nineteenth century and the beginning of the twentieth. It is especially revealing that the number of prescriptions was much greater during the sugarcane harvests, because of the strain on both health and family relations of the long hours and exceedingly hard work of harvesting. The boticarios' work, of course, was doubly profitable during such periods: they prepared their own medicinal prescriptions while selling the products needed by espiritistas, curanderos, and brujos for preparing theirs (p. 47).

Today botánicas continue the tradition of yerbateros and boticarios, but they have also added dried herbs and magical potions and healing emulsions packaged in mass-produced bottles and aerosols. Also, the assortment of amulets, candles, magical perfumes, lotions, and figurines has increased considerably, and it seems that the whole globe has become a supplier. This trend was facilitated by the rapid economic growth of the island between World War II and the 1970s, when annual personal income rocketed from $118 to $1,200 (Wagenheim and Wagenheim [1994] 1996:183–184). Local and imported icons representing the gamut of ethnicity, race, class, and gender make up an ever-changing pantheon of cosmopolitan spirits.

Interestingly, the foreign origins of many of the icons does not limit their ritual efficacy among local devotees; on the contrary, the translocal specifics of their essential powers are drawn into a comprehensive spiritual world, regardless of their or their devotees' gender, national, or ethnic identity—proof of the nondiscriminatory power of spiritual commodities.

In addition to icons of Catholic saints, one can find the Indio (a Native American warrior), the Madama (a powerful black woman), and Don Gregorio (a white Colombian medical doctor), as well as Japanese and Hindu deities, each with its own character. To increase your "luck," for example, you can choose among Ekeko, the Peruvian midget, spirit of wealth; Kwan Yin, the Buddhist goddess of fortune; and Ganesh, the elephant-headed Hindu deity of opulence. Catering to the younger generation of a spiritually minded yuppie public, New Age paraphernalia have also found their way into botánicas in recent years, making it possible for additional intergenerational and interclass connections.

Afro-Latin religious goods—along with products imported from India, Mexico, Japan, and Peru—have the power to gradually reshape healing and magic rituals as each has a particular area of influence and form of offering. Such trends toward spiritual entrepreneurship point to the potential for a commodity-based transnational syncretism, which erases

3.2 From left to right: Changó (lower left corner), La Madama (behind Changó), and San Lázaro; Yemanyá; and Don Gregorio

apparent differences via encounters very unlike those of colonial times. Even if inter-Caribbean migration and the revolving-door migration to and from the United States are important in shaping the practices of brujería, the circulation of commodities has an added effect. Indeed, in contrast to Walters's (1995) depiction of Sri Lanka's multireligious fields, this process does not depend solely on actual contact between believers of different cultures. The movement of religious commodities seems to be doing it instead. One item may be substituted for a compatible other, even if it originated in another belief system that has no history on the island.

Although not originating directly from client motivation, commercially based translocal practices have an additional impact on the status of practitioners in the local social hierarchy. On one occasion, while I was assisting at my host's botánica, a young woman and her mother came in asking for a Ganesh. They had heard Walter Mercado (a famous Puerto Rican spiritual consultant and astrologer) discussing the attributes of this Hindu deity in one of his regular televised astrological readings and decided to enshrine it among their pantheon of icons at home. There were several on the shelf, all made of various materials and in different sizes; some were of cheap (depending on the size, $15–$45), poorly colored plaster, others of expensive ($40–$120), gold-laden porcelain. Examining only

3.3
From top left to
bottom right: Indios,
San Judas Tadeo,
Árabes, and
La Caridad

the latter, very costly versions, the two affluently dressed women appeared more interested in exploring the size that would better suit their home altar than comparing prices—as I often had seen less well-off clients do. It appears as if, by means of keeping up with what is new in the spiritual realm, especially expensive, imported ritual commodities, people indicate their place on the social ladder or, equally probable, invite the newly adopted spirits to help them to climb it more vigorously. In particular, Western reworkings of ancient Southeast Asian and Native American spiritual procedures in New Age practices have been welcomed mostly by the rising middle classes as a way to enhance their social status. In one of my many conversations with a young espiritista who had been born into a family of traditional espiritistas, for example, I learned that she had been updating herself by participating in New Age–type metafísica work-shops.[3] With a sense of national pride and a tinge of self-inflicted sarcasm, she observed: "We all know that metafísica is nothing but an embellished yuppie version of our Puerto Rican espiritismo."

Some botánica owners whose merchandise reflects the idiom of New Age healing systems set up their stores more as "herbal pharmacies," that is, as the offspring of the traditional yerbateros and boticas. In addition to stocking their stores with the standard figurines and candles, they pro-vide at affordable prices a wide variety of fresh medicinal plants, flowers, imported dry herbs and seeds, and the essences of exotic roots imported form East Asia and South America. Items range from just $1.00 to $15.00, and the average buyer spends about $12.00 on prayer sheets ($0.20 each), candles ($1.20 each), flowers ($3.00 a bunch), and small bottles of cleans-ing essences ($3.00 each). Botánicas are usually located in or near large municipal fresh-produce markets. A botánica in the market may have so many pots of plants and herbs that from afar it looks more like a nursery. It may also offer selected organically grown fruit and vegetables, groceries, and herbal drugs commonly sold at health food stores.

Catering to the specific needs of a local clientele is common, of course. For example, in areas where there is a concentration of immigrants from the Dominican Republic, botánicas will likely sell more iron cauldrons and plastic skulls, products related to Dominican variants of Puerto Rican san-terismo and Haitian Vodou,[4] and fewer New Age items. Some botánicas on busy commercial streets also sell gifts, novelties, and jewelry, which can be used or not as religious offerings. Some of the jewelry is embellished with religious or esoteric symbols, such as a popular ring with the head of the Indio, or imbued with religious meaning, like the Afro-Cuban *collares* (colored bead necklaces, each color representing the power, or *ashé,* of a particular orisha). Talismans of different shapes and made of semiprecious stones can just as readily be marketed simply as unusual trinkets to be hung on necklaces and bracelets. For instance, the same doll or stuffed animal might be purchased as a birthday or an anniversary gift and also as an offering to Eleggua, the orisha of the crossroads that manifests itself part of the time as a trickster or child that devours sweets and likes dolls. Fol-lowing what seem to be smart business practices, these botánicas—while catering primarily to religious practitioners—also attract clients looking merely for gifts.

Most likely as a sort of advertisement, botánicas will exhibit their own shrines with offerings to their *protecciones,* or guardian spirits (see chap. 5).

Offerings include, according to the deity, candy, tobacco, coins, dough-nuts, sugarcane, or grains of corn. More prosperous botánicas exhibit as promotional devices—though seldom sell—a few very expensive crystal items or multicolored, gilded porcelain pieces. Some of these objects, such as Asian dragons and European Renaissance-style angels, serve purely veneration purposes; others fulfill mostly practical purposes, as in the case of luxuriously decorated receptacles for ritual offerings.

One of the botánica owners I met during my first week in Puerto Rico became a very good friend and teacher and eventually my host for almost a year. In our lengthy conversations throughout the workday, while wait-ing for clients and wholesalers, Basi told me how she became a botánica owner. Like most of the botánica owners I spoke with, throughout her life Basi has been engaged in a search for spiritual answers and in develop-ing her mediumistic powers. She had started her business as a health food store, selling vitamins and medicinal teas, shortly thereafter becoming the sole distributor of a Spanish brand of the latter. She told me that her guardian spirits apparently had something else in mind for her. While re-building her health food store after it had been destroyed by Hurricane Hugo in 1989, she realized that her store had gradually evolved into a botá-nica. Reframing the "tragic" event of the hurricane as a life-transforming sign from God, she later devoted herself to Spiritism. Today she offers her services as a medium to those clients who come to her botánica seeking spiritual help in addition to santos and herbs.

That a botánica is not "just any store" is evident from the ways in which their owners conceive their entrepreneurship. More than a source of in-come, the botánica is perceived as a mission, reflecting its owner's spiritual blessings. A fully stocked store points to economic success, on the one hand, and to being blessed by the spirits, on the other, very much as pro-fessional brujos regard their practice. This is why Basi never refused to buy new stock and try "new improved" products, even when sales that month were poor and she needed to pay for the new merchandise in cash. It is better to take a loan than to have an understocked botánica, she explained to me. When a botánica has empty shelves or looks untidy, it gives the im-pression of paucity and deprivation, which has a combined negative effect on the clientele: It shows that the owner is not blessed and, by extension, that everyone and everything that comes into contact with this individual (products and clients alike) will become devoid of spiritual blessings. This explains why the owner of a botánica in Canóvanas was taken aback one day when the bruja with whom I was working said to him, after buying the

3.4
*Offerings for
ancestors and
"cosmopolitan
spirits"*

regular candles and flowers: "You have to fix this broken glass [pointing to the counter]. You know it is bad luck—and it gives a bad impression." Indeed, in her capacity as a regular client and a professional bruja, she was giving him a free consultation, both warning and counsel, suggesting that his better judgment was being clouded by a spell cast by the owners of a competitive botánica that had just opened nearby. Not only was it huge and well equipped, but it also sold gifts and jewelry, attracting numerous passersby as clients. "Están tumbándola" (They are destroying your botánica, i.e., through witchcraft), she said, "unless you do something." The owner then listened carefully to the bruja as she gave him advice on how to *levantar,* or raise up, his botánica. That day, of course, he did not charge for the candles.

By and large, prosperity is the most sought after power. A prosperous-looking botánica attracts clients with the hope that its good fortune will also affect them. The sign of prosperity is not the size of the botánica but its displayed stock, in terms of both variety and quantity (the latter related to availability, the ongoing bountifulness of supply). The general advice, then: Never run out of stock!

Further, the ability to carry prodigiously expensive items is one of the proofs that a botánica has good protecciones. Seeking to know about the manufacture and distribution of religious goods, I drove to Río Piedras

to meet one of the largest wholesale distributors in Puerto Rico—a fairly young man—at his own botánica. His botánica, he told me, is known for its selection of imported goods, especially of porcelain saints. We went though the shelves, and when I admired the carefully crafted and hand-painted figurines made in Spain, he proudly said that judges, lawyers, and politicians arrive at his store in their limousines in search of the most finely made figurines in Puerto Rico. "It is impossible to compare those mass-produced plaster and coarsely painted figurines that are sold everywhere," he said, "with these carefully made images that express the mystical aura of the saints." I sense a circularity that connects the entrepreneurial impetus of store owners, spirits, and clients: the exquisite selection of religious goods is proof of the spiritual power of the store, while financially and publicly powerful clients, themselves endowed with spiritual powers thanks to the unique spiritual goods bought at this botánica, also testify to its success; its success, of course, depending on powerful religious goods that . . . and so forth.

For purely economic reasons, manufacturers and suppliers of ritual goods cater to these spiritually based exigencies, blurring the hitherto separated realms of commerce and sanctity. International suppliers and local distributors are responsible for the immense selection and constant variety of products that are manufactured and distributed among differ-

3.5 Basi's botánica with "new and improved" products

ent centers around the world. Local distributors act as go-betweens, informing each end of the trade—botánicas and manufacturers—of changing supply and demand. Hence, in addition to the impact of both local and televised brujos, espiritistas, and astrologers, manufacturers as well as distributors have no small part in influencing the very forms of ritual and offerings and even their meaning. A wholesale supplier shows me the labels of some products and explains that some of the alcoholados are imported from China, certain candles from Tampa and New York City, rosaries and chromolithographs from Italy, and hand-painted santos from Spain. "The Ekekos are imported from Venezuela," he goes on. "I import most of the amulets from Santo Domingo and Thailand, and also from Santo Domingo I get all the different cauldrons, pieces of lodestone, Shark Oil, and some of the cleansing bath emulsions." Because these forces seem to operate in between and in spite of national boundaries, one could reasonably argue that inadvertently they are creating new belief patterns that increasingly come to resemble each other, despite being practiced in distant places (see Appadurai 1990).

Books sold in botánicas are one of the ways in which religious symbols and meanings migrate. For instance, the *Manual Esotérico* (1988), by the Venezuelan popularizer Celia Blanco, and *El Monte* ([1954] 1975), by the Cuban folklorist Lydia Cabrera, contain detailed directions for concocting the potions and assembling the trabajos used to accomplish spiritual purposes. These imported books sell well among not just novices but also experienced santeros and babalawos. The books on Yoruba divination systems, *Ifa* and *Sixteen Cowries,* by the American anthropologist William Bascom, are bought by santeros and babalawos as references for their trade, probably not the scholarly use Bascom had in mind when he wrote them. I was astounded to see espiritistas-santeras and babalawos consult *El Monte* and *Ifa* in determining how to handle an unusual situation. In this case the idea of tradition, assumed to be handed down from one generation to another by word of mouth or by example, without written instruction, becomes obsolete.[5]

Some commercial entrepreneurs also engage in the apparently more lucrative endeavor of creating, similar to the market of nonspiritual manufactured goods, "new and improved" products. On one occasion when I was in charge of Basi's botánica, a well-known supplier bragged about his exclusive deal with a Miami-based Argentinean wholesaler who had recently become a manufacturer. This Argentinean has given him the sole rights to market in Puerto Rico his new and improved "best-selling" *velones* (tall candles set in cylindrical glass containers). This more expensive version of velones contains the herb associated with the saint mixed into the colored wax. Obviously, following the mainstream belief that new equals better, this form of commercially based spiritual entrepreneurship finds a favorable reception among the public—clients and witch-healers alike.

While brujos regularly go to botánicas to buy supplies, these shopping excursions provide another essential space for networking and gossiping about other brujos and botánicas. On our way to our third botánica one morning, Haydée said to me, "I always like to check out what's new here, . . . check out the latest novelty." Previously she had told me that she likes to buy her products from various botánicas in order to distribute her business equally among them. For these reasons, she regularly seeks out new botánicas in addition to the ones she already knows. She can also begin to weave new networks for herself. While positioned literally on the other side, behind the counter of Basi's botánica, I witnessed the interactions among brujos, santeros, and espiritistas. These encounters, however, end up becoming "spiritual duels" in which the prowess of each is displayed under the guise of innocent descriptions. This is what happened once to Haydée. While we were visiting a new botánica, she met its owner, a baba-lawo, and one of his godchildren, Armando, an espiritista initiated in San-tería. Immediately all three began to compare their spiritual experiences, a discussion that, after each account, escalated in terms of the extraordinary nature and results of their interventions. From what can only be charac-terized as an introductory informative encounter, a future friendship and partnership was to develop among them—at least for a while.

Brujería as a Protected Free Enterprise

Unlike the previous colonial persecution of brujería by the church and the 1950s medical reformation carried out by the state, roughly since the 1980s there seems to have been no state interest in controlling brujería unless (as with any practice) it is seen to violate some legal right, private or pub-lic. Puerto Rico, as a commonwealth, is under the same federal laws as the U.S. mainland regarding the commercial control of commodity trade. There are no legal provisions that regulate the sale, import, or production of the types of ritual paraphernalia sold in botánicas, either at the retail or the supplier level, for they are included under the rubric "Food and Gifts." And because they do not fall under any of the other categories—Jewelry, Cigarettes, Gasoline, Arms, and so forth—the kinds of merchandise sold in botánicas are of no interest to the federal or state government. How-ever, there are legal provisions administered by local agencies such as DACO (the Puerto Rican agency for consumer protection) and the U.S. Food and Drug Administration to protect potential buyers. These provisions have to do with matters such as protecting consumers from false claims of a product's ability to effect miraculous healing.[6]

Registration of botánicas is required by federal corporation law (ap-proved on January 9, 1956, under the ELA, or Commonwealth), with spe-cial amendments for Puerto Rico.[7] To register as a corporation, a botánica has to have initial capital of between $20,000 and $30,000 and an im-porter no less than $100,000. If the initial capital is less than $5,000, then —contrary to previous tax regulations—there is no need to have a separate license issued by the municipality (following the 1994 law No. 120—under the new measures of the General Tax and Inheritance Code). Such is the case for countless botánicas located at the indoor and outdoor market-places of the Plazas de Mercado. For example, there are no separate licenses for each of the several botánicas of the Centro Comercial Rafael Hernández, an indoor marketplace in Río Piedras, because the latter obtained one license for all its stores. This is one of the obstacles to assessing the number of botánicas operating on the island. But there are other problems. Even for those botánicas that are registered individually by law, it is impossible—without going through the entire listing of the tens of thousands of Puerto Rican corporations, one by one—to arrive at an objective total number, for the alphabetical indexing is not by type of enterprise but only by company name. However, a resourceful employee, realizing that the names of at least some botánicas begin with the word *botánica* (e.g., Botánica Ganesh and Botánica San Lázaro), was able to access the computerized tax histories of fourteen such botánicas. Besides this bit of information, the rest was left for me to compose out of oral accounts, observations, and some written sources. After asking suppliers and checking the Yellow Pages and newspaper articles, I finally arrived not at a precise objective number but at least at a reasonably composite estimate: there are between three hundred and six hundred botánicas, which means that if there are approximately two million adults on the island and each botánica has a total of approximately three hundred clients, they supply between 5 and 10 percent of the adult population.

I also learned that at the corporations' archive, located in the old city of San Juan, the card files detailing each corporation are open to the public. Intrigued by how botánicas have been characterized under the protective wing of capitalist laissez-faire interpretations of religious freedom and equipped with the names of a few botánicas, I was able to find out how these stores were defined by their owners. Under the heading "Goal and Purposes" of corporations, one can read, for example, "to sell at the retail level religious objects, medicinal plants, flowers, ceramics, gift-wrapping paper, bows, cards, mementos, school supplies, metafísica books, and anything related to botánicas." Evidently, the existence, nature, and mode of operation of these stores (very much like their antecedent yerbateros and boticas) have not required—contrary to the censorship imposed on the sale and distribution of esoteric books during the Spanish colonial state's rule, for instance—any moral or religious interventions by the state.

Intrigued further by how the law had addressed "brujería" and "brujos," I went to the Law School of the University of Puerto Rico and began inquiries. To my surprise, after consulting the most recent edition (1990) of the *Leyes de Puerto Rico, Anotadas* (Annotated Collection of Laws of Puerto Rico), I learned that there are no official provisions concerning brujería and brujos. If a legal action were to be brought against brujería, under the present legal system it would have to be under the section Perturbación o Estorbo (Perturbation or Hindrance), in Chapter 229, Title 32, Section 2761: "Anything that perturbs the rights of other individuals in terms of their health and decency, actions that might be offensive to the senses, or that might hinder the free use of property and the enjoyment of life and property." It ends with two caveats: "This section cannot be applied to the public worship displayed by various religions"; and "Nothing stated here will limit the power of the Junta de Calidad Ambiental [Council for Environmental Quality] to promulgate the regulations which it is entitled to by law."

In matters of the law and religious practices, however, there is always room for unprecedented cases of creativity and innovation. In 1993 the sensationalist newspaper *El Vocero* told of a complaint filed at the labor organization Junta de Apelaciones del Sistema de Administración de Personal by Maritza Rivera Flores, an administrative secretary of the municipality of Patilla, accusing the mayor, Pilar Rodríguez Rivera, of "discrimination" in the workplace. The allegations of discrimination were framed by her lawyer as violating civil rights and the existing laws against religious discrimination in the workplace. The mayor had fired Maritza, the lawyer had claimed, as a punishment for not complying with her "spiritual" demands. Because Maritza was a churchgoing Catholic and did not believe in spirits, she had refused to follow the instructions given by the mayor to all the employees to have their desks "cleansed" of bad spirits every day and to participate on Saturdays in séances and collective ritual cleansing organized by the mayor (*El Vocero* 1994).[8]

From "Charlatanism" to "Popular Wisdom"

Since the 1980s the way in which brujería and brujos in Puerto Rico have been depicted in the public sphere has changed drastically. No longer condemned as practicing heresy, superstition, and charlatanism, brujos have recently been entering the more favorable space of "popular healing" and "folk medicine." How is it that brujos and curanderos have ceased to be imagined and portrayed as symbols of national stagnation and blamed for bogus, even deadly curing procedures? By what unforeseen change of paradigm have their practices come to no longer require being "extirpated" from society but rather salvaged—indeed prized—as repositories of "popular wisdom"?

It is noteworthy that until the 1980s the Instituto de Cultura Puertorriqueña's interest in vernacular religions centered on popular Catholicism (excluding African or Afro-Caribbean influences). Vernacular religions were carefully packaged for nationalist purposes: any controversies as to their heretical (in Catholic terms) or irrational or superstitious practices (in modernist parlance) were muffled by reframing them as "popular" or "esoteric" expressions of the Puerto Rican "religious soul." Ritual objects were presented as "folk art" and thereby cleansed of religious meaning. Ángel Suárez Rosado (1992:127) writes, "The wooden saints (Santos de Palo) had been isolated, fragmented, with their transformation into precious, commodified objects." Instead of seeing them as a whole, as a unity defined by worship, "the wooden saints were taken [from homemade altars] and integrated into private collections both on the island and the United States" (p. 127).[9]

Consider the idea of Puerto Rico as an "ethno-nation"—following Grosfoguel, Negrón-Muntaner, and Georas (1997:17)—that is, imagining the "nation" without a "Puerto Rican" state. This form of nationalism has been termed "cultural nationalism," suggesting that political sovereignty or the break with the United States is not taken to be a prerequisite for strong national sentiments to exist (Dávila 1997; Duany 2000, 2001; Morris 1995; Romberg 1996a). Then consider the value placed on the politics of ethnic identity in mainstream American definitions of "multiculturalism" (Taylor 1994).[10] In this context, it makes sense for Puerto Rico to stress its unique ethnonational identity. Brujería and curanderismo not only can be annexed to the widely accepted discourse of "alternative healing practices"[11] but also can become tokens of "our national heritage."

As part of this process, African-based religious and musical elements have been rescued from oblivion by government and university organizations by means of sponsored public festivals, conferences, and events intended to recover the African roots of Puerto Rican culture and history. This is significant, especially because the African "root"—one of the "three roots" of Puerto Rican identity, promoted since the mid-1950s—has been neglected compared to the Taíno and Hispanic legacies. For example, several biannual international symposiums on Afro-Caribbean religions were held at the University of Puerto Rico in the 1990s.[12] Also, beginning in the late 1980s, the Centro de Estudios de la Realidad Puertorriqueña (CEREP) published special issues on the forgotten African components of Puerto Rican culture and history.[13] While some municipal and university organizations have been promoting the African elements of Puerto Rican culture, commercial entrepreneurs have pursued this trend on their own terms by packaging and selling African-inspired ritual goods to local and mainland tourists.

For practitioners of Afro-Latin vernacular religions, the public and commercial revaluing of the African elements of Puerto Rican culture acquire yet another meaning. On a purely practical level—after centuries of religious censorship—Puerto Rico has opened to an international market that supplies all sorts of African-Latin and Asian religious commodities. Yet in a subtler way, religious practices have been enriched as well via the intense migration of espiritistas, santeros, brujos, and New Age healers from the Dominican Republic and Cuba and by the circulation of Puerto Ricans back and forth between the island and the mainland through a revolving-door migration. Spiritual empowerment has become geographically unbound.

It follows that the change of terminology in depicting brujería and brujos in the public sphere is having a remarkable impact on practitioners of vernacular religions in Puerto Rico, who are now aware of the part their practices played in the politics of national culture of the 1990s. Followers of Scientific Spiritism have enhanced their long-established cosmopolitanism, internationalizing their practices through the inclusion of New Age symbols. As for those concerned with the Africanization of Puerto Rico, the public revitalization of African–Puerto Rican identity enables them to identify with other Afro-Caribbean societies and mainland African Americans. Although the promoters of Scientific Spiritism and those who support the Africanization of Puerto Rican culture (popular espiritistas, brujos, and santeros) define Puerto Ricanness in opposite ways— the first by stressing its European heritage and the second by highlighting its African legacy—both tendencies bear indirectly on the political debates about the future status of the island. Especially when one considers an antiessentialist view of Puerto Rican national politics, the meager number of independence voters might not be surprising—given their insistence on promoting romanticized Hispanic, peasant-based national symbols. The majority of the more visibly ethnicized, lower-class Puerto Ricans, in contrast, seem to favor statehood for pragmatic reasons. As citizens of the United States they are protected by welfare benefits and civil rights (Grosfoguel 1997; Negrón-Muntaner and Grosfoguel 1997).

Both in reporting and in constituting class-based, ideological attitudes about African-based religious practices and Spiritism, the role of journalism has been as prominent in this period as in the previous one. The Puerto Rican intelligentsia has traditionally been involved in the publishing business. Their influence on larger social issues has been and is still remarkable. As intermediaries between global discourses of progress and development at the beginning of the twentieth century and of multiculturalism more recently, they have shaped in great measure the ways in which those in the public sphere react to these global discourses by both enabling practitioners to present their case in the media and interpreting their practices in a favorable light.

Individual practitioners of vernacular religions on the island have articulated these broader issues of a Puerto Rican version of multiculturalism and cultural nationalism in various ways, suggesting the emergence of a new legitimate space for brujería and other marginalized religious practices. The reincorporation or "revitalization" of African elements in Puerto Rican culture was addressed on the radio by a santero during an interview about Santería in summer 1996. He said that there was no need for "syncretism" today. He was referring to the "defensive syncretism" of colonial times, when the worship of African deities had to be camouflaged under the guise of devotional services to Catholic saints (see Romberg 2000). He expressed this idea aptly and tersely: "Today, [the African deity] Changó is Changó" (i.e., it no longer has to be worshiped through Santa Bárbara, its Catholic face).[14]

Intimately connected though not always in total agreement, a new form of cultural nationalism stressing the timeless or "folkloristic" aspects of indigenous Puerto Rican culture has been rehabilitating brujería and curanderismo to fit a renewed nationalist agenda. Instead of vilifying folkloristic practices as obstacles to progress, this nationalist program—largely through the sponsorship of the Instituto de Cultura Puertorriqueña—foregrounds Puerto Rico's own unique folkloristic criollo trajectory. Pride has replaced the criticism of the 1950s and 1960s, when the same practices were framed as superstitious and as survivals of medieval beliefs.

The media's perception of its role in reporting on these folkloric practices had also changed drastically. Newspapers had denounced them to help "educate the masses" under the halo of being the "saviors of progress and civility." Today, in striking contrast, some newspapers are engaged in unraveling or uncovering hidden traditions. Still saviors, certainly, but of quite another kind: saviors of "endangered" Puerto Rican traditions (see Romberg n.d.).

This trend seems to have started roughly twenty years ago. A series of articles appeared in the well-respected (but now defunct) newspaper *El Reportero* (July–August 1982) under the category *ocultismo* (occultism), exposing in a positive way the fact that Puerto Rico had been housing a variety of multicultural esoteric practices since the beginning of its history.[15]

In the first article, Santería appears not as a dubious import from Cuba but as evidence of a continuous Puerto Rican–African tradition (*El Reportero* 1982a).[16] Tracing its origins among slaves and maroons, the author of the article, María J. Peña Signo, refers to Loíza as the "land of maroons," where a predominantly black population had maintained its African traditions under the guise of Catholic festivities, such as the feast of Santiago Apóstol. The strong impact of African influences on Puerto Rican culture is poetically described in this article through the trope of African drumming: "Blacks continued sounding their most precious musical instrument, at times hardly and at times just softly throbbing their hides to prevent waking up any suspicions among ambitious *conquistadores* that the African continent was indeed setting up its own banners in these new lands." The author's revelation that previous indigenous Taíno beliefs had "survived" the persecution of the conquistadores is not as unusual as recognizing the African survival, which had not been recognized publicly until the 1980s. It seems rather awkward or maybe obvious that in Loíza—the "most African" township in Puerto Rico—its African roots had been systematically disregarded. When I visited the cultural center of Loíza, there was no mention of any "past" except its ancient Taíno one, as if the enslaved Africans—small in number as they might have been (compared to the rest of the Caribbean)—had not left any traces in the town.

In the second article of the series (*El Reportero* 1982b), the identity of the real author of one of the most famous Puerto Rican *danzas* (a genre of traditional folk music and dance) is unveiled. Don José Silvent, a former judge in Guayama and an espiritista, reveals (to the unnamed author of the article) that "the true author of the precious lyrics of 'Mil Amores' was 'a high-ranking spirit' who appeared in the dreams" of the composer, his friend Simón Madera, and "enabled him to regale the people of Puerto Rico with one of the most beautiful danzas ever heard." A few years earlier this same account, along with the detailed report of the journalist's visit to a Spiritist center, would have been ridiculed in the newspapers, as were many such stories, as examples of the "silly," "credulous," and "superstitious minds" of "ignorant people." Furthermore, the article foregrounds the central role of Spiritism—especially of Scientific Spiritism—in the process of national identity formation, in dramatic contrast to the political elite of the 1950s, who strived to make sure Puerto Rico disengaged itself from anything that appeared to threaten the idea of a modern society.

The third article in this series, by Charlie Aguilar, is titled "Botánicas and Spiritism" (*El Reportero* 1982c). Instead of portraying botánicas as gloomy places catering to "dark purposes," Aguilar, paraphrasing the words of a botánica owner, an espiritista, speaks of them as "spiritual pharmacies." In the words of the interviewee, "Botánicas are to Spiritist mediums as pharmacies are to doctors." The analogy goes even further, as espiritistas themselves often write a prescription that includes the same *medicinas patentizadas* (over-the-counter drugs) prescribed by doctors. This is why some pharmacy prescriptions can be bought at "spiritual pharmacies," and vice versa.

A profile of Doña Eustaquia, an espiritista healer from Lares, appears in the fourth article, also written by Charlie Aguilar (*El Reportero* 1982d). Unlike many of the editorials of previous decades, Aguilar describes Doña Eustaquia's spiritual visions and healing procedures respectfully. He relates in her words how she had miraculously cured a dying child who had been brought to her once—after nobody had been able to cure her. After this initial God-inspired healing experience, Doña Eustaquia explained, she began *a trabajar el espiritismo* (to work spiritually) and had not stopped since. In Aguilar's words, Doña Eustaquia recognized that it was not she "who was healing the sick[,] . . . she was only an instrument of God in doing good deeds." The article goes on to detail the economic sacrifices Doña Eustaquia had to make to fulfill her mission—to construct a temple next to her old home altar big enough to serve all the people who needed to come. The article's coda stresses the persistent "unjust" attacks from neighboring Catholic and especially Evangelical churches that were relentless in their efforts to undermine her sacred activities, by threatening her and her children and even by throwing stones at her car. Especially annoying, according to Doña Eustaquia, was a pastor who "used to perform all kinds of rituals near [her] home and insulted [her] by calling [her] 'sorceress, witch' [*hechicera, bruja*] and whatever they felt like." Finally, three months before the article was written, both the physical and the emotional injuries had stopped, she said, apparently after the courts had intervened.[17]

Recent accounts such as these show a clear shift of perception—probably as a result of the local multicultural move suggested earlier. Although an explanation for this shift is outside the scope of this book, it is evident that the respect for alternative worldviews stands in sharp contrast to reports written some forty years earlier, when people like Eustaquia were depicted by journalists as quacks, charlatans, or scoundrels who take advantage of peasants and primitive people who do not know any better. Further, practitioners are quoted directly, lending legitimacy to their agency, no longer despised and mocked as being undercivilized or premodern.

Expanding Choices: Faith in Money— and How Money Meets Faith

The transnational flow of Dominican, Cuban, and American New Age healers together with the proliferation of charismatic "electronic churches" have opened up an unprecedented array of choices for spiritual help in contemporary Puerto Rican society.[18] The vigorous commercial and cultural exchanges between the Latino communities on the mainland and on the island provide a wide audience for any spiritual enterprise. University-sponsored international symposiums, publications, and the media facilitate the flow of information between these and other centers in Latin America and the Spanish Caribbean, making it possible for some cable TV mediums and astrologers to become famous throughout the Americas.

The famous spiritual entrepreneur Anita Casandra, who was called La Mentalista de América (the Mentalist of America) in an editorial on *esoterismo* published in *El Vocero* (1995), is most certainly *the* model of success and prosperity in the esoteric domain and is most surely still emulated by local brujos and espiritistas. (The only other Puerto Rican in this field who is equally successful is Walter Mercado.) The editorial presents Anita Casandra in hyperbolic terms, saying that she had managed to rise beyond Puerto Rican spheres of influence to become an internationally acclaimed and respected representative of mediums, astrologers, brujos, and santeros. As an example of her fame, the editorial mentions that there were some in Puerto Rico and New York who had to wait up to six months to be seen and that several heads of state, such as President Calderón Fournier of Costa Rica, were among her friends.

This editorial profile also publicized the upcoming creation of Casandra's own *línea síquica* (psychic phone line). It was portrayed as the epitome of success in matters of the unseen. Anita Casandra is depicted here as "a businesswoman," "a successful Puerto Rican who triumphed over thousands of obstacles" since she started out with a botánica in an Anglo neighborhood in Queens, New York, in the 1960s, "when nobody there knew what a botánica was." She had turned the botánica into a successful business and "one of the most beautiful known in the world. . . . Each item is bought with the utmost care and love. These are things she buys around the world."

The editorial continues,

[This] untiring, industrious woman [*trabajadora incansable*] is now negotiating several contracts with companies in the U.S and Puerto Rico who are interested in her new line of cosmetics, especially her patented perfume Magic. Her next step? To syndicate her horoscope all over the world and to make public her *dieta espiritual* [spiritual diet], designed over a period of more than eight years. Her goal is to improve on a previous diet, which appeared in her book *Yo no puedo rebajar por más que quiera* [I Cannot Lose Weight No Matter How Much I Want To]. The improved version would be appearing, she says, in a book titled *No más excusas: Embellece a ese ser que tienes ante tu espejo* [No More Excuses: Embellish That Being That You Have in Front of Your Mirror]. (*El Vocero* 1995)

There are other, less acknowledged forms of entrepreneurship in esoteric matters. David Basnueva, a young local santero-astrologer, created for the local newspaper *De Todo* a new format for writing horoscopes in the mid-1990s. In addition to including his telephone number (unusual in a horoscope) for those who might want to arrange a personal consultation, he added Afro-Latin deities and ritual procedures to the more conventional, neutral-sounding, Western style of prediction. Previously unthinkable, Basnueva's style of horoscope writing was another example of the recently relaxed, even favorable attitude toward African cultural elements in Puerto Rico and the rest of the Spanish Caribbean. A full range of advice and recipes inspired by the worlds of espiritismo and santerismo make his words sound more like the advice provided in a session with a brujo or a santero than in a horoscope. Indeed, while reading his section, Haydée referred to him as a brujo, not an astrologer.

Basnueva gives detailed guidance on how to win the favor of *los muertos,* of Catholic saints, and of Santería deities, how to prepare herbal and magical cleansing baths, and so forth. One entry reads as follows:

> Beware of careless accidents with fire in your home, be sure that candles, stoves, electric heaters, and matches are far from the reach of children—there's a warning of danger. There will be talk about inheritance or division of estates. Get a good lawyer in order to get a fair deal. You need to prepare yourself spiritually because there will be three persons who will throw witchcraft on you [bewitch you] and will want to keep you sidelined. But *un muerto* [the spirit of a dead person] that did not give you anything in life will reward you now. Pray for this [muerto] in your home, put out flowers [for this muerto], two dry coconuts with water, a white velón and a glass of water for nine days. You will pray for this *servicio* [offering]. You will shed many tears due to the loss of an acquaintance who will die in a tragic death. Lucky number: 710. (*De Todo* 1996)

As shown so far, various processes were involved in creating a commodified, multicultural space for brujería, in clear contrast to a previous era, when it was considered a threat to the development of a modern state. Botánica owners, manufacturers and suppliers of religious commodities, cable mediums and astrologers, and horoscope writers—all enjoy the benefits of economic and spiritual laissez-faire. They serve all kinds of agendas—nationalist, multicultural, and political. Nevertheless, they and their activities share one important corollary: novelty is good and increases business.

In this spiritual laissez-faire context, clients, seeking solutions for problems that mainstream treatments have failed to solve, can experiment with an array of choices—in addition to the services offered by traditional and nontraditional churches. Expecting less personal commitment, in terms of both time and money, than do other self-help or religious practitioners, brujos through various degrees of intervention and sophistication offer what one can refer to broadly as their "spiritual services" in a supply-and-demand relationship; and as in other areas of social life, innovation and expansion are signs of their prosperity.

Responding to an increasingly competitive market for clients, various kinds of mediums, espiritistas, New Age healers, and brujos construct their own system of differences. In spite of the visible incorporation of saints, deities, and spiritual techniques from all over the world, they articulate a nationalist-localist discourse of espiritismo, for example, either according to their own origins or the purposes of their spiritual work. If it is a "good" purpose, then it is Puerto Rican espiritismo. Indeed, some espiritistas envision an "authentic" Puerto Rican espiritismo that excludes extraneous, "bad" elements (usually black magic) that are believed to have been introduced by immigrants. For some espiritistas, knowledge about Spiritism should be gained through the canon of Scientific Spiritism. For other espiritistas, however, learning about espiritismo in books might place a practitioner outside authentic Puerto Rican espiritismo, as the ability to communicate with the spirits, even if used for solving worldly matters, should be a gift from God.

In a world obsessed with the expansion of economic choices, brujería leaves its previously marginal place and enters the transnational space of commodified goods and services. Matters of faith, like other areas of social life, become objects of commercial entrepreneurship, advertisement, and global influences. Enlarging previous face-to-face processes of transmission, new mediated forms of transmission of esoteric knowledge and expertise from all over the world produce an increasing market for spiritual commodities.

Although brujos operate today within this new space of "spiritualized materialism," their practices also entail traces of the previous tribulations of brujería—its history of persecution and exclusion resurfacing now as a form of empowerment.

Part II

*THE TECHNOLOGIES
OF COSMIC AND
WORLDLY SUCCESS*

CHAPTER

FOUR

BRUJOS, SAINTS OR BROKERS?

"Getting Spiritually Ready"

"O my God and celestial father, in this moment and in this precise instant and solemn day I sit again at this humble but sacred seat of yours, and precious and humble seat of mine, in order to thank you, my God, for the rich blessings that you have placed on my shoulders. In order to thank you, my God, for this precious labor that you have put in my hands because, my God, this is not mine. This is yours, together with my Caridad del Cobre. You, my Caridad, are the patron, owner, and princess of this home, of this humble and precious but sacred home, because for you and due to you it was bought. I live in it but you inhabit it. I pay for it but you govern it.

"I beg you, God of the Armies, that in this moment you look at how my matter is feeling, my God, look at how my body is feeling. I know that you have always fed my spirit, but my matter is debilitated today. Look how much pain I feel in my body, God of the Armies. But, my Christ, I beg you that in this moment you place your healing hands upon me, that you carry away all the pain, all the bitterness, all the sufferings, and all the torments that I carry upon my shoulders, and set me free to continue today with the spiritual labor that I have begun. Because, my God, remember that while I was on my sick bed, with my foot hurting, I promised La Caridad del Cobre that I would serve her every day until you determine otherwise; that I would go to my altar; that I would not open the gate to go out but only would open it to let in, and consult those in need. Because I know, my God, that when you bring them to me it is because they need the spiritual bread. Because the entire world claims to know, claims to do, but it is you who are the one who gives. And since it is you who gives, you give it right, otherwise it can't be right. . . .

"Now, I present you my friend, Reina, and this woman, my reportera. Bestow her with health, give her peace, and give her serenity. If there is a problem lingering over [these women], provide me the instruments to help them. I ask you for health for my son, health and serenity for my son. I beg you for health for me, nothing else. All the rest, I know, my God, you will provide. In the name of God Almighty, I leave everything in your care with the blessings of the Father, the Son, and the Holy Spirit. Amen."

Having completed her improvised morning prayer, Haydée had officially opened her altar for the day and become "spiritually ready" to begin consulting her clients. She had been ill for a few weeks, and she looked forward to resuming her consultations. As on many other occasions when she explained the sacrifice involved in her mission as a bruja to clients and friends, she expressed it in this prayer, asking for strength and direction from God so as to help those in need. I saw how powerful her words could be, even for occasional clients who might have been invited to attend the morning prayers, in conveying her perception of the role of a true bruja. Listening to her broken, at times sobbing, imploring voice communicating with God and the saints was—on this and several other occasions—a moving, cathartic experience. In those mystical moments I found even skeptical clients, as well as myself, moved to tears—probably experiencing what faith in a saintly bruja might mean to and do for us.

Godly Gifts

Paradoxically, if any words can describe the character of brujos, "humility" would not be one of them. Usually brujos are characterized by arrogance and acquisitiveness. Nevertheless, even the most powerful brujos would credit God for their power as, in Haydée's words, "it is He who governs matters on earth" and the only one "who can govern even the strongest of brujos." Simultaneously meek and playful, Haydée would acknowledge both God's cosmic rule and her own indomitable character: "Only God governs me, and sleep defeats me." Also as most brujos do when events do not proceed as planned, she would remind her listeners that it is the power of God that ultimately governs all matters of life.

As usual, on one occasion when the waiting room was full of clients, Haydée nonchalantly excused herself to a group of people who had arrived at 7:00 A.M. and been waiting for hours—first outside and then inside the house—for their consultations: "I propose, but God and my Caridad decide. I had planned to make some despojos this morning at 10:30. But I do not govern myself. La Caridad does.[1] I say I will leave my house at a certain time, and I can never do it—always I leave later." A couple of hours later, after consulting a few clients, Haydée came out of the altar and, standing in the middle of the waiting room/garage, turned to a client who was waiting to go with her to the monte about a half-hour drive away to finish a trabajo. Combining the sacred with the profane aspects of her life, Haydée laughingly said to her, "It's twelve o'clock now and I'm *so-o-o* hungry," expecting (half joking, half serious) that this client might buy her lunch on the way to the monte. Of course, the client drove Haydée, Reina, and me to the monte, stopping at a small restaurant on the way (we all shared the expenses), while the rest of the clients stayed at the house awaiting our return some three hours later.

God directs all things. In addition to justifying unplanned lunches and packed waiting rooms, this statement opens up a whole set of logical explanations for the occasional failure of trabajos, implying that God might have different plans for one, plans that might not be known even to brujos. Indeed, although brujos *pueden revocar* (can revoke)[2] human-caused disasters, whenever expected outcomes fail to occur it is apparently God's will. Nothing can change that. On the positive side, tapping into the sacred powers of God assures that trabajos will succeed and that brujos will be protected against evil machinations. This holds true for their entire lives. Invoking God in every endeavor thus is a logical, even if often seemingly obsessive attempt to protect themselves. Constantly referencing God might protect against liability as well as serve as a disclaimer in the presence of people who still connect brujos with the devil. Claiming God as the guiding force behind their spiritual endeavors assures brujos that they are endowed with unlimited yet—crucially as important—positive powers. In one of her daily prayers, Haydée said, "God gave me the blessings and the abilities [*dones*] to heal, and in abundance! . . . Without God, I don't do anything. God is the one [who heals]."[3]

Owing their power to heal and "see" to God's grace explains why brujos draw on stories from the life of Jesus for inspiration. If their labor is indeed guided by personal sacrifices and *pruebas,* or tests, it is because their life work follows Jesus's exemplary life of sacrifice and miraculous healing. Following Spiritist interpretations of the Gospel, brujos say that charity (*caridad*) is what motivates their actions, just as it motivated the deeds of Jesus. Although brujos charge for their services, they claim that charity is their ultimate mission on earth. As a bruja who was also initiated in

Santería once explained, "Sometimes we ask for a *derecho* [small money offering] for expenses, because we have to go to a river, the shore, we have to buy a small [prescribed] animal for cleansing the person, and sometimes one is left with the burden of that person. That's why fees are asked for. We don't get rich from these, and we ask a fee from both the poor and the rich because it's fair. Because these [our spiritual powers] are a gift that God had given us to help humanity."

"*Trabajar la obra espiritual* [doing the spiritual work] is not for the money," Bolina, an old bruja initiated in Santería and Palo Monte,[4] said the first time I met her at her altar in summer 1995, after several failed attempts. In that first conversation she mentioned how busy she was, and she showed me a local newspaper that carried a full-page photograph of her on the front page, below which was the headline "La Bruja de Loíza." As we sat in the small, tin-roofed waiting room by her house, surrounded by paper wedding bells and other decorations (kept as anniversary mementos) and chromolithographs of saints decorated with plastic flowers, she explained to me, "My husband and I are retired, so what I do now is to help the people who need me. . . . Interviews [like the one we were having] take up my time, and I need time to help my people." In subsequent, more informal visits, when I finally entered her small but crowded altar, I saw on one of the shelves, which were fully stocked with santos and figurines of all kinds, a small basket reserved for the kind of sliding-scale donations (between $2 and $10) clients would leave "for buying candles" after they had asked, "How much is it?"

That their gifts lead to a sense of mission is a leitmotiv in the discourse of brujos and may be conveyed in many ways. Haydée proudly stated, "I will be a bruja until I die. I was born a bruja, I was raised as a bruja, I will die as a bruja, and I want only brujos at my burial." Yet to have been chosen by God to carry out his divine providence means that brujos will have to undergo innumerable pruebas of their faith and to be committed to a life of perpetual sacrifice and charity.

Pruebas and the Professionalization of Brujos

One can only wonder about the oddity of having been blessed by spiritual powers only to have one's life marked by acute personal misfortunes. Brujos may be the object of the most heartbreaking events; but these afflictions, unlike those of regular people, would be seen not as the result of causas but as pruebas that God assigns them to prove their unconditional, unshakable faith. Depending on the way they respond to these pruebas, brujos may enhance their ability to heal others. *Pruebas* are one of the means to develop their *cuadro espiritual* (lit. "spiritual frame"; i.e., personal spiritual power).

While attending a series of lectures at a Spiritist center in Santurce, I met Yoli, the daughter of an espiritista, who told me that after experiencing a series of misfortunes she realized that she should follow in her mother's footsteps and become a healer. This insight is what drove her to the center. After a stroke left her paralyzed and without speech, Yoli managed a complete recovery "thanks to [her] faith." "The doctor couldn't believe it!" she told me. If that were not a sufficient test, after the stroke she was diagnosed with cancer. "I was operated on six months ago and look at me—I'm here! These things . . . are pruebas that one undergoes, they are signs that you have to develop your cuadro." To prove her point, she mentioned her mother's case: "My mother stopped giving consultations to people when my brother was caught carrying drugs. She rebelled against God. But after suffering subsequent misfortunes, she resumed giving consultations even better than before. As a result, my brother now studies in Boston."

Bolina's ordeals have not been much different. She underwent an operation twelve years ago to have plastic prostheses inserted in both knees. The doctor had told her she would have to walk with crutches the rest of her life. Devoting herself and praying to San Lázaro (always depicted on crutches and with a dog licking his wounds), she promised him that if she got better she would remove his crutches (i.e., she would remove the crutches from the santo on the altar of her shrine). "Y así fue" (And so it happened), Bolina said. In all the years she had waited to be healed she had "walked barefoot, as a penitent," everywhere. The trope "I walked barefoot" was used often by several other brujos as well to refer to the sacrifice involved in their obra espiritual—apparently a collective image that resonates in Puerto Rico with the image of Jesus walking barefoot on his way to be crucified. It is as if, mimetically, by "walking barefoot" Bolina had relived his torment, thereby inducing a miraculous outcome. Today she walks without crutches, and the San Lázaro she keeps in her altar stands without his usual crutches. She literally removed the crutches from the plaster figurine.

Even after this testimony to her faith, a series of new pruebas awaited her. Lifting her shirt, she exposed several scars on her torso. She had six additional operations. The scars on her breasts were the result of a tumor that had been extracted; those on her belly, the result of surgery on a vesicle and on her uterus. These material vestiges, living proof of the pruebas she has endured to become an even stronger bruja, compose a living map that substantiates the ordeals she underwent to become a true healer and unerasable marks of her unshakable faith in God.

Reflecting on her own endless pruebas, Haydée repeated the words God once told her, "'You're not going to suffer anymore, you had enough suffering already.' I suffered from the death of a daughter, the death of a son, the death of parents, and the death of my nephews. That is why my body is purified on earth with suffering for the love of human beings. The suffering for my husband destroyed me. But God, La Caridad, and I said that I would not suffer anymore."

Common to all the pruebas that brujos have to endure—not unlike testimonies of charismatic Protestant converts—is that God will reward them with astonishing deeds for their unwavering faith. In front of a group of five clients and me, for example, Bolina reenacted the essence of her faith in God and its rewards. Bolina had interrupted her session with a client and come out to the small waiting room, followed by the puzzled client, to see how many were still waiting for a consultation. After exchanging a few words with each of the women, she suddenly changed her expression. Now in trance, she began performing a dramatic account of what had happened to her when three years earlier her husband of more than fifty years left her for another woman—a matter, I would learn later, that was directly related to the type of problem afflicting the client she had just excused herself from.

> My husband had even started making the other woman a house; I saw the foundation pillars, the cement, the stones and sand, I saw it. [She tried to kneel and while gazing above as if talking to God, she then addressed the women, saying,] I cannot kneel because of the operation on the knees. [Continuing the dramatization] But then, then, because of you, Papacito [God],[5] the house was never seen, and she was never seen again. I think she had a car accident and her car was totally destroyed. One works hard, washes, cooks, and after a while the husband gets tired of eating the same *bacala'o* [codfish] every day [touching her pubis as she, and every one else, laughs]. That's why in the afternoon I put on perfume and don't hang around like this [points to her washed-out robe]. If you scold him, he leaves with another; if you give him your back [refuse to have sex], others will give it to him. I wanted him to

give me a masonry-made house and he asked me, "What do you need it for?" I said, "I want it made of masonry." And now I have it [said with her hands on her waist as she moves her pelvis mimicking the sex act, evoking laughter from everyone]. And yesterday, I drank nine beers at the Fiesta de Santiago Apóstol, all dressed up . . . ! Last May we celebrated our fiftieth wedding anniversary, *ha!* [contemptuously, while touching the mementos—crepe adornments, a large golden "50" and a paper bell, and photographs on the wall]. *Ha!* I get the goosebumps [touching her arms] when I think of what God did for me. I have such *fluídos* [mediumistic powers]. . . . I have such fluídos I'm working since seven o'clock!

Enacting publicly in the present the amazement she once felt while having her wishes miraculously come true—the disappearance of the other woman, the erection of her own masonry house—Bolina had asserted God's endorsement of her actions. Because Bolina is a bruja, the miraculously achieved solutions to her problems bore on both her good standing with God and her success in performing a *trabajo malo*[6] against the other woman. In the waiting room, a general sense of trust and faith in her powers to heal and help the clients could immediately be felt. If she had indeed been endowed with God's blessings at that time and if the trabajos malos she had performed did work as they appear to have, it means these women had come to the right bruja!

Mimesis, Sanctity, and Sacrifices of the Flesh

One morning Haydée was not feeling very well and decided to cancel all the consultations for the day. She would usually do this after several days of overworking or when she had personal problems. While conversing with her in her refreshingly air-conditioned, shuttered bedroom she told me, "Sometimes They[7] wake me up at 3:00 A.M. when we usually enjoy the best [kind of] sleep. I have to wake up; I have to open the Bible, pray, and meditate. I know already what will happen during the following day, and I try to modify it. I wash up; I prepare my bath and start the day. It's not easy because we are doctors, the doctors of the soul."

On another occasion, when she was feeling well, Haydée expressed less dramatically but no less powerfully her complete dedication to her mission as a bruja, regardless of material considerations and personal sacrifice.

What follows are her spontaneous poetic words, which I have transcribed in verse form:

Lo que haya para comer, comeremos
Lo que haya que tomar, tomaremos
Lo que haya que bailar, bailaremos
Y lo que haya que brujear, brujearemos.

[Whatever there is to eat, we will eat
Whatever there is to drink, we will drink
Whatever there is to dance, we will dance
And whatever there is to witch-heal, we will witch-heal.]

Although pruebas are not chosen, leading an unselfish life is. Personal sacrifices of worldly goods, of relationships, and of physical well-being are the ultimate expressions of truly being brujos and recipients of God's grace. Essentially, like the sacrifices of Jesus, the idea behind sacrifices of the *materia* (flesh) is that spiritual healing powers will be multiplied. But sacrifice of the flesh does not mean asceticism. Modern brujos fancy sassy clothes, glamorous jewels, flashy cars, and the latest technological gadgets. Outwardly these commodities mark their affluence, which also indexes their spiritual prosperity. Their altares must reflect prosperity as well. In contrast to the consumption of banal objects, having their altar well equipped with several santos, crowned with expensive charms and amulets, is necessary to show where their true loyalties lie. Thus, even if they have to forgo their basic needs—use up savings or take out a loan, for example—they will buy the most lavish ritual objects. Personal sacrifice is an indispensable investment in the realm of spiritual power.

Economic sacrifices such as these were made by Armando: he lived modestly in his in-laws' house; worked at a full-time, salaried job (often also on weekends); and dedicated free time to helping people. By means of getting a loan and setting aside a large part of his salary, Armando managed to pay for a *coronación*—a big fiesta for his spiritual guide and patron saint. Haydée, whom he had met at a botánica and with whom he was planning to consult, offered her home for the fiesta. In preparation for the coronación of Santa Bárbara, he not only bought a life-size image of his patron saint but also commissioned a special tailor to make a gold-embroidered costume and crown for it. Conspicuous consumption is one of the channels through which to increase one's material and spiritual power. This is what had inspired Armando to give a lavish fiesta, at great

4.1 Offerings for Santa Bárbara before her coronación

personal sacrifice, involving plenty of food and drink, elaborate offerings, flowers, and decorations (see figure 4.1). The riches—spiritual and material—that his patron saint and spiritual guide had given him deserved no less.

For a more ordinary but no less spiritually significant purpose, Haydée made similar economic and physical sacrifices for her patron saint. After a busy morning, she, Reina, and I went to a botánica to buy a tall Virgen de la Caridad for the altar she had recently constructed in her living room. A week earlier, while workers had been tearing down a wall to enlarge the space devoted to the new altar, Haydée had undergone an operation on her foot. A couple of days after the operation, still recovering and with her toes wrapped in a bandage, Haydée decided to buy the Caridad at any price, even if she had to go barefoot. On our way—reminding me of Bolina's account—I heard Haydée stress several times the fact that she was going barefoot. When we parked the car, Haydée pointed dramatically at the dirty, uneven pavement and said that despite all obstacles she was determined to complete her mission to buy a Caridad. Because she knew that the botánicas she regularly visited did not sell figurines of La Caridad that were as tall as she wanted, we set out to a more distant new botánica in Fajardo. On arriving and learning that the owner was herself a devotee of La Caridad, Haydée said to her, "As I promised [La Caridad], with the money I made this morning I will buy a Caridad. You see, I came barefoot and even though I will be left *pelá* [colloquialism for "broke"] I will keep my promise. She [La Caridad] always gives back amply."

Sacrifices of the flesh made in doing obra espiritual—in this case, the pain in her foot and the expense of buying this Caridad—were some of the ways in which Haydée signaled her mission as a bruja. Indeed, by mentioning the deprivation of food, sleep, or health that entails doing obra espiritual, brujos personalize the meaning of "making sacrifices." On our way to the monte to perform some trabajos after a whole morning of consulting, for example, Haydée told me that she was extremely hungry and tired and had a headache and that she needed to stop for a rest. "But my Caridad says I can't rest until I finish the devotion I started on this day. And then I will rest my materia, because my spirit is always nourished." Reina added, "You're always tired because even in bed at night you don't sleep; you spend the nights *brincando* ["leaping," evoking, in this context, the stereotypical flight of European witches on brooms at night], to help your people. You use up the night leaping to help people, doing charity here, charity there."

Working long hours, sometimes through the night, brujos, in Haydée's words, "have a time to begin their work but not to end it." This is in part what makes a "true" brujo. Both physical and spiritual exhaustion define what sacrifice entails among brujos. Being worn out spiritually, of course, is the most dangerous, and only experienced brujos know how to recognize its warning signs and avoid its dangerous consequences. Mabi, a newly practicing espiritista, told me that sometimes people "drain her." She explained that she often wakes up at dawn, for instance, because somebody wanting to consult her has already begun "holding" (*agarrando*) her attention with their thoughts, instead of waiting until the morning. Once, after healing a client, she ended up in a hospital as a result of being left totally "empty"—with no life energy or defenses. She had experienced what brujos call "spiritual drainage," the most feared price for being a witch-healer.

More experienced brujos would be alert to signs of extreme exhaustion and take measures to prevent it. A brujo might avoid certain clients or postpone counseling someone because of a perceived threat to her spiritual energies. For example, I saw Basi take the preventive measure of cleansing herself for several minutes both before and after counseling a certain person, as in previous contacts she had sensed the signs of spiritual drainage. She explained to me that on another occasion she "even had to be hospitalized for helping a person heal from cancer." "But," she continued, "my protecciones take care of me — San Gregorio, for curing. . . . There is also energy in nature. Sometimes you only need to hug a tree. The Indios are my personal protecciones. Congos are fierce. La Madama is always with me — she is La Caridad, Cachita. All the spirits dwell in the Yunque [a famous Puerto Rican rain forest, today an ecological preserve]."

Inescapably, personal relationships, too, are likely to be sacrificed as tolls that are paid for the obra espiritual. Marriages and love relationships might fall apart or be difficult to sustain, generally because the profession of brujería involves total dedication: clients' needs come first — before everything or everyone else. Leading a "normal" family life is thus quite impossible unless spouses assume, without resentment, most of the responsibilities of caring for the family's needs. As a general rule, spouses rarely encourage the work of their spouse-brujos. I heard some brujos say that the attitude of their spouses was merely one of acceptance. A bruja I met in Cabo Rojo said her husband was often jealous of her work, of the time she spent with her clients. A respected aging brujo, reminiscing about his recently deceased wife, said, "When clients started coming at dawn, my wife just used to go inside the house. She kept a low profile. Though she was a Pentecostal, she never interfered with my work."

But other less fortunate brujos often have to manage not only their spouses' but also their in-laws' negative attitudes. Armando, for example, had to counsel his clients outside of his home because his in-laws, partly influenced by his wife, refused to let him work in their shared home. This was extremely inconvenient for him, for after long hours of working at his paid job, he had to drive to Haydée's house, where he had set up, free of charge, his new consultation place.

In the most extreme cases, marriages end. Haydée is a case in point: "This espiritismo and brujería cost me my marriage; [my husband] never accepted what I was doing, and said to me, 'Decide: the saints — or me!' I kicked him out. Everything around me has to be positive; whatever becomes negative has to go. He was afraid of me — he couldn't hide it. For me, the obra espiritual was the most important thing. And I was, like, 'You ate — you ate, you left — you left.'" She would care only for her clients, in other words, and nothing except her children would interrupt her work, not even dinner or leisure time with her husband — which, for most Latin American women, is an unusual attitude.

In the process of healing, sharing their spiritual power, and helping others at the expense of their own and their spouses' well-being, brujos can enhance their spiritual abilities. Haydée expressed this in a militant mood: "I'm proud to be a bruja. I'm the number one bruja of Villas. Espiritismo is my food and brujería is my companion, my bedroom consort; I will not leave it for anybody. This is my mission, like that of the governor in Fortaleza [the governor's home]." Perseverance in their mission might grant brujos the ultimate power—that of becoming *un espíritu de luz* (a spirit of light) as Jesus was, according to Spiritism. Emulating Jesus's life enhances the possibility of becoming sanctified by a similar spiritual godly gift. Unlike the powers gained through trabajos malos, God-given powers are sacred. Haydée proudly said of her spiritual power (in contrast to that of some other brujos, which had been gained through black magic), "Lo que Dios da no hay quien lo quite. Han tratado y no han podido" (Whatever God gives no one can take away. [Enemies] had tried but had not succeeded).

The miracles and sacrifice connected with Jesus's life are an inspiration to brujos; indeed, they are the building blocks of their own claims to sanctity. These stories resonate with the great majority of Puerto Ricans, who heard them as children in religious schools and at church. Hence emulating the parables connected to the healing miracles of Jesus bestows evocative power on the work of brujos, which by apparent similarity taps into associative chains that link the sanctity of Jesus's ability to heal with their own.

The idea that spiritual power can be attained by mimesis, or imitation, of God follows a long tradition initiated in the Gospels and codified in *De Imitatione Christi* (The Imitation of Christ), the set of fifteenth-century Christian devotional books attributed to Thomas à Kempis (1380–1471). Influential ever since, it proposes the emulation of the life of Christ as a way to achieve a personal, direct spiritual unity with Christ. The Catholic notion of salvation and sanctity achieved through mimesis has become part and parcel of the ways in which brujos relate to their profession. Their particular form of this is expressed in discourse through aphorisms, proverbs, and stories of the life of Christ, as well as in action, through healing performances that emulate those of Jesus and thus are framed as "miraculous" acts of mercy and charity.

Once at noon, Haydée had Manuel, one of her clients, sit in the waiting room with his leg stretched out in front of her and placed on her lap in order to first spiritually cleanse it with the sacred smoke of the Indio and

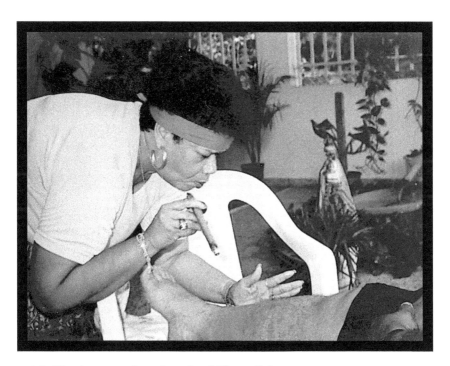

4.2 Blowing sacred smoke to heal Manuel's leg

then dress it with a special mixture of healing, sacred herbs. Lunchtime came, but Haydée was still curing Manuel. Nina brought her a plate of food, and while applying herbal compresses to the ulcerated leg, Haydée began eating her lunch of fried eggs and said, "I eat while I heal, like Papá Dios [Jesus] did with the lepers. He lifted up San Lázaro from misery. I live happy: *yo doy y recibo* [I give and receive]."

Near the end of the session, Haydée insisted, "Manuel, if you let your legs [the one she had cured once before and this one] get sick again, don't come back to me, because I will not use my hands again to cure you. Remember also that Papá Dios got angry in the temple and threw [the Pharisees] out. You do know that, right? As Papá Dios got annoyed, I also get annoyed." In making these two very different allusions, Haydée was aligning her work with that of Jesus: first, in reference to her vital mission to heal through the unselfish sacrifice of the flesh; and second, in reference to her ultimate lack of tolerance for those who do not respect true healers. By alluding to the only reported case in which Jesus expressed anger, she was making the point that even an espíritu de luz like Jesus can lose his temper

4.3 "I eat while I heal."

when faced with noncompliance. On another occasion, when Haydée felt that everything around her was crumbling, she made a direct connection between the weight of the Cross and the weight of her own misfortunes. Comforted by this simile, she concluded: "If Christ was helped to carry the Cross, I too will be helped [by Christ] to carry mine."

It was at dawn on a Sunday in October when Haydée, accompanied by a group of close clients, her family, her assistant, and me, set out for one of two yearly personal pilgrimages to the Santuario de Schoenstatt, a distant Marian chapel in the mountains of Juana Díaz. Haydée explained to me that brujos occasionally go to a chapel to worship and make special petitions, but usually they journey to a distant one where they will not be recognized and expelled.

In keeping with the holiness of the day and as a complementary sacramental act, Haydée had decided that on her way back she would also visit the ailing mother of one of her clients, Rosa, who had also joined our group, to effect a healing. Rosa's mother lived in Barranquitas, a town on a mountaintop in the central cordillera that crosses the island from east

4.4 Santuario de Schoenstatt

to west. It was a three-hour drive along very steep roads from Juana Díaz, but because Rosa's mother could not come to Haydée's altar, Haydée felt she had to come to Rosa's mother. For Haydée it was a pure act of charity. Near the end of the serpentine roads, heavy rain accompanied by lightning and thunder suddenly turned into a hailstorm. In Puerto Rico, where the daily temperature hovers around 80° Fahrenheit during most of the year, a hailstorm is an unusual event. Everybody in the car was exhilarated, laughing and crying at once, catching hailstones through the open windows. I was also terrified, driving with almost no visibility along very narrow roads. In the midst of this merriment, overriding the rest of the voices, Haydée said, "It's the Virgen de la Caridad who sent [the hailstorm]—it's the work of La Caridad! . . . She's turned the seawater into hailstones for us!" On arriving at the mother's house, we sprang to gathering this hail water into buckets, and with this "blessed water" Haydée set out to heal the aching leg and spirit of the old woman (photo 4.6).

Similar to the teaching and healing journeys of Jesus, Haydée's spontaneous journey through the mountains also involved personal sacrifice and

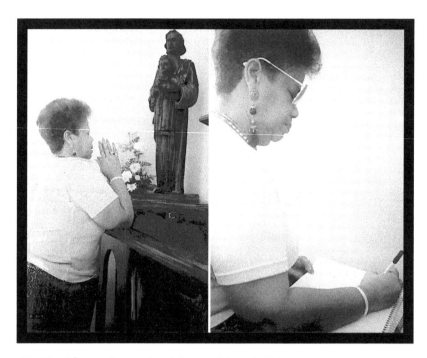

4.5 Haydée praying and writing petitions in Schoenstatt

charity and was finally blessed by La Caridad herself. We saw how the sad and feeble woman had transformed into a vivacious, reinvigorated person by the end of the day. We were in a heightened state, participating (in Haydée's words) in la obra de La Caridad—the spiritual work of La Caridad. Haydée closed the healing session with an emotional homily delivered to Rosa's mother and the rest of the group on the duty of offspring to make sacrifices for their aging parents. It was a mystical moment, infused with layers of religious significance. It was as if one of Jesus's healing miracles had come to life in the present through a mimetic performance connecting the mythical elsewhere with a Puerto Rican mountaintop.

A Second Chance: Charity and Reincarnation

Another layer of spiritual baggage that lies beneath the work of brujos originates in the ethos of espiritismo. According to one of its tenets, quite different from Catholic doctrine, any kind of social and moral transgressions must be "paid for" on earth. Debts contracted on earth are paid on earth, not in the next world, espiritistas of all kinds often say, quoting a

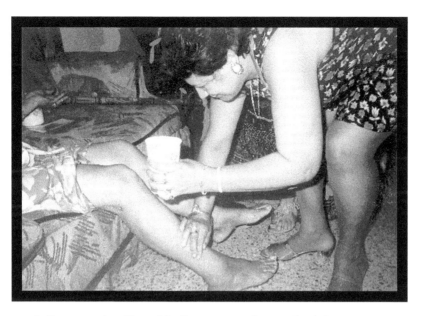

4.6 Rosa pouring blessed hail water over her mother's leg

famous Spiritist aphorism. Hence illness and other misfortunes, in addition to being pruebas, might—unbeknown to the sufferer—also be ways of atonement. This was the case, for instance, of a man who came to consult with Haydée after having suffered a stroke. In divination, he was told that he had "gathered" (*recogió*) bad energies from "two different trabajos malos made by two women [his life companions]" who were rivals and that, unfortunately, he was "caught in the middle." As he had been unfaithful to both, Haydée admonished, "You're getting what you in fact deserve. One has to pay [for one's wrongdoing] because hell is on this planet Earth, not there [in hell]. Sometimes we have to pay for what we do—*not* sometimes but always."

But any wrongdoing can be mended, if one cares to do so. Befitting the notion of the modern self, espiritismo provides the ground for limitless opportunities for expiating unpaid debts and for self-improvement through reincarnation. This is why God is a *Dios de misericordia* (God of mercy), Haydée once told me in a conversation about espiritismo. A few weeks later I heard similar attitudes about reincarnation when I attended a class on espiritismo at one of the most well known Spiritist centers in Santurce. The audience (most of whom were, or wanted to be, mediums) engaged in a passionate debate about the idea of reincarnation and its relation to charity: "People who were enemies in previous lives are given the opportunity to purge their hatred and negative deeds through reincarnations"; "Enemies can reincarnate as members of the same family"; "Those who hated each other in another life may be found in the same family today." A woman then quoted the proverb "El que no quiere caldo se le da tres tazas" (One who doesn't want soup is given three cups), pointing to the Spiritist belief in reincarnation and free will. She gave a few personal examples showing that individuals are given the opportunity to overcome any irrational, antagonistic feelings toward fellow human beings through personal will.

Free will, most of the speakers ended up agreeing, is the ultimate opportunity for redemption, as well as the force behind one's chance of "working up the ladder of spiritual betterment." Volunteering a personal experience in this regard, another woman said, "If someone disgusts me, I approach that person; one has to settle the balance of that debt [contracted in other lives] here and now." As to the morality of "paying our debts in this world," some speakers suggested in one way or another that it meant giving human beings the opportunity to learn to resolve conflicts with other people during the "material life—while we are incarnated [*encarnados;* i.e., alive]—in order to enhance the level of our spiritual growth [*desarrollo espiritual*] after we disincarnate [*desencarnamos;* i.e., die]."

Brujos are not exempt from falling prey to unresolved spiritual clashes with their fellow humans, of course, even when these are their clients. Such was the case between Haydée and a new client, Norma. Untypically, Haydée kept Norma, who often came with her two toddlers, waiting hour after hour for her first consultation; each time Norma's turn came, she would be asked to let yet another person go ahead of her. Although clients come without appointments to consult brujos, the unspoken rule is that people will be consulted in the order in which they arrive unless someone has a good reason to ask for permission to go before their turn. At the end of the day Haydée developed a headache and sent Reina to ask Norma to come back "tomorrow." The same thing happened the next day and the next. After nearly a week of this, it had become obvious to all—especially to Haydée herself—that something extremely awkward, not to say bizarre, was happening. Because her repudiation of Norma had no objective explanation, Haydée suspected that some "unfinished spiritual business" from one of her own previous existences was interfering with her ability to take Norma as a client. "I know that she and I don't match—we have a spiritual clash [*choque espiritual*]. I treat her badly, I push her away, and I know she has many problems, and I need to help her. That's why I will help her, even though she repulses me [*me repugna*]."

She expressed these problematic feelings to the client herself, who up to that point had accepted her inability to get a consultation with Haydée as further proof of her general current crumbling luck. Once in the altar, both women wondered about the source and nature of the animosity that was shutting Haydée off from Norma. At the end of what appeared to be a spiritual battle with negative forces, while Haydée was still in trance, the spirits revealed that those negative forces had intended to destroy Norma's life to the point that they had tried, obviously unsuccessfully, to cut her off from any possible help she could receive. First by reflecting on and then by fighting against her own ill disposition toward Norma, Haydée assured Norma that the fight against these evil forces had already begun. Now Haydée promised she would fight back with full force against the evil forces that had cursed (*salaron*) Norma, those forces that had closed off all the paths laying in front of her. After several consultations and all sorts of trabajos—all performed free of charge because Norma was indigent—Haydée gradually restored Norma's self-confidence and vital energy.

What motivated Haydée to overcome her baffling rejection of her client was her belief in the opportunities granted by incarnations to purify one's soul and her belief in the power of free will to make the sacrifices necessary to help others. In keeping with the Spiritist dictum "No hay casualidad, hay causalidad" (There is no coincidence, there is causation), Haydée admitted that it was not a coincidence. She acknowledged that her initial "refusal" arose from a spiritual source and therefore had to be identified and resisted.

Again and again, the Spiritist message is that human weaknesses have to be put aside to become true healers. Only through repeated acts of charity can healers elevate, in Spiritist terms, the "light frequency" of their spiritual powers—each reincarnation offering an additional opportunity to rise above the "frequency" reached in previous lives.

I met Roberto, an espiritista and photographer who lives as a hermit in a small house in the mountain town of Cidra, through a Puerto Rican colleague. When we arrived unannounced at his house one afternoon, he received us in a robe and invited us inside his modest home, which to my surprise was almost empty but for a computer. He told us that many years ago he saw in a dream a previous reincarnation of himself as an Egyptian pharaoh, and from then on he had dedicated his life to performing

4.7 Preparing a trabajo free of charge for Norma

charitable acts. Because his premonitions and visions are given to him in dreams, Roberto explained, he cannot let anything or anybody distract him after he wakes up. Living as a hermit is therefore a necessity as well as a sacrifice that enables him to concentrate totally on the images he is given by the spirits.

Once, Roberto told us, he woke up in the middle of the night and, in a zombielike state, walked as if "driven by a strange force" to a house where a crime was about to be committed. He arrived during a quarrel that had been going on between two brothers. While one of them was pointing a gun at the other, Roberto stood in front of the revolver held by the assailant and managed to stop him from firing. Roberto told us that on another occasion he was given the winning lottery number in a dream. Realizing that a poor neighbor needed money to feed her children, he gave her the winning number, which she then played the next day and won about $1,000. "Helping others," he said, "is my mission since God gave me the gift of clairvoyance."

The idea that charity is the main mission of brujos on earth was a

leitmotiv running through every one of my encounters with them. The healing stories of Jesus not only become sources of emulation that guide the healing performances of brujos but also become tropes that evoke retrospectively the motives that had inspired these performances. For instance, Haydée once made it clear to me and some of her closest clients that although everyone sees that she loves flashy dresses and jewels and is "spoiled," she also has a very generous nature. "I am a charitable person, but I give from what I have, not from what I have in excess [leftovers]. That, I throw in the garbage. I let go of my possessions—this is how Jesus did it." Contrary to the rich who engage in philanthropic actions, Haydée was defining the ultimate act of giving as a true act of sacrifice, and who other than Jesus could be raised as an exemplar?

Living according to the paradigm set by the life and deeds of Jesus—dedicating one's life to helping others through acts of charity and sacrifice, even in the worst of times—publicly asserts the spiritual mission of brujos on earth. In contrast to other professions, the legitimacy of brujería is not based on the legal or medical system. Nor is it bound by moralizing agendas for improving the world. The ultimate claim of brujos is based on their mediating function between the will "of God and the spirits" and that of humans on earth. In Haydée's words, "I'm happy with being a bruja. God gave me these powers in order to help. But God is first; without God I can't do anything. And remember that God had [mediators like] the Apostles, also the Antichrist. . . . Many are the signs, the miracles [that need to be deciphered]. We have to understand the mysteries of God. I do understand the miracles of God. Many things are revealed to me; these are the mysteries of God."

From a purely pragmatic standpoint, it is hard to see why brujos would want to endure personal sacrifices and to accept so much pain in modeling their actions after the life of Jesus. It would be quite incomprehensible without delving into the ways in which brujos depict the source of their calling.

Miraculous Beginnings and Personal Revelations

The sense of mission and empowerment on earth seems to originate with the miraculous encounters brujos usually report having had with God or a saint, either at an early age or at the outset of their obra espiritual.[8] Miraculous stories depicting the moment at which spiritual powers were bestowed on them reveal their enormous power in summoning them to a life of sacrifice and spiritual mission. Personal experiences of apparitions of Jesus or the Virgin are commonly reported in Puerto Rico among both Catholics and Protestants. Julia, an elderly Catholic woman who lived in my neighborhood in Old San Juan, had an almost life-size crucifix, surrounded by candles and flowers, in her tiny apartment. She told me that on several occasions she had heard God talk to her and even warn her once that someone was trying to break in her house.

Individuals might indeed be the private recipients of divine messages. Yet when brujos refer to their own experiences of having seen apparitions, they endow them with a special public claim — their sense of sacred mission and of being chosen to heal their fellow humans through their ability to communicate with the spirits.

Tonio, an old, well-known brujo in Loíza, told me he had started healing people when he was six years old, after seeing an apparition of the Virgin. It was during our first encounter, as we sat together on the porch, he in his wheelchair, that he reminisced about his life-changing experience:

One day I had gone as usual to fetch some water from a stream far from the house, where there was fresh water. I saw a mysterious woman with a long dress down to her feet. I filled one of the buckets with water and then lay down to rest in the center of some palm trees. When the woman approached me, [seeing her distraught] I asked, "Señora, what's the matter with you?" The woman said, "Give me a little water." She took the bucket full of water [and said,] "O, My Father, San Antonio, child of God [Antonio], help me. They are persecuting me. Where should I go?" After filling another bucket of water for her, I told her to follow me to my house. But she had arrived at my house before me. When I arrived, my aunt Jacinta scolded me for arriving so late, saying, "You should have come earlier, you left about three o'clock to bring water." But what Aunt Jacinta did not know was that I had had a miraculous encounter. Seeing that I had gotten into trouble for helping her, the Virgin said to me, "I won't say anything more to you, but I'll leave you with something"—it was the power to "see" and heal.

Tonio, like Haydée, was born in a *surrón* (caul)—believed to be an omen of good luck and, especially, *facultades* ([spiritual] powers).[9] He remembers that as a child he used to say to people, "You have a causa." His mother had to lock him in the house to protect him from the constant flow of people seeking his help. About his spiritual powers, Tonio said, "I see the spirits and they talk to me, but above all is God; faith in God is the most important thing."

As a child, Haydée also started to show signs of having spiritual experiences. "When I was a child I used to get revelations in dreams," she said. "I used to have fluídos. The events were given to me in visions, and I had the urge to tell about them, and they would then happen." Reinforcing the idea that spiritual power is a gift of God, not a learned ability, Haydée said, "One doesn't do this, one is born with it. God gave this to me, and each day he gives me more knowledge. Each day that passes by I come to this realization."

Like Haydée's encounter with God at the beach, Bolina had a revelation on the seashore of Loíza, after which she became a professional bruja. But hers was an encounter with another breed of spiritual forces. She had encountered the spirits of her African ancestors—who had been brought to Puerto Rico during slavery—and was possessed by them. "I started with brujería thirty years ago. . . . I used to wake up in the middle of the night and find myself in my nightgown on the seashore, not knowing how I got there. My spirits were African, you know." She uttered the last sentence with a sense of pride in her spirits' indomitable character, as she did on other occasions, here expressed through the image of the spirits being stubbornly drawn to the seashore, apparently in their longing for Africa.

Fame, Acquisitiveness, and the Trope of Excess

Worldly fame mixed with a sense of mission and sacrifice is an irresistible combination. The social enchantment with quick upward mobility and the need to regain good fortune once it has been lost place prosperous and famous brujos in high demand. Having been "blessed" has a twofold meaning: it means that brujos are endowed with spiritual gifts and that these gifts will eventually be translated into prosperity for them and those around them. Brujos thereby need to constantly reassert in public their riches, avid consuming nature, and fame. There are several ways in which bendiciones are signaled: the number of clients they have, the hours or weeks clients need to wait for a consultation, the distance clients have to travel to come to their altares, the socioeconomic status or fame of selected clients, the complexity and elaboration of their altares, and the lavishness of the feasts given in honor of the saints.[10]

One often hears, "La marquesina está llena" (The waiting room is full); "People started arriving for consultations at dawn"; "Some have to wait a whole day to be seen." Having a large number of clients who make the sacrifice of coming from great distances and of waiting many hours are certainly indications of fame, but this does not necessarily translate into more money, as some needy clients are given discounts, make payments in installments, or are given exemptions when a fee or a suggested donation is expected for consultations and trabajos. Yet a huge congregation of followers testifies to the unique spiritual powers of any bruja or brujo who is the object of such loyalty.

Interestingly, brujos boast about having many clients but do so in artfully disguised ways, for example, by "complaining." They might endlessly bemoan the number of clients disturbing their privacy or their leisure time or draining their physical and spiritual energies. One explanation for this rhetorical posture might have to do with the rhetoric of bemoaned excesses in media reports concerning public devotions. These reports usually depict, in Pantagruelian dimensions, the kind of public commotion that occurs where an apparition has been reported or around a person who has been shown to be endowed with unique spiritual powers. They often de-

4.8 "La marquesina está llena."

scribe in great detail the nuisance produced by the huge number of devotees and the curious who, in their efforts to come closer to these powers, "cause traffic jams" and "disrupt the privacy of fellow neighbors."[11] Inspired by this rhetoric, brujos stir up a great deal of reverence among their followers through, ironically, their charity-motivated "surrender" to often vexing clients who would stop at nothing to be seen by them.

An additional effective way to publicly assert fame is by tapping into some sort of intercontinental, Caribbean, mainland-island or at least intraisland circuit. Mentioning the city or town from which clients have journeyed enhances the fame of brujos.[12] "The woman from Camuy" or "The man from Cabo Rojo" serves not only the mnemonic needs of brujos to identify a particular client for themselves but also implicitly serves to indicate to interlocutors who might have come from nearby towns that their clients make huge sacrifices (a three-hour drive or more) to be seen by them. The distance between the client's and the witch-healer's residence is thereby directly proportional to the spiritual caliber of the witch-healer. Therefore, if the Atlantic Ocean has been crossed from the mainland to arrive at the altar of a witch-healer, the power of that witch-healer has been forcefully demonstrated. Indeed, clients coming from anywhere

abroad enhance the prestige of brujos, for it shows that their power transcends local boundaries.

Brujos make sure that when a client comes directly from the conti-
nental United States to consult specifically with them, everybody knows
about it. "He arrived from New York on Saturday and came to 'Haydée, La
Bruja de Villas,' even before going to see his mother," Haydée proudly said
in front of her clients in the waiting room when she saw that young man
seated, waiting to be seen. Often Puerto Ricans living on the mainland
use their visits to the island as an opportunity to seek the help of islander
brujos. It is always a source of pride to a witch-healer to have a "commuter" choose him or her over the other brujos on the island—and surely
over those on the mainland. On another occasion, Haydée came out from
the altar to check on the number of clients waiting to see her. In the presence of the rest of the clients, Haydée then approached one of the women
and asked, "You are the one from North Carolina, aren't you? And of all
the brujos on the island it is to me that you come—why?" Similarly, on
various occasions Haydée pondered publicly (with only halfhearted mod-
esty) why it was that—of all the brujos in Puerto Rico—I, a researcher,
was drawn to *her* to write my book? We all knew that what she was saying through these rhetorical questions was that the spirits, supporting her
enormously, drove me as well as her overseas clients to her.

Not unlike professionals in other fields, the fame of brujos can be signaled by invitations to participate in activities, to open consultations on
specific days, and to participate in veladas given by brujos in other towns.
With an air of smugness, Haydée would say, "I have been invited to come
to Villa Carolina, Río Grande, and even Cabo Rojo and Rincón," or "He
was the best brujo but now he calls *me* to help him in his veladas—*why
would that be?*"

In addition to indicating the extent of their devotion to their patron
saints, the lavishness of the yearly fiestas dedicated to them, as stipulated
by the devotional calendar, signals the prosperity and power of brujos. For
example, when Haydée organized a big fiesta for her patron saint, La Caridad del Cobre, to be held on her day, September 8, she had a new altar
for the Virgin built ahead of time, turning the fiesta into a kind of public housewarming for it. She recounted the event to me on my return to
Puerto Rico after a two-week leave:

> We were seven women—*Las siete potencias africanas* [the Seven African
> Powers]. We went to the beach, we cleansed ourselves [in the water];

it was beautiful. We came home, we had breakfast, we danced, and at night I conducted the *misa* [mass]. But I would say that it wasn't just a misa, it was a misa-velada; it was everything—trance on the floor, dancing—except Santería, because I don't go with Santería. There were people that I had never seen before. I told them truths [*verdades*], and I mentioned names [i.e., details during divination]. My house was full. All the furniture in the living room, the dining room, and even the porch was used, and still there were people standing. Rain and storm were announced, but fortunately it did not rain until the next day. I can't explain how beautiful it was. We were [feasting] until two o'clock in the morning, whereas I had said that it was a one-hour misa! That day I opened my house, we gave fruits—of La Caridad del Cobre— we made *asopa'o* [rice stew]. That was a fiesta, a fiesta espiritual. A man from the municipality of Carolina was there. I told him everything [that I had seen in a trance]. I saw many things that were happening to him—he is coming this Saturday.

Hedonistic obsession with worldly success is central to brujería. Even in less fortunate times and situations, brujos will express their acquisitive, ostentatious, boasting, and ungovernable natures. If skillfully orchestrated, these attributes send a double message: one directed to their clients, the other to their enemies. For clients, signs of the material, sensual, and spiritual power of brujos are a guarantee that they have come to the right witch-healer for help, with the belief that the positive energies of that witch-healer's patron saint and guardian spirits will eventually be transmitted to them. For manifest enemies or those harboring hostile thoughts, the visible signs of the power of brujos act as forewarnings. Boasting is therefore indispensable.

Assertiveness becomes their weapon. But it is also apparent that it stems directly from the power given to them by the spirits. During the divining process, in whichever form it is carried out—by "reading *cartas*" (Spanish cards), "reading the *fuente*" (lit. "fountain," a spherical, transparent bowl filled with clear water),[13] or by being possessed or in trance— whenever the words of brujos are harsh, it is a sign that the spirits are making them speak without censorship, "blinds," or "confusion." Once after a woman who had come for a consultation had left the altar, Haydée spoke to Reina and me of this woman's apprehension during the divination session, saying, "Today I'm direct [*estoy directa*], and it's not me who's talking. That's why I was surly. [When the words of the spirits are

spoken,] *hay que joderse*" (vulgar Spanish, lit., "One has to fuck oneself";
here, one has to live with it). In fact, *estar directo/a* means that the words
brujos are speaking are authored by the spirits, and as in a state of trance
or possession, the words uttered by brujos are in fact "theirs," that is, the
words of the spirits.[14] Just as in a trance, nothing is left conveniently hidden. If the client has been involved in some sort of antisocial behavior,
the spirits will surely uncover it. This is one of the moments most feared
by clients, and, paradoxically, it is the one most desired too. The ability to
uncover whatever remains hidden, even to clients themselves, is also proof
of the unique spiritual powers of endowed brujos, who can "see through"
and "uncover" the truth. Especially in difficult cases, brujos often urge
clients to confess any misconduct right at the beginning of the consultation, warning them that if they do not "come clean" they will be discovered anyway.

When foul language is spoken during the divination process, it is an indication that brujos, in trance, are speaking the direct words of the spirits.
Perhaps hard to believe, this foul speech is the ultimate sign of their being
fully developed brujos—clearly in total disregard of mediumship instructions given by Scientific Spiritists and metafísica workshop instructors.
Half joking, half arrogant, the brujos Lucy, Haydée, Bolina, Armando,
Mina, and Tonio have said on several occasions that their spirits *hablan
malo* (speak bad). The goal of every brujo is to *hablar claro* (speak clearly),
directo (in a direct manner), which entails using "bad" words. Because
spirits are above social conventions, they can *llamar las cosas por su nombre*
(lit., "call things by their name"; i.e., say things as they are). For example,
when a client is developing his or her cuadro espiritual, brujos help by
exhorting the novice to let the spirits speak clearly: "Habla claro!" they
shout. "Aquí no queremos confusiones!" (Speak clearly! Here we don't
want any confusion!).[15]

Showing off what one has is a good advertisement of one's abilities
and promotes progress while deterring evildoers. In a vicious circle, however, boasting can also be a source of evil. It promotes and feeds on others'
envidia (envy)—one of the most common motives for causas and trabajos malos—and thus of misfortune. But unlike people in general, brujos
would never feel intimidated by the threat of envidia. They have the power
to "revocar," to deactivate it, by all kinds of spiritual means.[16] In exposing
their material success regardless of the potential envidia it might create,
brujos reassert that they are in control of their powers and that the spirits
favor them. These are important messages that need to be conveyed, espe-

cially to clients, yet no less to their actual or potential enemies. Material success indexes the bendiciones of brujos, which—the logic goes—they would not have been able to uphold had they not also been protected from evil attacks by their cuadro and protecciones.

At the end of every day, Haydée proudly counts the money she has received for her consultations. Likewise, the bruja Lucy opens her basket and joyfully counts the money in it. Neither Haydée nor Lucy needs the money to survive. One has her disability benefits, the other the profits of her health food store. In both cases the exhilaration stems from a double realization—the purchasing power of their work and the bendiciones it entails. The two are intimately connected. Material prosperity enables brujos to reinvest in their altares and their personas. Buying new clothes, new and bigger santos, and expensive gold-filled amulets and throwing a feast for a saint—with lots of food and a live band—are not just so many ways of rewarding oneself materially and emotionally for one's financial success; they are different modes of "investment" in the maintenance of "spiritual capital." The fame of brujos, the number of people who follow them, and the richness of their environments simultaneously attest and increase their own "blessings." This double meaning of being "blessed" constitutes the core of brujería in its present face, defining it as a form of spiritualized materialism.

Liability and Condemnation

To limit their liability brujos always argue that their role is confined to deciphering the past, forecasting the future, and warning and advising about the present. It is entirely up to clients whether to heed the warnings and follow the advice they have been offered, or to request to have any suggested trabajo be performed for them. Brujos are not liable for the actions of their clients, even though they often complain, of course, that their advice is not always followed. Mina, a bruja initiated in Santería and Kimbisa,[17] once said, "This [spiritual work] is very nice, but not everybody does what you tell them to or what the spirits want. We [brujos] can't make them [clients] change or do things. Unfortunately, people don't do what they are told to do." Similarly, Haydée, in an exculpatory tone and playing with double meanings, once said about a client who did not follow her instructions: "Yo le di el remedio pero no lo tomó" (I gave him the medicine [remedy, help], but he didn't take it). Both cases illustrate the exact point where the responsibility of brujos vis-à-vis their clients stops. In terms of the relative success of their performance as brujos, Mina added, "El efecto de que todo sea positivo depende del por ciento que la gente haga" (The overall positive effect [of anything that brujos do for their clients] depends on the percentage of what people do). That is, the success of brujos in helping their clients is directly proportionate to how much of the total advice that had been given to them is actually followed.

When Manuel came to Haydée for a consultation about his second case of a swollen, infected leg (after she had already cured his other leg), Haydée warned him that it was the last time she was going to cure his legs. Since the first leg had healed completely, Haydée admonished him this time for "letting" his other leg become infected when he did not act on the spiritually based follow-up measures she had recommended the first time. She reasoned that obviously her protecciones agreed to aid him again this time. Yet she added—half serious, half teasing—*this* was the last time she would treat him.[18]

If up to now I have stressed the commonalities among the practices of various brujos, I do not wish to argue that their practices are identical. In fact, the modes of practicing brujería are as varied as the individual personalities of brujos. If asked, some would define their practice by referring to a specialization in performing divination by "reading the cards" or "reading the fountain," their healing techniques, the modes of performing rituals or preparing talismans and trabajos. Others would define their specialization by reference to the motives or kind of gifts that bear on their practices. Contrary to popular stereotypes about brujos, almost all of the brujos who perform trabajos argue that these are limited to "good" (*buenos*), "clean" (*limpios*), or "white" (*blancos*) ones.[19] When Tonio referred me to Haydée, he characterized her by simply saying that her mediumship is positive: "Es una mediumnidad positiva."[20] Indeed, when I met her for the first time, Haydée introduced herself by saying, "Mi brujería es blanca [My witch-healing is white]. . . . In my house there is always peace, love and tranquillity. But I'm human, I'm proud, lively, provocative, glamorous, and [therefore] I ask God not to let me host hate in my heart since my [trabajo] has to be clean."

Perplexing as it may seem, brujos argue that their services do not include making trabajos malos (evil works)—those aimed directly at causing misfortune to others. They would only make them, they say, in order to retaliate against trabajos malos that had been solicited or "bought" from *brujos malos* (evil witch-healers) with the aim of harming their clients.

Sitting in her altar, with all the herbs, powders, oils, and candles spread on the table in front of her, Haydée was getting ready to perform a set of trabajos, one of which was aimed at creating animosity between some people who had been threatening one of her clients. In the presence of the client for whom the trabajos were being made, Haydée addressed Reina and me just before performing them: "I'm going to make some trabajos for the benefit of my client, but their purpose is not to cause evil [*hacer daño*], because I do not harm unless harm is inflicted to my people [clients]." Also, Tonio, who was known to many as a brujo who performed all kinds of trabajos, especially malos, made it clear to me that he makes a trabajo malo only when he aims at punishing somebody else's evil actions; he never suggested that his trabajos were inspired by evil motives—just the opposite.

To the observer, statements such as these might appear politically convenient yet also very tricky, as the underlying assumption is that making trabajos malos is always the result of others making them first. Diverting the blame to an alleged original antisocial act would not thereby preclude the fact that trabajos malos could be made. It could also be a misleading assumption. The *power* to harm, even if never exercised, is one of the most vital legitimations of the social power enjoyed by brujos. Recognition of their potential power is what seems to matter the most. Indeed, referring to Tonio as a famous, respected, and feared brujo, Haydée commented about her own power: "He is the Brujo Número Uno (Witch-healer Number One) of Puerto Rico. He gave me his instruments, gold and silver [i.e., his knowledge and power]. I am a mediumnidad positiva of light, I don't harm. . . . [My motive] is love. But I can make any [trabajo] you want; I have the instruments [knowledge and power]. I'm La Bruja de Villas de Loíza." In sum, famous brujos are those who have managed to be both feared and admired for their ability to make powerful trabajos malos when needed. Unquestionably, fear and admiration can best characterize the social standing of famous brujos, who appear to the public as simultaneously pious and wicked.

Holistic Brokers of Prosperity

I have argued that under the laissez-faire context of consumer capitalism brujería has become a form of spiritualized materialism, speaking with one voice about godly gifts and holiness and of fame, consumerism, and prosperity. Thereby, brujos help clients to pursue the material goods needed for constructing their constantly shifting self-identities and at the same time transform otherwise conspicuous consumption into spiritual pursuits. Drawing its legitimation from an awkward combination of consumerism and sanctity, brujería today appears to bear little resemblance to brujería under colonial Catholic rule or nation-building periods during the colonial Spanish liberal interlude and U.S. rule. The ways in which brujos publicly and privately define their work in the present—as actual bendiciones—suggest that the quest for economic power is quasi-religious and that the roles of brujos shift on a continuum between being saints and brokers. As mediators between worldly and supernatural forces (*fuerzas del cosmos*), the tropes they use to convey the source of their expertise seem amazingly similar. In complex ways that combine the popular stereotypical image of brujos as sensual and unscrupulous beings with the image of them as pious unselfish saints, they claim their unique power in society somewhere in the interface of spiritual surrender and material acquisitiveness.[21] Legitimized by their spiritual power and charity, brujos assert their expertise as professionals who intercede between worldly and supernatural realms in order to help their clients maximize their worldly potential.

In "classical" witchcraft anthropological theory, "witches" and "sorcerers" are characterized by an innate greed, which is identified as a potentially socially disruptive force. I can hardly picture the same effects under consumerism. In industrialized, capitalist societies, for instance, acquisitiveness ceases to operate solely within social relations guided by reciprocity, and thus material desires do not necessarily or inevitably destabilize social relations. Rather, greed-acquisitiveness-desire is elevated under the quest for individualism as a legitimate conduit for attaining prosperity. In conditions of high modernity, brujería ties in perfectly with the pursuit of material goals and commodification by averting any potentially negative consequences.

On yet another level, if one looks closer at the ways in which, say, both white-collar professionals and brujos make claims on a certain area of human endeavor and legitimize their expertise in terms of a recognized system,[22] more similarities than differences arise. Like the former, the latter sell their services to help "clients" or "patients." Whereas mainstream professionals draw solely on the technological system, brujos add a moral layer stemming from core beliefs of Christianity, Spiritism, and African religious systems. They specialize in mediating between supernatural forces and the client-patient's personal power,[23] which would also have an impact on clients' health, labor, and family relations—each of the latter being separate fields of expertise among mainstream professionals.

Surprisingly, at the doorsteps of brujos appear people from all walks of life—nurses, physicians, lawyers, business owners, secretaries, and teachers. Often physicians and nurses—trained to suggest treatments according to statistics—consult brujos when they themselves become ill before they decide on a treatment, whereas their patients usually follow their statistically based advice and seek brujos only after this system has failed them. Among the most common causes that drive people to seek the services of brujos are illness, financial problems, love matters, and conflict with neighbors, kin, spouses, or coworkers. Especially when several aspects of life go wrong at the same time, it is time to consult a brujo.

Unlike other professionals, who have been trained to look at a problem in its specificity, brujos mainly investigate its complexity. Significantly, a singular explanation clients give for deciding to consult brujos is "Vengo a resolver" (I come to resolve). Since they do not specify *what* they have come to resolve, it is evident that they expect a total resolution of the problem. Indeed, brujos look at misfortune as the result of a *sum* of causes. Treating all aspects of life simultaneously, brujos orchestrate solutions that integrate usually dissonant domains of human action—employment, education, medicine, the legal system, and so on (see chaps. 7, 8). In more than one way, brujos take a holistic approach: just as the causes of misfortune are thus diagnosed holistically, so is the treatment administered holistically. Brujos combine different types of healing techniques, such as various forms of spiritual cleansing, various modes of divination, and herbal-based or purely spiritual healing rituals. Not only do they derive a diagnosis, but they also provide the remedy—seeing to its preparation in the presence of the client—and administer it. They also suggest preventive measures. Occasionally they become the arm that punishes their clients' wrongdoers, or expiates their clients' offences to their victims, in the spiritual realm by performing special trabajos. In matters that concern the material and spiritual well-being of their clients, nothing evades brujos. As spiritual entrepreneurs, they constantly look for ways to improve their services, and this seems irresistible to anyone who comes into contact with them.

By means of an alchemy of prayers, visions, and magic manipulations, brujos manage to fuse the spiritual and material realms, creating a holistic "blessed" reality for those who have faith in their power.

CHAPTER

FIVE

SPIRITUAL ASSETS AND THE
ENTANGLEMENTS OF POWER

Cuadro

As I worked with Haydée in her altar on a regular basis, I gradually began to grasp what Tonio had meant when he said that Haydée was a medium-nidad positiva and that she had a beautiful, clean cuadro.

One's cuadro, or personal spiritual power, is also one's *dones,* spiritual baggage, and it comprises the spirits—the guardian angels—who follow our lives from birth to death.[1] It can simultaneously *promote* and *be a sign of having* prosperity, luck, love, and respect. Similar to Calvinist belief, prosperity is a sign of being "blessed" (*tener bendiciones*) by the spirits. But unlike the Calvinist concept of election, one's cuadro is not preordained. While it is considered a gift that is inherited, the cuadro lacks any deterministic feature. It must be developed and nurtured throughout one's life—in this and later reincarnations on earth.

In their raw form cuadros are usually inherited from close kin. The personal realization of having a cuadro sometimes occurs as early as childhood. Some brujos remember having had, between the ages of seven and ten, sudden visions of events that later occurred exactly as they had seen them in their dreams, or in the "back of their eyes," or in shadows reflected on walls. They say that their first awareness of this unusual ability was often accompanied by their own or a close kin's fear and distrust. Some recall having dreamed about a tragic event and having felt an urge to share this information with others. When the event they had envisioned was later confirmed, they remember that people reacted to them strangely, with a mixture of fear and admiration and anxiety and curiosity.

The cuadro may be developed positively, ruined, or eventually misused for negative purposes. When I asked Basi why she did not sell fabric dolls

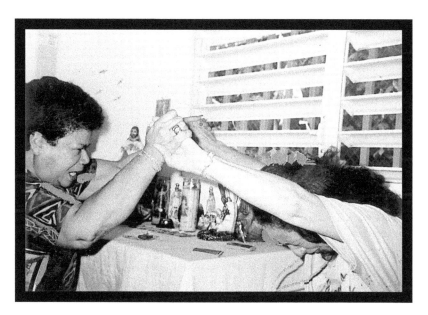

5.1 Haydée transferring her cuadro to a client in need

used in trabajos malos at her botánica, she replied, "I have a clean cuadro."
The danger of having both a strong and a developed cuadro that could
be put to various ominous uses always exists. Thus, reasserting that her
cuadro did not allow her to pursue, or sell, anything that could be used
for causing harm, she added, "I work my cuadro clean, clear. I'm a positive medium. I have a *cuadro de Dios.*" She meant by this that she would
use her cuadro—according to the Spiritist ethos—not only to heal but
also to help others develop their own cuadros. There are many opportunities in which brujos *pasan* (transfer) their cuadro to others, either to help
them solve problems or to empower them as future mediums.[2] Under the
Spiritist Law of Love and Charity, one's bendiciones (in this case, one's
cuadro) have to be shared, which assures that they will multiply: the more
we share, the more blessings and prosperity we are given back.

Speaking about the goodness of her cuadro and, implicitly, the rewards
that God had bestowed on her for unselfishly sharing it with others, Haydée said to Nora the first time they met at a botánica, "I have experienced
going into my altar at eight o'clock in the morning and not knowing when
I would finish. When I would look around I'd see that there were sixty
people [in the waiting room]. I would then leave [my altar] with $500 just
from reading the cards, not including the [fees for] trabajos. And I ask

myself, why is this? Because of the cuadro. . . . It was God who gave it to me."

Having a cuadro "open to the light" entails not only helping fellow human beings—especially since it is the cuadro itself that "tells you the needs of the other person"—but also helping yourself. For example, before a risky trip abroad, a prosecutor went to Tonio for advice and to have some trabajos done for him. Tonio told the prosecutor that he did not need trabajos because he had a very developed cuadro, which would stand "behind" him in all difficult endeavors, advise him on thorny decisions, and shield him from enemies.

Out of a sense of "infinite" charity, brujos lend their cuadro to others during veladas by having their spirits reveal and solve evenhandedly the misfortunes of each of those present. Such *cuadros de luz* (cuadros of light) are loaned to others to help them "see" the right path and get enough strength to solve their problems and prosper. In private consultations, the cuadros of professional brujos engage directly during the divination process, being responsible for revealing the problems to the client. This explains why when painful premonitions are told to a client, brujos might apologize, saying, "It's not me who talked 'bad' or predicted tragedies, it's my cuadro." In other words, don't blame me, blame my cuadro.

Having a *cuadro precioso* (precious cuadro) is only the beginning. Brujos often tell a client who shows special spiritual sensitivity in "seeing" beyond the evident that the person has a beautiful cuadro. To lead a truly moral, spiritual life and to prosper, one should properly develop one's cuadro. This is the message that a client endowed with an innately beautiful cuadro received when he complained that his neighbors were causing him great difficulties. Unless he stopped the negative thoughts about his enemies and rededicated his time and effort to the saints and his cuadro, he would not *salir pa'delante* (lit., "go forward"; vernacular, "prosper"). An outcome of having a highly developed cuadro is that one can eliminate the negative feelings that inevitably arise in daily interactions with others and thus lead a moral, just life.

Enhancing one's cuadro is a form of spiritual investment. As the bruja Lucy said when I came to see her for the first time, "I give money to help others with no fear, even if I am left with only $200 in my purse for the rest of the month. Because I then see [over the next few days] that I have [earned] $400! It is my cuadro that produces for me. It provides for me." Having a developed or enlightened cuadro assures success in every material and spiritual endeavor if it is "put to work." A teacher who came to Haydée for help was told, "Don't let anyone step on you [at work]. Profit from your cuadro! It's yours, that gift is yours." To another woman Haydée said, "You want to bring him [her husband] back to your feet, then how is it that with such a nice cuadro you've let this man humiliate you?" I have heard Haydée scolding a few of her clients who, regardless of their beautiful cuadros, still had serious problems, "But how come you have these problems? You always see whatever you plead for![3] Ellos grant your requests. You have to develop your cuadro; you have to lift it up. You have to open the road [darle paso] to your cuadro."

Spirits may communicate through any of the five senses via las cartas (Spanish cards), la fuente (fountain), and la clave (lit., the code).[4] Of all the senses, vision is the most important: one "sees" future events in dreams, or reflected in the fountain, or in the cards and the clave. Also, "hearing" is engaged when advice or warnings are "whispered" and the names of healing herbs and the recipes for healing concoctions are specified by the spirits during trance. In this sense, to have a highly developed cuadro means to be capable of deciphering the messages of the spirits and of harnessing the bodily sensations that signal the presence of spirits.

When clients appeared on the verge of entering into trance during consultations and "passing on" (letting their cuadro come about publicly), they were encouraged to let go of their fears—often in blunt, coarse terms. "Don't be afraid," a bruja might say. "Are you afraid of your cuadro? Coño [Shit]! Pass on that cuadro! Pass on that cuadro that you have. Let the spirits speak, puñeta [fuck]!"[5] The goal of what seems an abusive form of encouragement is to ease reluctant novice mediums into what might be a frightening experience of trance.

The ability to receive visions, even without going through the visible transformations of a trance, is what differentiates nonprofessional mediums from professional ones. This is a long-term process that requires regular participation in veladas and apprenticeship to professional brujos. Once, interrupting her consultation in the altar, Haydée came out to the packed waiting room and started a collective consultation, as in a velada. Among those present was Anita, a woman who came with her three grown children to solve various problems. On seeing Anita, Haydée was immediately drawn to her, exclaiming, "She has a beautiful cuadro and in the [next] velada she has to pass it on. [Prospective] mediums have to speak; they can't be mute. The twenty-seventh of this month I will have a velada. There you will pass on your precious cuadro."

Right there, Anita started to experience contortions. When Anita began to show signs of falling into a trance, Haydée and the other clients cheered her on, praying in chorus, "Que la paz de Dios quede aquí, ahora y para siempre. Amén" (May the peace of God stay here now and always. Amen).[6] Haydée then shouted at Anita to let the spirits speak freely. "Now and always! [Clapping hands] Now and always! [To the rest of us:] That woman has to put her cuadro to work and in what amazing ways! Now and always! Now and always! Always . . . lots of prosperity and progress for your spiritual cuadro." Showing signs of being in a trance herself, Haydée then voiced this acerbic pronouncement:

> And your husband, They tell me that he is going to go *pa'l carajo* [to hell]. He doesn't want you to work your cuadro espiritual. I had to kick my husband out of here, and They tell me that if your husband doesn't let you [develop your cuadro], your spirits will know about it, and he will have to put his tongue in his ass in order to let you *echar ese cuadro pa' delante* [launch your cuadro forward]. Because sometimes you want to ask [your spirits] for something and can't, or you want to light candles and don't because of him, because you're afraid of him. That fear . . . you have to let it go! [Shifting to her own voice:] I did it. I was afraid but I kicked him out, and it was for the best. It's better to retain your cuadro espiritual. And I gained bendiciones and bendiciones . . . in what amazing ways! *O'cará!*[7]

Generally, when novices attend veladas, they are encouraged to share their visions publicly under the close supervision of experienced mediums. The lead medium urges everyone, "Close your eyes and unite your thoughts" (Cierren los ojos en unión de pensamiento), in order to help the possessed novice bring about his or her cuadro. As the emotional level rises, the most powerful bruja passes on her own cuadro to the novice. The novice and the leader clasp hands and raise their arms. Then the leader steers the novice's arms and whole body in a frenzied waving movement. It is at this time that the energies of the former are passed on to the latter. When their hands unlock and the novice begins to deliver his or her vision, it is proof that the transmission has been successful and that the novice has been raised to a new level of spiritual development. The ultimate goal is *poner tu cuadro a trabajar en la obra espiritual* (to have your cuadro function in the spiritual work) for private or public purposes. In line with the ethos of espiritismo, the love and charity received by the novices in developing their cuadro have to be passed on to help others. The more one

5.2 *Unión de pensamientos in the Yunque*

shares one's spiritual power with others, the closer one is to having a *cuadro adelantado* (advanced cuadro) or a *cuadro de Dios* (God-given cuadro) and to being considered *un ser de luz* (an entity of light).

Once the cuadro has become highly developed, it can operate simultaneously in various places: it can "travel," "fly," and "work" through various [spiritual] "channels," to use the words of Doris, a Dominican medium I met at Basi's botánica. Doris, a short, thin, vivacious woman, described her mediumistic abilities as "channels, as electrical brain circuits that are

5.3 *Haydée, Reina, and Armando helping a novice to develop his cuadro*

open all the time [to receive spiritual signals]." She said she would travel in her dreams to places she had never seen before days or weeks prior to receiving a telephone call from someone who needed her. This person would send her tickets to fly—this time by plane—to the exact place she had dreamed about. In the dream she also would be given the herbs and recipes she would need to heal that person. Comparing them to pruebas, Doris suggested that because these spiritual and material voyages are extremely hard on her health, she sees them as part of the process of developing her cuadro. Hardships are meant "to see if you can bear with it. . . . Sometimes we even have to go through hunger in order to purify ourselves, to know if we could carry the burden. It's difficult." Doris said it was difficult for her to live a conventional life. There were times, she said, that she had "received" so much from her cuadro that she had felt exhausted and drained and had to be hospitalized several times.

In some cases, however, the cuadro can protect mediums by "telling" them not to *desenvolver* (untangle) clients who are "charged with negative energies." Such cases are few, but they indicate that "your own cuadro defends you." Lisi and Doris told me they had learned to tell some clients, "Today the spirits don't give me anything for you. Come back another day." Conversely, the cuadro can predispose a person to meet and engage in new relationships with previously unknown people — relationships that are meant to be positive. This, my host Basi and my mentor Haydée often said to me, is what drew different brujos to willingly enter a relationship with me. "My cuadro opened up the doors for you to my altar and my home," Haydée told me, reminiscing about our first encounter.

Protecciones

Some people, particularly brujos, acquire through their lifetimes a battery of protecciones embedded in the supernatural powers of *entidades* (entities) such as Catholic saints, Indios, Congos, Madamas, Gitanas (female Gypsies), and Árabes (Arabs). Apart from the specific features of each protección, which I discuss below, the general functions of the protecciones vis-à-vis the individual are similar if not identical to those of the cuadro; that is, they help their owners to succeed in life. The difference is that the essential aspects of one's cuadro are given at birth whereas protecciones are acquired and add up during the course of a lifetime.

Like humans, protecciones, I am told, can be audacious, wise, aggressive, sensuous, or mischievous. When I heard about their characteristics, it reminded me of stereotypical ethnically or socially based life stories. In the case of Catholic saints, the specific realm of human experience over which they are believed to have mystical influence is connected to some aspect of their legendary, miraculous lives on earth. Santa Bárbara, for instance, embodies the idea of "bravery during half of the year," when she appears on horseback, taking on the attributes of valiant men, and thus proffers a sense of courage to those whom she protects. During the other half of the year, when she appears on foot and takes on the attributes of

5.4 Haydée invoking her protecciones

"a female healer," Santa Bárbara protects her followers by endowing them with clarity of mind and with knowledge about the medicinal and magical properties of herbs.

There is great variation in the ways people define the attributes of their protecciones. Some refer to San Lázaro in relation to his "miraculous healing powers," to Indios with respect to "aggressiveness" and mischievous alertness, to Congos in relation to "playfulness and toughness," to Madamas in relation to "sensuousness and gregariousness," to Gitanas with respect to divining powers, and to La Caridad del Cobre in regard to mercy and prosperity. The importance of these attributes stems not only from the type of power that each entidad may grant its devotees but also from the ways in which they inspire the actions of devotees, who try to emulate them.[8] For instance, the Virgen de la Caridad is the main "shield" of Haydée; therefore, she constantly tries to direct her actions in ways that would emulate La Caridad. Reflecting on why she took a certain course of action and not another, she would say something like "This home is not mine, it is hers. I live in it, but she governs and commands it. Everything I have my Caridad del Cobre gave to me, and I have to be like her, do the Caridad to whomever may need it." And when she was the object of some unexpected help or gift, she would again draw on La Caridad, saying, "I give and receive plenty, as my Caridad."

Each entidad, similar to the orishas of Santería, is the "owner" of a color, an element of nature or culture, and healing plants, and influences specific body parts. Therefore, brujos "receive" from their protecciones the names of the plants and potions that must be used in each healing ritual. By means of a prayer that invokes a particular entidad and making an offering, for instance, brujos ask permission before cutting a piece of a sacred plant that is intended for a healing ritual. While healing Manuel's infected leg, Haydée pleaded for her patient's well-being. In trance and while blowing puffs of cigar smoke, offered to the Indio to cleanse the leg, she repeated several times the words *limpiando, recogiendo, botando* (cleansing, gathering, throwing). Then, while trembling, she said, "Virgen de la Regla fix this leg . . . Ouch! In the name of the Father, the Son, and the Holy Spirit I apply this *sábila* [*tuna,* aloe plant], but it's not sábila. It's the medicine to heal this leg, the medicine that my good protecciones have given me on this day and which will cleanse you completely, sir."

Because protecciones have a direct effect on specific organs or afflictions, brujos may lend one of their shields to a client to heal a specific ailment. During the course of consultation with a very troubled man in the back room of her botánica, Basi said, "It's my Gitana, the one who works for me [now]." The Gitana's mediumistic power and her vital energy was summoned to get to the bottom of the problem and help the client. Once, when a woman suffering from the HIV virus was leaving the altar with a series of healing recipes, Haydée bade her farewell, "You go now with your guardian angel and my *guerreros* [warrior spirits]," implying that her Indios, in accordance with their specific attributes, would also help the sick woman to fight the disease.

Protecciones not only guard by means of "sealing" the person (or, in New Age jargon, his or her aura) from malicious attacks, they also forewarn of upcoming unfavorable situations as well as bestow special weapons to fight against them. It is not uncommon to hear brujos publicly voice such power-affirming statements as "Those who work in Spiritism don't have to defend themselves, the shields do it" or "My shields take care of me" or "When my shields don't want me to work, they tell me—and if they don't want me to work for a certain person, I don't; I just look for an excuse." Strong brujos are fully protected and armed, made invulnerable by their protecciones: "Thanks to my shields, nothing can enter me."

Like the cuadro, protecciones also provide the "eyes" and "ears" that warn (by means of clairvoyance) their possessor of any impending spiritual or material attack on their well-being or property. They offer practical ways of diverting the paths of possible enemies, avoiding thereby a potentially deadly encounter. Protecciones "tell" people to go or not to go to a place and which path to take or when to make a critical decision, whether commercial, emotional, or political. In more active ways, protecciones also "do" things: they acquire and provide for spiritual and material needs to make things easier for their owner. Nora, commenting on her abilities, said to Haydée, "I always get what I want because *los nuestros* [our shields] fight for us."

Ordinary people who do not have these kinds of powerful armor have other ways to protect themselves, such as by regularly placing bits of camphor in the four corners of their houses or under their beds, by lighting candles to San Miguel Arcángel, or by placing goblets filled with rainwater in their homes. Any bad energy that might be sent to harm them would dissolve and evaporate, just as camphor and water do. The first thing that brujos usually do for clients who come "charged" with negative energies that might prevent them from receiving a good consultation is to cleanse them. The process involves proclaiming aloud several times, "Limpiando, recogiendo y botando," as the client—in a familiar Spiritist choreography—wraps himself or herself with both arms in a trembling motion from head to toe, as if gathering bad energies from the body, and then throws them into the fuente or onto the floor.

Protecciones are also in charge of alerting ordinary people to seek spiritual help. They may "bring" clients to a certain brujo. As Basi, for example, said about a client who was just leaving her botánica, "His very protecciones bring him here." In the same vein, I have heard clients and brujos say that when there is an obstacle to arriving at the destination, it is often interpreted as a sign that *los caminos están cerrados* (lit., "the roads are closed"). This means that the person's protecciones—or lack of them—had not been able to prevent the curse sent to harm a person from also blocking the attempt to get the help of a bruja.

If the divination process reveals that the cause of misfortune is a trabajo malo, brujos use their protecciones to launch a counterattack. The same protecciones redirect the trabajo malo to whoever commissioned it by a boomerang effect called *revocar* (to revoke), and in this process the defensive power of protecciones is automatically turned into an offensive one. While invoking her own protecciones to effect a *revocación* (revocation) in response to a trabajo malo that was apparently performed against one of her clients, Haydée said, "I'm a bruja and espiritista, so may nobody harm me or my clients or they will know *who* Haydée is. *Los míos* [my shields] take care of me. Anyone who harms my clients *tiene que vérselas* [has to contend] with my protecciones." The message is clear: protecciones not only protect, they also attack.

Los Muertos

Operating at a lower level of spirituality than the entidades, and closest to humankind, los muertos, or the spirits of the dead, add to the spiritual capital of brujos. But like any in-between category so close to human beings, los muertos occupy an ambiguous position. They can be commissioned (recruited) for the execution and deliverance of trabajos malos as well as *trabajos buenos*.[9] The Afro-Latin deity Papá Candelo is the "owner" of the dead, a role that is shared by his Catholic counterpart, San Elías, El Varón del Cementerio (Saint Elias, Lord of the Cemetery).[10] Brujos ask for permission from these entities before hiring the services of los muertos. Having good intimate relations with los muertos and no fear in dealing with even the most wicked muertos is what differentiates, by and large, espiritistas from brujos.

I have often heard people in Puerto Rico—even those who were not professional espiritistas or brujos—report having had nighttime experiences with los muertos, who appeared to them on a regular basis in their dreams, communicating important messages and warnings that needed to be deciphered. Some of those who were practitioners of Spiritism reported having had intimate interactions with los muertos. Los muertos can help and protect family members or friends. But by the same token, they tend to play tricks on humans, pestering them, "attaching" to them, or having sexual intercourse with them (incubus and succubus). Often people complain of having had a muerto come to their bedrooms, lie down in their beds, and kiss or bite them. They may show the blue marks on their arms or legs as proof of these nocturnal encounters. Armando, an espiritista initiated in Santería, showed me such marks while relating how he had to fight with all the strength that his protecciones had given him against the spirit of his wife's dead husband, who had come back to annoy them.

A more permanent—and thus excruciating—relationship can develop with *espíritus de existencia*.[11] These are evil spirits of people who after being dead for many years are still wandering among the living looking for a body to inhabit. In these cases a person diagnosed by an espiritista as having an espíritu de existencia is believed to have been born with a causa, a curse. Everything in the life of such a person will turn out to be bitter, tragic, or unsuccessful; failure will follow failure, every endeavor will end up being a fiasco. Misfortune will not end until the espíritu de existencia is driven away from the person—a difficult task that only strong brujos can accomplish. In most cases these kind of muertos live attached to the victim twenty-four hours a day, becoming their sole sexual partners and preventing their victims from ever getting a living spouse. This is what happened to Marta. She was diagnosed as having an espíritu de existencia who, in the words of Haydée's spirits during divination, is so possessive that he "even believes that he owns her and thus does not let any man approach her." Indeed, Haydée foretold, "Marta, you have seen many nice men get close to you and then watched them leave in a flash for no reason. And unless someone will be able to drive him [the espíritu de existencia] out of your life, you will never be happy."

Fortunately, los muertos can also intervene mischievously to help their protégées. For instance, bragging about her own spiritual power, Nora told Haydée and me that she doesn't need a husband, because her muerto provides for her sexually and financially.

My muerto provides me with everything. Once, I passed by a store and saw a golden chain worth 3,000 pesos. I looked at it [and said to myself,] "Wow . . . well, I don't have the money now," and [snapping her fingers] [a voice] behind me says, "But you'll have it," and I go on walking. One night I was sleeping and I hear "Get up," and I said, [in a complaining voice] "this muerto doesn't let me sleep!" And to my mother who was listening, [I explained,] "It's my muerto, who doesn't stop speaking, and he speaks and speaks and speaks. He doesn't shut up. He doesn't sleep; he is speaking for twenty-four hours, speaking and speaking." [Imitating his voice:] "No Norita, don't do this, do that, and that, look for the money." . . . [Interrupting herself, raises her voice to a shout, mimicking her response to the muerto:] I say to him, "Good, I'll do it!" You see, the next morning my uncle won the lottery and said, "Take these 2,000 pesos," and then I grabbed them. You see, I don't need a husband, because if I ask my husband for money to buy some 70-peso shoes he looks for "four excuses" or [says] maybe next week. And he gives you the money and gives you a *luk* [Spanglish for "look" (*y te da un luk*)]. [Laughing] No, the muerto gives it to you and already, immediately, immediately forgets about it. He only expects you to stay with him, working [the spiritual work].

A less colorful but equally positive nurturing relationship developed between Dominga and her dead husband's spirit. After the death of her husband, Dominga was engaged in a family feud over who was to inherit her home and land. She was told by Haydée, in consultation, that the spirit of her dead husband was making sure no prospective buyer would purchase the house. In contrast to what he used to do while alive—abuse her and make her work—the dead husband's spirit would now work for her and sustain her household. Therefore, Haydée advised her to light a white candle for him (said to feed the positive energies of muertos). "Now he wants to help you keep the house, Dominga. He doesn't want you to give the house to those sons of bitches [*a esos cabrones*], sons of his [previous wives] who didn't do anything and want a piece of that."

As pawns in a huge cosmic army, los muertos also work for brujos on a free-lance basis. In their dual role, they might either promote or thwart the success of the trabajos malos that are being performed by brujos. Occasionally, when the muerto who allegedly caused a misfortune is named during divination, it means that the brujo "saw" how the trabajo malo had been performed (*cómo se hizo el brujo*).[12] In these cases, because the source of misfortune was revealed in a detailed manner, the divination process is assumed to be extremely reliable, and the outcome of divination—especially the suggested trabajos—will be followed to the letter.

When the muerto summoned by a brujo is a departed loved one of the brujo, the commissioned trabajo is sure to be carried out by the muerto exactly in accordance with the directions. A high rate of success is thereby guaranteed. Haydée once promised a devoted client that for his trabajo she would summon her own dead son's spirit. Muertos can be paid in kind or with a symbolic amount of money; for example, for delivering a work they are rewarded with candles, flowers, prayers, or other offerings. The soil of cemeteries and cremains have strong magical power and are thus used for the preparation of trabajos malos. In exchange for a small quantity of cemetery soil, for instance, a small fee ($1) will be left in the cemetery for Papá Candelo, its "owner."

Causas and the Mimetic Power of Magic

If one has successfully accumulated the positive forces given by a highly developed cuadro, or a host of protecciones and favorable muertos, one can deal with causas or bewitchments. These are the primary causes of the worst personal tragedies and crises, deadly animosity among kin, impo-

5.5 Sweetening relationships of couples and siblings with honey

tence, infertility, substance abuse, criminal behavior, to name a few. Bad luck and extreme poverty are signs of having a *causa* or, just as possibly, of being *salá* or *tumbá* (disgraced through black magic). This means that everything one touches *se vuelve sal y agua* (turns to salt and water), one has *los pies y las manos atadas* (one's feet and hands tied), one *está envuelto* (is wrapped) or *lo tienen puesto en una caja* (has been placed in a coffin). These expressions are taken from typical *trabajos malos* that involve, among other things, tying a string around the extremities and body of a wax or cloth figure representing the victim, throwing into the sea an effigy of the victim after it has been wrapped with a spool of black thread, or burying the victim's photograph or effigy in a small replica of a coffin. Following the same mimetic logic, the passivity of the bewitched might be "untied" by the flight of a dove, their minds "cleared" with mint, and their personal attraction "recharged" with lodestone.

Various sets of homologies are magically exploited in all these *trabajos*. The words *menta* (mint) and *mente* (mind) connect mimetically the

5.6 *A Pepperidge Farm Three Layer Cake is "cooked" and entrusted to the Buddha.*

magic work and its effect. Likewise, the magnetic properties of lodestone, via the mimetic faculty, "attract" the people who are the object of the magic work. Thanks to the virtues of magical mimesis—semantic, onomatopoeic, sensual—the sexual energies of estranged spouses as well as relationships with one's children can be nourished with honey and perfumes, and their respective paths "cleared" and reunited after the "doors" that lead to each other have been "unlocked" with the aid of miniature keys. The love between a couple can be "guarded" forever by offering a luscious wedding cake—previously "cooked" by a brujo or bruja—to the deities of love that inhabit the Yunque.

The discourse of divination, therefore, reveals innumerable ways in which several series of homologies are weaved into the performance of trabajos. This discourse also suggests an idiom through which the effects of trabajos in general—both malos and buenos—might be experienced.[13] Both the misfortune that was allegedly inflicted by a causa and the relief that may be felt after a trabajo that was meant to "lift" the causa appear to be conveyed through a preestablished set of analogies—between a word and its meaning within the logic of spiritual and magical realms. For example, a client who had lost her job—and almost her house and car—heard the following prediction after a trabajo was performed for her at Haydée's altar: "You feel that financially they [your enemies] have 'closed all your doors.' But this is only until today." María, the manager of a grocery store chain, was given this prediction: "You have 'stones in your path.' Your bosses are expecting too much from you. [Your enemies] *te tienen todo vira'o al revés* [have turned everything that relates to you upside down] and your colleagues *están todos pendientes de ti* [are all scrutinizing what you do]."[14]

Failing businesses would be "lifted," that is, made to succeed—based on the expression *levantar causas* (lit., to lift causas)—to free people of their bewitchments. It is usually done by literally and magically burning obstacles that might be hindering customers. The treatment is usually completed once the store is protected and blessed with a calabash that has been stuffed with magical potions and topped with gold and silver glitter, and when the entrance to the store is "sweetened" (made attractive to potential customers) by spraying alluring herbal concoctions on the sidewalk. To restore parental control, offspring sometimes *hay que ponerlos de espaldas* (lit., have to be set with their backs facing each other) against undesirable company. *Hay que pisarlos* (They have to "be stepped on," that is, controlled) by stepping on *higuereta* leaf and by summoning the help of Santa Marta la Dominadora (Saint Martha, the Dominator). Coworkers or neighbors who are uniting against clients, causing them anguish, can be made to "quarrel and wander" by using mercury to cause among themselves a form of distress that resembles the erratic behavior of droplets of mercury.

The idiom of divination and magic encapsulates the very categories that describe the kind of magic effects that these procedures aim at achieving. In some cases, the word *levantar* means to spiritually lift a muerto from the body of its victim, thereby "freeing" the victim from the vicious parasitic effects of a muerto that has been sent by an enemy to pester the victim. Another common word that is heard during consultations is *desenredar* (to disentangle). The aim of producing a clave, or code, is to disentangle the threads that are tying down the victim's energies—presumably after a trabajo malo has been performed. Producing a clave is indeed a form of cleansing that can be performed in mild cases of suspected causas.

5.7
*"Hay que ponerlos
de espaldas."*

It is also a divination technique. As automatic writing generates a kind of spiritual map, the medium can proceed to decipher it, disclosing the present, past, and future problems of the client, as well as their solutions.

However, in what brujos perceive as life-threatening *causas*, a trance-induced *levantamiento de causas* (lifting of bewitchments) might be needed to "free" or "unwrap" the victim from a deadly outcome. This is a level of expertise that not every espiritista or medium reaches fully. In trance, brujos are expected to be possessed by the very muerto who had caused the misfortune, reenacting the exact moment when a muerto was commissioned to pester a victim. In this state, brujos are supposed to overpower the muerto and force it to leave the victim in peace. The whole process is called *coger muertos* (to catch, to grab, or to contain muertos).

During a very difficult levantamiento de causa that was performed for Eva, a forty-year-old client who came to Puerto Rico for a few weeks from the United States, Haydée began, in trance, to twist her neck and upper

5.8 *Reina cogiendo un muerto*

body like a chicken and speak in broken, cackling utterances, embodying the source of her client's bewitchment. "*O cará' . . . o cará' . . .* Its wings were cut off . . . its wings . . . its . . . its . . . its wings . . . to that black . . . ck . . . ck . . . chick . . . ck . . . ck . . . en [cackling for a few seconds unable to speak]." Also in trance, Reina, Haydée's assistant, in a heated quarrel, urged the alleged evil spirit that was possessing Haydée to leave the body of the client in peace, to go seek light and stop harming her. She then stated, voicing the spirits, "Exactly like this [like Haydée was possessed as a chicken without wings], they [Eva's enemies] had her like a chicken. . . . [Addressing the evil spirit:] Come on! Repent! And fly wherever you have to go. . . . Come on! Come on, spirit of light! [She sounds the bells] *Carajo!* (Damn it)." Recovering from her own trance, Haydée said in an imploring voice, "I ask my protecciones, the Indio, the Madama, to give light and progress to my spiritual cuadro. [Addressing the supernatural forces:] Why do they have her [Eva] like this *en el piso* [lit., on the ground; i.e., overpowered, beaten], *con las alas cortadas* [lit., with her wings cut off; i.e., passive, impotent]?" Recovering slightly from the emotional exhortations of Haydée and Reina, they started praying—together with

Eva—the Rosary, Hail Marys, and Our Fathers. With Haydée holding a big cross in the air, the event reminded me of Hollywood exorcisms, and it probably bore some similarities to actual exorcisms as, I was told, they occur in some Protestant and Catholic communities today. At the end of these exorcism-trance events, the evil forces that had been causing victims to lose their vital energies are allegedly deflected and "lanced" from the victim's body permanently. But the session is not complete until all the evil forces are also encouraged—through prayer—to seek the light (in line with the Spiritist belief in spiritual development).

Spiritual Investments and Their Risk

Threats to one's progress are always present. As long as others may covet it, one runs the risks of being the object of all sorts of negative forces that can be produced by unconscious ill thoughts, intentional curses, and black magic. *Envidia* (envy) of the cuadro of others or of newly acquired goods is the main cause of any form of black magic. A new car, a major appliance, or a piece of furniture; home improvements, vacations, and fashionable clothes; or being too generous to others—any of these can become a source of envidia. Any person can *salar* (lit., pour salt; i.e., curse, wish ill) others

5.9 Haydée is proud of her new living room altar and La Caridad del Cobre.

by "speaking badly" or even by "holding bad thoughts" against their victims, causing them to fall ill, lose their jobs, break up with spouses, or lose their good fortune.[15]

In the course of a few months, while I was working with Haydée, she changed the furniture in her living room, putting the old furniture in the waiting area in the garage. She renovated and expanded the living room in order to have—in addition to her backyard altar and small living room altar—a space inside the home for "meditation and communion with God" and her "Caridad." In just a few days, her house changed its appearance inside and out. Gallons of yellow paint (yellow is the color that symbolizes La Caridad) were applied to iron gates, window frames, doors, and walls, and white trim was added, to turn the whole house into an offering, a shrine dedicated to Haydée's patron saint, La Virgen de la Caridad.

5.10 Haydée's house freshly repainted in yellow (the color of her patron saint) with white trim

This large-scale iconic statement was preceded a few months earlier by a more practical though no less symbolic installation of a remote control–operated garage door. These innovations signaled Haydée's prosperity to everyone. She now needed special, expensive electronic devices to guard her privacy, to protect her from the harassment of numerous clients, who, she said, "knocked on my door at any time, day and night." Haydée said the electric garage door was the only one in the neighborhood and added that it had unleashed envidia among some neighbors—even her "loyal next-door neighbor."

If economic progress is a sign of being blessed, too much attention to the bendiciones of others can easily turn into envidia without the corresponding spiritual development. Thus the line dividing the positive, spiritually nurtured striving for economic progress and the negative desire to match the economic or social achievements of others, without the protection and guidance of the spirits, is very thin. *Brujería* under consumerism does not merely encourage material success. Rather, as a form of spiritualized materialism, it sets the moral boundaries of material progress in accordance with the relative spiritual development that is assumed to both sustain and be a reflection of it. This connection between material and spiritual bendiciones explains in part the great care that brujos take to manage the negative thoughts of those around them, clients and friends. *Pensamientos* (thoughts)—it is believed—are energies that can travel; and even if held unconsciously or not verbalized, they can become beneficial or harmful forces that either improve or destroy the life projects of those who are their objects.

If verbalized angrily in the form of curses (*maldiciones*), pensamientos can become very dangerous, almost like putting a contract out on an individual. For instance, during one divination process, Haydée told a school-teacher who came to consult her after realizing that her good fortune was being shattered, "You have to make an effort in order to have your 'doors open up' for you." And immediately after, Haydée asked this woman, as if she already "knew" the answer, "Usted maldice?" (Do you swear?). When the client answered affirmatively, Haydée replied, "Those who curse . . . I don't want them, neither in my home nor in my altar."

Haydée's dislike for people who swear points to the commonly held belief that a *pensamiento malo* (bad thought) or careless maldición functions like a spell that can make a person sick, unable to carry out the most basic daily chores, or have an accident. They can cause the victim to become "absentminded" by having their *pensamientos agarrados* (thoughts grabbed) or distracted by bad energies. If a chair suddenly breaks while one is sitting on it or if a pet unexpectedly dies, it can be an indication that the chair or pet inadvertently *recogieron* (picked up) evil energies that were sent to their owners. On one occasion, when Haydée's fish and dog died in the same week, she consoled herself by saying that they had most likely picked up the bad energies intended for *her*, sadly adding that it is crucial to have pets around the house if for no other reason than that alone. Haydée once told me that in order to pick up bad energies and be a source of meditation and peace, she placed a five-foot-tall fountain in her waiting room. The clear water constantly flowing in a cascade through the elaborate fountain into a pondlike basin was meant to recoger whatever negative energies might be intended for her and transform them into positive ones. For this purpose, every Friday Haydée deposits fresh flowers and drops a cleansing herbal mixture in the water.

Being too preoccupied with others' lives can be a sign of evil plans against them. The idea behind the suspicion of people who are *pendientes*, or overly involved with the lives of others, is that any information they might possess could be used to "make a copy" for the performance of a trabajo malo. This is what happened to Eva, who had come to the island from the United States to settle a financial dispute between her mother and her stepsiblings. The divination process revealed that Eva was the object of black magic. It also revealed that Eva, a prosperous person and knowledgeable about the American legal system and inheritance laws, was the object of dangerous intrigues that ended up in yet more black magic. In the presence of Eva's mother, who accompanied her, Haydée pointed out, "She [your daughter] is the strongest, and her enemies know that. She knows so many things about the family that if she spoke, the land would tremble. So in order to harm your family they have to prevent her from fighting for you." And then, in trance, addressing Eva, Haydée added, "They want to keep you aside, and since materially they don't dare, they have to do it spiritually. And remember that spiritually you can kill a person. [Said as a generalization about black magic:] You put a person in a bed and from there she won't get up."

Eva confirmed the latter, saying, "Last week I went to bed and something was holding me down—I couldn't lift an arm." She had come to consult Haydée because she had started to suffer unusual pain in her legs and arms after unexpectedly losing her excellent job with the government. Haydée diagnosed the cause of Eva's affliction: "*Usted tiene un cantazo que le tiraron* [You have a received a blow that had been directed to you] because your 'enemies' [stepsiblings] knew that you were the one who would fight [*bregar*] for your mother's inheritance." Stressing that a trabajo malo had been performed against Eva, Haydée added, while sounding a bell and banging vigorously on the desk a few times,

Tu tienes una vela negra perdida. Tienes que revocarla, ¿sabes? Tienes que comprar dos velas y traerlas: la vela negra y la vela roja de revocación—de San Miguel Arcángel. Dicen que te pusieron las copas al revés; que tú las vas a poner al derecho. Pero no son tres copas las que vamos a poner. Son tres velas.

You have a black candle [that has been lit for you by your enemies]. You have to revoke it, do you know? You need to buy two candles and bring them: a black candle and a red candle—of San Miguel Arcángel. [The spirits] say that [your enemies] "turned the goblets upside down" [i.e., performed black magic against you]; that you will turn them back up [i.e., revoke it]. We are not going to use three goblets, but instead three candles.

Addressing Eva directly, Haydée continued with the diagnosis:

O caramba,[16] ¿por qué la quieren tener así, señora? ¿Por qué la quieren tener con ese brazo en el piso? ¿A usted le tienen las alas cortadas, sabe? Esa gallina la preparó tu suegra, sabes. La gallina negra la preparó ayer para cortarte las alas en Puerto Rico y que tengas que volver sin resolver nada. Le trabajaron con un muerto, Edgardo.
[To Reina:] ¿Dónde esta el alcoholado?
[To Eva:] Llore, señora; que usted quiere llorar. Llore, llore, o cará', porque me dicen que tiene que llorar. Párese, señora. [While mimicking cleansing:] Limpiando, recogiendo y botando [said several times].

O shit, why do they [your enemies] want to have you like this, señora? Why do they want to have you with an arm hanging onto the floor? They are keeping your wings cut [helpless], do you know? That chicken was prepared by your mother-in-law, do you know? The black chicken was prepared yesterday in order to cut your wings [while you are] in Puerto Rico so that you will have to go back [to the United States] without having resolved anything. [Your enemies] worked against you with a muerto, Edgardo.
[To Reina:] Where is the alcoholado [for cleansing Eva]?
[To Eva:] Cry, cry; you want to cry. Cry, cry, o cará', because They tell me that you need to cry. Stand up, señora. "Cleansing, gathering, and throwing."

Haydée, Reina, Eva, and her mother concluded the divination session by praying several Our Fathers. The next day Eva and her mother brought the candles. The first part of the treatment, already described, was performed for Eva: el levantamiento de causa. The next consultation would consist of the second part of the treatment, la revocación, beginning with a cleansing ritual in the Yunque.

The forces of evil that one mobilizes to harm others for one's advantage always come back like a boomerang, Spiritists like to say. After revealing that Eva had been the object of black magic by her former mother-in-law's use of a black chicken, Haydée promised: "Like a chicken she will see herself, that santera [used disparagingly] mother-in-law of yours, *esa condená, cabrona, hija'e puta, desgraciada de la vida* [that doomed, quarrelsome bitch, daughter-of-a-bitch wretched woman] who prepared the trabajo. . . . I will revoke that thing [the trabajo]. I will revoke it."

5.11
The revocation for Eva continues in the Yunque with a black chicken.

Because it is believed that in all cases of black magic the perpetrator's malice eventually will be turned against the perpetrator and anyone who is related to that person in any way in future as well as present generations, it is imperative to push this spiritual justice forward by executing special *trabajos* as soon as possible. As had occurred in Eva's case, *brujos* perform *trabajos malos,* I am told, only to neutralize *trabajos malos* that had already been performed against their clients. Haydée advised Eva, "Light a

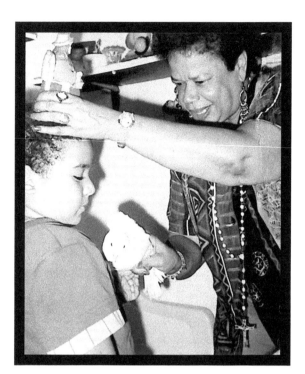

5.12
*Haydée blessing
a dove and then
cleansing the child
with the dove and
El Niño de Atocha*

candle of San Miguel Arcángel to neutralize the work done to you, *y voy
a voltear las copas que te tienene dadas vuelta con tu nombre* [and I will turn
back up the goblets they have turned down in your name]. . . . This velón
is for your ex-mother-in-law but not in order to kill her—*es para que deje
de joderla* [it is for her to stop mortifying you]." Haydée then revealed that
San Elías, Lord of the Cemetery, was the one who would "be in charge"
(*encargado*) of carrying out this trabajo and said, "We need to assemble
[*montar*] the trabajo today."

In keeping with the Spiritist theory of timeless and spaceless cosmic
justice, individuals inherit not only material goods but also any spiritual
debts not paid by their ancestors during their lifetimes. These have to be
"paid for" on earth by their spiritual offspring. Worldly misfortune, illness, and criminal behavior are often the outcome of an unpaid moral or
monetary debt.

Thus, once the divination process reveals the details of these unfinished transactions, brujos will perform some kind of atonement or payment to release the victim from these obligations. Five-year-old Claude
Marín was brought by his father and grandmother to Haydée to help him

with his insomnia and with his behavioral problems at school. The divination session revealed that the child was being haunted by *el espíritu intranquilo de su madre* (the troubled spirit of his dead mother), who had died of AIDS when the child was only a few months old. The mother had been a drug addict for many years. Claude Marín underwent a series of cleansing rituals at Haydée's, which involved the manipulation of a white dove (representing the spirit of his dead mother) and the application of various herbal cleansing baths accompanied by prayers at his home. The cleansing rituals ended with a moving ceremony aimed at freeing the child from the damaging effects of his mother's espíritu intranquilo. The child was taken for the first time to the grave site of his mother, and there he set the white dove free.[17]

Although illness and misfortune are interpreted as ways of atonement and payment, not everyone has to undergo these forms of repentance to clear the balance. Reincarnations offer the opportunity for expiating unpaid debts, offering the unlimited opportunity for self-improvement in each life on earth.

"I Feed My Enemies from the Wing, Not from the Breast"

In a vicious cycle, the rewards of economic success are coveted and then feared. Though essential in a consumer society, prodigal expenditures may attract dangerous evil forces. By the same token, signs of upward mobility may also indicate the possession of a strong cuadro and set of protecciones, which, following the idiom of brujería, should surely neutralize evil attacks. Caught between desire and the risks of maximizing acquisitive power, ideally unconditional kinship love and personal loyalties are entangled in webs of intrigue, envy, and black magic.

Rumors, albeit ethereal and invisible, feed a system of personal resources, investments that, given the right conditions, could be traded with a considerable margin of interest. For the outsider, the manipulation involved in the circulation of rumors, especially the gaps between actual events and their rendition in rumor, might seem to testify to chicanery. Yet the aggrandizement of past and future exploits, which can also be accomplished by conspicuous consumption, is not only a survival strategy. These attitudes, in addition to being part of the logic of brujería, are contained by and large in mainstream, capitalist modes of envisioning, producing, and marketing both material and social success.

Manu, a businessman, and Elena, a bruja, became lovers after he came to her altar for a consultation. Thereafter he became very successful in his business—thanks to her power, Elena liked to say. But after a few months Elena complained to me that he had suddenly stopped coming to see her: "Manu sacó el cuerpo" (Manu took his body out, left her). Convinced that someone had interfered in their relationship, she sent her assistant, Ronda, to speak to Manu on her behalf. Through various divination sessions that Ronda performed for Elena, both women determined that Manu's ex-wife was "seizing hold of his thoughts" (*lo tiene agarrado con el pensamiento*), that is, had resorted to evil machinations to cause Manu to leave Elena. Rody, Manu's brother, continued to visit Elena as he used to do, even after his brother's estrangement from her. These occasions soon became means for reciprocal accusations between Manu and Elena, which only worsened the already damaged relationship between them.

A major shift occurred when, on one of these occasions, Rody told Elena, "Those that eat with you are not your friends." This was a major accusation; it implied that her own assistant and go-between, Ronda, had betrayed her because she was envious of her power and her happiness.[18] Elena was in a difficult situation: she depended on Ronda's friendship but also feared her betrayal. On the one hand, Ronda had seen her prepare a trabajo malo against Manu when she felt betrayed, seeing that he was ignoring her and not returning her calls. On the other hand, Ronda heard Elena desperately defend her loyalty to Manu, saying to Rody that whatever people might say she "would never harm him." Manu's business had been declining since his falling out with Elena, however, so this confession of loyalty, besides being a lie, was meant to preclude suspicion on anyone's part that she had performed a trabajo malo against him. This would reassure Manu that Elena still wanted him as a lover and would not jeopardize his former trust in her. More important, it would also prevent him from going to a brujo to have a trabajo malo sent back to her. According to Ronda, she went several times to meet with Manu and explain to him personally that Elena had always been loyal to him, with the intention of dissipating any suspicions he might have about Elena's workings against him after they had separated. But Ronda knew the truth.

Accusations of envidia are the most feared, because it is considered the major cause of misfortune, even when experienced unconsciously. Because Elena's house was always filled with friends, assistants, and close clients, many people were under suspicion. Zulma, a friend who was also a medium, for example, defended Ronda's loyalty to Elena, saying that according to her own spiritual sources Rody's insinuations that Ronda was betraying her were not true. The problem, Zulma said, "is that you speak too much," implying that it was not only Ronda who knew that Elena used to go on spitefully about how much she had helped Manu and about the punishment he would get from her protecciones; any number of others could have carried gossip to Manu.

Having received many conflicting interpretations of her emotional misfortune, Elena did not act toward Ronda or Rody in any way that betrayed her suspicions of them. In private she said to me, "Yo me hago la pendeja pero no lo soy" (I'm playing the fool, but I'm not). In an attempt to reassert her status as a bruja who controls or "sees beyond" the webs of intrigue, she added, "Les doy de comer del ala pero no de la pechuga" (I feed [my enemies] from the wing but not from the breast), implying that although she seems to give out information about herself, it is not significant; she keeps the most important information to herself. She concluded—as most brujos do—by entrusting herself to her spiritual powers: "I put everything in the hands of God and my protecciones."

To acknowledge having done a trabajo malo for a former lover certainly weakens a bruja's reputation, for a powerful bruja would have her own protecciones punish the lover for having left. Also, a bruja would state her total faith in a higher spiritual plan by not taking any purposeful action against her former lover. By entrusting themselves completely to the transcendental forces that guide their lives on earth, brujos assert their credibility and humility. Matching their usual brassy arrogance, acknowledging that there might be designs that even they cannot know about— that are knowable only to God—brujos can convincingly argue that a certain trabajo has failed because it was God's design and thus avoid liability for its lack of effectiveness.

Spiritual capital in the form of cuadros, protecciones, and amicable muertos has many advantages for opening paths to prosperity and for preventing others from blocking them. Yet, as with any scarce resources, many might covet them, and thus inevitably threats and risks trouble even the most powerful brujos, who have to constantly find new ways to tackle them. Innovation and eclecticism are some of these ways.

CHAPTER SIX

THE GLOBAL BAZAAR OF
SPIRITUAL ENTERPRISE

Brujería Meets Santería and New Age

It is eight o'clock in the morning. As I arrive at Haydée's, tunes praising Ochún fill the street outside her house, sung to the rhythms of Santería music embellished with Afro-Cuban dance rhythms.[1] Inside, I see Haydée and Reina dancing and singing to the music, which comes from tapes that contain songs of praise for Yoruba orishas—not in Yoruba but in Spanish.[2] Every morning Haydée and Reina sing and dance together to these song-poem-prayers to the orishas-saints to ready themselves spiritually for the consultations. This is a way of cleansing oneself spiritually, Haydée tells me. Often while dancing they also enter a state of trance and deliver messages from the spirits that foretell the events of the day.

The tapes, an inexpensive commercial version of live ritual music, provide background music for spiritual gatherings of all kinds. Unlike tapes of ritual Santería rhythms that are sung in Yoruba in the sequence prescribed for initiation rituals, these are based on popular poems that re-create the mythical stories of the orishas and their associated Catholic saints. They are performed to the sounds of popular Caribbean rhythms such as *guaracha, rumba,* and *danzón.* For instance, during the closing ceremonies before Christmas at her private Spiritist center, located in Caguas, Carmen played such tapes intermittently as the congregants came forward one by one to be cleansed by Juan, her assistant. Now and then, a man or a woman would stand up in trance and dance, and the others would encourage the trance by singing along and clapping.

As on this occasion, in Spiritist consultation ceremonies and veladas, various elements of Catholic worship are combined with features of Santería.

6.1 Haydée dancing and spraying La Madama cleansing aerosol

For instance, trabajos intended to restore a husband's love are made with calabashes and then offered to Changó, king of love. In cleansing rituals, corn and beans, traditional offerings to Changó, are used in conjunction with the smoking of cigars (photo 6.2), associated with indigenous people and reverence of the Indio, exemplifying the merging of African, Creole, and indigenous deities, as well as Catholic saints, that occurs in Spiritist ceremonies such as Carmen's.

Likewise, dancing with colored bandannas (each color representing an Afro-Latin orisha-saint; see photo 6.3), dancing around a fire (also associated with Changó), and partaking of a mixture of grains and herbs (associated with Changó and the Indio) are related to the myths and symbols of Santería, espiritismo, popular Catholicism, and indigenous deities.[3] Also, at the end of successful trances, congregants—even those who are not initiated in Santería—commonly greet each other with *ashé*, a Yoruba word meaning "amen."

Notwithstanding the numerous similarities between brujos and santeros, the former differentiate themselves from the latter by rejecting animal sacrifice. At times the spirits might dictate the performance of a trabajo using a small lizard or a chicken, but this is not viewed as intrinsic to the ethos of Spiritism. On this point there are no compromises. Espiri-

6.2 Smoke for the Indio

tistas express this by saying, for instance, "God created animals to live. They also have a spirit, thus God did not create them to have them sacrificed. Noah's ark is a proof that God wanted to keep his creations alive, not annihilate them."

New Age practices rooted in Asian philosophies are also incorporated by brujos and espiritistas, santeros and curanderos. Some espiritistas have begun to integrate *círculos de oración y sanación* (prayer and healing circles) in their healing procedures. In response to New Age healing theories about the development of positive magnetic fields, chakras, and the colors of the personal aura, New Age–based spiritual objects, from rocks to perfumes, are now being incorporated into traditional Catholic and Spiritist worship and healing elements.

In line with these trends, María Dolores Hajosy Benedetti's *Hasta los baños te curan!* (Even Baths Can Cure You! [1991]), based on interviews with curanderos and espiritistas, celebrates Puerto Rican traditional healing practices. Unlike the terms used in the public sphere during the nation-building period, Hajosy Benedetti frames her interest in folk-healing practices in accordance with the revivalist approach of the 1980s and 1990s. In line with this naturalist-environmentalist perspective, in-

6.3 *Haydée and Armando dancing with the colored bandannas of the Siete Potencias Africanas*

digenous herbal healing practices and home remedies are depicted as deriving from popular Puerto Rican wisdom and at the root of a local version of cosmopolitan yuppie spirituality. The message is that Puerto Rican curanderismo and espiritismo should not be discarded as primitive but recognized for their benefits not only among illiterate peasants but also among the literate urban elite. Hajosy Benedetti presented her book and was the subject of a series of lectures at the Taller Puertorriqueño, the Puerto Rican Cultural Center, in Philadelphia. One of Hajosy Benedetti's interviewees is Bolina—the bruja I met during my fieldwork in Puerto Rico. Although the interview format of the book offers a somewhat realistic picture of Bolina's practices, some aspects—those that do not match the image of a native Puerto Rican medicine woman—are carefully downplayed. For example, Hajosy Benedetti mentions only in passing the fact that Bolina uses Lydia Cabrera's *El Monte*—a book that contains recipes for herbal healing as well as all sorts of trabajos from Cuban Santería— as a source for her healing procedures. Nor does she mention the use of manufactured products in making home remedies and the performance of trabajos malos and trance. The section "Remedios caseros y mucho más" (Homemade Remedies and Much More) contains recipes made only with natural herbs.

Contrary to the naturalist-environmentalist image constructed by Hajosy Benedetti, I noticed another side of Bolina's practices. For instance, in one of our encounters Bolina proudly showed me a special gift she had received from a foreign journalist and which she incorporated in her divining process. It was a battery-operated Disney-type "wizard" that barked random omens in English. Apparently Hajosy Benedetti excluded this wizard from her book because it was not natural. However, it had a very personal significance for Bolina. When I asked her why she used the mechanical wizard in the divination process, she explained that she saw it as a message: "No existe la casualidad, existe sólo la causalidad" (There is no coincidence, there is only causality). Indeed, the incorporation of new, often foreign elements in the practices of Puerto Rican brujos is an essential part of their enterprise, provided it has a spiritual rationale.

Haydée added the figurines of Eleggua (the orisha at the top of the Santería pantheon), the Congo (representing Changó) and the Monja (represented by a figure of a nun) to her altar after a divining session in which they were revealed as her new protecciones. Although Haydée said she was not in favor of Santería, she saw no conflict in adopting these new spirits and their ritual paraphernalia, for the possibilities of encountering spiritual powers embodied in traditions and religions of all kinds are limitless within the ethos of espiritismo and brujería.

Every spiritual consultation, or gathering, has the potential to enrich previous practices. On these occasions vicarious learning and transmission occur. Unlike traditional ethnographic depictions of African witchcraft and sorcery as practiced in apparently isolated societies, people from different backgrounds meet today in Puerto Rico to perform all types of spiritual ceremonies. Different styles of performing the same ritual, new symbols and potions, and additional stories about saints and deities are available at these transcultural gatherings, visible and ready to be incorporated in subsequent rituals.

Haydée and Armando, an espiritista initiated in Santería and Palo Monte, decided to work together after they realized their "spiritual affinity" during an intimate, private velada, which they had planned a few weeks after meeting at a botánica. The velada was held in the house of a babalawo, Armando's godfather, who asked to remain anonymous, for babalawos are not supposed to organize let alone participate in veladas.

As Haydée, Reina, and I arrive, the host calls Armando and the other five guests at the velada—two middle-aged women and three young men, all experienced mediums, who were gathered in an enclosed balcony adjacent to the living room—to greet us. The host introduces Haydée as "La Bruja de Loíza" and Reina as her assistant. To reassure the group, Haydée introduces me (as she usually does) as "Raquel, my reportera," adding that I had come from Philadelphia to work with her and that wherever she goes I go with her.

Immediately afterward, Haydée and Armando engage in spiritual dancing to the sounds of mixed Santería-Spiritist music playing very loudly while the rest of the group returns to the balcony. I recognize the tunes: I have heard them at Haydée's every morning. In the meantime I have a chance to glance over the glamorous altar that is placed along a whole wall—following Santería practice—on bamboo mats on the ground. Peacock feathers and huge fans pinned to pieces of golden fabric hanging from the wall extend the sacred area of the offerings. Several orishas are being honored, as I recognize by the profusion of offerings and gifts placed around the many figurines, everything from toys and teddy bears to perfumes, alcoholic beverages, cigars, and food. After about ten minutes, Haydée, Reina, Armando, and I go into the next room, an enclosed balcony on which chairs have been arranged in a circle and a table placed on the side. We all join in spiritual dancing. The excitement rises as we celebrate the orishas-saints by dancing to each of their prayer tunes. In the meantime the host is busy bringing various candles and preparing the fuente with a sacred mixture of herbs, oils, Florida Water, and fresh flowers, not concluding before he asks Haydée, "Do you need anything else?" Checking if the right ingredients are being used, he adds, "Do you normally use camphor in la fuente?" It is essential that he check each item with Haydée, as this is to be a unique velada—a joint venture of santeros, espiritistas, and brujos.

Haydée, Reina, and Armando continue dancing to the sacred music with the other guests—mediums who are at different levels of initiation in Santería—while I take some pictures and videotape the event. Suddenly Armando becomes possessed by Yemanyá, a goddess of the sea, who makes him dance in her own undulating style. We understand that

Yemanyá is the orisha who opens the velada when we hear Armando utter her words of greeting, mixed with low-pitched sighs, to all the participants: "I'm arriving at this home to give light and understanding to all present. But I see a bigger light coming, and I tell you this because it's Eleggua, who arrives with all his force to bring more light and understanding to this place." Armando's face breaks into a wide and sensuous smile. We hear a dramatically voiced "Ha, ha, ha!" before being asked, with equally deliberate phrasing, "Do you know who I am?" Announcing the forthcoming words of another spirit, Armando exhales loudly and repeatedly through the nose: "The Madama has arrived. I am the *prieta* [informal for "Black woman"]! [Shrieking:] Yes, I'm the Madama, and I have light for everyone here! But I'll tell you something, I come to break [*romper;* in this context, to lift causas], you know? I come to break!"

The rest answer in unison, "Yeah, yeah, *luz y progreso* [light and progress], yeah." Facing one of the younger mediums, Armando, possessed by the Madama, says, "You came here with troubles, you know, but I'll give you something, a ray of light to protect you, you know?" Haydée joins in, adding to the spiritual message, "O cará', o cará'." Somebody rings the bell, as I saw Haydée do in her altar just before the words of spirits are spoken while somebody is in trance. Haydée, who has been trembling all over and showing signs of being possessed, is now in trance, clapping and sighing. She continues, "O cará', o cará', *paz y progreso* [peace and progress] for all. That person whom you're waiting for will arrive and, kneeling, will ask for forgiveness for what she did and said. . . . Oh, but tell me my good spirits, my good cuadros espirituales and protecciones that *lo que pasó fue hasta hoy* [past troubles are a matter of the past, a Spiritist expression] because all the bad things will be broken and cleansed today in this home. Light and peace for this home." One by one, each participant receives a message, gives messages to others, and—in a few cases—is cleansed and blessed with the sacred mixture of herbs and flowers. Joining forces, santeros and brujos—each with their own prayers—set out to lift causas and restore positive energies to those who need it.

It seems as if the orishas and the spirits have always worked together. With an ease that looks totally natural, African orishas had joined Spiritist entities in this fiesta espiritual. Santeros and brujos spoke in similar ways, communicating in a transspiritual lingua franca to reveal and revoke the cause of misfortunes. Indeed, while the Madama was delivering messages, Haydée explained, "I'm a bruja, but it is the same saint, the same cuadro espiritual [of the Madama, who is also a healer], because I work with La Caridad del Cobre. That's my woman, my patron, and my princess. That woman, whatever I ask her, she never says no." Haydée was articulating for those present the idea of materialization that allows for African entities to appear as Catholic saints and vice versa.[4] Only when one of the santeros reached for a saber—one of the components of the regalia of Ogún, the warrior-blacksmith orisha—that was placed on the floor by the fuente, raising it above his head to symbolically "cut" (*cortar*) a causa or trabajo malo, did Haydée and Reina hint to the host that they would rather he not use it, explaining that it was not "necessary in *this* type of velada."

After three hours of intense divination, cleansing, and curing rituals, the host brought food and drinks. Exhausted, we all sat down. Armando and Haydée started a provocative dialogue about the nature of spiritual work in general and theirs in particular. Armando spoke about his spiritual development in New York, where he had lived from the time he was thirteen until just a few years ago. In New York he met curanderos, brujos, espiritistas, and santeros from Cuba and South and Central America. One of them gave him a protective amulet prepared with the powers of South American Indians, which he wears all the time, along with the colored bead necklaces of Santería. In Puerto Rico he met a Cuban babalawo— his padrino—and a Puerto Rican bruja—Haydée. Armando's trajectory exemplifies the transnational nature of vernacular religious transmission, which occurs via several circuits—along the routes to and from the mainland and the island, further mediated by Caribbean and Latin American migration (see Cornelius 1992). Borrowing from Duany's (2000, 2001) characterization of Puerto Rico as a "nation on the move," cases like Armando's suggest that brujería is a vernacular religion on the move.

At work (he is a machinist in a paper factory), Armando has to hide all his collares under his shirt, as he must never take them off: they are his protecciones. "Some people are ashamed to show that they are Spiritists or santeros," he explained, unbuttoning his white shirt to proudly expose all his necklaces. "I, on the contrary, like to go dressed all in white with my beads and tons of jewelry. This is what I like." Haydée agreed, saying that she also wears her amulets and jewelry all the time, proud of being a bruja and showing it publicly. I added, "I remember that the first day I met Haydée, she said, 'I'm a bruja, and a very proud one indeed.'" Armando, shifting the conversation back to himself, responded, "I may be an espiritista and a santero—I have no religion, though I follow Yoruba beliefs—but I like to call myself neither espiritista nor santero but *consejero espiritual* [spiritual consultant]. And this is what I give to people, spiritual advice. Sometimes I begin with a psychological insight, then I go to consult the spirits, the muertos, or whichever entity can help me aid people." Interrupting his obvious grandiloquent self-presentation (and as if asserting her spiritual power over Armando by "seeing" beyond), Haydée teasingly told him, "You are an Indio. You can be whatever you want, but for me you're an Indio spirit." We all laughed at her volatile cheekiness. And from then on she kept calling him—without any objection on Armando's part—*mi* Indio (my Indio).

Armando and Haydée continued to exchange opinions and darts while I taped the conversation. In addition to measuring each other, they seemed also to compete for my attention, outdoing each other in having had miraculous experiences, extraordinary healing successes, and having had to endure ferocious attacks from all sorts of enemies. Speaking about their expertise in dealing with the often untamable forces of los muertos, both Haydée and Armando agreed, for example, that some people (not themselves, of course) who do not know how to deal with powerful forces might summon muertos and, without realizing it, bring death and misfortune to themselves and their clients. "We have to know how to deal with these forces," Haydée concluded ceremoniously. After a few more rounds of mixed shared sympathy and defiance, they found that their spiritual affinity allowed them to collaborate in doing the obra espiritual: both were granted powerful, positive forces, and both were sensuous and competitive.

At about midnight, the host closed the velada by thanking all the guests in the name of God, who join him in praying the Our Father. Having felt that the velada was a success, he expressed the wish "that gatherings such as this will follow whenever healing and purification are needed." Haydée joined him in wishing for future collaborations: "With our heads held high, and united in goodwill, we will always triumph, because where there's faith there's always goodness." Before everybody departed, the host and guests exchanged addresses and telephone numbers, pledging to continue meeting in spiritual gatherings such as this.

Retrospectively, I realize that this had been an unprecedented opportunity to trace emergent syncretic processes between Santería and Spiritism. Unlike the particular understanding one might gain from the observation of the iconographic bricolage of saints and figurines, symbols and potions from Spiritism and Santería, this velada—and the partnership that developed between Haydée and Armando — offered the opportunity to see this process in the making, at the moment when expert practitioners articulate and negotiate this partnership in ritual and verbal forms.

In the following days, Armando came to Haydée's altar several times. The first time he brought her a gift: a huge platter of fruits and vegetables. They talked at length about their plans to do obra espiritual together and how it would help Armando to overcome his in-laws' refusal to let him work at their shared home. Because Armando had a regular job, they could only consult together on Saturdays and, in special cases — only by appointment — on Sundays. Spiritual dancing, trance, and divination took place during the next visits, which became spiritual gatherings that were also attended by Reina, Haydée's son, and some close friends and clients.

Slowly, Armando (or "El Indio," as Haydée used to call him) had become a known personage in Haydée's altar, dropping in for a few minutes before he went to work in the morning and for a couple of hours after work. Finally, having gotten acquainted with a few clients and friends of the house, Armando's first Saturday joint consultation with Haydée was perceived as the natural next step in a process. Thus in a fairly smooth way Armando and Haydée initiated a collaborative divination-healing practice and mutual learning process, even though — because of eventual personal conflicts and jealousy — it lasted for only about six months. Remarkably, clients adapted very easily to this new arrangement; they showed no doubts or awkwardness in being treated by both Haydée and Armando, although they had different styles. Haydée would invoke La Virgen de la Caridad, the Indios, and other saints, and Armando would invoke Eleggua, Changó and Yemanyá. Then both would summon Papá Dios, praying the Our Father and Hail Mary in litany.[5] Sometimes Haydée consulted clients and sometimes Armando consulted, enabling one of them to go out to perform trabajos in the monte, for example, without leaving the altar unattended. But the confirmation of the merging of Spiritism, brujería, and Santería at Haydée's altar was most evident when Armando brought his predominantly Santería-based *instrumentos* (instruments) and herbal magical potions (e.g., *cascarilla* [white powder], seven colored handkerchiefs representing the seven African powers, and the bottle containing his own special mixture of sacred herbs).

When they worked as a team, the divination process for a client would be performed by Haydée and assisted by Armando and vice versa, and when one would enter trance, the other would assist (as is customary) by making sure the possessed person does not get hurt. Most of the time

Armando and Haydée gave spiritual recipes interchangeably and performed trabajos and cleansing rituals alternately, but on a few occasions they worked together, adding their own particular expertise. In fact, this type of collaboration opened an additional level of dialogue between Haydée and Armando with regard to the compatibility and possible unification of treatments that they used to perform separately—the former following the tradition of Puerto Rican brujería and espiritismo and the latter, the Afro-Cuban tradition of Santería and Palo Monte.[6]

The recent revival and public recognition of "folkloric" forms of healing (curanderismo) by mainstream medical institutions probably responds to the worldwide interest in herbal and other healing practices, which has come about only fifty years after these same institutions organized campaigns against them. In the first issue of *Buhiti* (July–August 1970), a quarterly publication of the Puerto Rican School of Medicine at the University of Puerto Rico, Francisco X. Veray, M.D., a researcher in the history of medicine in Puerto Rico, explained, "In giving the name *Buhiti* [the indigenous Taíno term for "shaman"] to our journal of medical education we want to honor that humble herbalist, healer of our first settlers—the *indios*—precursor of our trade." Also, the attempts made by Puerto Rican scientists since the 1970s—such as Doctor of Pharmacology Esteban Núñez Meléndez (1982)—to investigate empirically the medicinal properties of the island's plants have propelled a drastic change in the public perception of vernacular religious practices that include these plants. Several articles appeared in mainstream newspapers such as *El Mundo, El Reportero,* and *El Nuevo Día* during the 1980s that stressed popular healing as part of "our heritage."[7] In addition to highlighting the wisdom of popular healers and the availability of these wholesome plants on the island, some articles also warned against the danger of misuse. Reflecting the controversies about jurisdiction over the distribution and consumption of medicinal plants, these warnings also were disclaimers of the liability of the publishers for encouraging people to try home remedies.

The revival of interest in natural healing frees clients who come to consult with brujos and santeros from the fear of being labeled "primitive" or of being perceived as connected to dubious "occult forces." Instead, they can safely assert, using New Age lingo, that they are "healing their energies," "restoring the wholeness of their aura," and so forth. Under the rubric "self-healing workshops" and "magnetic healing," Armando and "spiritual consultants" like him define their expertise, regardless of what they actually do, and thus avoid the unpopular labels brujería and magia. Those who do not wish to include "retaliation" or "revocation" among their practices can publicize themselves as administering "works" that heal the energies of the individual through traditional herbal medicine, saint worship, and New Age and self-help techniques of Hindu, American Indian, and Chinese origins.

Such were the services offered by a young married couple in Santurce. Ken came from New York and married Lorena, who was from Puerto Rico, after they met and fell in love at a yuppie convention of espiritistas, mediums, and healers that took place in Puerto Rico. Originally a Spiritist medium, Ken had also been initiated in Reiki (a Japanese self-healing system) and related Asian spiritual healing methods. Lorena, daughter of an espiritista, was a medium who had also been initiated in Santería. Together they offered an "eclectic treatment" according to the particular needs, problems, and individual orientations of their many diverse clients. As Ken and Lorena did not have other jobs, their home was transformed into a spiritual treatment center, where courses for self-improvement and meditation—lasting from a few weeks to a couple of months—were offered in addition to private consultations.

These unorthodox mergings have been shown to be very successful. Espiritistas already initiated in Santería often incorporate Hindu, Japanese, or other healing systems into their own practices, enlarging the scope of their expertise in transcendental powers. By the same token, being able to offer "eclectic treatments" also enlarges their client base, attracting people from diverse social backgrounds. Broader expertise not only promises what I call "an extended care system" but also encourages an extension of circles of influence. Likewise, clients consult with multiple practitioners, developing a wider personal network of healers for themselves.

Commodification and Individualism

Because there is no institutional theology that guides them, the religious practices of brujos as a whole are essentially eclectic. Through various social networks, the exploits of brujos circulate among coworkers, family members, neighbors, and botánicas. Clients thereby can choose, according to their specific needs, from a host of services and approaches. Choice is the name of the game. The services rendered by brujos can range from divination (reading cards or the fuente), healing, and cleansing rituals to making trabajos. Conveniently, clients pay relatively small fees and are not obligated to return to any particular brujo or bruja. Because no long-term commitment is promised, they are free to look for a "better deal" elsewhere at any time. Similar to the consumer relationship prevalent among health care and social services providers and their clients, this relationship contrasts sharply with the all-or-nothing lifelong commitments to the ethical demands of religious institutions. Although brujos cater to identical spiritual needs, they expect only a modest financial compensation for their services, as do health providers in the public sphere.

The persistence of the belief in personal miraculous encounters and in spiritual grace as an individual personal matter—not requiring institutional approval, mediation, or involvement of any kind—accounts for the anti-institutional attitudes among brujos and clients alike. In contrast to previous centuries, spiritual eclecticism is protected today under the Freedom of Religion amendment to the U.S. Constitution. The church is within oneself, many clients and brujos like to say—probably referencing "The Kingdom of God is within you." When put into practice, this dictum inevitably fosters basic unorthodox approaches to experiencing the transcendental, in keeping with the ethos of free choice and the commodification of brujería.

Brujos in general undergo formal religious education during their childhood in either the Protestant or Catholic church.[8] As insiders, brujos in Puerto Rico are knowledgeable about churches, their rituals and paraphernalia. Haydée's father was an espiritista, but her mother was a Pentecostal. Because Haydée's mother disapproved of espiritismo, she used to take the young unwilling Haydée to church with her every Sunday. Just as Haydée does, almost all healers, having once been churchgoers, are able to draw on innumerable stories to justify their antagonism to institutional religious practices. So do many clients, who also occasionally still go to church.

Aiming at clearing their names before society and God, brujos claim that in spite of having been traditionally feared and marginalized, they are holier than most priests. We might be holier than any churchgoer could ever be, some like to say. In the words of one espiritista, "In Puerto Rico today there are many who believe in espiritismo. That's why God protects us. We espiritistas pray [*rezamos*] and plead [*pedimos*] to God. Our Father is in the church and here, too [in her home]; there's no need to be kneeling in church with a black heart, it's better to have a white heart and be an espiritista. *La religión se lleva en el corazón* [Religion is carried in the heart]."

As if to reinforce their legitimacy, clients and brujos circulate stories about the occasional dishonesty of otherwise pious congregants and their lack of charity. Yet the most powerful stories are those that tell of intentional impious actions by those who are the more zealous defenders of the religious demeanor and morals of the community. These outrageous stories seem to seek not only the vindication of brujos as religious people—after centuries of being vilified as heathens—but also the reframing of their basic nature as holy people. One client, Alba, responding to her sister-in-law "accusing" her of being a bruja, countered: "[Being a bruja] is a blessing. It's better to be a bruja than to harm others, as those who are Pentecostal do and are always on everybody else's case." Alba explained, "My sister-in-law claims that she doesn't eat in my house because I'm a professional bruja who 'blesses' (*santigua;* i.e., makes the sign of the cross) over the plates [of food]; these are the blessings that God sends to multiply your food." In this context, counteraccusations by espiritistas and brujos against churchgoers make sense as part of the collective imagination, paralleling as they do those accusations made against them for centuries. "One day," Alba said, "my sister started a rumor in my community that she 'smelled candles' in my house.⁹ This meant that I was involved in brujería. To avoid these rumors I hid all my santos, and from then on I only lit candles during electricity shortages. My sister kept insisting that she 'smelled candles' in my house when I wasn't doing anything, and so she had the congregants of her Evangelist church perform a *limpia* [cleansing ritual] in my house. Haydée had told me that I was wrong in hiding my santos—'You should never hide your *santos.*'" Indeed, on several occasions I have heard Haydée admonish clients who had decided to abandon the worship of their saints and entidades because of family pressure. Because brujería was no longer under legal pressure, they should not fear, Haydée always stressed, "man-made churches"; they should fear the rage of their own saints and entidades for their lack of loyalty to and faith in them.

As an example of the stereotypes of brujos promoted by religious leaders, Haydée mentioned her brother, an Evangelical pastor who lived in California. Stressing the obvious lack of a public ban against lighting candles (or of worshiping the saints in the privacy of one's home), Haydée manifested her unquestionable authority as a bruja, proudly saying to Alba, "When my brother comes to visit me, I leave everything as it is. I don't hide anything from him. This is my home and he has to respect what I am. Although my brother reprimands people for lighting candles [worshiping the saints], when he visits me, I light them as usual." Pretending not to worship the saints because one is afraid of what others might think is the same as dishonoring them, she explained to me. "I don't let anyone intimidate me, not even my brother, since I know that although I don't spend the whole day praying like my brother does, when my parents were alive, I was the one who gave them *chavos* [slang for "money"] under the table [secretly], not my brother, the minister."

Not surprisingly, the public admonitions of brujos against institutional churches usually find a receptive audience among clients, who add their own stories critical of fervent churchgoers who, praying and pleading to God while they are in church, fail to behave in compassionate ways toward their fellow humans when they step out of church. Tomasa, a woman in her late fifties, said she had converted to the Evangelical church but soon left it because she saw things that offended her, such as pastors in limousines and elegant suits, always asking for chavos for social activities in addition to the *mensualidad* (monthly fee; i.e., tithe). She tried the Catholic church but was disillusioned as well. She found that the great majority of parishioners "were not good Christians." "Out of a hundred, only one [was a good Christian]," she said. In line with a widespread Spiritist notion, Tomasa argued that "because God is to be carried inside, the church is oneself; if one follows the commandments, you don't need to go to church." This realization—expressed while waiting for a consultation with a brujo—would not prevent Tomasa from joining another church sometime in the near future, just to keep up with what others in her neighborhood were doing.

Haydée, reflecting on the ambivalent attitudes of her clients toward institutional churches said to me, "Today you can see a person in a church and tomorrow in the house of an espiritista. I've had them in my house. Pentecostals are forbidden from [going to brujos], but the minister doesn't have to know. I ask them, 'But you have faith in God, why are you here?'" Haydée often referred to those who zealously follow the liturgy dictated by institutional churches with suspicion, for they pay too much attention to external behavior. Moreover, as a kind of common ground on which to legitimize the relationship clients have with brujos, I have heard clients and brujos alike express variations of the following justification: Those who attend Mass fanatically or go every week to church (Protestant or Catholic) may be sinners who hate others. Claiming to follow a pious religious life by attending the rituals and reading the Bible does not ensure that a person is not gossiping about neighbors or wishing someone ill.

Manuel's wife, who accompanied him in all his consultations with

Haydée, confided, "My brother-in-law had tried many times to woo my husband and me to the Pentecostal church, claiming that we could be saved if we converted. But I don't believe in this. Too many people who don't use makeup [referring to radical Pentecostal women] *te dejan sin pellejo* [gossip about you].[10] But I don't care about[11] those who get out of church, and standing on the corner, te dejan sin pellejo."

The power of the Bible is unquestionable among brujos. Bolina, for example, leaves an open Bible on her consultation table to prevent evil from reaching her. Catholics, Protestants, brujos, and espiritistas—all, in various ways, agree on the power of the Bible, but they also warn against its potential misuse. Someone well versed in the Bible can misuse its psalms[12] if they invoke them to bestow extra power on the negative thoughts they hold against a person. That is why brujos tend to mock people who, assuming a righteous and spiritually enlightened air, hold on to their Bibles twenty-four hours a day.

The lingering danger of misuse of the Bible was discussed once during a divination consultation at Haydée's altar. A distraught young man, Leo, came to see Haydée to figure out what to do about his wife, who had just left him. Having stated in divination that his wife truly loved him, Haydée suddenly proclaimed, while knocking on the table to indicate the upcoming words of the spirits, "Your mother-in-law, with the very Bible, is the one who's separating you from your wife!" Satisfied with Leo's silent acknowledgment of the truth of her diagnosis, Haydée reaffirmed it with a laugh. Leo, as if recovering from his astonishment at having heard something he must have known before, said, "She [the mother-in-law] always used to cite the Bible and I'd get goosebumps. [Whispering] And, you see, once I said to her, 'I won't go back to church because I saw in church much hypocrisy.' And I'm a person who has a big soul. . . . [I give my] *cuerpo y alma* [body and spirit] for my wife. I told her, 'You're a hypocrite with God.' 'Why?' [she asked]. 'Because of many things I've seen.' She said that the pastor-woman touched her head and told her [in a revelation] that I'll fall very low and sink deep, and this and that, and that she'll sing [thanks] to the Señor [God] for my fall." Continuing her vision, Haydée said, "Your mother-in-law has her *peticiones* [petitions] written on parchment paper [for executing trabajos malos][13] and inserted between the very pages of the Bible." A dialogue between the client and Haydée about the secrets embedded in the Bible and its magical power followed. Haydée said, "You know, Sir, in the Bible there's a novena that . . . you don't know, . . . the Song of Songs. It's the novena that we pray for nine days, each day one psalm. . . . We read it as psalms [in the making of trabajos]. You have to know how to do [trabajos with] the novena of the Song of Songs." Through the lengthy divination process that ensued, the basis of the mother-in-law's antagonism toward Leo was finally revealed: She believed her daughter married below her social status—that Leo was "not good enough for her"—and thus when a more desirable man, in her view, began courting her daughter, she even protected her unfaithful daughter and began scheming to get rid of Leo.

On another occasion, the misuse of the Bible came up in relation to a mother-in-law who, this time, plotted against her son's wife. The wife, a young teacher, came to consult after having all kinds of problems—at work and at home. During divination, Haydée suggested to this woman, Carla, that her mother-in-law was the main cause of her misfortunes. Carla refused to believe it because she said her mother-in-law "spends her days and nights holding her Bible and praying in church." Haydée insisted she should be wary of this woman. Further into the divining consultation, after disclosing the nature of Carla's problems with her children from her first marriage who were antagonizing her husband, she finally said, "It's her [your mother-in law]! That bruja! She hides her ill petitions and her wishes to harm you inside the Bible!" The ill wishes this woman had for her daughter-in-law, the divination revealed, were the result of her loyalty to her son's first wife, the mother of her grandchildren.

All the criticism of the Catholic and Protestant churches aside, their rituals and functions are in fact undertaken by brujos, who not only recognize their spiritual power but also aim at partaking in it. Many espiritistas and brujos who were raised as Catholics protest the persecution the Catholic Church waged against them for "lighting candles and for burning incense." Emotionally, pointing to the evident injustice behind these factitious accusations, they argue that priests also light candles and burn incense. What brujos and espiritistas mean when they state that "Our temple is our home"[14] becomes evident when one observes how their home altars are arranged and hears their prayers. Ritual objects that are part of the Catholic material world are now shared by brujería and espiritismo. It is telling that since some of the most venerated saints—Santa Bárbara and La Caridad del Cobre, for example—have been taken out of the churches on the island by the ecclesiastical authorities (probably because they attracted so many unorthodox forms of veneration), they can be venerated today only in the homes and in the altares of espiritistas, santeros, and brujos. Liturgical prayers and objects like the rosary also play

6.4 *Haydée improvising a prayer as she opens her altar in the morning*

an important role in mediums' rituals, as do medals, *resguardos* (badges for protection against evil spirits), and *escapularios* (scapulars).[15]

Furthermore, according to Catholic tradition, these sacred objects need to be blessed in order to acquire spiritual powers, and brujos and espiritistas are the ones who consecrate them outside the church. Resguardos and escapularios can be bought at any botánica as well as at stores sponsored by the Catholic Church, but before they have been "prepared" by brujos they are powerless. According to Ortiz (1975:90), when an escapulario is properly blessed it becomes a "sacred passport" and a "spiritual insurance policy." Brujos transfer transcendental power to escapularios and resguardos in many ways. They usually keep them in their altares and wear them on their bodies for a certain number of days. After the healing and protective properties of herbs and prayers have been magically conferred on these objects, they are "baptized" in their owner's name, thereby becoming an indivisible part of their being. The fuente used in divination serves the function of the Catholic baptismal font in blessing these sacred objects before their owners can touch them.

6.5 *The collares are empowered with the Indio and then baptized in the fuente.*

In slightly different contexts, the traditional functions of priests that pertain to the life cycle—baptism, marriage, and funeral rites—are performed also by brujos. Adults might undergo baptism to mark a rebirth after a misfortune has befallen them or to mark their recovery from alcoholism. Such a baptism includes a cleansing process and a restoring process—both part of a despojo. The first stage is performed in the sea and serves to lift the *salazón* (causa or curse) by means of immersing the person in the saltwater. The second, or restoring, stage is the actual baptism, which is also performed by immersion but in a river, not the ocean.[16] At the beginning of our relationship, Haydée took me to the places she always goes to perform the second part of the despojo. At the Yunque, we stopped the car at the exact spot near the bank of a river—hidden from the main track by a profusion of foliage—where Haydée usually performs the despojos for her clients.

"When the tide is high," Haydée explained, "I come here and I make them throw their old clothes over there [pointing to a spot underneath a huge tree], and then they receive the blessings in this pure, clear, sweet water of the Guzmán [river]—similar to the Jordan River of God. We let the old clothes wash out to the sea, since this river, like all rivers, pours out into the sea—the water disposes of all that is bad. This is a marvel. The current is constantly cleansing and disposing of all the bad things and bringing new life. This is how God brought you [the author] to my home.

These are God's mysteries; only he knows them, and this is why I feel so happy." She added: "At times, when the river is flooded and carries too much debris, I don't perform despojos for my people. I wait. *Yo soy amiga del tiempo* [I am patient; lit., "I'm a friend of time"). You can't stop the current, and that's why I let myself drift with the current."

Adopting the role of a priest, brujos also perform "spiritual marriages" (photo 6.6). With only slight external variations, they enact their empowerment as representatives of God on earth, following the tradition of the church. Spiritual marriages are performed by brujos even when the participants have already been married or when there is an impediment to legalizing their relationship in a civil or church wedding. It is a wedding after all, and for those who believe in the spirits, brujos are the right mediators. When couples who have marital conflicts come to brujos, they go through a series of divination, cleansing, and healing rituals. Trabajos, like those performed with calabashes or wedding cakes, may be performed to restore their relationship. As the culmination of the process of healing, they may have to undergo a "spiritual wedding" as well.

Haydée explained, "There are some cases like my cousin. If she married her partner at a judge, she would lose her benefits [from a previous husband]. Instead of marrying before a judge, we marry them here [in the altar]. [I say, for example:] 'You receive Juana as a wife' and then they are united [spiritually] for all their lives. Because whatever God unites, man cannot untie. I will perform a spiritual wedding for my cousin because she has to collect her benefits; they are hers. And since they are hers, she's going to get them."

The participation in life-cycle rituals bestows on brujos traditional rights and duties comparable to the *madrina* (godmother) and the *padrino* (godfather). A woman who after years of infertility became pregnant through the assistance of herbal and spiritual treatments provided by Haydée said that Haydée had the right to choose the name of the baby and to baptize her when she was born. Haydée was called to be the madrina. Joyfully, Haydée expressed her commitment to protect the unborn child in the future, saying, "Esa niña es mía!" (That girl is mine!).

Her success with infertility cases provided Haydée with a large number of *ahijados* (godchildren). People would stop her in a mall and show her the baby or child she had "helped" to conceive. Not only women but men too sought her help. A young man in his thirties who was suffering from impotence came to Haydée for help after years of shame and frustration. Conceiving a child right after a ritual that was performed for him and

following the birth of his child, the man and his wife came to the altar one day. The man announced emotionally, "I have a baby boy thanks to what you did to me—he's yours!" When they left, Haydée explained to me that after a series of consultations, the last treatment had included a ritual in the rain forest, which was conducted in the presence of his close kin. In addition to prayers and *unión de pensamientos* (joining of the spiritual power of the present; lit., "unity of thoughts"), she had performed a very "powerful cleansing ritual" by pouring the sacrificial blood of a rooster on his penis.[17]

According to Catholic and Spiritist customs, when death hits a family the Rosary has to be prayed for nine consecutive days, during the novenas. Brujos take on this role as well for families who are nominal Catholics and who believe in espiritismo. Since they may not have close relationships with priests, brujos may conduct funeral rites when asked by family members. If brujos knew the deceased personally, they are expected to come to the *velorio* (wake)—conducted in funeral homes or the home of the deceased—and to lead the prayers. It is a great honor and a good omen for the families of the deceased to have brujos join in praying the Rosary and making the novenas for the departed. Since brujos are well versed in Catholic ceremonies and also know the deceased family in a spiritual way—their problems and conflicts—who better than they to make sure

6.6
A spiritual wedding
in the Yunque

the deceased's soul departs this world in peace? As a prerequisite to preventing future afflictions from striking the living kin, it is crucial, according to Spiritism, that the living kin properly bid farewell to the spirit of the deceased from this world; they must also make sure that the spirit of the dead person does not wish to come back to the world of the living as an espíritu de existencia. For instance, on the anniversary of the death of Tonio's wife, Haydée and many other mediums and espiritistas came to Tonio's house to join in prayer, honoring the spirit of Tonio's wife and wishing for its development. After some refreshments were served, all the mediums and friends of the family gathered in Tonio's backyard shed-altar for a velada.

Haydée has a special string of rosary beads reserved for when she is invited to "rezarle el rosario a los muertos" (pray the Rosary for the dead). She explained:

> We perform the *letanías* [litanies] for the deceased. In Puerto Rico we have an obligation . . . no, not an obligation, rather a devotion to pray for nine nights. We do the novenario [novenas] until twelve o'clock. It's called novenario when we complete the nine days. With these prayers we withdraw the dead from the living and elevate [the departed] to the celestial mansions. Because, independent of being good

or bad, they have to be elevated to where God will want to take them, right? We take the flower bouquets, we pray, and on the tenth day we go to the cemetery to bring flowers and the rosary. I am used to praying with this rosary [points to the string of beads]; that's why I tell the family of the deceased to bring their own rosary, because I don't give to anybody my rosary. My rosary is of San Judas Tadeo.

After seeing how Haydée and other brujos react when they are called on to pay their respects to a deceased person they have known well, it became evident to me that those who were not only well known but also well loved by brujos are the object of heartfelt treatment. This is what happened when the father of a boy that Haydée had treated came crying to her, announcing that his son had just been gunned down. Haydée told me that since the father knew she had warned the son he would soon get killed unless he left the island, he asked her to come to the funeral home to pray for him, for his spirit. "And I did go to pray for him," she added. "And I cried for that boy. . . . I prayed [for him] the complete novenas." For family members who believe in Spiritism, this kind of intervention is an immense source of solace. Suggesting that the appropriate honors had been given to their loved ones, sometimes family members would proudly mention, for instance, that a certain witch-healer came and stayed for many hours at the funeral home or that a witch-healer had sent an impressively large personalized funeral wreath for the deceased.

But those who were disrespectful to brujos during their lives should expect nothing of that sort at the time of their death. Rather, by refusing to come to pray for them, brujos publicly dishonor the spirit of the deceased and indicate that there is still an unresolved conflict between them. It is a way to publicly announce the resentment held by a witch-healer toward the deceased's family. Mourning families dread this situation almost as much as the death of their loved ones. It means that further misfortune awaits them. A bruja who refused to pray for a girl who had just died a couple of days before explained to me why she did not respond to the constant telephone calls from family members begging her to come to pray for the girl. "I didn't pray for her [a relative's daughter] because I didn't feel like it. I was very annoyed with my relative. It was not the girl's fault. I'm quite defiant [but also] loving, kind; but when it's no, it's no!"

Rosaries are also prayed during the performance of trabajos malos. A woman came to Haydée after she had a stroke and a series of mishaps. The divination process revealed that another woman was responsible for it and

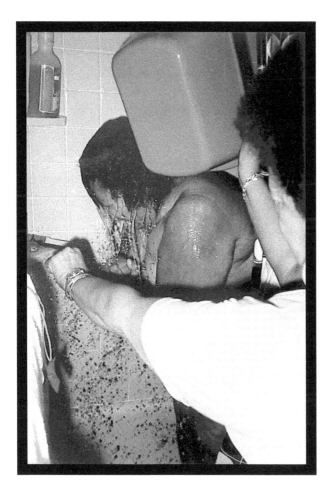

6.7
After preparing a despojo, Haydée pours it over the client, praying for its success.

that a trabajo malo was to be made to punish her. This trabajo consisted of placing a lizard—representing the evil woman—after it had been ritually anesthetized, inside a fancy soap box made into a coffin. She/it was given the proper funerary rites, including the preparation of the "corpse" with *polvos mágicos* (magical powders) and herbs. Intended to mimic a real funeral rite, the symbolic death of the perpetrator was accompanied by several Our Fathers and Hail Marys: "Dios te salve María. . . . Santa María madre de Dios. . . . Por el alma de Natividad que Dios la saque de pena. . . . En el monte murió Cristo, no murió por sus pecados pero murió por los ajenos. . . ." At the conclusion of the prayers Haydée rang the small bell she has on the table, signaling the presence of the spirits. In front of the open casket/soap box, Haydée, Reina, and the client started praying the Rosary. The woman was given a series of cleansing baths right there at

Haydée's home—an unusual practice but necessary because of the gravity of the situation. This person had already been the object of serious attacks on her health. This enabled Haydée to pray while she poured the solution of sweet herbs on her naked body, very much like Haydée does when she performs these despojos in the river.

Brujos also perform restorative funeral rituals, especially when the surviving kin suffer the effects of a wandering soul that haunts them. Haydée's special ritual to free Claude Marín from the spirit of his dead mother is an example. Indeed, until the day of the restorative ritual, the child, now five years old, had never visited the grave, though his mother had died when he was just a few months old. Because his mother died from AIDS, she had not received a proper burial, nor had her son ever been given the opportunity to make a proper farewell. By the time Haydée performed the special rite he had developed serious problems, which were interpreted by Haydée as a sign that the spirit of a possessive, resentful dead mother was haunting him.

The ritual started early that morning at Haydée's altar. After the usual opening prayer, which invoked the spirits to assist her in treating the little boy, Haydée took her rosary and said to the child,

Put your arms down—and everybody, in unión de pensamientos . . . [say with me,] "In the name of the Father and the Holy Spirit, Amen. [Holding a dove above the child's head:] With this white dove, which is the symbol of the Holy Spirit, I [will] strip off [*despojar*] and cleanse this boy, his soul, body and matter. [Passing the dove around the child's body in a upward and downward motion:] I gather, deposit and throw away, I strip off and cleanse this boy [of a causa]—his soul, body and matter; all that is bad in this boy will be thrown away inside this bowl and be deposited in these crystal waters, because this boy has to become, from now on, clean, happy, and satisfied—especially calm." [To the child:] This little dove is for you; give her a kiss.

Haydée and her assistant, Reina, along with the little boy, his father, and me, drove to the cemetery. The ritual continued, under a light rain, in front of the monument. Haydée began praying the Rosary for the mother as the boy put flowers on her grave. With the power invested in the cross and the rosary, Haydée helped to "set free the spirit of the dead mother." Represented by a white dove—"symbol of the holy Spirit"—the wandering soul of the mother would be sent to the "celestial mansions." Haydée

6.8 *Claude Marín sadly looks back as "his" dove flies away.*

took the dove, which had been ritually prepared beforehand at her altar with magical powders and herbs, blessed it, and put it in the hands of the child. Claude Marín, who during the ceremony had kept the dove tightly secured in his hands, allowed it to fly away at the end—but only reluctantly, after Haydée insisted he release it as marking the culmination of the ritual.

On returning to her altar, Haydée cleansed and baptized Claude Marín in the presence of all those who had taken part in the special services. She sprayed an aerosol despojo, then rubbed alcoholado—Florida Water, in this case—over the child's body and head. Having previously "prepared" it spiritually, she gave him a plaster figure of El Santo de Atocha (the Infant of Prague),[18] who thereby was installed as his patron saint, and advised him to keep the santo near his bed as a protection.

In addition to rituals connected to the life cycle, brujos perform exorcisms in extreme cases, such as when a person is suspected of being possessed by an evil spirit. Aided by the most sacred Catholic symbol—the

Cross—and a complement of Catholic prayers, candles, alcholados (usually Florida Water, sometimes mixed with healing herbs), flowers, perfumes, and polvos, brujos in trance engage in a spiritual battle with the evil spirit. At the end of the battle, which usually ends with the brujos victorious, they encourage the evil spirit to repent and, following the humanistic approach of espiritismo, to "seek the light" and transform into an espíritu de luz.

The intrinsic relationship of Catholicism and brujería, particularly curanderismo, is evident in healing performances. Contrary to what students of folk medicine usually highlight, these healers do not stress their knowledge of medicinal plants. Instead, they allude to the power and knowledge invested in them by God or a saint via a miraculous encounter as the key determinant of their ability to cure. I met one such healer from a shantytown in the countryside on his way to cure a patient. He told me he always went to heal his patients dressed as San Martín de Porres—called "the Black Saint"—wearing a white tunic, a brown leather belt, a black cap on his head, and sandals. His tall, thin figure and his long hair framing both sides of his face reminded me, except for the color of the skin and hair, of the typical blue-eyed, blond-haired images of Christ sold in botánicas in Puerto Rico. "I started healing when I was sixteen," he said, "but I didn't learn it from anybody—only from the Lord God." This is why he makes the healing concoctions he needs to cure his patients by himself out of plants and roots he finds in the surroundings. His "spiritual relationship" to all kinds of herbs, roots, and plants is what enhances their healing effects and brings forth, in his words, "some miraculous healing" in cases where others had failed.

The main idea behind herbal healing is that the healing capacities of plants are part of God's design but need the sacred power of a healer to become manifest and effective. As Anita, a woman in her fifties who regularly consults with brujos and mediums (and is herself the daughter of a medium), said, "Healing miracles are produced by means of the holiness of the healer." In other words, the efficacy of the ritual depends on the spiritual state of the ritual expert (*ex opere operantis*), as opposed to rituals that in themselves effect the desired transformation regardless of the disposition of the ritual expert involved (*ex opere operato*).[19] Anita reminisced about healers she had met throughout her lifetime who were famous for performing or for being the object of miracles. When Anita was about nine years old, her grandmother was in an accident that left her in a wheelchair. "She was an invalid. They [the family] took her to Canóvanas to

6.9
"My matas
flourish."

see a Señor called Don Rafa and he was able to heal her." Also, Anita remembered having seen "a man who was there [when the grandmother consulted the healer] who apparently was ill in the chest. After Don Rafa waved a white handkerchief in front of and behind the man's chest, the handkerchief [suddenly] turned red," the disease now transferred to it, a sign that the man had been healed. "When Don Rafa died," Anita added, "the doves standing on the casket cried. I tell it because I saw it." As she grew up, Anita met many other healers. "Among those I knew was El Indio de Fajardo [the Indian of Fajardo], who was of the Hindu race [sic]; [he was] famous because everything that he prognosticated did happen."[20]

The healing power of plants (matas) depends not only on their successful growth, final cut, and appropriate use in medicinal and magical potions; as noted above, it is the spiritual level of the healer who owns them that largely determines their efficacy. Most brujos grow their own medicinal plants in their gardens. When they do not own a mata they need for a trabajo, they borrow buds or stems from another healer in order to grow it, or they go to a place in the countryside where they expect it may be found. Tonio, for example, was very knowledgeable about where

6.10 *"It's the power of my hands."*

to find a variety of native matas and how to recognize areas in which they might grow. The manner in which these matas subsequently flourish and develop once they are planted indicates the blessing of the brujos, that is, the power of their hands.

Tonio's expertise reminded me of Haydée's joy in her own power: "Look, look at how this mata 'gives birth' [*pare*, usually used only of mammals] here in my altar!" Every time Haydée checked on her front-yard matas, she would call me to see how fast and strong they were growing. Driven by the spirits' advice and her own desire to show the world how blessed her hands are, she urged me to take pictures not only of the thirty or so different types of medicinal plants flourishing in her garden but also of her carefully manicured *manos poderosas* (powerful hands).

One of the most popular and widespread healing practices, shared by

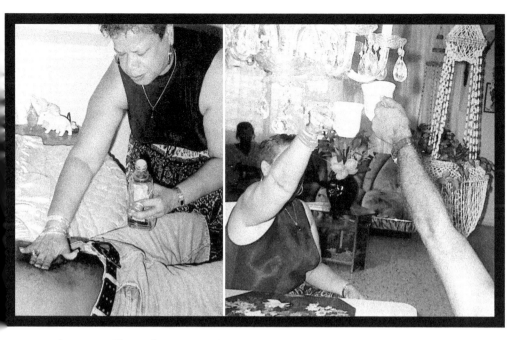

6.11 Haydée performs a santiguo, then drinks Guanábano tea with the client.

brujos and curanderos all over Latin America, combines popular Catholicism with herbal healing in the santiguo, or blessing by making the sign of the cross.[21] *Santiguar* means to cure illnesses of the digestive system that have a spiritual cause. The cure involves making the sign of the cross over the abdomen of the patient while rubbing it with pure olive oil and chanting prayers such as the Our Father. Haydée once performed a santiguo on a man who had suffered a series of family, work, and health mishaps within a period of only several weeks. It was determined in divination that his misfortunes originated when his former wife "le dio un café" (gave him a black magic potion made by mixing regular coffee with her own vaginal secretions). At the end of the actual santiguo and marking the conclusion of the entire curing event itself, the bruja and the patient drink together an infusion of the medicinal leaves of the Guanábano tree.

Although quite unusual, santiguos may be performed to free not only adults from a curse but also unborn children from a curse-driven future life. During divination, a pregnant woman named Marta was "diagnosed" as carrying a fetus that had been cursed to develop with "a physical disability." To revoke the curse, Haydée and Armando performed an impro-

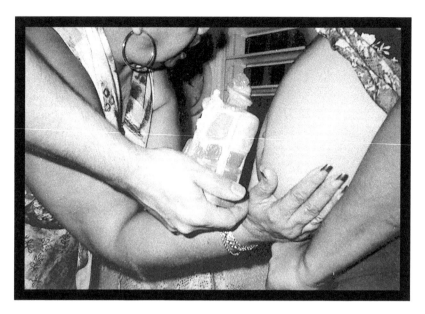

6.12 An unborn child is cleansed and blessed with El Niño de Atocha.

vised version of the traditional santiguo. It combined a cleansing ritual performed with a mixture of Florida Water and white flowers and the invocation of the santo de Atocha, patron of children. Gently rubbing the cleansing mixture on the woman's abdomen while invoking the santo de Atocha, Haydée and Armando aimed at both cleansing and invigorating the spiritual power of the mother and freeing the unborn child from a malicious causa that was meant to harm the mother by harming the child.

Technological Expansion and Global Marketing

"Los santos se cogen igual en los Estados Unidos; los espíritus son pájaros—están las palomas, las golondrinas, las cotorras, el alcatraz" (You can get possessed by the spirits the same in the United States; spirits are birds—there are doves, swallows, parrots, and seagulls). Tonio once said this to me as he was reminiscing about the spiritual work he used to perform on his frequent trips to the Bronx and Washington, D.C., where his sister and niece lived, respectively.

Adding to the expansion of healing circles and techniques, technological advancements extend the reach of brujos and medium-healers beyond territorial boundaries. Nowadays brujos not only "fly" to the Yunque to meet spiritually with other brujos but also "fly" overseas to cure or retaliate for the harm done to their international clients. For example, Doris, the Dominican medium-healer, received a request—with accompanying plane tickets—to help a woman in the United States. In less expensive ways, long-distance consultations are given over the telephone, and trabajos, cleansing baths, or resguardos are sent via Federal Express. One day Haydée received a telephone message from a military base in Kansas requesting that she call back, collect, for a consultation. On the conclusion of such consultations, she sends the client a package with the appropriate remedy, which can be a trabajo, resguardo, or cleansing bath.

On one occasion Tonio was sitting in his wheelchair watching television when the telephone rang. It was a lifelong client from New York who had been worrying about the consequences of a recent hurricane in Puerto Rico and was calling to see if Tonio was all right. The conversation soon became a consultation. Although Tonio had stopped working in his altar because of deteriorating health, he was still actively involved in helping his long-standing clients on the island and on the mainland. This time Tonio advised the man about his work and his wife and suggested he go to a nearby botánica (in New York) to buy some printed prayers and promised to mail him some other things, including a trabajo, which the client would be able to spiritually activate once he read the appropriate prayers. Seeing my surprise at hearing about mailing trabajos, Tonio proudly showed me a box with a trabajo—carefully assembled and wrapped to protect it from shipping and handling hazards—that he was about to mail to a client in Georgia.

Within a few minutes another client called, this time from the island of Vieques. Since it was almost noon, Tonio, following a brujo's custom, rapidly *se santiguó* (crossed himself) by his ear and over his chest before putting the receiver to his ear.[22] It was a woman worried about her married daughter. Tonio said, "You don't want to add to the fire. This will be resolved. This is what happens when strange ideas are put in those kids' heads. . . . Leave her alone. . . . You didn't seduce her, didn't marry her, so you're not going to [help] her divorce either. . . . In San Sebastián people [referring specifically to her daughter's husband] drink. . . . Don't worry, you think I'm doing nothing? . . . 'La rata esta haciendo nido en palo seco'" (lit., "The rat is making a nest in a dry tree," an aphorism implying, in this case, that the husband is trying uselessly to regain the heart of the client's daughter). The consultation was taking a long time, and Tonio was getting impatient. He made all kinds of faces to me indicating that this person talked too much and that she did not really understand what he was trying to tell her. Apparently in response to the woman's threat that she was going to stop helping her daughter if the daughter didn't stop responding to her abusive husband's financial and emotional demands, Tonio, in an admonishing tone, gave the woman a piece of his mind, quoting another aphorism: "Una madre nunca echa los hijos para afuera, siempre los recoge" (A mother never kicks her children out, she always gathers them near her). Seeing that this woman was going on endlessly about her problems, he conveyed that he was going to resolve her problems by saying, "Yo se dónde está el monte" (lit., "I know where the rain forest is"; i.e., I am the brujo).

Widening the range of influence overseas by initiation into other famous Afro-Caribbean religions (such as Haitian and Dominican Vodou or Cuban Santería) takes a considerable investment. For brujos, it is a way to widen their expertise and powers. For clients, it is a way of acquiring more protecciones and of extending spiritual empowerment. Sara, my neighbor in the apartment house in Old San Juan, is a retired government employee who remains very active in Puerto Rican politics; a nonprofessional espiritista, she decided to get initiated in Santería as part of a personal healing process. She explained, "*Me hice un santo* [I got initiated; lit., "I made myself a santo"]²³ in order to cure myself." Since her initiation, she has not missed an opportunity to participate in Santería ceremonies not only in Puerto Rico but also in New York, Chicago, and Miami. She makes regular trips to Haiti as well, to participate in Vodou ceremonies.

Like Sara, brujos aim at tapping into a transnational circle of spirits and occult forces and expanding markets of religious goods and services as a way to enhance their spiritual powers. From this standpoint, for professional brujos, innovation combined with cosmopolitan expansion of their spiritual expertise is not only a positive, often lucrative quest but also, and primarily, a necessity, as it helps to widen the scope of their spiritual power. A brujo I met while I was working at Basi's botánica explained to me why he had become a habitué of botánicas: "In botánicas there are always new things, new dictates [*mandatos*] [given by spiritual forces]. This is like science. Clients like to go on exploring, and exploring [different brujos] until [they] get to the essence [*llegan al grano*], until [they] discover whatever can help [them], [just as] new cures are being discovered for AIDS. The cure exists, but it has to be revealed [to all], [those who have it] haven't made it known to all yet." This was one last, very powerful reason for brujos to welcome innovation and to continue checking what is new in the area of spiritual healing procedures in general and in botánicas in particular.

Basi discovered her spiritual powers as a child by means of being close to a curandera. She developed them in Spiritist centers and enhanced them through courses in metafísica, círculos de oración, Reiki, and meditation. Nowadays she lights candles to the saints regularly; she places food, herbs, and other offerings next to the santos on her altar; and she uses quartz in the healing process. On my return to Basi's house after a day's work, we had dinner together as usual before she showed me her latest acquisition in the area of spiritual help: a particular stuffed dog that embodies what "South American *indios* believe to be incredible spiritual powers." She had purchased it from an "Ecuadorian indio at an open market for a reasonable price, $200." Stressing that she had made a great financial as well as spiritual deal, she added, "Small bits of the fur of these dogs, which are now used in healing rituals, are sold in different botánicas for at least $30 each." (Although I now realize that through my many experiences with brujería I had learned to see santos as the embodiments of enlightened Catholic, indigenous, or African spirits, it was hard for me then to immediately see in Basi's stuffed dog the embodiment of the powerful South American spirit she recognized in it.)

Once the spiritual world is seen as an ecumenical, vast, yet attainable resource, the combination of healing techniques and philosophies—regardless of their ethnic or national origin—become limitless. Bountiful innovations can only mean more blessings. The more, the better. In both the spiritual and material realms, inventiveness and progress increase in direct proportion to each other, resonating well with the ethos of brujería and complementing the high value placed in consumer societies on novelty and improvement at the same time. Thus when new religious commodities appear on the market or when brujos have the chance to meet healers from other countries and exchange information about different cosmologies, these occasions are perceived as opportunities offered to them, the larger purpose of which might escape them at the moment but will surely be conducive to additional blessings. Albeit probably unknowable to humans, these occasions have an ultimate, spiritual purpose. As the Spiritist adage goes, "No hay casualidad, hay causalidad."

Spiritual Free Trade

The social space in which brujos operate today is far from being situated on the margins of society, in the bush, or in communal huts. Surely its transmission does not depend solely on face-to-face interactions or on the existence of a preestablished local community (Appadurai 1990, 1996; Bhabha 1994; Ferguson and Gupta 1992). Individuality, technological innovation, extended services and choices, and the international circulation of ideas are some of the values directing both society and the practices of brujería. The same principles that apply to any other enterprise apply to brujería. Far from being a closed form that is centered in a locale or circumscribed to an ethnic group, brujería is an open form in constant change, its contours discontinuous and permeable. Healers from other parts of the Caribbean and the U.S. mainland, for example, influence practitioners in Puerto Rico. Indeed, rituals are often reshaped as a direct result of contact between them as well as the creation of new ritual technologies, showing constant innovation.

This poses an unprecedented problem in academic assessments of the "authenticity" of shamans, brujos, sorcerers, and other ritual experts—whatever their particular noninstitutional mode of mediating transcendental forces. Carol Laderman (1997), for example, writes of a Malaysian woman who offered her clients a combined system that included her own traditional seances with the techniques of an urban healer. This system made them both wealthy and acceptable to their urban clients "at a time when traditional Malaysian shamanism, primarily based in agrarian communities, was on the wane" (p. 341). The contrast between "traditional" shamanism and this woman's style suggests that hers is an idiosyncratic mixture of traditional and urban healing techniques, not "the" tradition (i.e., as it had been practiced in rural Malaysia). Not unique to Malaysia or to Puerto Rico, what I want to suggest is that there are alternative criteria for assessing the authenticity or legitimacy of vernacular healers that are based on their success in appealing to and communicating with urbanites with whom they share common lifestyle values and attitudes. Indeed, today the success of brujos does not depend on their adherence to an imagined pastoral spiritual healing tradition, or on their fitting in with the atavistic expectations of a certain ethnicity or race. One may hear Puerto Rican brujos and their clients voice stereotypical statements such as "Haitian brujos are the most powerful" or "Dominican brujos perform trabajos malos for Puerto Ricans." At most, these expressions usually serve pragmatic conversational purposes. Yet for all practical purposes, when choosing brujos, it is not their ethnic origin, color, or "traditional" healing technique that attracts clients; rather, it is their fame and connections with commercial and public institutions and with socially influential individuals.

With the prominence of brujos from the Caribbean and the flow of brujos to and from the U.S. mainland, the divining and healing styles as well as the types of trabajos performed in Puerto Rico have expanded considerably.[24] In addition to the combination of traditional-urban healing styles mentioned by Laderman, the importation of "traditional" healing styles is a source of change. The global circulation of "exotic" products and spiritual practices has destabilized any assumed fixity of vernacular rituals, such as those of brujería, on ethnic grounds. And with this, any possible legitimation of brujería based on its folkloric, national character has also crumbled away. Unlike the previous reframing of brujería as *medicina popular* that had been endorsed by the school of medicine, the latest global circulation of religious commodities and ritual experts has not contributed to similar approval of brujería among top administrators of the medical school today. Nor has this global circulation generated a global form of brujería. Because meaning is not intrinsic to objects but is attributed to them in the course of human thought and practices, objects have the ability to change meanings in their lifetimes over time and space (Appadurai 1986; Errington 1989). Any object that circulates would then lose the meaning of its source society and be prone to acquire new meanings in a new context, contradicting those theorists of globalization that assume that the circulation of goods over different spaces creates a homogeneous global culture. Instead of eliminating differences between cultures, intense circulation of goods could re-create or strengthen differences. For example, "the seemingly empty and universalist signs circulating in the world informational system can be recast into different configurations of meaning . . . [and]—in the context of traditional and self-reflexive social practices—instead inform the (re)constitution and creation of individual and communal identities" (Featherstone, Lash, and Robertson 1995:2–3). Contrary to the predictions of some globalization theories, homogenized witch-healing practices that would erase local differences in favor of a generic ritual lingua franca does not seem to be emerging in the near future either. On the contrary, and this is what I find particularly telling, global flows of people, goods, and ideas have promoted further particularization and individualization of spiritual practices. While feeding into a boundless need for spiritual renewal and growth, imported "exotic" healing systems are selectively added by individual brujos with the aim of securing additional translocal spiritual power.

Concomitantly, recent critical debates over the idea of an ahistorical, bounded tradition or culture have suggested that more than portraying actual practices, the notion of a bounded tradition reflects rather a romantic idealization of how cultures have formed and changed (see Wolf 1982). Following this critique, I have suggested (in part 1) that brujería cannot be understood as a bounded, ahistorical practice. Furthermore, as the ethnographic accounts have revealed so far, new technologies, innovative commercial products, and the input of foreign religious practitioners have been drawn into the practices of brujería today. The unobtrusive, easy incorporation of new elements into the practice of brujería deserves to be looked at more closely. Two possible explanations are, first, that the commercialization of culture encourages religious unorthodoxy, or, second, that perhaps there is something inherent in past and current forms of brujería that eschews orthodoxy altogether. Does the intensity of eclecticism in brujería emerge directly from historical contacts with other groups and their religious practices? Might commercial openness facilitate the unorthodox practices of brujería by fostering a larger pool of material and spiritual resources?

Wande Abimbola (1996), a Nigerian scholar initiated in the religion of the orishas, has argued that the incorporation of Catholic saints into Santería was in line with the African cosmology of the orishas. Building on this idea, it could be argued that the incessant and effortless incorporation of innovative elements into brujería practices, such as the South American dog, is the outcome of an inherent attribute of brujería. It might be the result of a systemic attribute. Assuming that the mechanisms of magic — namely, homeopathy and contagion, as depicted by Frazer ([1922] 1960) — are also operating in the practices of brujería today, these mechanisms may offer an explanation for the ease with which new homologous features are swiftly incorporated without necessarily modifying the essential meaning of witch-healing rituals.

While encouraging certain built-in attributes of brujería — its unorthodoxy and eclecticism — not all the attributes traditionally associated with the threatening aspects of brujería disappear under the liberal state and free market. Some secrecy, although no longer serving to protect brujos from the stake or from the "civilizing" arm of the state, is still necessary, notwithstanding the laissez-faire context in which brujería operates today.

Today's secrecy can hardly be regarded as putting any constraints on the trade. Instead, it protects brujos from the dangers of their trade: from counterattacks, rumors and accusations of bewitchment, and disclosure of their healing procedures.

Evidently the influence of a commercial free market frame of action has had a remarkable impact on the practices of brujería, both with regard to the professionalization of brujos and with regard to the way clients relate to them. Certainly the availability of ritual choices favors clients, who gain from a competitive spiritual arena of professionals who swiftly generate ritual changes and treatments to encompass the constantly expanding pantheon of spirits. Although globalization theorists have emphasized the role of transnational media and commercial forces as well as new communication technologies in shaping local cultures, I wish to stress the grassroots interplay with these international forces by examining how local brujos turn to these forces in order to expand their blessings. In the case of brujería, a great deal of its commodification and eclecticism results with little or no direct intervention of large-scale global extrareligious forces. Rather, the creation of an extremely malleable and prolific spiritual realm that transcends local boundaries is owed to a great extent to brujos, who—living up to the expectation of acquiring infinite bendiciones—take an active part in the transmission and formation of brujería, refueling its practices with yet further unexpected energies. In the next two chapters another level of their spiritual entrepreneurship is discussed in relation to the sociopolitical realities of Puerto Rico insofar as they set up the conditions for their expanding roles as practical and spiritual mediators between state agencies, businesses, and individual clients—another type of expansion of the practices of brujería.

CHAPTER

SEVEN

THE MORAL ECONOMY OF
BUREAUCRATIC PROVIDENCE

Brujos and the Modern State

The modern bureaucratic system has been viewed by a number of historical and political sociologists, for example, Max Weber (1983) and Reinhard Bendix (1978), as a positive development that turns away from traditional, irrational forms of governance. Briefly, the modern state, with its
functional compartmentalization of bureaucratic organizations, was to be
guided instead by rationality and technology. Notwithstanding its Kafka-
esque dehumanization, the technical expertise of bureaucratic officials—
responding only to the functional orientations of their organizations—
would have an equalizing effect on citizens. This, it was assumed, would
forestall partisan forms of mediation between individuals and the state.
All this sounds good. But even in the most democratic systems, these assumptions have not withstood experience. Bureaucratic systems have generated their own intrinsic, ambiguous areas of legality. Equity and uni-
versalism—the principles of state bureaucracies—are debased whenever
internal sources leak information, say, of upcoming economic or health
policy changes. This invaluable information could favor some people over
others, especially when the state takes on the role of redistributing public
wealth under a welfare system.

Since the invasion of Puerto Rico in 1898, the American state-bureau-
cratic system, with its ethos and modes of operation, has been exported—
under classic colonialism—along with American military and economic
control. On becoming a U.S. commonwealth in 1952, the island created
new local state agencies such as social security, labor, and housing and
judicial, health, and education systems following the U.S. model. In addition, economic incentives and tax exemptions have facilitated the reloca-

tion of many multinational enterprises to the island. Since the launching of Operation Bootstrap, Puerto Rican society has been struggling between the economic advantages of and the social and political prices wrought by this program as it shifted from promoting first labor-intensive and then capital-intensive export-oriented industrialization (Grosfoguel 1997: 58–59).

Currently, propelled by the constant flow of federal moneys for the administration of Puerto Rico and of American investments in local industries, the prevailing sense among the people I met was that a pool of unlimited goods was there to be appropriated—or otherwise lost. These goods may be in the form of public positions, jobs, housing, and educational opportunities and of government loans, pensions, and compensation for natural disasters and work-related damages. In addition, in the wake of the debates over the future status of the island, people employed by American-owned corporations are aware of how extremely sensitive these corporations are to developments in the political arena and ready to adjust their modes of operation accordingly.[1] Federal regulations tend to change as well. In this respect, the availability of jobs in the private and public sectors and federal assistance on the island fluctuate accordingly.

Awareness of changes in the rules and regulations governing corporate benefits, labor, welfare, and social security rights thereby becomes essential. Because the stakes for the rapid accumulation of wealth by individuals in public redistribution and corporate production circles are high (compared to the internal market), individual investment in these areas of human endeavor is worthwhile. Through what appears a resilient world of public and corporate resources, maximizing one's position in these spheres seems an astute move. Indeed, as important as participating in the internal economic market, knowing where and how to get these American freebies from welfare and corporate systems is central to advancing one's interests.

Contrary to the ideal rational bureaucratic system, official and corporate positions are not always assigned solely on the basis of professional expertise. Rather, securing these highly desirable positions often depends on the capacity of candidates to manipulate personal alliances in their favor. For those who lose the post to others, these positions appear—in the eyes and parlance of individuals who consult with brujos—grabbed or "stolen" from them by the other candidates, not because they have better qualifications, but through "cosmic and magical interventions." Through these cunning interventions, they believe, a candidate may "snatch" a certain position by causing an opponent to suddenly fall ill, or by swaying the minds of top executives. From a purely sociological perspective, the allocation of behind-the-scenes information—such as the names of key contact officials, upcoming layoff plans, or new deadlines for submitting petitions to state agencies—becomes a vital survival strategy for individuals who want to compete in such a social environment. In this context, networking and accumulating interpersonal cultural capital are the means by which such social assets can be acquired.

Brujos become valuable at these times. Not only are they endowed with spiritual and magical resources that can cripple one's competitors and enemies, they are also resourceful in more worldly, practical matters. Being at the center of influential relationships among high-ranking officials and business managers, brujos tap in to critical information regarding available positions, upcoming changes in the market, and federal regulations. Thus, by means of their responsiveness to spiritual as well as material obstacles, brujos best qualify to counteract any adversities their clients might encounter—adversities assumed to be the result of trabajos made against them by rivals—in pursuing their economic well-being and personal power. By endowing their clients with material and spiritual positive energies, brujos can also turn past adversities into future bendiciones.

Besides encouraging assertiveness and alertness in the material sphere, brujos redirect their clients toward a morally oriented attitude in pursuing these very goals. In line with the Spiritist Law of Cause and Effect and the notions of spiritual justice and reincarnation (see chap. 2), the advice given by brujos can transform merely instrumental advantages into ones that are spiritually endowed. In the context of Puerto Rican society, brujos thereby provide not only the "eyes and ears" for clients to find possible resources in bureaucratic organizations and capitalist enterprises but also the "soul" or moral charter behind the demands and profits that could be made, legitimizing the righteousness of accumulating state- and corporate-administered social goods. By and large, as mediators between clients and society, brujos certainly manage the needs of the first side of the equation under the constraints of the second.

An important point needs to be kept in mind with regard to the mediating abilities of contemporary brujos. Without aiming at demystifying the spiritual powers at the core of their vision and advice, there are other sources that contribute to the factual knowledge, sensibility, and effectiveness of brujos in dealing with current problems. Perhaps as a result of the pruebas, or tests they "have to" undergo to become healers, their life experiences have typically also included struggling with the state's medical, educational, employment, and legal agencies. These otherwise devastating experiences contribute in the present to boosting their insights into the conflicts intrinsic to a capitalist- and welfare-oriented society. Indeed, a few snapshots from the life histories of brujos reveal that, far from being an endangered species on the margins of modern society, they are adroit in managing current social adversities.

Tonio, who fathered ten children, had worked all his life as a plantation overseer. He had to lead his workers in times of personal conflicts as well as mediate between high- and low-ranking plantation workers with the aid of his spiritual and magical resources. His clients used to be found not only among poor plantation workers but also in administrative and managerial circles.[2] Bolina, having raised eleven children, had worked at a foreign-owned canning factory from the early decades of the twentieth century until her retirement. It was an experience that had prepared her to better relate to her clients' work problems under current multinational constraints. Haydée had worked for twenty-three years at a local Centro Médico (government-operated medical center), having worked previously in a law firm as a legal secretary and as assistant to the manager of an international corporation's factory. Through these wide-ranging work experiences she developed a keen understanding of legal procedures and the health care apparatus, which she now applies in her consultations (see chap. 8). Last, Basi, raised as an orphan, became a self-made businesswoman in the 1950s and since the 1970s has been a real estate investor, botánica owner, and importer of health food products. A single mother, she not only understands the pressures of those Puerto Rican women who have to contend with neglectful fathers who fail to meet their child support obligations, but she is aware of convenient state provisions for starting small businesses and for arranging short-term loans. Today she attends to her clients' well-being, helping them to maximize their economic opportunities.

In addition to the insights derived from their life experiences, the centrality and variability of their clients' endeavors further enhance the expertise of brujos. Depending on their relative fame, brujos are usually at the center of various social networks that might include members of the political, professional, and commercial elite. Brujos thus often find themselves at the crossroads of crucial channels of information. This pool of knowledge, gathered during consultation and then exchanged in gossip among other brujos, comes in handy when informing their clients how to apply—on time and in the right manner—for federal help, a job, housing, social security benefits, and the like. Knowledge of social and welfare services regulations is also crucial. Brujos can help their clients to avoid losing custody of children, to protect their legal rights as parents or common-law couples, to apply for social security benefits after an accident, and so forth. Brujos also provide assistance in more direct ways, for example, by putting managers and directors in touch with potential employees. Invariably, a letter of recommendation or personal request signed by a bruja or brujo opens many doors.

The Commonwealth and the Mobilization of Wealth

Puerto Rico under the Estado Libre Asociado occupies an ambiguous position between total independence from and total annexation to the United States. Rather than the result of positive political action, the commonwealth seems to be the result of an irresolute electorate. After decades of deferred controversies, visible in the enactment of endless plebiscites, the future of Puerto Rico's status is still blurred by issues of legal sovereignty and cultural identity. According to Grosfoguel (1997:66–67), Puerto Rico—like French and Dutch colonies in the postwar Caribbean—could be defined as a "modern colony," or, as Duany (2001:6) suggested, a "postcolonial colony." The benefits enjoyed by modern colonies (vis-à-vis neocolonial neighbors in the Caribbean) include "annual transfers of billions of dollars of social capital from the metropolitan state to the modern colony (e.g., food stamps, health, education, and unemployment benefits), constitutional recognition of metropolitan citizenship and democratic/civil rights, the possibility of migration without the risks of illegality, and the extension of Fordist social relations that incorporated the colonial people to metropolitan standards of mass consumption" (Grosfoguel 1997:66–67).

Motivated by the elections of 1996, debates about the future of the island vis-à-vis the United States were in the air. A brujo who is also an activist in the Partido Nuevo Progresista (PNP), a party that promotes statehood for Puerto Rico—as the fifty-first state in the Union—did not see any conflict in also advocating a nationalist Puerto Rican identity. In his view, "Puerto Rico will never become the fifty-first state. The ELA will continue, the United States has to accept our rights, we'll not be left without them, but also there will be no independence, communism, or statehood. Since I love the American money—governments are anyhow the same—I want statehood, but it'll not happen. If we became the fifty-first state, that's good, but they'd raise our taxes, and we'd have to learn English. Now [with the ELA] we have the very same benefits, *el welfear* [Spanglish for "welfare"] without having the negative aspects."[3]

Before and during elections, brujos, mediums, and psychics get involved in political events at various levels. Regardless of political affiliation, brujos generally show a deep concern for the sociopolitical situation of the island and get involved as citizens and as spiritual consultants in conceiving possible solutions for its political future. Some express their dismay at the island's problems in their daily prayers, urging God's help to resolve them. Others make public predictions about the elections or put a certain santo in charge of a candidate by making special offerings and lighting candles. Some brujos support their candidates by performing trabajos that aim at "sweetening" voters' attitudes toward that candidate, at "tying up" the tongues of contenders, or at neutralizing their rivals' energies by "putting [the rivals' doubles] in a coffin."

Also, brujos stay well informed about the latest developments in state and government affairs and local events. I have seen brujos quickly browse through their daily newspapers early in the morning, before they begin their consultations. This gives them a good idea of the latest crimes, legal cases, and government affairs and occasionally provides them with the names of judges, attorneys, and police officers who were involved in these events—some of whom they recognize from previous cases and later make use of when advising their clients or performing trabajos. Often this information is later exchanged during regular visits with other brujos, who might add their own inside stories about these people and cases, opening new circles of very useful exchanges.

After Hurricane Bertha hit the island in summer 1996, a subject that came up frequently in consultations was the Federal Emergency Management Agency (FEMA), which, among other things, deals with hurricane victims' complaints and demands. Federal funds allocated for these purposes were distributed according to the specifications and under the administration of the Puerto Rican government. Haydée, Basi, and other brujos were well informed as to who was eligible to claim losses from FEMA and how, where, and when to file for them. Few knew that just by making a telephone call, a small but meaningful payment could be received without undergoing annoying appraisals. Because Haydée had an *ahijado* (spiritual protégé; lit., "godson") whose sole job responsibility was answering hurricane-related emergency telephone calls for the government, she was fully aware of this pool of easily available money that had recently arrived;

she directed her clients who had suffered the aftermath of the hurricane to make the best of it. Many were encouraged to make the first move by Haydée's saying, as she read the cards, "You'll cry when you receive this gift from FEMA. The money will help you resolve many things."

Among the general public, the laws and regulations governing eligibility for government housing, loans, technical education, and the like, are not always known to those who might be qualified. In their role of enlightening, guiding, and advising their clients in the spiritual realm, brujos also open clients' eyes to the possibilities awaiting them in the bureaucratic system. Basi, for example, encouraged a poor widow to apply for public housing after the woman had expressed hopelessness about her future following the death of her husband. Basi helped her to acquire a home in one of the best public housing neighborhoods. Through the mediation of brujos, many young high school dropouts find their way to technical schools that are sponsored by the government and businesspeople. Unemployed men and women were able to take out loans in order to invest in small business ventures. All of this was done thanks to the interventions of brujos who wisely counseled clients to take advantage of public assistance programs.

Transactions among the Living and Blessings from the Dead

During consultations, kaleidoscopic perspectives on a situation may arise as the various voices of the spirits, the dead, and brujos merge. Clients thus hear several types of explanations for their afflictions, illuminating all sides of the problem. This holistic approach may be what makes brujos so attractive to urbanites, some of whom are health care professionals themselves, accustomed to the fragmentation of services of the modern state and the compartmentalization of professional help. Infusing words with an irresistible and incisive resonance, brujos can speak in the voice of a spirit, a public official, a betrayed former wife, or the client. Meshing narrative with other speech styles and combining the material and spiritual aspects of a misfortune, the divination process becomes a complex exchange.

More than an encounter limited to verbal linguistic exchanges, the process is a performance that combines gestures typically made by bureaucrats, howls and tears, trance, and dancing. It might be initiated by the client's confessional account, unexpectedly shifting to corrosive warnings voiced by the bruja as she takes on a judge's role, then to accusations of the guilt of a third party, and finally ending with emotional exhortations that provide detailed reckoning of events, supernatural measures, and even down-to-earth advice. The whole spiritual event is often convoluted: crisp remarks expressed by a bruja in trance are interrupted with long ruminations on personal experiences that interpret the voices of the spirits, first from a moral and then from a practical standpoint. Usually proceeding more rapidly than ordinary speech and disregarding rules of conversation, the multilevel dialogue among brujos, clients, spirits, and the dead might end up in a cryptic cacophony of voices. In these cases, brujos take on the additional role of docents, translating what transpired during the divination process to apprehensive, inexperienced, or just bedazzled clients.

The aim of these consultations is to resolve conflicts among the living through the blessings of the spirits. Brujos, as spiritual entrepreneurs in a consumer and welfare society, are called to intervene in personal matters that, most of the time, concern public services and private businesses. The following cases illustrate the intricate process by which brujos bring together, in a multilevel performance, a variety of spiritual forces and ritual manipulations and practical expertise and connections to solve housing, labor, and family problems.

Haydée had advised Dominga (Eva's mother), a sixty-year-old widow, to take out a government loan to pay off the mortgage on the house she had been sharing with her lifelong companion before he died and thus avoid losing the property. The government loan was taken out by Eva so that Dominga's "enemies" (her stepchildren) could not lay claim to it. Most important, Haydée had also advised her to pay each of her stepchildren for their share of the house. Dominga came back to consult Haydée because of the conflict that arose after her stepchildren unexpectedly made claims on the house. While in trance, Haydée voiced the spirits' verdict: "The house is yours, you worked for that house, you were the *macho* in the household. Your [former] husband wasn't any good in life, but now, as a muerto, he's helping you get the house." Moved by this, Dominga immediately felt the fluídos, and while she was starting to show signs of being possessed by the spirits, Haydée cheered on the imminent trance, calling out, "Despójate! despójate!" (Strip, cleanse yourself of bad spirits!). She was implicitly addressing the negative energies of the stepchildren, who—envious of Dominga's well-being—were wishing evil on her, even though she had already settled their inheritance years before. Reiterating the voices of the spirits, who often "speak the truth" in harsh and irreverent ways, Haydée called out, "Keep the house! The money you gave to those sons of bitches—sons of his—they ate it and now they want the house. Now, [the spirit] of your *cabrón* [fucking husband] should flog them; they want you to be left with nothing." Continuing the prediction, Haydée assured Dominga that "the government agents will come to appraise the house either on Thursday or Friday and will extend the loan." Until then, Haydée suggested she place four goblets filled with water at the four corners of her house in order to cleanse the home of any bad spirits her enemies might have conjured to harm her.

In keeping with the Spiritist ethos of individual and civil responsibility, spirits often admonish humans who commit any—even the slightest —interpersonal misdemeanor. Because the spirits enable brujos to "see" simultaneously the present, past, and future, the cautionary premonitions of the latter are to be taken seriously. The repercussions might be transgenerational. According to Spiritism, any social transgression is paid for during this or other reincarnated lives on earth and might be passed on to one's descendants. Like those of the ancient prophets, the admonitions of brujos contain simultaneously directives as to the right course to be taken and warnings of the tragic consequences of not following them. Indeed, what for clients might appear a straightforward, down-to-earth personal problem can turn into a cosmic moral issue. And following the Spiritist ethos of individual responsibility, instead of being constrained by human-made laws, this problem is set against universal spiritual ethics.

The Puerto Rican state has several ways to intervene in matters related to the well-being of children, especially children of single or divorced parents; Social Services, in particular, takes responsibility for ensuring child support, proper education, and fulfillment of the physical and emotional needs of underage children. Brujos warn men and women about extramarital love affairs, not so much to protect the idea of the bourgeois family as to open their eyes to the legal consequences of their actions and to protect them from punitive state interventions.

For example, divorced fathers or legal guardians who have not made support payments in time would hear the warnings of spirits urging them to comply with the rulings of worldly judges regarding alimony and visitations. If fathers or mothers fail to meet their moral and financial obligations, grandmothers or other close relatives are morally, not legally, expected to carry the burden for them. Brujos warn grandmothers that if they do not want to see their adult sons in legal trouble, they can either coax them to pay child support or pay it themselves. For the sake of the child's physical and spiritual well-being, brujos put moral pressure on all the relatives, irrespective of who is legally responsible.

By and large, clients know that if a breach of social and moral rules has been committed it will be revealed during consultation with brujos. When clients hear brujos utter the words, "They [the spirits] give it to me [inform me]: 'One has to know how to do things well,'" they know these are the words of the spirits; whatever follows will be endowed with the ultimate power of the spiritual realm and thus should be taken as cosmic edicts.

When an ex-wife remarries, the bruja or brujo intervenes to neutralize the animosity of the former mother-in-law, especially when the latter tries to meddle in the former daughter-in-law's new marriage by turning the grandchildren against her or the stepfather. This was the problem presented by Flora, a thirty-year-old client who came to consult with Haydée. She complained that her children were very disrespectful to her and their new stepfather. Haydée saw it in a vision:

> Your ex-husband's mother is trying to undermine your new marriage by pitting your three sons against your new husband, who is very young —twenty-five years old, right? And you ask yourself [reciting in the client's voice, as given to her by the spirits], 'How is it that this young man, who could have younger women, is interested in me?' [Shifting to an assertive tone:] We have to work with these children. They are treating him so badly that he will gradually take his clothes away from the house. You'll see. That's why we have to control them. That bitch of an ex-mother-in-law of yours *los puso de espaldas* [has pitted them against] your new husband and incites them against him at every opportunity. She even sends them to spy on your financial state. You have to open your eyes! Be aware! You husband is afraid of your sons, and one day he'll pack his stuff.

Haydée suggested that Flora talk with her children, for at ages eighteen, sixteen, and thirteen they were old enough to understand the situation. Otherwise, Haydée warned, Flora would suffer tremendously by losing her new husband. Haydée then started dictating a recipe for a trabajo aimed at predisposing Flora's sons positively to their stepfather: "For the boys, I need three unwashed socks, one from each. I'll prepare them. Bring a

7.1 Clients burying trabajos buenos in the monte and trabajos malos in the cemetery

pot of honey, and the rest I'll give to you. We'll sweeten the boys toward your new husband, and then we'll prepare something for that meddling grandmother, who doesn't want you to be happy since you didn't make her son happy." Haydée explained that she would take the trabajo made to sweeten the sons toward their stepfather to the monte, the abode of the spirits of love, so they could be united spiritually with him. But for the trabajo planned for the grandmother, Haydée would need to go to the cemetery, where she would summon one of her own muertos to carry it out, thereby assuring its success.

Trading with Connections and Revelations

Contrary to the idea that only people on the margins of society seek out the services of witch-healers, today's brujos are in contact with clients who occupy important positions in government agencies and private businesses. In exchange for their spiritual services, brujos acquire favors in goods and services and connections that can be used personally or transmitted to their clients. One can imagine the range of resources that might be accumulated and then distributed by brujos whose clients are police detectives, high-ranking municipal clerks, district attorneys, government workers, and managers of hotels, car rental agencies, and fast-food chains. In addition to finding out about their past, present, and future actions, brujos may learn about jobs or new career opportunities. Thanks to Haydée's connections, for example, a young unemployed woman found a job with a restaurant chain. Because the manager of one of the restaurants is a client of Haydée's, on several occasions when she had come to consult at the altar, she brought Haydée complete lunches from the restaurant or gave her dinner vouchers as gifts. On this occasion, the manager had offered a job to one of Haydée's clients, proving once more her indebtedness to Haydée and her commitment to extending such favors in the future. Through another client, the manager of a hotel chain and car rental agency, Haydée secured a receptionist job for a young Nuyorican man just arrived from the mainland. The young man's mother, also a client, brought him directly from the airport to see Haydée. He had been having work- and drug-related problems in New York, and, on Haydée's advice, the mother had sent for him a couple of months earlier. Getting a job and starting a new life on the island would solve a major problem for the client and his worried mother. For Haydée, the intervention of the car rental agency's manager was public testimony to her power as a bruja, as well as a display of the bendiciones—acquired through her trabajo espiritual—she was able to share with her clients.

Another of Haydée's clients, María, is the assistant director of a local government labor agency. Haydée directs those clients who need to resolve problems such as benefit claims and layoff settlements to María. On several occasions María was at Haydée's service, either by offering her professional advice or by direct involvement with regard to Haydée's clients, such as Diana, a schoolteacher. Diana was advised by her friends to ask for Haydée's help concerning a file she had submitted to the Fondo, the government agency that handles work claims. During her first consultation, she told Haydée how—after ten years at the same school—she began having problems with the principal, who apparently wanted to get rid of her so that she could hire a friend. Haydée immediately checked into whether the case fell under the jurisdiction of María's agency. Remembering that María was scheduled to come to the altar in a couple of days, Haydée wrote down the pertinent details of Diana's case—a smart move that was intended to facilitate María's inquiry into Diana's case. While

Haydée was writing down her name, I saw the relief on Diana's face: Haydée would make a personal request of this government agent to rule in her favor.

The consultation continued, and after Haydée read another pile of cards for Diana, she said: "First, I will deal with your son and with his father and then with your colleagues at work and with the principal who wanted to drive you out of that school. [Acknowledging Diana's spiritual powers:] *Pero con usted no hay quien pueda* [But with you, there's no one who can harm you]." Implicitly affirming Haydée's divinatory statement, Diana offered further evidence of her alleged spiritual power as she continued her complaint.

> The principal had fallen down and broken her leg and said it happened because *le hice un brujo* [I had cursed her]. She started to look for material evidence for trabajos [that I had allegedly made]; [implying the source for the principal's enmity toward her:] she's a pastor of an Evangelical church. When the school year ended the principal said that since my position depended on a special [government] budget, there was a chance that I might keep the position, but she suggested I apply for other jobs [offered by the school], such as that of computer assistant, in case the budget wasn't renewed. But she told a colleague of mine—and I also dreamed it—that the principal was saving my position for a friend of hers. For the principal likes to come in [to work] and go out freely, and with me in the school she can't do it [implying that, unlike the principal, she has a strong work ethic].

Interrupting her client's detailed narrative, Haydée began dictating a recipe inspired by the spirits: "For you, I want a despojo [mass-produced cleansing concoction] 'Against Envy'; a despojo 'Demolish Everything' [Arrasa con Todo]; a despojo 'Good Luck'; and a despojo 'The Just' [El Justiciero]. May you have justice! That's what you need, because you didn't harm anybody, giving no reason for others to harm you." When Diana said that the lawyer had already submitted her case to the Fondo, Haydée already "knew" the end of the story. Indeed, before Diana could finish explaining how and why her case was delayed, Haydée, implying a deliberate mishandling of the case due to black magic, immediately said: "I tell you, it had been [purposely] tangled [*lo han enredado*]." In the same breath she offered the solution: "[The spirit] of El Vencedor [the Conqueror] will conquer it; [the spirit of] El Justiciero [the Just] will assure that justice is done. It's the first time I'm working with these spirits, but these are the names given to me [by my cuadro]."

Many other clients who were facing work problems also found strong encouragement and were provided with the spiritual backing of powerful deities to turn unfavorable situations into positive ones. In some cases, knowledge about the particular system within which clients work enhances the advice given to them by brujos, for their words are not only empowered by the spirits but imbued with practical savvy as well. For example, Martita, a forty-five-year-old woman with several misfortunes behind her, used to work as a clerk in a federal agency. Haydée's knowledge of the system in which Martita had worked arose during the consultation, giving Martita additional confidence in Haydée's ability to help her. Because of a lack of funding, Martita's office had been downsized, and, to her dismay, at the end of the fiscal year she was dismissed. During a consultation right after she was laid off, Haydée had a vision that Martita would be interviewed for another job in a few days. A week later, during the second consultation, Haydée prepared a special "luck bath" for Martita. As Haydée customarily does in preparing cleansing baths and trabajos, she carefully went through her written recipe, naming each component while mixing it with others in order to endow the ingredients, previously bought by Martita at a botánica, with the desired spiritual power. In the presence of Martita, Haydée named each component and its expected effect: "*Ruda* [a medicinal plant] symbolizes money. . . . A piece of lodestone to attract good fortune . . ." Interrupting the preparation of the concoction with a sudden vision about a new job Martita had applied for, she said, "They interviewed you and hired you, right? During the next few months [after the probationary period], you'll also be given a permanent appointment. How glad I am for you, Martita, sincerely from the bottom of my heart!" A big smile appeared on Martita's face. Haydée was glad for Martita and for herself: Martita got a job, and Haydée had another corroboration of her visionary powers.

In less fortunate cases, when clients do not immediately find a job or are unable to continue working because of health problems, brujos' knowledge of how and where to file unemployment claims becomes essential. Yet unlike social workers, brujos can also summon other forces to speed up resolution of a problem. Indeed, in a fleeting moment the emotional premonitions of brujos can shift to sharp practical counsels, back into the sacred realm, and then continue with the promise of a holy fiat. Sori, for example, had come to her first consultation with Haydée accompanied by her mother and her two young children and newborn baby. Among the various subjects touched on (including her husband's indifference and her meddling neighbor's acerbic comments), Sori mentioned her inability to return to her secretarial job at a factory because of a swelling in her leg and foot that had persisted for three months after she had delivered her last baby. The swelling resisted all treatment and appeared to be a permanent, disabling condition. She gave Haydée a couple of government letters to read and then asked: "Haydée, look at what I bring you here, maybe you can put your hands on this social security thing?" Haydée replied, "But this has to be prepared *Mama* [a term of endearment]. Did you appeal?" Sori explained, "The Fondo says that the swelling is due to bad circulation. The doctors say it's cellulitis and that I'll have it all my life; they tell me, 'You should appeal because it's not bad circulation.'" Haydée confirmed the doctors' diagnosis in front of Sori, proclaiming vehemently:

[Pointing to Sori's feet] You have cellulitis, not bad circulation . . . this is cellulitis, you know! This swelling of yours needs to be lowered with *saúco* [a medicinal plant]. And it's hard, because whatever you have there, it's a *cantazo* [causa; lit., "blow"]. . . . The spirits say, "Why do you sometimes think that everything around you is negative when you know that it's not so?" When you apply to Social Security, it [your claim] will be approved. But we have to work with those papers. We have to work with that leg—you know, spiritually not materially. [Snapping her fingers, signaling the presence of spirits] *Uy carajo!* [Oh, shit!]. The spirits say [while she knocks on the table], "Time has come for that swelling to leave that leg because there's no more pregnancy." They say, "On what did you step? . . . That, that [trabajo] wasn't for you. That's a trabajo." . . . [Silence] . . . [No], it *was* a trabajo [her emphasis implying that at this moment the curse was over]. But They say that first I have to treat the left leg and then the right one. And They tell me that today I have to give you a despojo with brazo fuerte.

While applying herbal compresses to Sori's leg and foot, Haydée began to examine the forms Sori had received from the government. In analyzing these papers, she changed her attitude from that of a healer to that of a state official. For a few minutes she scrutinized the official signatures on the document that specified the status of Sori's claim, the institutional definition of the problem as established by the labor agency and social security agency. After commenting on the names of the officials who had

7.2 Haydée examining social security claims

signed the forms—some of whom she knew—Haydée told Sori to leave the case in her care. Sori was instructed to deposit the forms on one of the altar's shelves right under the Buddha itself for a few days, then wait until the next consultation to further "infuse the case with good luck and positive energies." Sori came to consult several more times, and eventually the swelling in her leg and foot was reduced. Also, one of Haydée's clients who worked for a labor agency got involved in Sori's case, and by the time I left Puerto Rico, it seemed that Sori's problem would soon be resolved.

As the previous cases have shown, in contrast to social workers and psychologists, brujos examine a problem from different angles and integrate several realms of reality in working toward its resolution. In this process they change their roles and styles of speech accordingly. Abusive judgments voiced by spirits can easily become poetic exhortations addressing the deep emotional states of clients in aphoristic or metaphorical expression, turning the divination process into an all-encompassing performative reflection of the client's predicament. The divination experience seems to have a more forceful influence on clients in inducing them to follow a suggested course of action, at least when compared to the contractual exchanges with psychologists or social workers. For the drama that results in enacting the alleged cause and solution to a problem during consultation with brujos tends to leave little room for dissociating the different levels of reality that are bought together. At least under the effect of the divination performance, whatever the spirits and brujos enact is perceived as a totalizing reality, an all-or-nothing experience.

On one occasion, León, a handsome police officer in his thirties, came to consult Haydée, fearing the loss of his marriage due, as he put it, to his "angry, uncontrollable" wife. León, who was quite desperate at that moment, heard a heartfelt prediction delivered in a lecture style by Haydée, who, inspired by the wisdom of the spirits and her insider's knowledge of the legal system, was able to make a compelling connection between the hostility he was feeling toward an ex-lover, the legal ramifications of that failed relationship, and his powerlessness to straighten out his relationship with his wife. In a subtle, nonjudgmental way, Haydée's forecast was tinged with an edifying tone aimed at making him understand the kinds of feelings his present wife must be experiencing toward a child León had fathered with another woman while married to her. In addition, the child's mother was filing child support claims against León in her child's name, which obviously caused León substantial marital problems. The first part of the treatment, therefore, included the preparation of a trabajo that was meant to sweeten his wife toward him, especially since she had become estranged from him after this child suddenly popped into her life. Haydée solemnly stated, "This trabajo is made to unite a matrimony; you love each other, but this problem with this illegitimate child you had with another woman is causing lots of bitterness between you."

A second trabajo was aimed at neutralizing his ex-lover's interference in his present marriage. While preparing it, Haydée continued the divinatory process, unraveling his many other previous extramarital affairs and the problems they posed, and then stated, "This trabajo is for the one who meddled in your marriage. If the husband doesn't love the wife, she feels it and suffers. I forgave my husband two times . . . [Interrupting to finish the trabajo:] Give me the name of the mother of that child. I'll put her back to back with you [i.e., estrange her from you for good]. But you used to love her; wearing your police officer uniform, you thought you could profit from [women falling for your looks], and you had two, three women at a time. You didn't think about the consequences. [Back to mixing the ingredients of the trabajo:] This is powder of sulfur, now powder Arrasa con Todo [Wipes Out Everything]." To make her case about betrayal even stronger, Haydée told him about her own experience as a betrayed wife who had to struggle with her first husband's infidelities. "We wives have to accept whatever our husbands do in the streets. These are mistakes, but we can forgive one mistake, even two. But after the third . . . I threw him out."

León was mute, his eyes lowered in shame and consternation. As if in a court of law, Haydée—acting as his defense attorney in front of a sort of cosmic jury—verbalized Leon's deep repentance: "He regrets it, he is sorry, he regrets being unfaithful, is it or isn't it right? You almost lost your marriage because of that, do you know? You regret the mistake you made, right?" Immediately, taking the child's perspective, she then continued: "But no, that child is not culpable; he needs to be treated well, needs to be loved as [you love] your other children. More than that, I would say to you, León, that you should give more love to that child than to the others. The others have the love of their father in the house—warmth, love, passion, and tenderness. That child is left without a family, sees you only when you look for him. And giving only twenty or thirty pesos a week is not true love for a son—not in these days we live in. The child is not to blame; you have to give him more." Assuming the client's perspective again, she continued her vision: "But if the child's mother continues bothering you, you'll have the obligation to turn to other means, as you already have done, right?" Haydée then asked him if he had already gone to the social services courts. But before he could reply affirmatively, she already "knew" the answer and said, "But they didn't do anything. They didn't do anything because the very supervisor is a friend of hers. But do you know that you can present a *moción por derecho propio* [motion on your own behalf] to prevent that señora from bothering you?"

Complementing this legal advice, given as a trabajo was being made to sever for good the ex-lover's attachment to León, Haydée performed another trabajo, this one aimed at restoring Leon's loving relationship with his wife. "This is to unite a couple, not to curse them. With a leaf of *higuereta* you will step on [control] your wife to make her stop distrusting you, León. To smooth your relationship she needs to be controlled, for she is right to be angry with you." Haydée reminded him that his wife had obviously felt betrayed. Voicing the wife's lamentations, Haydée then added, "How much it hurts. That child is the product of a betrayal." When the trabajo was finished, to protect her client's secrecy and to avoid having his wife discover the trabajo aimed at controlling her, Haydée suggested that he leave it in the altar. As he placed his bundled trabajo beside Marta la Dominadora and next to the trabajos that had been left by other clients, Haydée said, laughing, "You are going to step on your wife! [Implying that his wife should not know about it:] She believes in brujería. If she finds this trabajo you'll be in trouble. [Pointing to a santo standing on the floor:] Leave it there with San Judas Tadeo, [the patron] of difficult cases, for nine days."

Doctors of the Soul and the Pocket

Brujos help their clients to adapt to their social and emotional circumstances while ensuring that they take advantage of all the resources, both material and spiritual, available to them. Yet for brujos a distinction can hardly be drawn between economic and spiritual prosperity: they are seen as inseparable. Economic well-being attests to spiritual and emotional bliss and vice versa, so brujos address every aspect of their clients' well-being with the same attention in a holistic manner. If a client has a problem related to a government agency, a brujo intervenes through a trabajo while also contending with institutional constraints. Trabajos are thus aimed at influencing the actions of people who although total strangers to the client, might play a fundamental role just because of the positions they hold.

Carmen, an old woman who has lived with her partner for more than twenty-five years, was extremely anxious about his approaching death as, legally, he was still married to another woman. When Carmen came to consult with Haydée, she expressed in a symbolic way her concern about the inheritance problems she would be facing after he died: "That woman would claim his body and would hold the wake in her house." Cutting her short, Haydée stated, "You want him to divorce her. I will intervene to help your husband divorce her; otherwise you won't be able to enjoy all your rights. He says you are his woman, but she is his wife according to the [legal] papers. . . . You'll have to put a battery up his ass to get what you want, he won't do it voluntarily."

Having thus bluntly verbalized the fears that were disturbing the client's peace of mind and which she could only express via tropes such as the wake, Haydée took an active role in devising a viable, legally sound solution—one that took into account the weakness that prevented the husband from divorcing his wife in the first place. Agreeing with Haydée's depiction of the problem, Carmen said, "I know that. I had already told him many times and he does nothing. He says [mimicking his voice], 'One of these days! You don't help me, you don't come with me.' I say, 'Shit, you're not a child!'" Without waiting for Carmen to finish her account, Haydée started dictating to Reina the recipe for a trabajo that aimed at cutting (on the transcendental level) the legal ties that still bound the man to his first wife. As the relationship would be severed on the transcendental level, so their ties would be cut in this world as well. Reina began to write. Carmen was to take the recipe to a botánica and buy the products for the trabajo, then bring it and the products she purchased so that Haydée could make the trabajo at the altar the next time she came. While Reina was writing, Haydée added some explanations about the products that Carmen needed to buy:

> Abre Camino [Path Opener; a manufactured essence]; a photograph of the husband; Abre Puertas [Doors Opener; a manufactured essence]; Oil of Rosemary; three leaves of *tártago,* called also brazo fuerte. When you buy it, buy it in the name of that *cabrona.* A small locket; Water of Sunflower; a small can of sardines—you'll be puzzled, but it's for divorce. And bring me one—they sell three for one peso— of those oval ones, so I can eat one with white rice [laughs]. Now the powders: Polvo Volador (Flying Powder), "The Señora Can but She Doesn't," Water of Mint, three leaves of *llantén,* but don't buy it [the llantén]. I'll give it to you from my yard. Three lemons; and the name of that cabrona because you don't have her photograph. And last, a red ribbon to lash the whole trabajo together. I will charge less for this than the lawyer will charge him for the divorce, which, I assure you, will be by mutual agreement. He will initiate it, but she'll agree to it. You'll see. And it'll happen before January.

Even when the advice given by brujos is practical, it carries supernatural force. Legitimized and empowered by guardian spirits and a host of muertos, any premonition or advice voiced by brujos while in trance is no ordinary kind of suggestion and thus should not be taken lightly. For they may attain the status of magical wishes or prophecies, which, depending on higher-level designs, will surely occur at any given time. Brujos usually brag about their power to *reclamar,* or endow, wishes with magical powers and make things happen if they only wish or think about something, saying, "Yo reclamo y veo" (I wish and I see). This can also become a threat that can intimidate potential enemies or even clients who might turn against them at some point in their lives. But the power of brujos to reclamar can have positive effects as well. Invigorated by the power to envision positive outcomes at will, brujos can also transfer it to clients, who are thereby reinforced spiritually to fight any adversity that might be causing them worldly or cosmic misfortunes, as the next case clearly shows.

Jessica, a confused sixteen-year-old nursing student, appeared once at the altar. It required great effort to make the trip as she had little money for transportation. She finally arrived after overcoming all kinds of physical and logistical obstacles—several buses, walking the last mile with a cast on her leg. When Jessica entered the altar she was exhausted, breathing with difficulty. But most of all, she seemed utterly depressed. Haydée immediately asked about her mother. Having heard that her mother was neglecting her and refusing to give her any money, Haydée suddenly rang the small bell on her table, signaling that what was about to follow was the result of a sudden vision inspired by the words of the spirits.

> You are angry and thinking about suicide; and now answer the truth, have you had thoughts about selling your body? Don't do it! You'll catch AIDS with the first one if you sell your body. Evil spirits want to see you 'up and down' [on the street like a whore]. You have negative thoughts; don't do it. . . . I want to see you as a nurse, a nice young woman. If I tell you, would you be willing to pour on yourself some [spiritual] stuff—herbal [solutions] and a cleansing bath? Here, take ten pesos to buy the stuff. Your mother shouldn't deal with you in this way, but leave that to me. And if your mother insists on refusing to drive you to school—especially now that you have a cast—and refuses to give you money for the bus, you tell me, and I'll tell her that you can file against her at social services.

All those present became very emotional at hearing Haydée's passionate words, which seemed to have touched the young woman deeply. In subsequent visits Haydée took care of Jessica's leg when it became infected under the cast, charging her nothing for this or for the despojos and trabajos she performed. After several despojos and healing rituals, Jessica underwent an amazing transformation. Less depressed than when she first came and with a big smile, she expressed her willingness to continue with her studies. She soon got a job as a hairdresser's assistant, thanks to one of Haydée's connections. Cured of her infection and encouraged by her ability to earn some honest money, she felt that in Haydée's altar she had found a second home if she ever needed one and began to call Haydée

"Mom." Jessica became one of the group of clients who drop in on Haydée just to say hello and visit for a while.

When Haydée became Jessica's doctor of the soul and body, job hunter, advocate of training school, and defender of her rights as a child, I saw a new, softer side of Haydée. Haydée, like a tightrope walker, chose her words and demeanor carefully, aware that an apparently insignificant slip could throw Jessica into a dangerous, maybe even fatal path. But in less acute cases, brujos often take the attitude of a spiritual coach, driving their clients to fight their internal fears or lack of self-esteem by becoming fervent advocates and defenders of their rights.

In these cases, the defining quality of the divinatory performance is the direct, often harsh and painful style in which brujos voice the words of the spirits to their clients. I emphasize this feature because it characterizes the general tenor of consultations with brujos, setting them apart from any other type of consultation with care providers. If rude and abusive expressions are heard during a consultation, brujos generally point out that it is not their own choice of words but that of the spirits, who above all wish to put things in clear, straightforward ways. Amazingly, straightforward depictions of their situations produce neither anger nor desperation in clients. On the contrary, listening to their problems rendered bluntly by brujos seems to produce a positive reaction, as we saw in Jessica's case. Perhaps brujos can speak the socially unspeakable, regardless of social decorum, because, in the idiom of brujería, the clarity of their words—when voicing the spirits—"opens up even the most entangled paths."

When Miriam, a twenty-year-old yuppie, came in the altar smiling and full of confidence, she heard the following painful depiction of her "real" situation during divination: "Miriam, nowadays you don't have anything. You have no job, no car, no house, no boyfriend. You're, like, forsaken in the world." If the forecast would have ended there, it could have sent poor Miriam into despair. But it did not end there. After a few more cards were read, Haydée said, "But you're not alone, because you have me [rings the bell, implying the words of the spirits]. Don't cry, They say that these tears that you're now spilling you should have spilled before." At this cathartic moment, Miriam changed her initial arrogant attitude and was ready to examine closely what was really behind the facade she presented. Stripped of her social pretenses, she was able to contend with her most unappealing parts: her insecurity about a boyfriend, her feared pregnancy, her overall lack of luck, and her imminent financial downfall. During this lengthy exposition, Haydée suddenly interrupted her with a vision: "You'll get a job!" She continued the divining process through a series of questions that she answered. "Have you applied for one? In the government, right? You'll get a white card offering you an interview. And you'll be asked to come. Then you'll get another recruitment card; you'll get accepted, and then you'll move up to a supervisor position. But you, like me, are *come-mierda* [vulgar expression for "arrogant"; lit., "shit-eater") since we have studied and prepared ourselves. The spirits say, 'Don't worry . . . you'll get that job.'"

The divinatory performance not only entails the venting of often excruciating or embarrassing aspects of clients' lives but also leaves no room for pleasantries. For in the process of defending their clients' rights as neglected daughters or in capturing the desires of unemployed professionals, the mediation of brujos between spirits and clients is in itself the beginning of a healing or restorative process. Puzzled about the motives driving psychologists and medical doctors to consult with brujos when their own systems could have provided the answers they were looking for, I asked myself, what is the added value of brujería for people who are part of the mainstream care system? One of the advantages of brujería seems to be its timeless and spaceless cosmology: any problem can be traced not just to one source but many, not to one realm but several; and its solution can depend not only on what had been already laid down, but on prospective paths not yet recognized. Indeed, unlike mainstream law and health care professionals or social workers, brujos do not follow proscribed ways of proceeding and therefore are free to respond in an impromptu manner to what the spirits reveal during the divinatory performance, as well as to the specific character and emotional situation of clients.

I remember my surprise at seeing a physician who came to consult with Haydée when he was diagnosed with cancer. Although aware of the statistical success rates of the various treatments he had been offered, he was unable to decide which would save *his* life. In spite of the doctor's belief and trust in scientific knowledge, he searched for an alternative form of reasoning to find the "real" answer to his dilemma. Knowing the hard facts was not enough. This client was still confronted with uncertainty as to the outcome and thus consulted with a bruja to help him with a difficult choice, sorting out possible, equally rational modes of solving his predicament.

Another side to the effectiveness of brujos lies in the artfully persuasive mode of conveying practical advice to often confused, disoriented, or misinformed clients. Once a solution has been envisioned, brujos coach their clients in the appropriate moral and spiritual disposition required to take full advantage of, say, new opportunities in regard to work or love and to prevent future misfortunes. But the manner in which these directives are given varies greatly in tone and mood, according to the specific character and needs of the client. One can hear brujos exchange relevant information with their clients and pass on invaluable advice and values in the form of predictions, prophecies, and forewarnings that are intertwined with aphorisms, narratives of personal experience, and sermons.

Such was the case when Lily, a beautiful young woman in her twenties, came to consult after she had been told—on a previous visit—that she would get a new job and that her husband would not leave her even though he had already filed for divorce. All these were decoded from the clave that had been performed for her at a previous consultation. In light of the accuracy of Haydée's predictions, Lily returned a few weeks later. On this occasion she heard new premonitions about a baby that she would conceive with the magical intervention of Haydée. But before Haydée went on about this matter, she elaborated on an important issue left unresolved from the previous visit. Meticulously reminding Lily about the legal rights she had as a dismissed employee and the eventual material or social obstacles that might hinder their actualization, Haydée insisted on making sure she would get the rightful unemployment compensation from her previous employer. "Did they pay you what they had to pay you in the other job? When are they going to pay? Remember that you are the one who has to be on top of them until they pay you. How many years did you work for them? Three years? *Pero tenías hora de entrada pero no de salida* [You always worked extra hours and never left right at the end of the workday; lit., "You used to have a beginning but not an ending time for your work"]. If you figure all the extra hours that you have worked, it will add up to two more years, and they didn't pay for them, and you were in charge of that office. [Addressing me:] She's an accountant. [Shifting to a premonition:] Now, you're going to work in a factory up there [in the office], and those women downstairs [in the production line] will envy you; one of them will want your job for a relative."

At this point Haydée's speech shifted again to a moving personal account.[4] The previous voice—that of a calculating, savvy bruja—became a revealing confessional tone that aimed at pointing out the business ethics that ought to guide this accomplished, though inexperienced, client in the future. Haydée delivered an affable sermon, filled with tender remarks about her own previous coworkers, suited for Lily's future job environment as envisioned during the divination process. Because social conflict had been predicted, the meticulous exposition of a moral working code, based on respect and the protection of less privileged workers, had a purpose. Through her narrative of personal experience, Haydée was gently coaching Lily on the ways she might want to treat workers under her if she wished to gain their respect and love. Lily was to follow this basic attitude—Haydée implied—if she was to avoid encountering ill-willed co-workers who would sabotage her position at her future place of employment and thereby change the outcome of the ominous picture painted by Haydée's premonition.

Several thousands of Puerto Ricans—between 10 and 45 percent of the total migration flow between the island and the mainland—participate in a revolving door or circular migration between the island and the mainland (Duany 2000:19) with the aim of improving their business or employment prospects. For example, Duany (2000:6) reports that according to the 1993 census of the U.S. Department of Commerce, "in 1990, more than 321,000 residents of Puerto Rico, or nine percent of the total population, had been born abroad—most of whom were persons of Puerto Rican parentage born on the U.S. mainland." In addition to the cultural issues involved, this migration also produces awkward situations for people under federal plans or Medicare. In such cases, brujos operate in the interface between social security and other social and medical services on the mainland and the island, thereby maximizing their clients' chances in the gray areas of institutional jurisdiction. Haydée followed in great detail the peregrinations of Mariana, a woman in her forties, through various state agencies in New York and on the island after Mariana discovered that she was infected with AIDS. Mariana had recently returned from New York, where she had filed her case with Social Security. She came directly from the airport to Haydée's altar for a follow-up consultation. Haydée welcomed her: "I told you that you'd come back before August—and here you are! You had to come back, proof of your faith and a testimonial [of my visions]. Everything is positive [around you]. You're better. Although you have AIDS, the *teces* [healing teas] I gave you are healing you. The drugs you take make you constipated. Use Metamucil. I have worked with doctors, so I know about material as well as spiritual cures. Eat *guineos* [plantains] and mango, they're good for you." On this occasion Haydée also gave Mariana an additional recipe "for controlling and healing the immune system."

Mariana then discussed her health problems at length, her possible employment on the island, and the available social services. Immediately afterward, Haydée expressed a vision—part vengeance, part practical information, but mostly a reassurance that Mariana was under the aegis of Haydée's protecciones and cuadro: "Your man will die first—he has tuberculosis. . . . You're not alone; you're with your guardian angel and my good protecciones. There will be a *desenlace* [denouement]; you'll get some money when he dies, but you're not married to him [implying that she has to do something about it]. He is a scoundrel and he'll confess [that he passed the virus] to you. You came back to the island during this rainstorm, crying. [You came back] with a mission, and we'll achieve it."

In search of ultimate justice in this world, brujos promise their clients to intervene in their names and for their own good among the living, the dead, and the spirits. As I have shown, helping clients to maximize their chances by encouraging them to take advantage of resources available in the system is done with a sense of ultimate moral right. Likewise, empowered by the voices of spirits, brujos act as brokers between business managers and employees and between providers of government social services and citizen-clients. As spiritual entrepreneurs, their intervention is always in harmony with Spiritist morals and the parameters set by the legal system, both of which they take into account in examining the particularities of each case brought to them. Contrary to lay beliefs, brujos are hardly at the margins of society; rather, they are at the very center of contemporary life as the material and spiritual mediators between the system and individuals, as well as unofficial brokers between the welfare bureaucracy and its subjects.

CHAPTER

EIGHT

ADVOCATES AND LAWYERS
OF ANOTHER ORDER

....

The Law of Love

The ultimate law that governs the spiritual sphere, the Law of Love, supersedes all human-made laws. All actions are to be measured against the life and teachings of Jesus, and it is left to the conscience of each person to determine the righteousness of an action. Even when human laws protect one's actions, it is in the spiritual sphere that these actions will eventually be judged. Given the Spiritist Law of Cause and Effect and Law of Reincarnation, the consequences of one's actions might reverberate for generations. Thus debts to society are expected to be paid at the spiritual level as well. Ultimately, regardless of one's social position or profession, the social and spiritual worlds are interconnected. In this sense brujería in Puerto Rico seems to recuperate, in the words of Anthony Giddens (1991:207), the "moral meaning of existence which modern institutions so thoroughly tend to dissolve." Because some conflicts may have originated in previous lives, transactions among offenders, victims, and the judicial system are conducted through a combination of worldly and cosmic rulings. These rulings emerge during trance and contain ethical advice as well as practical ways to follow it.

Rumors about brujos' connections—real or fabricated—with judges, prosecutors, policemen, defense attorneys, and government agents (all of whom might also be clients) enhance their resources and reputations. These connections can be actualized in real cases when needed, or they can just be mentioned when a deterrent force is enough. The mere presence of a brujo or bruja in a courtroom (or merely the mention of his or her name) might serve as a deterrent. Witnesses, lawyers, and judges may be swayed to turn matters in favor of the brujo's or bruja's friends.

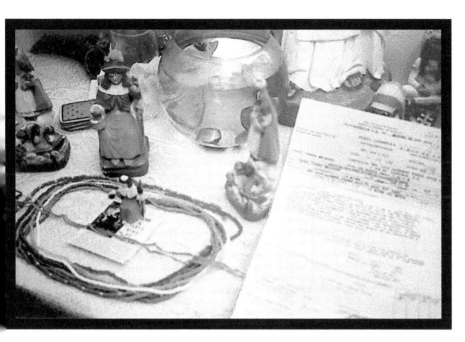

8.1 Court papers are empowered with an escapulario and El Niño de Atocha.

Sometimes long-distance magical interventions can achieve this purpose. For example, brujos can help from their altares by "tying the tongues" of witnesses, "hiding" victims from persecutors, and "sweetening" the disposition of judges or administrators in favor of their clients.

Legal documents might be brought for the bruja to examine. If necessary, these documents may be "prepared" and then placed beneath the figurine of a deity such as the Buddha or San Judas Tadeo for protection. Brujos thus can operate behind the scenes, pulling strings and advising their clients as invisible jurisprudence experts and advocates. In matters of civil, family, and criminal law and in dealings with state agencies, it is therefore a wise decision and a good investment for clients to maintain close relations with brujos.

In legal matters such as drug prosecutions, restraining orders, crimes of passion, spousal abuse, or inheritance and labor disputes, brujos help their clients to manage their affairs, combining the functions of the liberal professions with their mediumistic expertise in the spiritual realm. During the day, brujos might recommend efficient lawyers or friendly court clerks to their clients and during the night, intervene in court proceedings through their altares. Contrary to centuries-old representations of brujos as lawbreakers of some sort, Puerto Rican brujos today seem to defend the law. Not only do they manage the best outcome for clients, but in most cases they prevent clients from breaking the law in the first place. Like an external social and moral conscience directing their clients' actions, brujos prevent criminal acts from occurring by offering alternative courses of action. And if clients have already broken a minor law, the ability of brujos to "see" and "hear" everything, even their thoughts, is extremely effective in extracting confessions of the truth during divination.

In these cases, for example, brujos will compel their clients to negotiate a fair settlement with the injured party before the case reaches the court. Indeed, the spiritual guidance of brujos, which stresses opting for spiritual justice in lieu of its mere material execution, might often suffice as a deterrent powerful enough to thwart possible criminal actions. Given that ill intentions might be known to the spirits, clients know that the consequences of not complying with their warnings could be more devastating than failing to comply with human laws. As spiritual lawyers and judges, brujos draw on the cosmic Law of Cause and Effect and the Law of Love, which propel them—following the Spiritist ethos—to weigh carefully all the possible material and spiritual components of a conflict.

Protecting Human Laws

Risky human endeavors call for extra protection. The spiritual world can be summoned for this purpose. Brujería can be used during police actions for various purposes, such as to protect police officers from being killed by shielding them from their attackers, to help them hunt criminals, and to open their eyes and ears. Several police officers of various ranks came to consult with Haydée, and the risks of their profession inevitably came up during consultation in addition to other issues they had come to resolve. For example, Haydée's niece, Lisandra, who worked as an undercover agent in a special police drug unit, was often in Haydée's mind. While waiting for a client to come to the altar, Haydée said,

> I have to call my niece, the police detective, to talk to her about something she had wanted to ask me. [Emotionally, in a spiritual state:] Shit! I thank you [looking up as if talking to God] for everything, for what I had asked. For six months I have fought [spiritually] with that [helping Lisandra chase down a criminal], but last night I accom-

plished it. [Before Lisandra worked as an undercover agent] they [her colleagues] had made Lisandra's life difficult; she had been assigned to tactical operations, and a sergeant was fucking with her [*jodiendo,* vulgar for "bothering"] — I took her [with the aid of material and spiritual connections] out of there. Then she asked me to help her [to arrest] some people [drug dealers] and, see, last night she accomplished it, and they didn't kill her [thanks to my spiritual intervention] in this maneuver. I have been telling her, "You'll succeed" . . . and she was not killed. I have to call her now because she sent me a message [on her beeper] saying she was leaving for New York [on a secret mission].

Most likely, police officers who do not have brujos in their families, like Lisandra does, would seek to be included in brujos' close circle of acquaintances. The bendiciones that brujos are assumed to be endowed with could provide for them as well, if needed, protecting them from the possible dangers inherent in their work. For example, a police lieutenant once came to one of Haydée's veladas and, befitting his rank, was received with great honors. When a person holding a high position in any field is seen interacting with brujos, the immediate assumption is that this person had attained such a prestigious position only with the strong backing of the spiritual world, which evidently has protected him from the negative energies he would have had to come into contact with over the years. The first thing the lieutenant had to do was to undergo a thorough despojo. Unlike others in a velada, who are called publicly to receive a message from the spirits, all those involved with the law are given private messages. In one such confidential moment, after Haydée introduced me to the officer by saying, "She's with me" (to reassure him of my total discretion), Haydée told him, "How come you can control criminals and you can't control your own family?" Having heard what seemed a blunt and provocative but accurate diagnosis, he immediately set up an appointment for a private consultation that week.

Because criminal lawyers are exposed to life-threatening situations, they too are likely to seek the protection of the spiritual world. One way is to become mediums themselves. Camilo, one of Tonio's clients, is a district attorney who, with Tonio's guidance, was trying to develop his cuadro. In the belief that a strong cuadro would better protect him in his criminal law practice, he maintained close relations with Tonio to enhance his spiritual powers. Tonio also helped Camilo with his cases, advising him what action to take and from whom to distance himself—in legal terms—and which forces to summon—in transcendental terms.

Tonio also sent several of his clients who had legal problems to Camilo. Camilo charged them lower fees because they were recommended by his padrino. Conflict arose when Tonio felt that Camilo—his most loved ahijado, or spiritual godchild—had been ungrateful to him. Tonio complained that Camilo had attributed to himself alone the success of the cases he pursued, ignoring the trabajos Tonio had made for their mutual clients before the legal proceedings. Tonio was so distraught by Camilo's ingratitude that every time Haydée and I came to visit him, he would complain about him, making sure Haydée, too, was warned against Camilo —to whom, he knew, she also directed clients. In various ways, Tonio suggested that if Camilo did not come to his senses, Tonio would disavow him, meaning that he would not share his spiritual power with him anymore, and as a result we should expect to see Camilo's business decline rapidly. Why would a brujo resent the ingratitude of his godchild? Although I did not ask Tonio this question, my observation of similar situations suggests two, apparently contradictory explanations. One explanation relates to the moral tenets of Spiritism—which condemn ingratitude—the other to the dynamics of power between brujos and their protégés, which are informed by a strong sense of hierarchy and loyalty and can be summarized as follows: although brujos might be good to you, beware of falling out of grace with them.

Crime Prevention, Pardons, and Restitution

One morning a young woman, Joanna, came with her child to see Haydée. Because Haydée was ill that day, Nina, her housekeeper, sent the woman away with an apology, as she did the other clients who came that morning. But this woman would not leave. Communicating through the gates—as I had to do the first time I came to meet Haydée—she asked Nina to tell Haydée that it was a very urgent matter. On being admitted to the living room, where Haydée was lying on a sofa and chatting with me, she told Haydée that she had been on her way to the police station when she realized that before doing anything else she first needed to consult with Haydée, so she turned back to see her. In a convoluted narrative, Joanna tried to explain to Haydée the core of the problem. That very morning her former husband had come to visit their daughter, and finding that Joanna had another man in the house, he immediately threatened her with a gun.

Although they had been divorced for some time, he ordered her not to see the man again. Haydée promptly applauded her decision to come first to consult, even insisting that she be seen. It was an especially wise decision given that in these cases one usually goes first to the police. "You were guided by your *protecciones*," Haydée told her. "Seeing" that the former husband would become violent if she brought charges against him, Haydée said, "Don't even *think* about filing against him. He might kill you." She advised her instead to move for a few days to a friend's house with her daughter and then devised a plan that included spiritual as well as material protections.

In a similar way, a timely consultation before a crime could be committed helped a man to resolve his conflicts on a spiritual level. Ángel, a government employee living in a housing development, and his wife came for a consultation in a total state of despair because of the continuous conflict—verbal and physical—he was having with the members of one of the largest families in the housing development. Ángel was the victim not only of his neighbors but also of his own thoughts: he wanted to leave the neighborhood altogether, yet envisioned how he would stay and personally carry out revenge. Through the divining process he was given the solution: have a despojo performed for him so as to cleanse him of hostile energies and clear his path to a renewed sense of well-being and have trabajos made to punish his troublesome neighbors instead of killing them. Ángel and his wife came for the second time that week, bringing a calf's tongue from the supermarket along with peppercorns, tart green oranges, and other kinds of ritually "hot" ingredients from a botánica. These elements would be combined together with spells and candles in a trabajo malo against his neighbors who, in Haydée's words, "have been bothering Ángel for a long time." "This trabajo is 'heavy duty' [her English] in order to prevent them from pestering Ángel with their aggressions. It [the trabajo] will be taken to the cemetery."

Haydée suggested making the trabajo for Ángel and his wife after she "saw" in the cards that Ángel's neighbors were indeed making his life miserable. Empowered with the spirits' voices, Haydée expressed Ángel's anger and internal wish to kill them. Almost in tears, Ángel pointed to the unfairness of their attack: "They have provoked me when in fact I was minding my own business." Haydée then asked sarcastically, "And you were going to go to jail for *that* garbage? They are not worth going to jail for." She promised that they would be punished instead by supernatural forces in a way that would hurt them even more. "With the aid of San

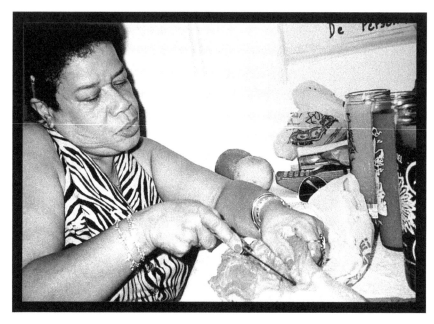

8.2 "This trabajo is heavy duty."

Miguel Arcángel, who cuts everything [i.e., invalidates curses], you'll be free. They will not bother you anymore. Now as this candle is burning, *they* will burn—and may they ask for forgiveness. And now you make your petición [wish, plea]."

Although police officers, abused women, and criminals alike come to brujos for protection, a line is drawn: if the action of brujos is sought as a cover for felonious acts, then their involvement becomes conspiratorial. Thus those who have already engaged in illegal actions are not helped unless they repent and express a wish to radically reform their lives. Demonstrating that spiritual interventions could not be "bought" or recruited for unlawful purposes, Haydée once told me about "a man, very elegant, from Collar [a wealthy neighborhood], [who] came asking me to prepare him a trabajo that would make him invisible to the police and promised to pay me $2,000 for that. I told him, 'I'll give *you* $5,000 to leave immediately!' Any day he can have me killed [for saying no to him]. But he's afraid of me. [Addressing me:] Remember, 'De cualquier malla sale un ratón' [A mouse can come out from any mesh, a proverb related to the unpredictability of people]."

According to the ethos of espiritismo, a person who might have violated both spiritual and human laws should be helped, healed, and enlightened by those who have achieved a higher spiritual stage. Since there is no way to go unpunished, emphasis is placed on bringing out each person's potential for rehabilitation as well as on alternative forms of compensation or restitution—as established by the philosophy of free will in espiritismo. Doris, the healer-medium mentioned above, had worked extensively in rehabilitation clinics. In her view, people who trespass societal laws are in fact "spiritually ill." Clarifying her position on these matters to me, she said that although they are treated by "psychologists who give them drugs that put them to sleep, they're in fact possessed—they have a wickedness that they've caught from who knows whom and where." She mentioned the case of an adolescent—from a well-to-do family—who had been heavily involved in using and selling drugs. He was brought in for a consultation by his father in a last attempt to help him. Because the boy was involved in drugs, Doris explained, she stipulated the conditions. "I told the father, 'If [your son] wants to get out of the *fango* [mud, slang for lowlife] I'll help him but not [if he's wanting simply] to hide.'" The father, who was an affluent professional, emotionally told of his son's depression and gradual involvement with drugs. It was not until Doris met privately with the adolescent in subsequent visits that she was able to heal him. During several consultations, he underwent a series of cleansing rituals, after which he received protective amulets during a rebirth baptism at a river in the rain forest. Healing him left Doris sick for a few days. "The bad energies that I extracted from him in order to cure him almost emptied me," she said.

Judicial Interference

For a few weeks, as a result of minor surgery Haydée had undergone on her foot, she received only her closest clients who came for help, seeing them in her living room, where she lay down on her sofa, instead of in the altar. One of these people was Hada, a young woman who had recently become pregnant with the aid of Haydée's treatment. She came in despair one morning to resolve a legal problem she was having with her uncle, who was making claims on the land where her house—which had belonged to her recently deceased mother—was located. Although he also had a house on the same property—originally owned by Hada's grandparents—he wished to evict Hada from her mother's house, sell it, and get the money as part of his inheritance. After learning that the uncle had just

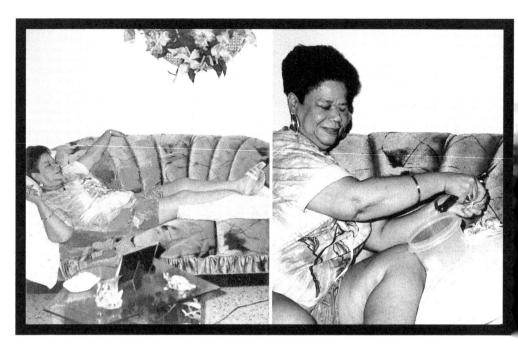

8.3 A consultation and preparation of a trabajo in the living room

filed a lawsuit against Hada, Haydée sent her immediately to the market for a head of garlic. Because Hada was a devoted client, Haydée decided to perform a trabajo for protecting her interests in court.

On her return Hada said that, unsure of what kind of garlic would be the most appropriate for the trabajo, she had purchased three. Carefully choosing the largest one, Haydée jokingly said she would use that for the trabajo and keep the others for cooking. Holding the chosen bulb of garlic as if it were a trophy, Haydée said, "This is the one I want for your trabajo." . . . [Mimicking Hada's desperate state of mind:] You're like, 'I can't deal with my life.'" Shifting to a down-to-earth tone, she then ordered Hada to "write down the names [of those involved in the grievance] on the parchment paper." Haydée proceeded to painstakingly thread each clove of the chosen head of garlic—as if they were beads—onto a ribbon, murmuring a spell after each one had been secured with a knot:

> This is a trabajo for a court case, meant to [stop] some people who are jodiendo with that woman while that house is hers and the land is hers as well. [In a self-assured tone:] Because there are people who *joden* in

this world, and people who joden others *hay que joderlos* [have to be fucked], right? [Laughs aloud, making all those present laugh as well.] [Reassuring Hada:] I will be there *en pensamiento* [lit., in thought; i.e., spiritually invoking your success with my spiritual powers]. I know where [the courthouse] is. [She recounts aloud her vision:] Marcial [a town], first floor to the right when you enter. I know it, even if I have never been there. The spirits tell me, "The constable that checks those who come in is on the right and, further, there is a sign [by the door] that reads 'Querellas' [Disputes]."

Then, reflecting on her client's conflict, Haydée said, "It's better for you that the land be divided, so your uncle will leave you alone." And continuing with the preparation of the trabajo: "How many [people involved] are they? This trabajo goes to the court *bien preparadito* [pretty well prepared, i.e., embedded with special powers]; it goes with the name of the lawyer, the name of the police officer. You, Hada, you don't have to go." Looking then at the court notice, Haydée read aloud: "'At three o'clock . . . the one who is in charge of presenting the case is Florinda Rosario.'" To Hada she said, "Write the name of Florinda Rosario together with Hada and Gerardo [Hada's husband]." Gathering the garlic string into a tight bundle and securing it with pins, she recapped, "How many people are there? Of the bad [your enemies], four; of the good [you, your husband, and your lawyer] there are three . . . this goes to the court." On concluding the trabajo and realizing that the bulb of garlic she had chosen had yielded exactly seven cloves (the exact number of people involved in the court case), Haydée expressed her amazement at what she saw as a supernatural coincidence—a sign from the spirits.

In times of family conflicts and divorce, brujos are the best defense attorneys that money can buy. They not only attend to economic and legal interests, but also to the emotional states that these might generate. For instance, José, a young man about to divorce his wife and living with another woman, came to see what the spirits had to say about his situation. In a lengthy exchange about Haydée's premonitions and José's confessions, vital information circulated in a variety of forms—each legitimated differently. For instance, warnings were empowered by the spirits, guidelines for action were based on the legal system, and persuasive personal narratives were contextualized by universal propositions about human nature— all intermingling in one complex speech event.

At one point José said, "My wife wants $500 for alimony and wants to keep the house." Unleashing a series of legal questions, Haydée asked, "Did you file for divorce? If it's by Mutuo Acuerdo [Mutual Agreement], you have to give her that." When Haydée learned that his wife had not filed for Mutuo Acuerdo but for Trato Cruel (Cruel Treatment), she asked, "You never mistreated her, so why did she file for Trato Cruel? She responded to your petition with Trato Cruel?" Then José revealed another vital piece of information that would tilt things in his favor: "She had sex with me [after we separated] in my own house, even as she filed [for Trato Cruel]. And now she canceled the request." Haydée's legal-spiritual consultation moved to another area: proof and its impact in judicial terms.

- How can you prove that she was in your house?
- She stayed until the morning and my mother and neighbors saw her.
- Did you take pictures?
- No.
- What a mistake you made! She's afraid because if she slept in your house there is no basis for Trato Cruel. But there will be litigation because there's a controversy in the middle. . . . I assume they will wait now for a two-year separation before the divorce. Now, don't agree to Mutuo Acuerdo; there are witnesses that you [came and stayed the night] in your house. . . .

Having "seen" that José still loved his wife, Haydée continued her vision and warned him, "Do you think about getting her? Don't even think about a crime of passion."

The consultation then evolved to yet another sphere. Haydée said,

The spirits say, "Whatever you didn't see then, you can't see now." When she filed for the Ley de Protección [Restraining Order] were you arrested? The police brought the citation to your home to prevent you from coming near [her], right? I'm seeing this, be careful, you know, *Todo lo que brilla no es oro* [All that glitters is not gold]; make sure she doesn't make your bed [set a trap for you][1] in order to turn the case in the courts [against you and] in her favor. Now she knows that you have witnesses, and you think the case was dismissed because the lawyer told you that; but the judge is the one who has to rule, and he hasn't done so yet. He has to determine whether the request [for a restraining order] should be dismissed because she herself violated the Ley de Protección.

Haydée concluded, "The spirits say, 'Many tears were shed and many more will be shed.' You love that woman. [The spirits say,] 'Time decides everything. That woman will be your wife, and your marriage will begin anew, [you'll begin] a new life.'" Knocking on the table, she voiced the final verdict: "The divorce [papers] will not arrive." After José left the altar, Haydée explained to Reina and me, "This fellow wanted to know too much about his wife's past. I told him, 'Don't make me speak' [tell all my visions]. He might kill her if he knew [all that I saw]; these cases can turn into those crimes of passion [we hear about in the news]."

In many cases the shifting attitudes of brujos show that they have more than a short-term concern in mind when dealing with their clients' well-being. This can make the difference between hiring a lawyer and consulting a brujo. In the following case, the victim of an unlawful act is put under the accusing eye of the spirits, who determine that she has largely been at fault and is paying for her mistakes. Although Haydée had taken a day off from work, she received Mili, who came to resolve a very urgent problem. Her sister Laura accompanied Mili. Carlos, Mili's former husband, was filing for custody of their two children after they had spent some time with him during a vacation. He refused to send them back to their mother in the United States, thereby violating an agreement made through the mother's lawyer. The sister, Laura, was supposed to put them on a plane home, but Carlos, deciding to file for custody, canceled their trip just hours before the flight.

Haydée attacked the problem from another angle, already thinking ahead to the upcoming judicial process. "Look," she began addressing Mili. "Germán [a lawyer whom Haydée knows] has a preliminary deposition today down in Serena. He's there at this moment. Go there [right now] and ask the constable for the lawyer Germán Rodríguez. You'll find him there, and you tell him that I sent you. . . . The social workers are on the third floor, in Family Relations. [Perusing the citation:] This case is being tried in Serena, and on Monday they will decide the custody case. But that wretched son of hell knew how to do it, and he did it in time, one week earlier."

Turning again to the citation, Haydée reflected a few seconds and continued planning her offensive. "That judge . . . for Monday [the day of the proceedings], we have to take her tongue and *amarrársela* [tie it up] in order to put her on Mili's side. Her name is Gutiérrez Sánchez; she is the short-haired, red-headed judge." Complementing her plan for a spiritual offensive involving the execution of a trabajo with the aid of her muertos, Haydée turned to Mili and urged her to explain her side convincingly among the living according to the rigorous standards of the legal system. "You have to know how to speak." Reina then added, "And don't dress in black—wear light colors." Completing her briefing like a good lawyer, Haydée probed her client to determine the possible allegations Carlos might make against her. To prepare Mili with counterarguments, she set to weighing all the charges that might be brought against her. Among the issues at hand were the following: "He works"; "You haven't abused them, right?" "What might the children say?"; "The neighbors might have said something"; "Remember, they will ask you why you sent the oldest son [who is a problem] before the school year ended."

At the end of the consultation, Haydée encouraged Mili to fight for her children at any cost and to avoid making mistakes like "not coming in person to take them back home because of a boyfriend who was holding [her] back there in the United States." Sensing that Mili was about to make another mistake regarding her boyfriend, Haydée, making her suggestion look more like a threat, said, "And don't make me *montarme* [ride myself, be possessed]. You know that if I did ride myself you'd be *jodida* [fucked]. I would have revealed everything [of your blunders as a somewhat careless mother]." She warned Mili not to repeat the same behavior that led her to put the needs of her boyfriend before her children. In doing so, Haydée not only reminded Mili what was really important in her life but also predicted that she would lose her children if she did not follow her advice.

Cosmic Verdicts

Brujos, believing that people have to answer to the ultimate Law of Love, are often more humanitarian judges than those who hold law degrees. By advising their clients to take a more lenient, charitable attitude toward those who have offended them, they intercede between worldly laws and spiritual ones. With the Law of Cause and Effect in mind, brujos tend, in cases in which a desirable outcome might not be within reach, to leave the ultimate punishment of worldly aggressors in the hands of cosmic laws. Tonio, for example, reprimanded Camilo, the lawyer, for being narrow-minded and intolerant when he sued one of his clients for not paying all his fees. Tonio reminded him that although the penniless woman was in dire straits, she had paid him some money and then invited him for a wonderful meal. She cooked several of the very elaborate traditional Puerto

Rican dishes eaten at Christmas. With that feast, Tonio said, "she had paid you more than what she owed you in money." Had Camilo showed more generosity, Tonio concluded, his earnings would have doubled, for the spirits would have provided him with more clients.

Exploiting or taking advantage of an offender's misfortune, even if human judges rule in favor of the alleged victim, is morally questionable according to the Spiritist ethos. Worldly punishments are sometimes the result of bigoted or unjust rulings according to other levels of existence, and thus the conscience of the victim should determine whether the monetary reparation was just or simply the result obtained by a sharp lawyer. Because the final judgment does not depend on a clever lawyer but on transcendental rulings, the individual is ultimately liable only to God.

When I lived with Basi, I had the opportunity to see how the Spiritist ethos is put to work in legal matters. At that time Basi was involved in a court case with one of her tenants. This woman, Basi recounted, arrived one day in her botánica. She was pregnant and had no roof over her head after her boyfriend had thrown her out on the street. Interpreting her arrival as answering a transcendental purpose, Basi tried to help her by renting one of her apartments to the woman. Basi soon saw that the welfare money the pregnant woman received for rent was being spent on alcohol and drugs.

After more than a year, in spite of numerous attempts on Basi's part to help her pay the rent, and only after neighbors of the apartment building complained about the disturbances that she and her shady visitors were causing, Basi sought a court order. Even near the end of the process, Basi felt that if the judge suggested she evict her tenant she would not do it. Basi had hoped that the judge would intervene either by forcing the woman to get treatment for her addiction or by having the welfare money paid directly to Basi. She would try to find a solution, a compromise for the "pitiable" woman. Profit evidently had another meaning for Basi. Indeed, recognizing how well off she was, Basi said, "I'm prosperous, and the more I give, the more I receive." She meant that her cuadro and protecciones had always helped her in difficult times and provided for her prosperity as a way of repaying her charity and consideration for others less fortunate than herself.

In similar fashion Haydée advised one of her clients, Tomasa, who had won a court case awarding her past-due rent money (plus interest) from a tenant who was a single mother on welfare. During divination, Haydée stated via an aphorism which course of action was the right one according to the spirits. "Lo mal quitado no luce" (Whatever is maliciously seized won't shine; i.e., you won't be able to enjoy anything you've achieved through unlawful or antisocial acts). As far as Haydée was concerned, given the financial circumstances of the tenant, the judge's ruling was immoral (according to the Spiritist ethos), and thus she urged her client to consider a fairer deal by lowering the amount of the monetary compensation ordered by the judge.[2] "Remember, 'Lo mal quitado no luce.' How much does she owe you specifically for the rent?"

When Haydée realized that the judge stipulated that Tomasa's tenant had to pay her past-due rent plus interest plus attorney fees, Haydée became very upset, suggesting that it was not morally right to ask the wretched woman to do that. Shifting to a personal narrative form, Haydée continued:

> Because for me, *lo que no es mío no lo quiero* [what's not mine, I don't want]. . . . You have to decide what is yours [the rent money], . . . what you are asking for. . . . You're not taking what is not yours [interest money plus attorney fees], you're asking for what is yours; the lawyer is asking for more than he should, for what is not yours, but you'll pay [the consequences]. . . . The lawyer knows how to [trick the law]. . . . "La soga revienta por lo mas débil" [The rope breaks at its weakest point; i.e., you are going to suffer, not the lawyer]. . . . If that girl takes you to the Treasury [Hacienda] or to DACO [the Puerto Rican consumer protection agency]—You didn't think about that, eh?

Voicing the words of the spirits directly, Haydée then firmly stated, "They say again—They tell me to tell you—that 'lo mal quitado no luce.' And [They tell me] that it's not you, They say again, 'It's not you, it's the lawyer.'"

Shifting again to personal narrative, Haydée continued,

> I understand that "money wants money." You see, I have no food here, Tomasa, none, and she [pointing at me] knows it, and the car is broken in the garage. But I [don't worry about] anything; I'm happy. Lo que no es mío no lo quiero. [In an admonishing tone:] If you and your husband have social security . . . why take the money from those that need it? But [I know that] greed for money. . . . That's terrible. "Cuanto uno más tiene, más quiere" [The more you have, the more you want]. That woman doesn't have even a place to fall dead.

Proving her point from yet another personal angle:

> I could charge [here] whatever I want, because whatever I do here you
> see the results. I bring back husbands. People will pay anything. But I
> don't profit from anybody because I know the kinds of sacrifice they
> have to make to pay $200 to me. Maybe they are left without food in
> their house for it. I don't take away from anybody; I prefer not to have
> food in my house myself before leaving you without your food, because
> I earn more.

Finally, in a last attempt to make Tomasa aware not only of the moral but
also the practical consequences of her unnecessary greed, Haydée ended
her own personal narrative exemplar saying, "Look how I speak to you!"

By means of the aphorism "Lo mal quitado no luce" a temporal co-
herence was created in the divination ritual, integrating all the rhetorical
strategies that were used to convince the client to opt for a morally just
decision. Each time the same aphorism was applied to convey another
idea it had created associative chains of meaning, all around its same universal, timeless truth. Contrary to the rulings of judges, the success of a
divination process in attaining the status of a cosmic verdict depends on
whether the temporal selves of the client and the bruja and the timeless
spiritual entities have managed to coalesce into a morally cohesive "we."[3]
With this goal in mind, Haydée had thoroughly examined the judge's
ruling, Tomasa's lawyer's intervention, Tomasa's financial standing and
legal responsibility vis-à-vis the IRS and the Department of Commerce
and Labor. By means of an interrogation that meshed ethical with monetary dilemmas, Haydée managed to show Tomasa how unfair and unwise
it was for her to ask the tenant to pay for the past-due rent plus interest
plus attorney fees. Finally agreeing with Haydée's and her spirits' verdict,
Tomasa decided to lower significantly the amount of money she was adju-
dicated to collect from her tenant, thus overriding the judge's ruling and
accepting that of the spirits.

Cosmic Outlaws and Remedial Punishment

Some behaviors are considered "crimes" according to the ethos of Spiritism because they violate the cosmic Law of Love and thus are liable to
be punished within the spiritual realm. Diana, a young married woman,
came for a consultation because she was having problems with her hus-

band. Unexpectedly for Diana—and for me—the focus of the divination session soon shifted to her husband's mother, who—the cards revealed—was the main cause of the recent marital difficulties. A trabajo malo was needed, Haydée stated, to punish a mother who had been *pendiente* (excessively involved, meddlesome)[4] in her son's marriage. She had interfered in their lives, ruining their relationship. "Mothers have to accept whoever their sons choose [as wives]," Haydée said. To save the marriage, Haydée first planned a trabajo bueno to *amarrar* (tie up, unite) the couple spiritually through a Spiritist wedding. A trabajo malo then would be performed to complement it. Haydée said,

> This mother, this cabrona has to be put back to back [*ponerla de espaldas*], pitted against her son. . . . Papá Dios, forgive me for this [kind of trabajo], but when a mother-in-law is bad [she has to be punished], . . . because children cannot always choose the wives that mothers want. . . . We [mothers in general] didn't follow our mother's advice, so how can we say to our children which wife to choose? "Look, [I would say to my children] you have chosen your [wife] and you eat it yourself [deal with it], and if she doesn't suit you [any longer], throw her the hell out." Mothers always back up their children, [but] they are not supposed to search out women for their sons.

Through magic, this mother who had exceeded her nurturing role and was destroying a marriage, would have to be put "back to back" with her son (see fig. 5.7 for a similar trabajo). Having attached two black wax figures at their backs, she accompanied the magical procedure with a prescribed formula in which the names of mother and son are pronounced. While tying the wax figurines, she solemnly stated, "I hereby tie back to back not wax figurines but a mother and a son—the names follow. [As if talking to an antagonistic audience:] And listen carefully, mother and son [are] tied back to back, may anyone hear it, like it or not!" Using pins to hold the parchment paper on which their names were written, Haydée explained: "And these pins are introduced in order to step on their names." And then she continued, "I hereby put all the five senses and five thoughts of [the mother's name] back to back, even if they are mother and son. And if anyone tries to pit my [son] against me, fuck them! I don't care, they can do it, because here I can untie it."

Each time a new element was added to the trabajo, its name and expected effect were mentioned.

Now, the *polvos* [powders]. I pour the *polvo San Alejo*⁵ over the heads of [names of mother and son] to drive them apart. . . . I deposit the *polvo Guerrero* [Warrior] on the heads of [names of mother and son], for them to be at war; . . . hot peppers to make their relationship hot like peppers; . . . the juice of a tart orange to make their relations as tart as this juice; . . . the *polvo de Olvido* [Forgetting]. . . . And now, the powder of a [cremated] dead man and woman. I'll put also the little nails [of the coffins] that were used in cremating them. . . . We'll take the trabajo to the cemetery after nine days. Remember to bring a black candle of San Elías, El Gran Varón del Cementerio [San Elías, the Great Male of the Cemetery], and the other [the good trabajo] we'll take to the monte [Yunque].

Addressing the righteousness of the trabajo malo, Haydée invoked an ultimate sense of justice: "I'm happy doing this; I'm happy because I know that Papá Dios will not punish me. If God wanted to punish me, he wouldn't have given me these gifts, right?" After Diana deposited both trabajos, which were supposed to remain in the altar for nine days—the "mean" one on a shelf near San Elías and the other on the floor—Haydée bade her farewell: "May your husband come back to your home, and God go with you, may God protect you."

Brujos mediate between human laws and spiritual laws in various ways. This ability to fulfill positive rational rules as well as emotional ones is an essential quality of their profession. Yet the realm that always wins out— if a choice between them needs to be made—is the spiritual one, with God as the ultimate arbiter of how conscientiously and sincerely brujos and their clients have abided by the Spiritist Law of Love.

EPILOGUE

THE HALLOWEEN EXTRAVAGANZA

··

Between Seduction and Fear

At Halloween I was somewhat shocked to see how a "real," professional Puerto Rican bruja—the one I had been working with for nearly a year—transformed herself into a pop culture, black-bonneted "witch." In preparation for this Anglo festivity, Haydée had decorated her altar and house with plastic posters of caricatures of Halloween witches (pointed chins, crooked noses) flying on brooms. She also proudly exhibited a portrait by a nine-year-old girl depicting her bruja neighbor—according to another stereotypical image of witches—as a frightening old gypsy with big red lips and covered with jewelry. As part of this middlebrow seasonal extravaganza, all the participants, Haydée's clients and close friends, celebrated "her day" by eating a white and orange, cat-shaped cake that her close clients bought in her honor at a nearby Walgreens pharmacy and by munching on candy corn that the bruja provided as seasonal treats for clients.

Obviously, although impressive to her clients, her conspicuous consumption of "witchy" media images would not have spoken to other types of guests—those who, adhering to elite, academic, or nationalist quests for essential identities, would have refused to see the event as part of what constitutes "authentic" Puerto Rican brujería and this woman as an "authentic" bruja. If anything, this event would have been dismissed for the most part as a carnivalesque mainstream presentation of the archetypal witch; or, in the words of a hypothetical Frankfurt School–inspired critic, as a clear sign of the decadence of genuine Puerto Rican folk religious practices resulting from the infiltration of foreign mass-produced images. It would have been perceived—not unlike the case of "tribal" shamans

E.1
A Halloween
"witch"

wearing Nike sneakers, or African ritual dancers in jeans and Malcolm X T-shirts—as clear evidence of the inauthenticity of both the event and the bruja.

But the fiesta espiritual, as Haydée called this event, did not end there. Soon the initial play with commercially produced images of witchcraft and magic receded, opening the stage for an awesome ritual fight between demons and enlightened spirits. Haydée in her golden gown—the color of Ochún and of her patron saint, La Caridad—once in trance, substituted the black-pointed hat with a headband, enacting (in the popular Spiritist tradition), one after the other, the Indio, the fearsome spirit of the Americas; the Madama, the old African woman healer; and Papá Candelo, the old African man, owner of muertos. Stopping at each of the participants, she voiced the spirits' messages for them and at times grabbed a cross and a rosary from her altar to perform exorcisms, praying in litany the Rosary, Hail Marys, and Our Fathers with the rest of the participants. She offered spiritual advice to some, performed despojos in the Spiritist and Santería ways, and, with the same authority as a government official, recommended to a few that they consult a physician or lawyer. As she continued the fiesta espiritual, she embodied the power of brujos past and present, commercialized and traditional, until at midnight, exhausted, she fell into an armchair.

Some might think that this bruja was by all means a postmodern one—one who collapses time and space and is involved in disembedding meanings and recombining them in novel forms. For these same reasons, some researchers might have excluded her from their research for not fitting their idea of an authentic, traditional bruja. Actually, it might be clear by now that what this bruja does—in an admittedly extreme form—defines vernacular religions in general and brujería in particular.

Authenticity in the Looking Glass

One of the tropes of authenticity is anachronism (Handler and Linnekin 1984). It is paradoxical that in a world marked by rapid change, timelessness is a desired commodity. With few exceptions, authenticity is imagined as a pristine, frozen connection between the lore of a people and a locale (see Hanson 1989). Notably, one can easily identify a host of diverse groups, such as radical intellectuals, international tourists, and researchers of culture, being drawn into this imaginary relation and sharing much of its unspoken assumptions. And in their various modes of operation and their differing practices, one can discern a shared political economy of authenticity at work (see Bendix 1997; Taylor 1991, 1994). But the most important reason for discussing authenticity here is not to show its constructed nature—that is hardly an interesting venture today—but its constitutive role in shaping the practices of vernacular religions.

In the context of globalized processes of consumption, the quest for a pristine "natural" experience is a quest that does not escape vernacular religions. It explains the success of tourist resorts that reenact an "authentic" way of life, as Edward Bruner and Barbara Kirshenblatt-Gimblett (1994:435) show, for example, in their depiction of the elaborate way in which the "colonial drama of the savage/pastoral Maasai and the genteel British" is enacted daily for an international audience of tourists and visi-

tors. "The tourists are made to feel that they are watching the Mayers [the owners of the ranch–tourist attraction] and the Maasai in their natural state" (p. 457). In staging, curating, and editing the Maasai in their natural state, one of the owners "does not permit the Maasai to wear their digital watches, T-shirts, or football socks, and all radios, walkmen, metal containers, plastics, aluminum cans, and mass-produced kitchen equipment must be locked away and hidden from the tourist view" (p. 457).

The folklorization of Brazilian Candomblé (Ryle 1987) and Cuban Santería (Hagedorn 2001; Menéndez Vázquez 1995) for tourist consumption is also a case in point. Having been under attack or condemned at various times in history, Candomblé and Santería have reached, respectively, the pinnacles of Brazilian and Cuban "heritage." The following extended case illustrates this thorny process.

In colonial times, the sacred *batá* drums of Santería were confiscated for fear of slave revolts. And although Santería practitioners had proved their loyalty to the Cuban nation when they joined in the wars of independence in the late nineteenth century, they again became the object of state persecution and criminalization during the first republic (1902–

E.2
A witchy bruja

1934) because they were perceived as a threat to "progress"[1] while the elite members of the Afrocubanismo art movement celebrated their practices for boostering Cuban national identity with idiosyncratic local color (Matibag 1996; Moore 1997). Santeros were finally vindicated when they supported Castro's 1959 socialist revolution, but it was only a few years before Castro would limit their access to ritual goods when he felt they were betraying the revolution.[2] Since roughly the 1980s, in light of increased international interest in Santería, Castro's government has begun to promote Santería in heritage-type state programs without, however, necessarily tolerating the open practice of the religion (Matibag 1996). Within the last decade (1990–2000), Santería has become a tourist attraction fully endorsed by the government (Hagedorn 2001). Indeed, based on the amount of material I have received as a scholar interested in Santería and the reports of visitors, Santería seems to have been converted into an exotic venue for lay and academic groups touring the island and has become, as well, a typically Cuban subject matter around which yearly international conferences are organized. In offering tourists as well as international practitioners various Santería-related services—for example,

initiation rites, consultations, and ritual objects—in the very place Santería originated, the promoters can guarantee a supply of the most "traditional" and "real" forms of Santería experiences for consumption at the
best prices. For example, an initiation ceremony that costs $15,000 to
$20,000 in the United States can be performed in Cuba for about $4,000
(Hagedorn 2001:220–221).

Not surprisingly, a countermovement is emerging. Some high-ranking
religious practitioners call for a return to the "real" origins of Santería. To
mend what they regard as the detrimental effects of syncretic processes
and their commodification (read: adulteration), some santeros and babalawos propose to increase the secrecy and control of the liturgical practices
of their religion. The Cuban author Lázara Menéndez Vázquez (1995)
mentions the recent "yorubización" (Yorubanization) of Santería, tracing
the invention of this term to the 1992 International Workshop on Problems of Yoruba Culture in Cuba. "Yorubanization," the author explains,
signifies the quest for recovering the ritual orthodoxy of Santería through
a "return" to Africa, particularly its Nigerian origins (p. 38).[3]

Social scientists and cultural critics sometimes share these fears, more
in terms of recent academic concerns about the potential negative ho-
mogenizing effects of globalization processes than in terms of what could
have been lost as a result of colonialism. In a 1994 *New York Times* article,
for example, a sociologist reacting to the comments of a santero in Miami
warns about the possible detrimental effects that Americanization (perceived as a globalizing force) can have on Santería and questions the future
of this Afro-Cuban religion in the context of American culture (Miller
1994). Both groups—Cuban practitioners and American social commen-
tators on Santería—seem to share an atavistic nostalgia for an "authentic"
religion, originating, for the former, among preenslaved Yoruba people
and, for the latter, among pre–American contact Cubans.

Responding to a different agenda but also motivated by the quest for
authenticity free of American influence, the "revival" of "traditional" cultural elements in Puerto Rico unfolds in national political and cultural
events. As mentioned in chapters 3 and 6, some cultural experts as well as
a certain sector of the media have ceased to perceive magia and brujería as
signs of "national stagnation"; instead these experts repackage these "traditional" practices as "traditional wisdom" and "popular medicine" for a
local public hungry for alternative healing systems. Protected by the halo
of tradition (Hobsbawm and Ranger 1983), these representations recast
syncretism in a positive light. Serving wider political nationalist agendas

of modern states in a "global ecumene" (Foster 1991), these "fragile traditions" (Errington 1989) help to construct or recover an integrated indigenous and Afro-Latin national identity.

The quest for authenticity also explains researchers' occasional expressions of disillusionment or nostalgia over the sudden realization that their fields of research have changed under the effects of capitalism. Laurel Kendall (1996:512), an anthropologist who began her research on Korean shamanism in the 1970s, comments on this commonly held perception: "I am often told that I am lucky to have worked with Korean shamans in the mid-1970s, for certainly by now such practices as I described in my dissertation and subsequent book must all have died out." Disparaging these worries, she continues, "Then, as now, I found a vital practice in the immediate environs of Seoul, invigorated by young and dynamic practitioners."

It is arguably a new realization in the social sciences that cultures— geographically forsaken as they may be—are not isolated wholes that could have possibly managed to escape being changed, even in the most tangential ways, by worldwide economic and symbolic processes. Wolf's (1982) work has been especially influential in pointing out that throughout the routes of trade between different regions of the world the lives and cultures of allegedly isolated tribes and villages were structurally modified.

Yet the purposeful incorporation of these macroprocesses in ethnographic accounts is a current preoccupation (Comaroff and Comaroff 1993; Ferguson and Gupta 1992; Gupta and Ferguson 1997; Roseberry 1989; Taussig 1987). Among other things, it points to the willingness to confront the epistemological discomfort produced by people and events that do not fit traditional ethnographic expectations that they be "unique," "pure," or "authentic" (Fabian 1983; Handler and Linnekin 1984).

These expectations, Bhabha (1994) suggests, could not but be confounded by games of mirroring within postcolonial societies, where mimicry is at once expected as a precondition of civility and feared as a subversive force that might reveal the king is naked. In this respect, "mimicry" is at the same time the means to become "like" powerful others and the menace resulting from not being "quite like" them.

Ethnographic encounters might also be mediated by ambiguous expectations of authenticity. The anthropologist Vincanne Adams (1997) candidly points out that at first she was struck by the acceptance of the Sherpas of the name given to them by British mountaineers: "Tigers of the Snow." This designation seemed to her very "un-Sherpa" as it was attached to "a people who, before the arrival of Westerners, did not climb the Himalayan peaks" (p. 92). The Halloween event I attended could be viewed similarly, as very un–Puerto Rican, even if the un–Puerto Rican-ness was undertaken by the bruja herself and not by outsiders.

A new rapprochement with the already much debated trope of the ethnographic present, its phenomenology, and its role in essentializing identities (Fabian 1983) seems under way. Especially worthy of mention are the various attempts to incorporate analytically the indeterminacies of cultural production of complex societies (Appadurai 1990, 1996; Ferguson and Gupta 1992; Gupta and Ferguson 1997; Rosaldo 1988). How does one account for the discrepancies between the expected timeless essential-ness of "Others" and the actual participation of "real Others" in a world that was supposed to be foreign to them? Maybe there is not a way to totally contain "real Others," not even through scholarly representations that "silence" their voices, as some might have feared. For in shaping their own identities, "real Others" might be willing to avidly consume foreign commodities as a way of life—regardless of expectations that they hold on to some dubious form of preindustrial purity outside of global markets (see Rowe and Schelling 1991). In line with the reflexive move in the social sciences, it is often as hard to credit "real Others" with the willingness of purposely playing the part of the Other. Furthermore, how to explain their fascination with recognizing themselves in the romanticizing eyes of foreigners or scholars, those same eyes that might be freezing them in a timeless time?

But relinquishing the academic search for authentic Others is not an easy task. Often researchers are confounded by their own expectations of genuineness and unknowingly play into a local politics of authenticity. When the anthropologist Carol Laderman (1997:336), working with tra-ditional healers in Malaysia, decided to play for other "traditional" sha-mans the tapes she had recorded of Cik Su—a female healer whom she depicted as "atypical"—she was putting Cik Su to the test. The "tradi-tional" shamans told her that Cik Su was "clever" but not to be "trusted"; and, criticizing her ways of healing, they advised Laderman to throw away the tapes of Cik Su, because they did not represent "traditional" Malay-sian shamanism. Unlike traditional female shamans, Laderman pointed out, Cik Su had adopted the ceremonial dress of men in conducting heal-ing performances. "Her spirit guide was masculine," and her "expressions of fury when under his influence were far from normal" for a female healer,

Laderman explains. "The control Cik Su exerted was unusual in a culture where flexibility is stressed" (p. 337). Implicitly espousing the negative evaluation of Cik Su by "traditional" shamans and further legitimizing it with a timeless sense of what Malaysian culture is, Laderman seems to have unwillingly ended up playing into their local politics. Cik Su's success among Malaysian urbanites is portrayed by Laderman as an anomaly because it was not based on traditional Malaysian etiological explanations of illness but on "unorthodox" methods (p. 340).

I cannot avoid noticing the similarities between Cik Su and Haydée, and I ask myself how many Cik Sus or Haydées have been disregarded or excluded from scholarly attention for not being "traditional" or for being anomalies—whatever these categories may have meant for different researchers. When are practices "typical" enough to be the object of scholarly work? As an ethnographer working in mostly urban postcapitalist and transnational contexts, I cannot be oblivious to the countless instances in which the rationale for determining who and what are the objects of research becomes problematic.

Specifically regarding the subject of vernacular religions, having done fieldwork among practitioners of various competing practices, I have learned that practitioners—even if they operate in a similar manner, say, as santeros—tend to delegitimize each other for not being authentic or knowledgeable enough in what they do compared to themselves, of course. As mentioned in chapter 4, this is also a built-in characteristic of brujería. In a competitive circle, while brujos build their own fame by means of their bendiciones, alleged attacks by other brujos increase their fame and vice versa.

Because expertise is not granted by initiation or sustained by a hierarchy of healers—as in Santería, for example—it becomes an even subtler and more malleable position to maintain. Lacking any agreed-on legitimizing authority, a researcher might very easily be driven from one religious expert to another on the promise of getting to meet the most or only "authentic" expert. Or researchers might enter unwittingly into an already controversial situation between healers (as seems to have happened to Laderman), which in extreme cases could jeopardize their work and personal relationships. In listening to the ways in which practitioners assert their expertise and power, researchers might realize that they have become pawns in their local power struggles. Instead of succumbing to this role, an important insight might be attained if researchers were aware of the role they play in defining authenticity and expertise—a role that might not have been the initial object of the study but may nonetheless be part of the very nature of the field under investigation.

The purpose of what may seem an ethnographical confession-digression is to portray the conditions under which the investigation of vernacular religious practices in conditions of high modernity and transnationalism is carried out. If the trope of consumption and syncretism or "cross-fertilization" (Laguerre 1984:131) directs the content, transmission, and prevalence of brujería, is that by definition a sign of its inauthenticity? Paraphrasing Abrahams (n.d.), folklore in the marketplace seems a contradiction in terms to many guardians of the sacred words of tradition and authenticity, for such a site implies that the most treasured embodiments of a culture are commodified and thus distrusted. Or does the ease with which marketplace forces are incorporated into brujería point to the unboundedness of magical powers? Most likely, outsiders might be engaged by the first question, but practitioners and clients might be inclined to address the second.

If brujos provide the best service for the least amount of money invested in competitively effective ways, seduce their audiences with attractive yet frightening witchy tropes, refer clients to friendly lawyers, state agents, or businesspeople, and also engage in communal spiritual exorcism and healing rituals, does this make them "atypical" brujos or, instead, simply prove the limitless aspect of their magic? In some situations and for some groups in search of authenticity and origins, ritual innovation, like the Puerto Rican bruja enacting a Halloween witch, may be seen as emblematic of its inauthenticity. Interestingly, the assumption underlying such an allegation could be shared, albeit for different reasons, by the intellectual elite and by practitioners. For the former, it may indicate a priori rejection of any practice that might contest the notion of a timeless Puerto Rican tradition. For brujos, claiming the inauthenticity of other brujos may serve personal agendas that aim to delegitimize competing healers by ways of assigning them extraspiritual motives such as profit—despite the fact that prosperity is an index of legitimate spiritual power. Accusations of false pretenses and of being driven by profit are the most powerful ways brujos have to neutralize competitors in their profession. And yet prosperity attests their spiritual power.

Local social and trade politics aside, ritual innovations like the Halloween event illustrate the intricacies involved in integrating, in this case, the local and the imported and the sacred and the mundane signs and meanings of magic. In a flash, time and space boundaries had collapsed; signs and meanings produced in the present by media and commercial forces were endowed with new meanings just by being fused with centuries-old signs and meanings of "flying witches."[4] It would seem that for observers like Laderman (1997), the Halloween event—when constrained by a priori notions of what traditional magic is—would, in effect, illustrate the "limits of magic." Yet, bearing in mind that in different situations and historical contexts, practices involving magic (such as sorcery, shamanism, witchcraft, or brujería) have absorbed selected features of the multifaceted sociocultural worlds in which they have operated, the idea of the "boundlessness" of magic practices becomes more tenable. Instead of being anchored in a specific form, magic draws on the potentialities of infinite materialization, creating new sets of correspondences in its trajectory as it irreverently crosses borders that should not be crossed.[5]

Evidently, considerations of "authenticity," defined in terms of either a fixed or a timeless form, are irrelevant to the process of ritual creativity within brujería to its practitioners and clients. Indeed, the creative power of ritual to reinvent itself, in the words of the Comaroffs (1993:xxi), "arises from the fact that (i) it exists in continuing *tension* with more mundane modes of action, of producing and communicating meanings and values; (ii) its constituent signs are ever open to the accumulation of new associations and referents; and (iii) it has the capacity to act in diverse ways on a contradictory world" (their emphasis). In a world driven by the transnational production of desires, the circulation and transmission of brujería becomes more complicated than a simple passing down of knowledge from the elders. Brujos are, like poets, "experimental practitioners [who] try to make universal signs speak to particular realities" (Comaroff and Comaroff 1993:xxii). Botánica owners and commercial entrepreneurs of religious goods provide a variety of such universal signs. Stirred by the potential empowerment that a rich supply of ritual innovations can have for increasing their spiritual capital, or cuadro, brujos are naturally eager to appropriate, transform, and recast these signs in their ever-changing rituals to enhance their efficacy.[6]

Must brujos be considered fake or inauthentic just because money, profit, and mass-produced ritual commodities are involved in their creative processes? Aware of present possibilities for enlarging the scope of their maneuvers and fame through a more effective seduction and commercialization of their powers, must these brujos be regarded as "frauds"? Or is it more fair to say that "ritual innovators" are simply redeploying variously empowered new signifiers to craft novel forms of practice (Co-maroff and Comaroff 1993:xxii)? Adams (1997) claims that the Sherpas' fascination with wearing the "Tigers of the Snow" title they were given and their wearing "Nike hiking boots, Patagonia mountain jackets, and Vuarnet glacier glasses" are markers of their "Sherpaness." As this form of mimesis "is not evidence of commodified subjectivity"—which typically would be indicative to Westerners of the loss of authenticity—but instead "is done in a manner that resonates with Sherpa Buddhism and even sha-manism," it increases their *rlung rta,* translated by Adams as "luck," "en-lightened detachment," or "being unobstructed by attachment to material forms" (p. 89).

Material rewards in the form of fees or gifts for spiritual services have been part of alternative spirituality not only in Puerto Rican brujería, but elsewhere, perhaps everywhere, from Cuban Santería to Muslim healing practices. In one sense the commodification of brujería is not new, nor is the eclecticism of its rituals. But what has changed drastically in condi-tions of high modernity, transnationalism, and globalism is the efficiency and speed with which ritual innovations travel and the readiness of state and cultural experts to endorse some aspects of brujería, mainly its ethnic elements. Under these new conditions, the entrepreneurial aspect of bru-jería finds fertile ground for its prolific, carefree, eclectic development, far exceeding the expectations held by outsiders of its remaining a fairly "ethnicized" or, to again employ Urban's (1993) designation, "marked" practice.

Although the free enterprise aspect of spiritual work has been boom-ing recently in Puerto Rico, not every ritual innovation within brujería has been valorized to the same extent. In recent years the political ambi-guity of the future status of the island has promoted the development of a new form of cultural nationalism that stresses its difference from other states of the United States while at the same time asserting this difference by measuring up to American criteria for what constitutes cultural differ-ence. Thus the autochthonous, timeless, or "folkloric" aspects of Puerto Rican culture move center stage. Instead of denigrating folkloric prac-tices as obstacles to progress, this nationalist program foregrounds Puerto Rico's criollo Hispanic heritage and, lately, highlights its Taíno and Afri-can trajectory. In a series of articles that appeared in the 1980s, the idea of Puerto Rico as housing a variety of multicultural esoteric practices is presented in a positive light. Pride replaces the criticism of the 1950s and 1960s, when the same practices were framed as superstitious and as survivals of medieval beliefs. The media's role has changed as well. Previously, journalists who presented themselves as saviors of progress and civility denounced brujería so as to help educate the masses. Now the media unravel or uncover hidden traditions and thus claim to be the saviors not of rationality and civil society but of endangered Puerto Rican Hispanic, Taíno, and African traditions. David Scott (1991:279) is right when he argues that cultural traditions "are not only authored; they are authorized."

In line with a cultural nationalistic spirit, some brujos are now featured in newspapers as heroes, as unique voices of Puerto Ricanness, and as saviors of ancient Taíno and African traditions. In this context brujos proudly consume "African"-based religious songs (imported from Cuba or New York) and exhibit Santería and Vodou paraphernalia. Strategically appropriated, some key commercialized icons of Santería, such as the seven powers and the beaded necklaces of the orishas, symbolize the strength of "African" ritual power (even without adopting the essential tenets of animal sacrifice and initiation rituals through which these symbols acquire their ritual power).

Although by now the reader may be aware of my politics as an ethnographer concerning questions of authenticity, my aim is to take these questions beyond the understanding of local politics of authenticity. Taking this ethnographic actuality as a stepping-stone for a reflexive, epistemological commentary, I aim to foreground the differential perceptions or frameworks that might mediate the understanding and experience of brujería, at least among two distinct groups—practitioners and clients, and outsiders and researchers.[7] In a modern world of global capitalism, what outsiders might perceive as deviation from tradition might be the result of the indeterminate dynamics of ritual innovation and evolution. For practitioners, the latter is an "innate" characteristic of brujería: Aren't the ways of the spirits *occult* for the layperson but *revealed* to ritual experts through divination, dreams, or visions? If so, who can stipulate whether or not a certain course of action or ritual innovation is authentic?

Although I show that vernacular religions have emerged historically as a contestation of official, often repressive forms of religiosity and healing, I cannot assert that this is what propels brujería today. The Halloween event captures in an extreme form an ongoing tendency that challenges the expectation that popular religions are liberating and transformative revolutionary forces in society (see Rowe and Schelling 1991). In similar ways, the idea that colonies will "naturally" seek sovereignty is put to the test by the great majority of Puerto Rican voters (95 percent) who reject

E.3
"I'm proud to be a bruja."

independence as a viable alternative to the island's ambiguous political colonial status.

Perhaps the fascination of a Puerto Rican bruja today with commodified versions of Anglo witches flying on brooms is liberating and transforming in her own terms. These images might be appropriated for their performative power to shape desired images of self-identity. Not that this is created in a vacuum, or that envy ceased to operate as a pretext of the new modes of spiritual empowerment. "Envy," as Taussig (1987:393–394) cogently notes, is a discourse, an "implicit social knowledge," and as such becomes "a theory of social relations that functions as . . . a presence immanent in the coloring of dialogue, setting its tones, feelings, and stock of imagery." Rather, commodified images of brujería feed in to the need for brujos to create updated images of themselves that do not necessarily betray the ways in which outsiders and insiders have historically imagined them while simultaneously playing with the magic of commodities or the "quirky flickering unity formed by thingification and spectrality" (Taussig 1992:4). Brujos seem to have recruited the "poetics of the commodity" (p. 4) to their own tactics of self-fashioning. Herein may lie their defiance. Contesting the repressive forces against innovation might thereby be a new way of envisioning liberation within brujería.

If the appropriation of Catholic narratives, Spiritist techniques, and African deities has been recognized as constituting brujería, why then not recognize bureaucratic gestures and consumer goods as part of it as well? For brujería has redefined itself, co-opting the ethos of welfare capitalism and consumerism for its practices. Making consumerism speak to the spiritual realm, unwillingly transforming it into a kind of spiritualized materialism, brujería not only has become an active yet undeclared partner and broker of mainstream Puerto Rican society but also a local provider of tactics through which the desired self-images of high modernity could be materialized.

NOTES

Preface

1. It has been remarked that even if the Catholicism of many Puerto Ricans is nominal, every Puerto Rican is Catholic. Agosto Cintrón (1996:112) found, ironically, that even those who converted to Protestantism used expressions such as "Oh Virgin" and "May the Virgin go with you."

2. *Espiritismo* refers to the belief in spirits as encoded by the French scientist and man of letters Allan Kardec. Its orthodox practice is referred to as Espiritismo Científico (Scientific Spiritism). Yet any follower of espiritismo, whether in its orthodox or popular form, is generally called—except by orthodox practitioners, as I show in chapter 2—an *espiritista* (male or female; pl. *espiritistas*).

3. Santería, also called La Religión de los Orishas or La Regla de Ocha, is an Afro-Cuban religion. *Ocha* in Spanish and *orisha* in English derive from the Yoruba word for deity, *òrìṣà*.

4. From a sociolinguistic perspective, when people in Puerto Rico label somebody who is not initiated in Santería a *santero/a*, they are actually saying that the person is not practicing a "typical" but a "foreign" form of vernacular religion. Sometimes, orthodox Spiritists refer disparagingly to a person practicing a "popular" form of espiritismo as either a santero/a or a brujo/a, as a way of delegitimizing their practices as foreign to mainstream Puerto Rico, as Cuban, African-based, "primitive," or simply "evil" (see Romberg 1998). Yet these practitioners label what they do in public—to the annoyance of Scientific Spiritists—under the general rubric "espiritismo."

5. *Brujería* is an emic or native term imported to the Spanish colonies at the time of conquest and in use ever since. Its closest translation in English is "witchcraft." Like *brujería*, curanderismo was a term used in the Spanish colonies to refer to the heretic folk healing practices of *curanderos*, "quacks" or "false doctors." When people refer to "curanderos" today they imply that these are traditional healers who live in the mountains far away from urban centers and use in their treatments only healing herbs accompanied by prayer, whereas the term "brujos" implies that in addition to healing, they have the ability to use "black magic."

6. According to Joan D. Koss (1964:5), "Witches (*brujos*) are *espiritistas* who choose to work at black magic in addition to their more altruistic pursuits. . . . It appears that every *espiritista*, after an initial period of practice, gains the reputation from some quarter of being a witch."

7. To differentiate between the negative connotations of "witchcraft" and to capture the ways in which practitioners refer to brujería, I suggest "witch-healing" as a more accurate translation.

8. Note that in Spanish *bruja* refers only to a female and *brujo* only to a male witch-healer; the plural *brujos*, however, refers not only to two or more male witch-healers but to a mix of males and females.

9. I refer to "postcapitalism," following Raymond Williams ([1976] 1983:76),

to point to the changes effected in traditional forms of capitalism by the "transfer of control from shareholders to professional management . . . or 'state-owned' industries."

10. Villas de Loíza is a development located east of Loíza, a town whose population is predominantly of African descent, but it belongs to another municipality, Canóvanas. Through my ethnographic experience I found that witch-healing is not limited by locality. Rather, it is a pervasive practice that cuts across regional, class, and ethnic boundaries. I met brujos working in places other than Loíza and met with clients who came to Canóvanas (in the metropolitan area, where I conducted the bulk of my fieldwork) from distant places on the island, such as Cayey or Aibonito.

11. Unlike the English word *altar*, Puerto Rican brujos use *altar* to refer not only to the table but also to the room in which the figurines of saints and sacred objects are located and displayed and where consultations take place.

12. The names of some places and people have been changed to protect their privacy. All the dialogue recorded in this book was spoken in Spanish, and the majority of the textual sources are in Spanish as well. All translations are mine.

Introduction

1. See Tambiah (1990) for an anthropological perspective; and Touraine (1995: 24–28, 33–34, 304–305) for a recent sociological critique of capitalism and rationality and attitudes toward religion.

2. There is some resonance here with the ideas put forward in the 1950s by the novelist Ayn Rand (1964) and the ideas later promulgated by L. Ron Hubbard (1972), founder of Scientology.

3. I thank Jorge Duany for this quote.

4. For these perspectives, see Bram (1957); Garrison (1977); Harwood ([1977] 1987); Koss (1964, 1970); Rogler and Hollingshead (1961); and Saavedra de Roca (1969).

5. See David Brown's (1999) excellent insiders' portrayal of the creative tactics that Santería practitioners need to devise in order to turn public and private spaces into new places of worship when they migrate to new urban frontiers. See also the other chapters in Orsi (1999) and Romberg (1996b).

6. For the purpose of my argument here, I encompass under "witchcraft and magic" the indigenous practices previously studied under shamanism, sorcery, witchcraft, and magic.

7. See Austen (1993) for a comparative historical treatment of the moral economy of witchcraft in Africa and Europe.

8. In Germany, Holland, France, England, and Scotland, national archives have been kept in notably good order, enabling researchers to study witchcraft accusations and their proceedings in detail and to compare them diachronically. For example, Larner (1984) was able to show the nature and dimensions of Scottish witchcraft, the periods of its peak activity through the centuries, the sites where witchcraft accusations occurred, and the number and identity of those accused.

9. See Larner (1984); Macfarlane (1970); Middelfort (1972); Monter (1976, 1983); Thomas (1971).

10. See Duany (2000, 2001) and Grosfoguel (1997) for excellent debates on the

ways in which Puerto Rico defies traditional definitions of the nation. Here I follow Duany's claim that Puerto Rico and its diaspora should be considered in assessing Puerto Rican identity and Grosfoguel's distinction between postcolonial and neo-colonial states.

11. I thank Roger Abrahams for this insight.

12. See Lionnet (1992) for similar processes in language use and in literature.

13. See Smith (1990:184) on vernacular mobilization, the role of the intelligentsia, and the politicization of culture within nationalist projects.

14. See Starrett's (1995) study on the effects of the global production and circulation of mass-produced Islamic paraphernalia on different religious experiences in Egypt.

15. For an excellent review of anthropological studies of Puerto Rican popular religions on the island and mainland, see Duany (1998).

Chapter One

1. *Trabajo(s)* is a general term that may refer to any of the types of work performed by brujos: cleansing, healing, and other practices that go under the rubric *magia* (magic). Fees for trabajos, ranging from $20 to $40—depending on the amount of time, effort, and travel that the performance of the *trabajos* require—do not include the materials used (though some of them might be supplied by brujos free of charge).

2. Bartolomé de Las Casas (1474-1566) was to have a decisive impact on the future demographics and history of the Spanish colonies, especially the Caribbean. Believing that the indigenous peoples were the lords of their land, he advised the king to free them from any form of enslaved labor and instead import slaves from Africa (Las Casas 1971).

3. For a compelling interdisciplinary study of the impact of the Inquisition on the social and political lives of marginalized groups in Spain and the New World, see Perry and Cruz (1991).

4. Based on stories told in the countryside, Garrido (1952) and Vidal (1989) show that popular devotions took many forms in Puerto Rico, from *décimas* (oral literature) to popular sayings and proverbs. Biased by Enlightenment assumptions, however, both Garrido and Vidal see these folkloric forms as inspired by ignorance, therefore implying their basic falsity.

5. See Thomas (1971) for similar processes in England.

6. Compared to English and French Inquisition trials, the "Spanish Inquisition regarded witchcraft as a form of superstition, treated it leniently, and saw many more trials of sorcerers (hechiceros) than of witches (brujas)" (Monter 1983:102). The Inquisition in Spain was suppressed by Joseph Bonaparte in 1808, restored by Ferdinand VII in 1814, suppressed in 1820, restored in 1823, and finally suppressed in 1834.

7. Here I draw from Bourdieu's (1977, 1980) notion of "misrecognition." About its place in the formation of categories, Bourdieu (1977:163) writes, "Practical taxonomies, which are a transformed, misrecognizable form of the real divisions of the social order, contribute to the reproduction of that order by producing objectively orchestrated practices adjusted to those divisions."

8. It seems that what Ramos had believed was—and those neighbors that testified against these "black sorcerers" had seen as—the materialization of the devil was in fact a goat that was being offered, as was customary in Africa, in ritual sacrifice to an African orisha. See Ortiz (1975).

9. The connection with West African spirit-possession practices is evident and is recognized by Fernández Méndez (1976). For a recent account about Cameroonian witchcraft (its alleged animal form, its location in the belly, and its genetic inheritance through females), see Geschiere ([1995] 1997). Two discourses about witchcraft converge in Puerto Rico: the West African and the Mediterranean. The similarities between West African and Mediterranean accounts of flying witches is well documented but still unexplained (cf. the stories of flying witches in Cabrera [1954] 1975; Geschiere [1995] 1997; Vidal 1989).

10. The details of this case—for example, the green candle and the banishment to Seville—are puzzling to me, as they were to the historian Perea, who mentioned that there was very scant information available.

11. Bishop Valdivia blamed the untimely deaths of his predecessors on the "diabolic workings of those non-Christians who want to live in this city as in Geneva, in ways worst than the Huguenots and atheists" (quoted in Murga and Huerga 1990:82–83).

12. The lack of historical research on these matters makes it necessary to draw from chronicles written for the king by priests such as Fray Iñigo Abbad y Lasierra ([1788] 1970) and Torres Vargas. Reports by military envoys such as Fernando Miyares González (1749-1818), a militia captain, also help to reconstruct Puerto Rico's colonial past. In his chronicles (compiled and introduced by the anthropologist Fernández Méndez [Miyares González [1775] 1954]) he included valuable information about the economic, political, and religious lives of Puerto Ricans in 1775.

13. By and large, scholarly historical works mention "unauthorized" spiritual practices by slaves or peasants only in passing, usually in figurative language and without archival references. For an eye-opening study of the different silencing practices in the production of history, see Trouillot (1995).

14. Unlike in European countries or the more vital colonies of Spain, primary archival materials on Puerto Rican vernacular religious practices are almost nonexistent. Evidently these practices were not the usual subject of institutional documentation in colonial times—except, of course, for the Inquisition or other persecutory proceedings. Due, first, to the destruction of the ecclesiastical archives during the invasion of the Dutch in 1625; later, to their incriminating nature in regard to the Spanish colonial state; and finally, presumably as a result of governmental inefficiency, these types of documentation have been lost to history.

15. See Caro Costas (1983) for the beginning of the colonization and settlement of the island.

16. "In 1765, the Island had only about forty-five thousand inhabitants" (Knight 1990:258).

17. See Knight (1990:88-119) for a comprehensive account of the intense inter-Caribbean and intraisland informal systems of trade during the seventeenth and eighteenth centuries.

18. Some aspects of the history of Puerto Rican popular devotions in the eighteenth century are well documented in López Cantos (1992) and Vidal (1986). For a

current representation of these popular devotions, see the catalog of the exhibition on popular religion in Puerto Rico curated by Alegría-Pons (1988). For an excellent study of popular devotions in Puerto Rico, see the volume edited by Quintero Rivera (1998).

19. Several authors find similar marginal forms of settlement and culture in the Caribbean (Price 1979) and Brazil (Bastide 1978).

20. This form of Catholicism was sustained in the countryside mainly as a form of anticlerical worship that took over the major functions of the church. Some analysts, such as Jaime R. Vidal (1994), argue that due to the perpetual underfunding on the part of the institutional church, it had never succeeded in controlling the faith and rituals of Puerto Ricans. For different forms of popular Catholic devotions, see Lange (1975); Nevárez Nieves (1994); Valle Ferrer (1985). Also, for the traditional art of carving wooden figurines of saints, see Curbelo de Díaz (1986) and Firpi (1973).

21. It is noteworthy that currently urbanites have adopted a form of folk healing that just involves praying. These groups are called *círculos de oración* or *sanación*.

22. See Sued Badillo and López Cantos (1986:41-42, 138-141, 151-154, 286-294) for the problematic relationship of the Catholic Church to slavery.

23. See Coll y Toste (1920:147-150) on the *carimbo* (branding iron, branding).

24. Essential differences in the required mode of conversion of the slaves brought to the Americas might explain in part the comparatively much more visible organization and persistence of African religious expressive culture in the Spanish colonies, especially the Caribbean, than in the northern colonies. According to Murphy ([1988] 1993:111), Catholicism offered a "wide gate" to entrants, admitting all those who were sacramentally initiated. Protestantism, in contrast, opened a "narrow gate" to prospective entrants, expecting a "personal conversion experience" that entailed a "sincere commitment to the example of Jesus and a working knowledge of Scripture."

25. By 1873 (when slavery was abolished) the number of slaves had decreased to 31,635 because of the export of slaves to Cuba during the 1850s cholera epidemic there and because of new laws enabling slaves to buy their freedom (Baralt 1981; Coll y Toste [1969] 1972; Negrón Portillo and Mayo Santana 1992). Overall, the proportion of black slaves in the population never exceeded 10 percent in Puerto Rico, the lowest in the Caribbean (far lower than in Cuba, where at the height of the sugar boom in the 1820s the ratio was 40 percent slaves)(see Pérez 1988).

26. The history of slavery in Puerto Rico has been recovered, especially with the aid of the archival materials collected since the beginning of the twentieth century by the historian Coll y Toste ([1969] 1972). These parochial registrations have become an important source of information for several aspects of slave life on the island. Notwithstanding these renewed efforts and even with the copious documentation of insurrection movements, a void still exists in regard to the religious practices of slaves.

27. Díaz Soler ([1953] 1974) claims that slaves in Puerto Rico lost all connection with their African traditions. Negrón Portillo and Mayo Santana (1992:24), however, argue that Soler's portrayal "obviously does not match reality." "[C]oncerning the diligence with which evangelization was carried out, [Soler's claim], as far as it is known to us, has not been corroborated. To the contrary, it seems that the influ-

ence of the Church on the lives and evangelization of the slaves was less significant than what Soler supposes."

28. Although the examination of the transformation of free laborers into forced labor is not the object of this study, it is important to note that after the *Cédula de Gracias,* or Decree of Benefaction, was put into effect in 1815, Puerto Rico was opened not only to legal commerce but also to an increased flow of immigrants from the mainland and other Catholic colonies, setting in motion a series of far-reaching economic changes known as Puerto Rico's "Golden Age." One of the less praised effects was an increase in the number of *agregados* forming a new landless poor-white and free-colored peasantry that was forced, under carefully orchestrated vagrancy laws, to work in plantations or otherwise risk being incarcerated. According to the restrictive Police Edicts (Bandos de Policía y Buen Gobierno) of 1824, 1837, and then 1849, all landless unemployed were finally forced to carry the infamous *libretas,* or workbooks that recorded their services on a daily basis (Mintz [1974] 1989:90–92; Morales Carrión 1983).

29. See Nevárez Nieves (1994) on the tradition of *promesas* (promises) among nonslaves performed during the Epiphany in Puerto Rico.

30. It is revealing that on different islands in the Caribbean and in various historical circumstances, the playing of drums—even their mere existence—was perceived by the authorities as threatening the "social order" (however defined) and was therefore prohibited, and all drums were confiscated. One can see in Trinidadian pan-steel drumming and Cuban box drumming examples of Creole forms of creative innovation and contestation of these measures.

31. *La Gaceta Oficial* (the Official Gazette, a colonial broadsheet) mentions on July 10, 1826, the uncovering of a slave conspiracy that was conceived before the festivities of San Pedro and planned to take place in Ponce during an allegedly innocent gathering for bomba drumming and dancing. See Coll y Toste (1916c:347–349).

32. See Morales Carrión (1974) for how the litigation and punishment of slaves were conducted under the provisions of the state.

33. Alegría (1956) meticulously documented these festivities as he observed them in the early 1950s.

34. See Constitution LXXVIII, in Huerga (1989:102).

35. See the references made by Miyares González ([1755] 1954:33) to the civil and religious cofradías of the Cathedral.

36. In this edict there are also rules concerning the recreational activities of slaves, especially their bomba dances and songs.

37. Vidal (1986) gives an excellent account (and photographic documentation) of these additions and adornments (promesas). Although detailing the popular devotions specific to San Blas alone, Vidal's book exemplifies the scope of the material culture that developed in the Puerto Rican religious vernacular tradition. See also Quintero Rivera (1998) for more on contemporary photographs and accounts of popular religions in Puerto Rico.

38. This topic is developed further in chapter 4.

39. This unpublished case, based on primary archival sources (Archivo General de Puerto Rico, Fondo Gobernadores Españoles, Box 283), became available to me through what I can only call my own private "miracle." It was discovered accidentally, in one of the thousands of unindexed boxes housed in the General Archive

of Puerto Rico, by Rafael Nevárez Nieves, a young scholar who made a personal note of the case simply because he had found it interesting, even though it was not related to his own project. He generously, and by pure coincidence, made this documentation available to me when our paths crossed in the archive one morning and we happened to mention the topics of our separate research.

40. The complete name is La Virgen de la Caridad (Our Lady of Charity), or La Virgen de la Caridad del Cobre (the Virgin of the Charity of Cobre), the name given to her in Cuba and often shortened to La Virgen del Cobre. Sometime in the seventeenth century, folk tradition says, a statue of the Virgin was found floating on the sea off the eastern shores of Cuba by three fishermen, all named Juan: Juan the black slave, Juan the Indian, and Juan the Spaniard. Her statue was later enshrined in a village called Cobre (Copper) and became the object of popular devotion over the centuries. Because of the miraculous recovery of the statue of the Virgin by three ethnically different men and the subsequent intense devotion to this saint (especially during the wars of independence in the last quarter of the nineteenth century), and following the many miracles attributed to her intervention, she was eventually canonized, in 1915, as the patron saint of Cuba. She came to symbolize, mainly among the popular classes, the "Creole" character of the Cuban nation. (For a study of the contested nature of the meaning of La Virgen de La Caridad among Cuban exiles in Miami, see Tweed [1999].) The history of La Caridad in Puerto Rico and her resonance among Puerto Rican women is yet to be researched; but the actual migration of Cubans and the global circulation of religious icons—in addition to the folk narrative associated with her Creole trajectory—might explain in part her fame on the island.

41. See Ryle (1987) for similar processes regarding Brazilian popular religions and the church.

Chapter Two

Parts of this chapter appear in my article "Whose Spirits Are They? The Political Economy of Syncretism and Authenticity" (1998).

1. *Causa* can mean a curse, spell, or bewitchment, and it can be caused by black magic or by the spirit of a dead person who brings about all kinds of misfortune.

2. See Machuca (1982); Mesa Redonda Espírita de Puerto Rico (1969); Rodríguez Escudero (1991); Santiago (1983); Yañez (1963).

3. After I finished my research, Jorge Duany pointed out that some historical research has been done on the internal differentiation of the elites, which, I believe, will shed light on the development of political allegiances in Puerto Rican society.

4. According to Richard Greenleaf (1991:259-260), the persecution of Masons in Mexico by the Inquisition between 1751 and 1820 was on account of their alleged link to the independence movement: "The Holy Office of the Inquisition viewed Masons as social revolutionaries who were trying to subvert the established order."

5. In recent years revisionist historians have been exploring the connection of the great liberators of the Americas (e.g., San Martín, Bolívar, and Martí) to Freemasonry. I thank Duany for pointing out Martí's case. Interestingly, a Masonic Lodge paid for the studies of Albizu Campos at Harvard University. Campos would become the leader of the Puerto Rican nationalist party and later its martyr.

6. The newly created republic instituted the separation of state and religion, ended the Concordat (the agreement not to sell religious paraphernalia), ordered the expropriation of church property, eliminated Christian education in primary schools, abolished seminaries for the training of priests, suspended payment for clergy in public services, repealed the church power (*el fuero*), expelled certain religious orders from Spain, abolished the military orders, declared illegitimate those children born to couples who had not been married by civil judges, and appointed revolutionary priests to fill posts in the church (Silva Gotay 1985:60).

7. On the development of the different political movements of Puerto Rico, see Morales Carrión (1983).

8. Although short lived, the insurrection achieved, among other things, the end of the libreta system, symbolically marked by the burning of these notebooks in Lares Plaza on September 23, 1868, after which the Spanish government abolished the libreta system altogether (Juan Antonio Corretjer, quoted in Wagenheim and Wagenheim [1994] 1996:63).

9. Despite the institutional allegiance of the Puerto Rican church to Spain, many Puerto Rican clergy made a plea in favor of the prisoners of Lares, indicating a high degree of sympathy for the insurrection (Silva Gotay 1985:60).

10. In Puerto Rico, as in other Latin American societies, the professional elites were engaged in promoting their literary, antireligious, and political ideas through the media. Most doctors and lawyers, who were also writers and poets and sometimes owners of publishing companies, used the newspaper as an arena to discuss and disseminate their political ideologies. See Hess (1991) for a similar process in Brazil.

11. In this regard, as Cruz Monclova (1957) shows, the fate of Spiritists and Freemasons was very much the same.

12. Among other things, the decree allowed Protestants to gather freely for the first time in Puerto Rico. Silva Gotay (1985) remarks that even before this time Protestant congregations had existed outside the law. The first Protestant congregation was founded in 1860, thus inaugurating the history of this religion in Puerto Rico forty years before the 1898 arrival of the Americans (not *after* 1898, as most studies claim) (pp. 61–62).

13. Teresa Yáñez Vda. de Otero, an espiritista herself, compiled various documents, letters, and other historical sources (housed in the Mayagüez Section of the Federation of Spiritists in Puerto Rico) and collected the oral history of some of the founders of the first Spiritist center of Mayagüez, Luz y Progreso, while writing *El espiritismo en Puerto Rico* (published for institutional circulation)—the "unwritten" history of Spiritism in Puerto Rico.

14. Silva Gotay (1985:63) summarizes, as follows, several statements made in Protestant journals at the time of the 1898 invasion: "The Church's mission consisted in following the U.S. Army's military conquest of Catholic and non-Christian countries in order to impose American democratic institutions, capitalism, and Protestantism with a view toward launching world history into its final phase along the lines of true Christianity and progress."

15. The scientific-empirical aspect of Scientific Spiritism needs clarification. Kardec operated in the context of a general scientific interest in the observation and measurement of what was then called "metaphysical phenomena," which would be later established as the study of parapsychology.

16. For an account of a similar attitude, in Brazil, toward the role of Scientific Spiritism, see Hess (1991).

17. Note that I refer to curanderos, following anthropological practice, as popular healers that operate away from urban centers. Most present-day dictionaries, however, continue to define *curanderos* as "quacks" or "false doctors." Indeed, this is how they were labeled by those who persecuted them. This becomes clear in Quezada's (1991) study of the Inquisition's repression of curanderos in Mexico. She claims that they were persecuted because they had become a threat to the order of colonial Mexico, despite the fact that, because of the scarcity of doctors, they functioned as medical practitioners. Their "knowledge and skills contributed to the health of the oppressed and led to the formation of a traditional mestizo medicine that syncretized Indian, black, and Spanish folk medicines" (p. 37).

18. In Puerto Rico the word *santo* refers to the figurine of the saint and the word *santero* to the traditional carvers of the figurines. However, since the late 1950s, when Santería began to be practiced on the island, the word *santero* acquired another meaning—initiate of Santería.

19. The literal meaning of *santiguo* is making the sign of the cross. Traditionally, a santiguo is a curing ritual that involves, among other procedures, rubbing the patient's belly with pure olive oil, making the sign of the cross over the patient's body, and praying. (More about the *santiguo* is presented in chapter 6.)

20. Immediately after the 1950s (in part because of the influence of Cuban immigrants following Castro's revolution), Spiritism incorporated more visible ritual and musical elements related to Afro-Latin spirit possession religions such as Cuban Santería and Haitian Vodou, giving rise to what today has been labeled *santerismo* (the mixing of Santería and espiritismo), which evidently acquires a dismissive tone when spoken by orthodox Santería and espiritismo practitioners. In Brazil the African-based Candomblé has merged with Spiritism, creating Umbanda, which has many similarities to Puerto Rican santerismo.

21. It would be revealing to investigate the development of Kardecean Spiritism in Europe to see if it has been as eclectic as in the Americas.

22. The term "popular" is used here only to distinguish the vernacular forms of Spiritism from orthodox Scientific Spiritism. Practitioners of Spiritism do not make this distinction unless they are practitioners of Scientific Spiritism who wish to differentiate themselves from others.

23. The influence of these measures on the syncretic religious practices of the generation of Puerto Ricans growing up in those times is still to be studied. In the chapters that follow I suggest ethnographic evidence that points in this direction.

24. Some of these programs were the Federal Emergency Relief Administration (FERA)—known locally as the Puerto Rican Emergency Relief Administration (PRERA)—the National Recovery Act (NRA), and the Puerto Rican Reconstruction Administration (PRRA).

25. See Morales Carrión (1983:242–307) and Carr (1984:201–230, 279–304) for a critical assessment of Operation Bootstrap.

26. See Dávila (1997:34–37) for an excellent assessment of DIVEDCO as an agency reproducing the ideology of the state apparatus—in Althusserian terms—and of the goals of other programs devised by DIVEDCO.

27. It is worthwhile to note at this point how journalists and state officials, as well as Scientific Spiritists, raise the notion of "folklore" as a rhetorical strategy to

exclude from modern society what they consider primitive aspects of popular forms of Spiritism. Also, for a critical general review of the relation between "official" and "popular" forms of religion, see Vrijhof and Waardenburg (1981).

28. A caricatured narrative and a review test presented in the form of "riddles" included at the end of the story to persuade citizens speaks volumes about the Department of Health and Education's perception of their audience. Assuming their incapacity for abstract generalization, such use of "exempla," which is standard in sermons, was clearly intended to mobilize these supposedly superstitious audiences more effectively.

29. Paradoxically, in recent years there has been a tendency to reappropriate "popular medicine" within the Puerto Rican medical establishment. The first three issues between July 1970 and January 1971 of the journal *Buhiti*, published by the Puerto Rican School of Medicine, University of Puerto Rico, give a medical perspective on these renewed interests.

30. The senator's differentiation of curanderismo, brujería, and the practices of espiriteros from "true" espiritismo, or Scientific Spiritism, seems to result from very ambiguous criteria, as in the case of the *Código de las Siete Partidas*, mentioned in chapter 1. The senator's categories conform to the definition of Spiritism as expressed by orthodox Spiritists (e.g., see, below, Rodríguez Escudero's claims) but are certainly not appropriate in the discourse of government officials. In clarifying what Scientific Spiritism is, Rodríguez Escudero (1991:13–14) claims: "All the rest—sorcery, santerismo, *cumbandismo*, black magic, the use of candles, magnetic water, commercial healing colognes [*alcoholados*], saints, santos and Indios, stereotyped prayers that are learned by heart (spells), and curanderismo—all these have distorted, confused, and misinterpreted the teachings of Spiritism, which aims at revealing the truth—liberating people from lies that promote the fear of death—and at developing the hope of eternal life."

31. This is a derogatory popular word, composed of *fu* (fü), the onomatopoeia for the act of blowing, which here indexes the blowing of magic powders and hence its reference to esoteric, magical practices in general and to brujería in particular.

32. Compare this statement with the above-mentioned principles of Scientific Spiritism, particularly the one that refers to the important role of charity as a sign of "true" Spiritists. This type of legitimation claim resembles that of the early Catholic Church, which stated that ends, not means, determine whether a practice is holy or unholy (see pp. 35–36).

33. In Puerto Rico today, when people say they go to metafísica workshops or classes they might refer to classes in mediumship, some of which combine in various ways the teachings of Kardec and his contemporary exegetes, as well as those of paranormal and New Age esoteric schools.

34. The stress here is on verbalization, as mediums might also deliver the messages of the spirits through body movements, which are considered by some, like this instructor, to be novice forms of mediumistic trance.

35. For an interdisciplinary dialogue on syncretism among missionaries, philosophers, cultural anthropologists, and students of comparative religion, see Gort et al. (1989). See also Bendix (1997) and Romberg (1993) for critical approaches to authenticity in folklore.

36. By no means do I suggest that all Puerto Ricans share this belief. For a dis-

cussion of the politics of recognition and its problematic relation to an individualist thrust of authenticity and identity, see Appiah (1994).

37. Following Hannerz's (1990) lead, cosmopolitan intellectuals in Puerto Rico are thus able to play the "world culture" game by constituting diversity in their own locales.

Chapter Three

1. On June 11, 1993, the Supreme Court ruled in favor of his church, arguing that the ban was unconstitutional.

2. See also Gold's (1988) depiction of the Hindu Darshan bus tour.

3. Some more New Age–oriented metafísica workshops combine, in addition to the writings of Kardec and his followers, various techniques for spiritual growth and mediumship, all rooted in esoteric notions of magnetism, prayer, visualization, and so forth.

4. *Santerismo*, as noted above, is the native term for the visible mixture of Santería and espiritismo. In both Vodou and santerismo, Catholic saints are interchangeably called by their Catholic and African names. See Desmangles (1992) for the relation of Vodou to Catholicism and Fernández Olmos and Paravisini-Gebert (1996) for a cross-cultural depiction of the meaning of sacred objects in Vodou, Santería, and Trinidadian Obeah.

5. These ideas are further developed in Romberg (1993).

6. Even with the help of some well-intentioned employees at DACO, I have not been able to find out if there have ever been complaints registered against botánica owners or their products, as complaints are computer indexed in DACO by number, not by subject.

7. For example, real estate agencies in Puerto Rico cannot register as corporations and, unlike on the mainland, cannot buy more than a certain number of acres of land. The court's ruling in a case that threatened American control over the land in Puerto Rico during the 1950s resulted in a change in how developers were registered. According to the amendment, developers have to be registered in Puerto Rico not as corporations but under the rubric "professional endeavors."

8. I have attempted, without success, to discover the outcome of this case.

9. This process began in 1928 on the island and continued into the 1940s on the mainland, according to the Puerto Rican folklorist Marcelino Canino (1976). For more on the popular carvers of wooden santos, the role of the Instituto de Cultura Puertorriqueña and El Ateneo Puertorriqueño (founded in 1876 by Manuel Elzaburu Viscarrondo), the role of the group Rescate (Salvage) in the collection of these santos, and information on other collectors and collections, see Canino (1976:95-105).

10. See Taylor (1994) for a revealing discussion of the complex relations involved in "multiculturalism" and the "politics of recognition" in modern democracies, where particular claims for national, civil, gender, and ethnic identities seem to contest a universalistic notion of the "general will."

11. Abrahams (n.d.) refers to the romantic nationalist roots of New World postcolonial Anglophone and Francophone artists who draw on "creolite" cultures (identified as low-status lifestyles) as a way to speak for their "people." He argues that

by means of such "verbal wizardry," intellectuals "capitalize" on the most portable of the vernacular expressive practices as the seedbed of their art. For an example of how Puerto Rican literature has incorporated brujería, see Ferré (1989). Also, the attempt of Puerto Rican scientists such as Nuñez Meléndez (1982) to acknowledge the healing properties of plants used in vernacular religious practices legitimizes— and at the same time marks a change in—the public perceptions of these forms of healing.

12. For example, one catalog published by the University of Puerto Rico documents the international symposium, "Ancestor Religious Cults in the Caribbean," held on December 24-30, 1990. Another was published after the third symposium, "Afro-America and its Religious Culture," held on March 20-26, 1994.

13. For example, an illustrated catalog for popular distribution, "Ogún's Machete," published by CEREP in 1989, discussed the slave revolts in Puerto Rico during the nineteenth century. Another, "La Tercera Raíz: Presencia Africana en Puerto Rico," published in 1993, also by CEREP, illustrated the African contributions of the "third root" in Puerto Rican culture.

14. Changó (English, Shango) is the Santería orisha owner of fire, love, sensuousness, and thunder, associated with Santa Bárbara.

15. Indeed, Ocultismo is a popular section in local bookstores such as Thekes in the Plaza de las Américas mall (I thank Jorge Duany for this note).

16. During the 1980s, a series of articles appeared in *El Reportero* on Santería by the Cuban anthropologist Julio Sánchez, author of *La religión de los orichas*.

17. Unlike the judgment in the case of the woman of La Moca (related in chapter 1), who had also been the object of similar attacks and persecution by institutional churches in the 1860s, the courts of the 1980s seem to have protected Doña Eustaquia's right to freedom of religious worship, thereby ending her misery and allowing her to continue with her "mission."

18. See Ayala Álvarez (1992) for recent developments in Pentecostal, electronic, and other charismatic churches in Puerto Rico.

Chapter Four

1. Other brujos might have different personal patron saints, such as Santa Bárbara, or a host of different spirits.

2. *Revocar* is a complex term that means "to invalidate," "to default," and, sometimes, "to retaliate against black magic."

3. Haydée performs these prayers each day, one at the beginning and another at the end of her spiritual consultations, and refers to them respectively as "opening" and "closing" the altar.

4. Palo Monte is an Afro-Cuban religion based on what Cubans—in differentiating it from Santería and its Yoruba origins—term "Congo" beliefs. Its Bantu cosmology, unlike Santería, includes the recruitment of muertos by *paleros* (those initiated into Palo Monte) who manage to have total command over them in a master/slave, or master/pet, relationship. See Cabrera (1979).

5. Brujos often refer to Jesus as Papá Dios (Father God) or Papacito (Daddy), in addition to Dios (God).

6. *Trabajos malos* is the term for what is called "black magic" (see Marwick 1970) in the literature on Africa and *magia negra* in the literature on Latin America.

7. During divination, brujos often refer to the spirits as *ellos* (they), without specifying who "they" are, because everyone who comes to consult understands that *ellos* refer to the spirits. To distinguish between the pronoun "they" and "the spirits," I capitalize "They" to refer to the latter.

8. The convergence of these stories with those of Catholics and Protestants is striking. The interrelations are not casual. Most brujos have been educated in Catholic schools or have participated as children in Protestant services. Some have experienced both, having been born into a Catholic family that converted to Protestantism in the early decades of the twentieth century.

9. Notably, Thomas (1971:188, 625) mentions similar sixteenth- and seventeenth-century English beliefs in the good fortune of being born with an intact caul wrapped around one's head. Monter (1983:73) mentions the caul (*camiscola*) as the precondition of becoming a *benandante* who, according to Carlo Ginsburg's account of the first trial of a benandante in 1580, is one whose spirits fight at night four times a year "in favor of Christ against the witches [, who fight] in favor of the Devil."

10. Similar signs of fame of an African healer-diviner are reported by Redmayne (1970).

11. I base these remarks on one of the hundreds of reports that have appeared since the beginning of the twentieth century in the Puerto Rican newspaper *El Mundo* about apparitions that have resulted in the transformation of a number of public places into devotional sites.

12. Most brujos have notebooks in which they register the names and addresses of their clients. More than serving functional purposes, these notebooks are often skimmed by brujos to corroborate the magnitude of their work.

13. The *fuente* has been an indispensable ritual object for espiritistas of all kinds since the creation of the Spiritist centers in the nineteenth century. Among its many purposes, it is where the messages of the spirits *se plasman* (coagulate or coalesce). Reflections in the fuente can thus be "read." During cleansing rituals, the fuente can become the repository of bad energies; therefore, immediately after a cleansing, the impure water inside the bowl is carefully discarded and the bowl is refilled. Sometimes brujos add ice cubes to the clear water and then rub the frozen water on their or their clients' foreheads and necks if they feel that their minds need to be "cooled off."

14. Although I do not develop here the poetics of divination performances, it is worthwhile to point out an element shared with charismatic discourse. Following Csordas's (1997) analysis of the poetics of Catholic charismatic discourse, the words spoken during divination attain the sacredness of "a speakerless discourse." The power of this type of discourse lies in its ability to move people "by means of establishing the presence of the sacred and the manifestation of divine power" (p. 330). See also Lévi-Strauss (1963a) and Tambiah (1968).

15. See chapter 5 for more on the different meanings and ways of developing a cuadro.

16. I develop further the notion of *revocar* in chapter 5.

17. Kimbisa is an African-based religion that is organized in secret societies whose focus is the cult of the dead.

18. The protecciones and their role in Spiritism and brujería are discussed more fully in chapter 5.

19. "Good," "clean," and "white" trabajos correspond to what appears in both

scholarly and popular literature on witchcraft as *magia blanca* (white magic.) See, for instance, Marwick (1970:19–44) for similar oppositions between white/black and good/bad magic as they have been articulated by scholars writing about African witchcraft.

20. A *mediumnidad positiva* (positive medium) is one who works only with his or her "good energies" and invokes "positive" spirits. The dichotomy positive/negative can also be used to refer to people in general. Haydée says about her clients: "I have a nice, positive clientele, and also a negative one. Those clients that are negative I help them to reason."

21. As an example of the combination of pride and humility, Bolina proudly says that ever since a cover story about her was published in the newspaper, people have been arriving to take pictures of her and conduct interviews, but when receiving them she is always barefoot, wearing simply a housedress and a turban and with a cigarette dangling from her mouth—just as I am seeing her while we talk.

22. See Lewis-Fernández (1986) as well as Singer and García (1989) for life history approaches to the process of becoming an espiritista.

23. I have found several cross-cultural similarities between my observations of Puerto Rican witch-healing and Asian shamanism (Kendall 1996; Laderman 1997) and African mediumship (Beattie and Middleton 1969; Douglas 1970; Mair 1969; Middleton 1967).

Chapter Five

1. In recent years, apparently due to the influence of New Age books about angels, the notion of having a guardian angel is heard in conjunction with the Spiritist notion of cuadro.

2. "Pasar el cuadro" means to transfer momentarily one's cuadro to help others develop their own. When applied to novices, however, it means manifesting their cuadro publicly.

3. This is a phrase commonly used among brujos to express spiritual power. "Tu pides y ves" (You plead and then you see) means that the spirits grant whatever one desires. Another expression, "Te dan las cosas" (They [the spirits] give you things) points to the idea of receiving, through visions and premonitions, the necessary information to succeed.

4. *Clave* is a form of automatic writing inspired by the spirits. The marks (clave) scribbled on a piece of paper while brujos speak to their clients are kept and later deciphered.

5. *Coño* and *puñeta,* vulgar terms for "vagina" and "masturbation," are used to express an emotional exhortation. I have translated them into their English equivalents. In consultations, especially when spirits speak, a change in speech register occurs, marking the presence of the spirits. As mentioned in chapter 4, foul language or a break in "normal" rules of speech signifies the suprahuman power of spirits.

6. This is a formula used during seances and consultations as a greeting and as part of divination and trance events. When, as sometimes happen, the spirit is an evil or dubious one, the presiding medium will sometimes initiate a communal Our Father or Hail Mary.

7. This is a typical expression of amazement while in trance, apparently an abbreviation of "O'carajo!" (Oh, shit!).

8. There is no correlation between the medium's gender and the gender of the *entidad*. Male mediums might have female *protecciones*, and vice versa.

9. Unlike *protecciones*, who only protect their owners, or at the most redirect *trabajos malos* back to those who had commissioned them, *muertos* actively engage in carrying out and delivering *trabajos*. Although specific *protecciones* are invoked when performing a *trabajo* that relates to their area of influence, the *muertos* are the ones who carry them out.

10. This deity is similar to Bawon Samedi in Vodou.

11. There are no bad *cuadros*. So when somebody shows signs of constant lack of luck, the diagnosis is usually that he or she has an *espíritu de existencia*.

12. "Hacer un brujo" means to perform black magic against somebody. Here, *brujo* stands for a thing, not a person.

13. I develop these ideas further in Romberg (1999b).

14. *Estar pendiente*, to be excessively attentive to the actions of others, could in some cases—like this one—be the sign of ill feelings or evil intentions toward the object of such attention.

15. What other cultures term the "evil eye" is termed here "evil thoughts." Although an "envious gaze" might be involved, a curse could be cast by both conscious and unconscious "strong envious thoughts" against a person as well as by "coveting" (*reclamar*) something others have.

16. *Caramba* is used here as a euphemism for *carajo*.

17. A full account of this story appears in chapter 6.

18. Indeed, as Koss (1964:5) remarked, "It frequently happens that the best candidate for an interfering *brujo* is the medium's former teacher. Though formerly an intimate he is considered powerful enough to direct the 'bad work' and also is familiar with the details of the individual's personal life and spiritual protection."

Chapter Six

1. Ochún (English Oshun) is the orisha associated with La Virgen de la Caridad, La Madama, and Cachita.

2. Available at every *botánica*, these de-Africanized Santería dance tapes are very different from the live, or even the commercial versions of the sacred rhythms of Santería. These are basically chants in Yoruba, accompanied by drums (see Amira and Cornelius 1982; *Sacred Rhythms of Santería* 1995).

3. For an excellent account of the mutual influences of Santería and *espiritismo*, see Brandon (1993); Murphy (1988); and Suárez Rosado (1992). Also, see Stanford (1997) for a documentary video that portrays the Afro-Latin rituals of a Cuban "sorcerer" living in New Jersey.

4. See Abimbola's similar explanation in the last section of this chapter.

5. Santería does not include the Christian God in its system. Yet Armando, who in addition to being a santero is an espiritista, invokes the Christian God and Jesus together with the orishas.

6. I am developing these issues in a new research project.

7. I was fortunate to be entrusted with a set of newspaper articles compiled by the librarians of the Puerto Rican School of Medicine under the rubric "popular medicine." I analyze this collection in Romberg (n.d.).

8. Since 1898 Protestant churches in Puerto Rico have attracted a large number of

Catholic families (Partsch MacMillan 1994). As Agosto Cintrón (1996) shows, most of the families that converted to Pentecostalism were the poorest. Over the generations, numerous Puerto Rican families and individuals have shifted back and forth from participation in Catholic and Protestant churches, often changing not once but many times, making it almost impossible to determine the number of Catholics and Protestants on the island.

9. To "smell candles" is a popular expression meaning, "to accuse someone of being involved with brujería." It is based on the common practice among brujos to light candles as part of their worship of the saints and as part of their performance of trabajos.

10. Lit., "leave you without your skin."

11. She used the expression "Siete gotas de aceite para que me resbalen" (lit., "Seven drops of oil for it to slide on me").

12. Brujos refer to *salmos* (psalms) in relation to certain passages of the Bible—identified by their numbers—that are commonly used in trabajos.

13. Parish priests often have a book in which parishioners can write their *peticiones* (pleas to God). Writing peticiones on parchment is a direct allusion to the performance of trabajos malos, which, indeed, involves writing the names of the victims on parchment.

14. This expression shows that brujería shares important concepts with the Protestant Reformation besides the idea of merit revealed by worldly success.

15. Lately brujos have been adding the sacred objects of Santería, such as beaded necklaces and amulets, combining them with Catholic ones.

16. It is important to note that brujos consider the sea a receptacle of contamination, hence *salazón* (from the stem word *sal,* "salt"). In contrast, the river is perceived as a source of sweetness and goodness. Its waters thus "sweeten" and provide blessings and good luck.

17. The use of sacrificial blood is an extremely unusual procedure among espiritistas and brujos. This explains why Haydée referred to it as a "very powerful ritual."

18. This santo corresponds—within Santería—to one of the faces or paths (*caminos*) of Eleggua, when it manifests as a child.

19. I thank Bernard F. Stehle for bringing this distinction to my attention.

20. Indios are deities representing the indigenous people of the preconquest Americas (*indios*). Like "West Indies" indicates in English, *indios* in Spanish points to Columbus's confusion when he saw the native people of the Americas and thought they were natives of India. Indeed, in Spanish *indio* also means a person from India, as here.

21. *Santiguar* is the active verb of the reflexive form, *santiguarse,* which means to cross oneself. Catholics cross themselves in several contexts, mainly to honor the presence of a priest or anything related to the church. *Santiguar* means to bless somebody by symbolically making the sign of the cross over his or her body.

22. There is a prevalent belief among brujos today, which I suspect originated in medieval thinking about the order of the universe and the power inherent in spatial and temporal boundaries, that trabajos are most effective if done at the stroke of twelve o'clock noon or midnight. Making the sign of the cross serves to ward off any trabajos malos that might be on their way to you at that moment.

23. It means that one's "head" (being) acquires the attributes and powers of an

orisha-saint through initiation rituals. Correspondingly, the orisha is said to have been "seated" on the "head" of the novice and is responsible for its well-being.

24. See Brandon (1990, 1993); Pérez y Mena (1991); and Vidal (1994).

Chapter Seven

1. Section 936 of the U.S. Internal Revenue Code, which provided federal corporate tax exemptions to U.S. corporations located in Puerto Rico since the mid-1970s, recently has been eliminated. "The program will phase out by the year 2006" (Grosfoguel 1997:33 n. 4).

2. At the time of my research Tonio was ninety years old. He died in December 1998. In his memory, I wrote a paper (Romberg 1999a) in which I reminisce about the stories he told and gestures he made while describing his work as a brujo.

3. This position resonates with the idea that if Puerto Rico becomes a neocolony (politically sovereign but economically dependent), "the United States would be relieved from the expenses of a modern colony." The population most affected by this redefinition would be the Puerto Rican working classes (Grosfoguel 1997:66).

4. I explore the spiritual force of the shifting voices of brujos in divination rituals in Romberg (1999b).

Chapter Eight

1. This expression probably originates in another Hispanic phrase, "hacer la cama turca" (to make a Turkish-type bed), used in some Latin American countries. It obviously stems from fifteenth-century Iberian prejudice against Turkish people and means "to set a trap for someone."

2. For the sake of clarity, I include only the lines spoken by Haydée.

3. For an excellent analysis of the intersubjective and intertextual power of metaphor in charismatic prophecy see Csordas (1997).

4. When brujos say that a person is *pendiente*, they are implying a negative behavior liable to be transformed into an unconscious if not purposeful curse.

5. Alejo is a proper name used here in reference to the verb *alejar*, "to drive apart."

Epilogue

1. In this spirit, which he later would dismiss, Fernando Ortiz wrote his *La hampa afrocubana: Los negros brujos* (1906).

2. See Brandon's (1993) excellent analysis of the ambivalence of repression and resistance in the trajectories of Santería at different periods of Cuba's history. For the last period, see especially pp. 95–103. In this respect, Hagedorn (2001) traces the ambivalence of postrevolutionary Cuba toward Santería in relation to the role played by the Conjunto Folklórico Nacional de Cuba (founded in 1962) by performing the sacred on a secular stage.

3. Similarly, Ryle (1987) mentions the "yorubismo" of Candomblé *terreiros* (houses) in Brazil, which stresses their unbroken continuity with African Nagô (Yoruba) and Jeje (Fon) roots at the expense of including Bantu, Amerindian, and Catholic influences. This bias has been fueled in no small measure, according to

Ryle, by the concerns with "Africanity" of researchers, intellectuals, and artists who have neglected until very recently the rest of the terreiros, the majority of which practice a syncretic form of Candomblé.

4. See Bausinger (1990) for an illuminating debate about the creative aspects of the production of vernacular culture in a technological world.

5. See the volume edited by Patricia Spyer (1998) on the instability of the fetish as it relates to producing creative hybridities across borders. Another more rarely acknowledged source of unprecedented diversity, according to Daniel Miller (1995), is produced by "a posteriori difference," which is created "by the differential consumption of what had once been thought to be global and homogenising institutions." Novel forms, instead of being modifications or syncretisms of prior traditions, "arise through the contemporary exploration of new possibilities given by the experience of these new institutions" (pp. 2–3).

6. Elsewhere (Romberg 1999a) I explore the micropoetic aspects of these ritual innovations.

7. In a reflexive mode, Edith Turner (1992:1–17) looks back at the changes that she and Victor Turner experienced in their theorizing of the rituals among the Ndembu, acknowledging not only the factual changes that have affected the Ndembu since the 1950s but also the shifts of perspective throughout their own lives.

Abbad y Lasierra, Fray Iñigo. [1788] 1970. *Historia geográfica, civil y natural de la Isla de San Juan Bautista de Puerto Rico*. With a preliminary study by Isabel G. del Arroyo. Río Piedras: Editorial Universitaria, Universidad de Puerto Rico.

Abimbola, Wande. 1996. Lecture, Haverford College.

Abrahams, Roger D. 1977. "Toward an Enactment-centered Theory of Folklore." In William R. Bascom (ed.), *Frontiers of Folklore*. AAA Selected Symposium. Washington, D.C.: Westview Press, pp. 79–120.

———. 1993. "Phantoms of Romantic Nationalism in Folkloristics." *Journal of American Folklore* 106:3–37.

———. n.d. "Notes on Creolean Degeneracy and Vernacular Redemption." In process.

Adams, Vincanne. 1997. "Dreams of a Final Sherpa." *American Anthropologist* 99(1): 85–98.

Agosto Cintrón, Nélida. 1996. *Religión y cambio social en Puerto Rico (1898–1940)*. Río Piedras, Puerto Rico: Ediciones Huracán.

Aijmer, Göran, ed. 1995. *Syncretism and the Commerce of Symbols*. Göteborg, Sweden: Institute for Advanced Studies in Social Anthropology (IASSA) at Göteborg University.

Alegría, Ricardo E. 1956. "The Fiesta of Santiago Apóstol (St. James the Apostle) in Loíza, Puerto Rico." *Journal of American Folklore* 69(272):123–134.

Alegría-Pons, José Francisco. 1988. "Aspectos de la religiosidad popular en Puerto Rico." Exhibition catalog. San Juan, Puerto Rico: Centro de Estudios Avanzados de Puerto Rico y el Caribe. Appeared also in *La Revista del Centro de Estudios Avanzados de Puerto Rico y el Caribe* 7:105–109.

Amira, John, and Steven Cornelius. 1982. *The Music of Santería: Traditional Rhythms of the Bata Drums*. Crown Point, Ind.: White Cliffs Media.

Amorim, Deolindo. 1994. *Africanismo y espiritismo*. Trans. Pura Argelich Minguella. Caracas: Editora Cultural Espírita León Denis, Ediciones Cima.

Appadurai, Arjun. 1990. "Disjuncture and Difference in the Global Cultural Economy." *Public Culture* 2(2):1–24.

———. 1996. *Modernity at Large: Cultural Dimensions of Globalization*. Minneapolis: University of Minnesota Press.

———, ed. 1986. *The Social Life of Things: Commodities in Cultural Perspective*. Cambridge: Cambridge University Press.

Appiah, K. Anthony. 1994. "Identity, Authenticity, Survival." In Charles Taylor (ed.), *Multiculturalism: Examining the Politics of Recognition*. Ed. and introd. Amy Gutmann. Princeton: Princeton University Press [expanded from 1992 ed.], pp. 149–163.

Apter, Andrew. 1991. "Herskovits's Heritage: Rethinking Syncretism in the African Diaspora." *Diaspora* 1(3):235–260.

Archivo General de Puerto Rico. 1865. Documents about a woman in Moca. *Fondo Gobernadores Españoles*, box 283.

Asad, Talal. 1983. "Anthropological Conceptions of Religion: Reflections on Geertz." *Man* 18:237–239.

———. 1988. "Towards a Genealogy of the Concept of Ritual." In Wendy James and Douglas H. Johnson (eds.), *Vernacular Christianity: Essays in the Social Anthropology of Religion Presented to Godfrey Lienhardt*. Oxford: IASO, pp. 73–87.

Auslander, Mark. 1993. "Open the Wombs!": The Symbolic Politics of Modern Ngoni Witchfinding." In Jean Comaroff and John Comaroff (eds.), *Modernity and Its Malcontents: Ritual and Power in Postcolonial Africa*. Chicago: University of Chicago Press, pp. 167–192.

Austen, Ralph A. 1993. "The Moral Economy of Witchcraft: An Essay in Comparative History." In Jean Comaroff and John Comaroff (eds.), *Modernity and Its Malcontents: Ritual and Power in Postcolonial Africa*. Chicago: University of Chicago Press, pp. 89–110.

Ayala Álvarez, Laura Ivelisse. 1992. "Deprivación relativa: Una posible explicación de los movimientos milenarios de Puerto Rico." M.A. thesis, Programa de Estudios de Honor, Universidad de Puerto Rico.

Baird, Robert D. 1971. *Category Formation and the History of Religion*. The Hague: Mouton.

Baralt, Guillermo A. 1981. *Esclavos rebeldes, conspiraciones y sublevaciones de esclavos en Puerto Rico 1795–1873*. Río Piedras, Puerto Rico: Ediciones Huracán.

Barnet, Miguel. [1995] 2001. *Afro-Cuban Religions*. Princeton: Markus Wiener.

Bastide, Roger. 1978. *The African Religions of Brazil: Toward a Sociology of the Interpenetration of Civilizations*. Trans. Helen Sebba. Baltimore: Johns Hopkins University Press.

Bausinger, Hermann. 1990. *Folk Culture in a World of Technology*. Bloomington: Indiana University Press.

Beattie, John, and John Middleton. 1969. *Spirit Mediumship and Society in Africa*. London: Routledge and Kegan Paul.

Bendix, Regina. 1997. *In Search of Authenticity: The Formation of Folklore Studies*. Madison: University of Wisconsin Press.

Bendix, Reinhard. 1978. *Kings or People: Power and the Mandate to Rule*. Berkeley: University of California Press.

Benito Cantero, Juan José. 1886. *La magia disfrazada, o sea el espiritismo*. Madrid: R. Velasco.

Beyer, Peter. 1990. "Privatization and the Public Influence of Religion in a Global Society." In Mike Featherstone (ed.), *Global Culture, Nationalism, Globalization and Modernity*. London: Sage, pp. 373–395.

Bhabha, Homi K. 1990. "DissemiNation: Time, Narrative and the Margins of the Modern Nation." In Homi K. Bhabha (ed.), *Nation and Narration*. London: Routledge, pp. 291–322.

———. 1994. "Of Mimicry and Man: The Ambivalence of Colonial Discourse." In *The Location of Culture*. London: Routledge, pp. 85–92.

Blanco, Celia. 1988. *Manual esotérico*. Caracas: Representaciones Loga.

Borges, Dain. 2001. "Healing and Mischief in Brazilian Law and Literature, 1890–1922." In Ricardo D. Salvatore and Carlos Aguirre (eds.), *Crime and Punishment in Latin America: Law and Society since Late Colonial Times*. Durham: Duke University Press, pp. 181–210.

Bourdieu, Pierre. 1977. *Outline of a Theory of Practice*. Cambridge: Cambridge University Press.

———. 1980. "The Logic of Practice." In *The Logic of Practice*. Stanford: Stanford University Press, pp. 80–97.

Bram, Joseph. 1957. "Spirits, Mediums, and Believers in Contemporary Puerto Rico." *Transactions of the New York Academy of Sciences*, pp. 340–347.

Brandon, George. 1990. "African Religious Influences in Cuba, Puerto Rico and Hispaniola." *Journal of Caribbean Studies* 7(2–3):201–231.

———. 1993. *Santería from Africa to the New World: The Dead Sell Memories*. Bloomington: Indiana University Press.

Brown, David. 1999. "Altared Spaces: Afro-Cuban Religions and the Urban Landscape in Cuba and the U.S." In Robert A. Orsi (ed.), *Gods of the City: Religion and the American Urban Landscape*. Bloomington: Indiana University Press, pp. 155–230.

Brown, Karen McCarthy. 1991. *Mama Lola: A Vodou Priestess in Brooklyn*. Berkeley: University of California Press.

———. 1995a. "The Altar Room, A Dialogue." In Donald J. Consentino (ed.), *Sacred Arts of Haitian Vodou*. Exhibition catalog. Los Angeles: UCLA Fowler Museum of Cultural History, pp. 226–239.

———. 1995b. "Serving the Spirits: The Ritual Economy of Haitian Vodou." In Donald J. Consentino (ed.), *Sacred Arts of Haitian Vodou*. Exhibition catalog. Los Angeles: UCLA Fowler Museum of Cultural History, pp. 205–225.

———. 1999. "Staying Grounded in a High Rise Building: Ecological Dissonance and Ritual Accommodation in Haitian Vodou." In Robert A. Orsi (ed.), *Gods of the City: Religion and the American Urban Landscape*. Bloomington: Indiana University Press, pp. 79–102.

Bruner, Edward M., and Barbara Kirshenblatt-Gimblett. 1994. "Maasai on the Lawn: Tourist Realism in East Africa." *Cultural Anthropology* 9(4):435–470.

Cabrera, Lydia. [1954] 1975. *El Monte*. Miami: Ediciones Universal.

———. 1979. *Reglas de Congo, Palo Monte, Mayombe*. Miami: Colección del Chichereku en el Exilio.

Canino, Marcelino. 1976. *El folklore en Puerto Rico*, vol. 12 of *La gran enciclopedia de Puerto Rico*. Madrid: Ediciones R.

Caro Costas, Aida R. 1983. "The Organization of an Institutional and Social Life." In Arturo Morales Carrión (ed.), *Puerto Rico: A Political and Cultural History*. New York: W. W. Norton, pp. 25–40.

Carr, Raymond. 1984. *Puerto Rico: A Colonial Experiment*. New York: Vintage Books.

Chambers, Iain. 1994. *Migrancy, Culture, Identity*. London: Routledge.

Clifford, James. 1994. "Diasporas." *Cultural Anthropology* 9(3):302–338.

Club Amor y Ciencia. 1913. *Tesoros espirituales: Dictados de ultratumba obtenidos en Arecibo*. Arecibo, Puerto Rico: N.p.

Coll y Toste, Cayetano, comp. 1915. "Bando del General Prim contra la raza africana, 1848." In *Boletín histórico*, vol. 2. San Juan: N.p., pp. 122–130.

———. 1916a. "Bando contra ratería de 1829, con el fin de controlar las horas de descanso para que los esclavos no conspiren." In *Boletín histórico*, vol. 3. San Juan: N.p., p. 345.

———. 1916b. "Carta del Arzobispo de Santo Domingo a S. M. en su Real Consejo de Indias sobre lo ocurrido en San Juan de Puerto Rico con algunos negros hechiceros, siendo el obispo de aquella isla." In *Boletín histórico*, vol. 3. San Juan: N.p., pp. 48–49.

———. 1916c. "Conspiración de negros esclavos en Ponce, 10 de julio de 1826." In *Boletín histórico*, vol. 3. San Juan: N.p., pp. 347–349.

———. 1916d. "Sobre la inquisición en general, cartas del 1519, 1521, 1524, 1528." In *Boletín histórico*, vol. 3. San Juan: N.p., p. 143–149.

———. 1916e. "Los tiempos coloniales" (Real Orden de 1857 prohibiendo pronunciar discursos en los cementerios en el acto de inhumar cadáveres). In *Boletín histórico*, vol. 3. San Juan: N.p., pp. 138–139.

———. 1917. "1826, Reglamento sobre la educación, trato y ocupaciones que deben dar a sus esclavos los dueños o mayordomos de esta isla." In *Boletín histórico*, vol. 5. San Juan: N.p., p. 263.

———. 1920. "El carimbo." In *Boletín histórico*, vol. 7. San Juan: N.p., pp. 147–150.

———. 1923. "Reglamento para el trato de esclavos del gobernador Miguel de la Torre." In *Boletín histórico*, vol. 10. San Juan: N.p., pp. 262–273.

———. 1925. "Tres visitas para verificar si los esclavos recibían educación cristiana." In *Boletín histórico*, vol. 12. San Juan: N.p., p. 56.

———. 1926. "Historia de Puerto Rico, Conferencia 22, Estado de la iglesia católica en el siglo XVII, rectificaciones históricas." In *Boletín histórico*, vol. 13. San Juan: N.p., pp. 1–7.

———. [1969] 1972. *Historia de la esclavitud en Puerto Rico (Información y documentos)*. San Juan: Sociedad de Autores Puertorriqueños.

Comaroff, Jean, and John Comaroff. 1991. *Of Revelation and Revolution: Christianity, Colonialism, and Consciousness in South Africa*. Vol. 1. Chicago: University of Chicago Press.

———. 1992. "Ethnography and the Historical Imagination." In *Ethnography and the Historical Imagination*. Boulder, Colo.: Westview Press, pp. 3–48.

———, eds. 1993. *Modernity and Its Malcontents: Ritual and Power in Postcolonial Africa*. Chicago: University of Chicago Press.

Cornelius, Steven. 1992. "Drumming for the Orishas: The Reconstruction of Tradition in New York City." In Peter Manuel (ed.), *Essays on Cuban Music*. New York: University Press of America.

Cruz Monclova, Lidio. 1957. *Historia de Puerto Rico, siglo XIX*. Vol. 2, pt. 2. Río Piedras: Editorial Universitaria, Universidad de Puerto Rico.

———. 1958. *Historia de Puerto Rico, siglo XIX*. Vol. 1. 2d ed. Río Piedras: Editorial Universitaria, Universidad de Puerto Rico.

Csordas, Thomas J. 1997. "Prophecy and the Performance of Metaphor." *American Anthropologist* 99(2):321–332.

Curbelo de Díaz, Irene. 1986. *El arte de los santeros Puertorriqueños / The Art of the Puerto Rican Santeros*. San Juan: Instituto de Cultura Puertorriqueña, Sociedad de Amigos del Museo de Santos.

Dávila, Arlene. 1997. *Sponsored Identities: Cultural Politics in Puerto Rico*. Philadelphia: Temple University Press.

Dayan, Joan. 1995. *Haiti, History and the Gods*. Berkeley: University of California Press.

de Certeau, Michel. 1984. *The Practice of Everyday Life*. Berkeley: University of California Press.

Departamento de Instrucción. 1951. *La ciencia contra la superstición*. San Juan: División de Educación de la Comunidad.

Desmangles, Leslie G. 1992. *The Faces of the Gods: Vodou and Roman Catholicism in Haiti*. Chapel Hill: University of North Carolina Press.

De Todo. 1996. "Horóscopo por David Basnueva." September 25, p. 42.

Díaz Quiñones, Arcadio. 1996. Personal communication, Puerto Rican Studies Association conference, San Juan.

Díaz Soler, Luis M. [1953] 1974. *Historia de la esclavitud negra en Puerto Rico*. 4th ed. Río Piedras: Editorial Universitaria, Universidad de Puerto Rico.

Dietz, James. 1986. *An Economic History of Puerto Rico*. Princeton: Princeton University Press.

Douglas, Mary. 1970. *Witchcraft Confessions and Accusations*. London: Tavistock.

Droogers, André. 1989. "Syncretism: The Problem of Definition, the Definition of the Problem." In Jerald Gort, Hendrik Vroom, Rein Fernhout, and Anton Wessels (eds.), *Dialogue and Syncretism: An Interdisciplinary Approach*. Grand Rapids, Mich., and Amsterdam: Eerdmans and Rodopi, pp. 7–25.

Duany, Jorge. 1998. "La religiosidad popular en Puerto Rico: Una perspectiva antropológica." In Ángel Quintero Rivera (ed.), *Vírgenes, magos y escapularios: Imaginería, etnicidad y religiosidad popular en Puerto Rico*. Río Piedras: Centro de Investigaciones Sociales de la Universidad de Puerto Rico.

———. 2000. "Nation on the Move." *American Ethnologist* 27(1):5–30.

———. 2001. "Nation, Migration, Identity: Rethinking Colonialism and Transnationalism Apropos the Case of Puerto Rico." Department of Sociology and Anthropology, Swarthmore College, November 30.

El Mundo. 1948a. "Persiste el curandero." February 6, p. 6.

———. 1948b. "Los servicios médicos." February 8, p. 6.

———. 1948c. "Doctor Astor denuncia los daños causados por los curanderos." May 11, p. 1.

———. 1949. "Curandería y brujería florecen." April 17, p. 6.

———. 1951. "Distribuyen libro contra superstición." August 23, p. 10.

———. 1957. "Salud en Comerío, estudia influencia de curanderas." November 25, p. 5.

———. 1962. "Insta legislar para acabar con curanderas." January 11, p. 17.

———. 1968a. "Editorial." September 27, p. 7.

———. 1968b. "Editorial." October 10, p. 7.

———. 1968c. "Editorial." November 11, p. 7.

El Reportero. 1982a. "La Santería es un culto ritualista." July 24, p. 6.

———. 1982b. "Espíritu escribió famosa danza." August 3, p. 5.

———. 1982c. "Las botánicas y el espiritismo." August 5, p. 5.

———. 1982d. "Doña Eustaquia tiene su templo." August 21, p. 6.

El Vocero. 1994. "Imputan alcaldesa valerse brujería." November 21, p. 6.

———. 1995. "Anita Casandra pronto tendrá su línea síquica." February 6, p. 12.

Errington, Shelly. 1989. "Fragile Traditions and Contested Meanings." *Public Culture* 1(2):49–59.

Evans-Pritchard, E. E. 1937. *Witchcraft, Oracles and Magic among the Azande*. Oxford: Clarendon Press.

Fabian, Johannes. 1983. *Time and the Other: How Anthropology Makes Its Object*. New York: Columbia University Press.

Favret-Saada, Jeanne. [1977] 1980. *Deadly Words: Witchcraft in the Bocage.* Cambridge: Cambridge University Press.

Featherstone, Mike, ed. 1990. *Global Culture, Nationalism, Globalization and Modernity.* London: Sage.

Featherstone, Mike, Scott Lash, and Roland Robertson, eds. 1995. *Global Modernities.* London: Sage.

Ferguson, James, and Akhil Gupta, eds. 1992. "Space, Identity, and the Politics of Difference." Special issue. *Cultural Anthropology* 7(1):3-120.

Fernández Méndez, Eugenio. 1976. *Crónicas de Puerto Rico, desde la conquista hasta nuestros días (1493-1955).* Río Piedras: Editorial Universitaria, Universidad de Puerto Rico.

Fernández Olmos, M., and L. Paravisini-Gebert, eds. 1996. *Sacred Possessions: Vodou, Santería, Obeah and the Caribbean,* New Brunswick, N.J.: Rutgers University Press.

Ferré, Rosario. 1989. "La brujería en la literatura Puertorriqueña." *El Nuevo Día,* November 9, pp. 3-7.

Firpi, José. 1973. *El arte de la imaginería popular en Puerto Rico / The Art of Folk Imagery in Puerto Rico.* San Juan: Ediciones Tau.

Flores, Juan. 1993. *Divided Borders: Essays on Puerto Rican Identity.* Houston, Tex.: Arte Público Press.

Foster, Robert J. 1991. "Making National Cultures in the Global Ecumene." *Annual Review of Anthropology* 20:235-260.

Foucault, Michel. [1966] 1973. *The Order of Things: An Archeology of the Human Sciences.* New York: Vintage Books.

———. [1961] 1988. *Madness and Civilization: A History of Insanity in the Age of Reason.* New York: Vintage Books.

Frazer, Sir James George. [1922] 1960. *The Golden Bough: A Study in Magic and Religion.* Vol. 1. New York: Macmillan.

Garrido, Pablo. 1952. *Esotería y fervor populares de Puerto Rico.* Madrid: Ediciones Cultura Hispánica.

Garrison, Vivian. 1977. "The Puerto Rican Syndrome in Psychiatry and Espiritismo." In Vincent Crapanzano and V. Garrison (eds.), *Case Studies in Spirit Possession.* New York: John Wiley, pp. 383-449.

Geschiere, Peter. 1988. "Sorcery and the State." *Critique of Anthropology* 8(1):351-363.

———. [1995] 1997. *The Modernity of Witchcraft: Politics and the Occult in Postcolonial Africa.* Trans. Peter Geschiere and Janet Roitman. Charlottesville: University Press of Virginia.

Giddens, Anthony. 1991. *Modernity and Self-Identity: Self and Society in Late Modern Age.* Stanford, Calif.: Stanford University Press.

Glazier, Stephen D. 1996. "New World African Ritual: Genuine or Spurious." *Journal for the Scientific Study of Religion* 35(4):420-431.

Gluckman, Max. 1959. *Custom and Conflict in Africa.* Glencoe, Ill.: Free Press.

Gold, Ann. 1998. "Sweeping the Road Ahead: The Hindu Darshan Bus Tour." In *Fruitful Journeys.* Berkeley: University of California Press.

González, José Luis. 1993. *Puerto Rico: The Four Storeyed Country.* Princeton: Markus Wiener.

Gort, Jerald, Hendrik Vroom, Rein Fernhout, and Anton Wessels, eds. 1989. *Dia-*

logue and Syncretism: An Interdisciplinary Approach. Grand Rapids, Mich., and Amsterdam: Eerdmans and Rodopi.

Greenleaf, Richard. 1991. "Historiography of the Mexican Inquisition: Evolution of Interpretations and Methodologies." In Mary Elizabeth Perry and Anne J. Cruz (eds.), *Cultural Encounters: The Impact of the Inquisition in Spain and the New World.* Berkeley: University of California Press, pp. 248–276.

Grosfoguel, Ramón. 1997. "The Divorce of Nationalist Discourses from the Puerto Rican People: A Sociohistorical Perspective." In Frances Negrón-Muntaner and Ramón Grosfoguel (eds.), *Puerto Rican Jam: Essays on Culture and Politics.* Minneapolis: University of Minnesota Press, pp. 57–76.

Grosfoguel, Ramón, Frances Negrón-Muntaner, and Chloe Georas. 1997. "Beyond Nationalist and Colonialist Discourses: The Jaiba Politics of the Puerto Rican Ethno-Nation." In Frances Negrón-Muntaner and Ramón Grosfoguel (eds.), *Puerto Rican Jam: Essays on Culture and Politics.* Minneapolis: University of Minnesota Press, pp. 1–38.

Guerra, Lillian. 1998. *Popular Expression and National Identity in Puerto Rico: The Struggle for Self, Community and Nation.* Gainesville: University Press of Florida.

Gupta, Akhil, and James Ferguson, eds. 1997. *Culture, Power, Place: Explorations in Critical Anthropology.* Durham: Duke University Press.

Habermas, Jürgen. [1962] 1992. *The Structural Transformation of the Public Sphere: An Inquiry into a Category of Bourgeois Society.* Trans. Thomas Burgerwith with the assistance of Frederick Lawrence. Cambridge, Mass.: MIT Press.

Hagedorn, Katherine J. 2001. *Divine Utterances: The Performance of Afro-Cuban Santería.* Washington: Smithsonian Institution Press.

Hajosy Benedetti, María Dolores. 1991. *Hasta los baños te curan! Remedios caseros y mucho más de Puerto Rico.* Saline, Mich.: Editorial Cultural.

Hall, Stuart, and Paul du Gay, eds. 1996. *Questions of Cultural Identity.* London: Sage.

Handler, Richard, and Jocelyn Linnekin. 1984. "Tradition, Genuine or Spurious." *Journal of American Folklore* 97(385):273–290.

Hannerz, Ulf. 1990. "Cosmopolitans and Locals in World Culture." In Mike Featherstone (ed.), *Global Culture, Nationalism, Globalization and Modernity.* London: Sage, pp. 237–251.

———. 1996. *Transnational Connections: Culture, People, Places.* London: Routledge.

Hanson, Allan. 1989. "The Making of the Maori: Culture Invention and Its Logic." *American Anthropologist* 91(4):890–902.

Harwood, Alan. [1977] 1987. *RX/: Spiritist as Needed, a Study of a Puerto Rican Community Mental Health Resource.* Ithaca: Cornell University Press.

Herskovits, Melville J. 1937. "African Gods and Catholic Saints in New World Negro Belief." *American Anthropologist* 39(4, pt. 1):635–643.

———. 1958. *Acculturation: The Study of Culture Contact.* Gloucester, Mass.: P. Smith.

Hess, David J. 1991. *Spirits and Scientists: Ideology, Spiritism and Brazilian Culture.* University Park: Pennsylvania State University Press.

Hinkson, John. 1990. "Postmodernism and Structural Change." *Public Culture* 2(2): 82–101.

Hirschman, Albert O. 1977. *The Passions and the Interests: Political Arguments for Capitalism before Its Triumph.* Princeton: Princeton University Press.

Hobsbawm, Eric, and Terence Ranger, eds. 1983. *The Invention of Tradition.* Cambridge: Cambridge University Press.

Hubbard, L. Ron. 1972. *The Problems of Work: Scientology Applied to the Work-a-Day World.* Los Angeles: Church of Scientology.

Huerga, Álvaro, comp. 1989. *Damián López de Haro: Constituciones Sinodales de Puerto Rico 1645.* Ponce: Universidad Católica de Puerto Rico.

Kelly, John D., and Martha Kaplan. 1990. "History, Structure, and Ritual." *Annual Review of Anthropology* 19:119–150.

Kendall, Laurel. 1996. "Korean Shamans and the Spirits of Capitalism." *American Anthropologist* 98(3):512–527.

Knight, Franklin W. 1990. *The Caribbean: The Genesis of a Fragmented Nationalism.* 2d ed. New York: Oxford University Press.

Koss, Joan D. 1964. "Puerto Rican Spiritualism in Philadelphia: A Lady or the Tiger Dilemma." Paper presented at the annual meeting of the American Anthropological Association, November.

———. 1970. "Terapéutica del sistema de una secta en Puerto Rico." *Revista de Ciencias Sociales* 14(2):259–278.

Kramer, Karen. 1985. *Legacy of the Spirits.* Videorecording. Documental Educational Resources.

Laderman, Carol. 1997. "The Limits of Magic." *American Anthropologist* 99(2):333–341.

Laguerre, Michel S. 1984. *American Odyssey: Haitians in New York City.* Ithaca: Cornell University Press.

———. 1987. *Afro-Caribbean Folk Medicine.* South Hadley: Bergin and Garvey.

Lange, Yvonne. 1975. "Santos, the Household Wooden Saints of Puerto Rico, Philadelphia." Ph.D. dissertation, University of Pennsylvania.

Larner, Christina. 1984. *Witchcraft and Religion: The Politics of Popular Belief.* Oxford: Basil Blackwell.

Las Casas, Bartolomé de. 1971. *History of the Indies.* English. Selections. Trans. and ed. Andrée Collard. New York: Harper & Row.

Leinhardt, R. Godfrey. [1961] 1969. "Diviners in Dinkaland." In Roland Robertson (ed.), *Sociology of Religion: Selected Readings.* Harmondsworth: Penguin, pp. 419–431.

Lévi-Strauss, Claude. 1963a. "The Effectiveness of Symbols." In *Structural Anthropology.* Trans. C. Jacobson and B. G. Schoepf. New York: Basic Books, pp. 186–205.

———. 1963b. "The Sorcerer and His Magic." In *Structural Anthropology.* Trans. C. Jacobson and B. G. Schoepf. New York: Basic Books, pp. 167–185.

Lewis-Fernández, Roberto. 1986. "The Training of a Healer in Puerto Rican espiritismo." Ph.D. dissertation, Yale University.

Leyes de Puerto Rico Anotadas. 1990. "Título 32, No. 2761."

Lionnet, Françoise. 1992. "Logiques Métisses, Cultural Appropriation and Postcolonial Representations." *College Literature,* Special issue, *Teaching Postcolonial and Commonwealth Literatures* 19(3)–20(1): 100–120.

López Cantos, Ángel. 1992. *La religiosidad popular en Puerto Rico (siglo XVIII).*

Santurce, Puerto Rico: Centro de Estudios Avanzados de Puerto Rico y el Caribe.

Macfarlane, Alan. 1970. *Witchcraft in Tudor and Stuart England.* London: Routledge and Kegan Paul.

Machuca, Julio. 1982. *¿Qué es el espiritismo?* Santurce, Puerto Rico: Casa de las Almas.

Mair, Lucy. 1969. *Witchcraft.* New York: McGraw-Hill.

Malinowski, Bronislaw. 1948. *Magic, Science and Religion, and Other Essays.* Selected and with an introduction by Robert Redfield. Boston: Beacon Press.

Marwick, Max, ed. 1970. *Witchcraft and Sorcery, Selected Readings.* Harmondsworth: Penguin Education.

Masquelier, Adeline. 1993. "Narratives of Power, Images of Wealth: The Ritual Economy of Bori in the Market." In Jean Comaroff and John Comaroff (eds.), *Modernity and Its Malcontents: Ritual and Power in Postcolonial Africa.* Chicago: University of Chicago Press, pp. 3–33.

Matibag, Eugenio. 1996. *Afro-Cuban Religious Experience: Cultural Reflections in Narrative.* Gainesville: University Press of Florida.

Mauss, Marcel. [1950] 1972. *A General Theory of Magic.* London: Routledge and Kegan Paul.

Menéndez Vázquez, Lázara. 1995. "¿Un cake para Obatalá?!" *Temas* 4:38–51.

Mesa Redonda Espírita de Puerto Rico. 1969. *¿Qué es el espiritismo científico?* San Juan: N.p.

Middelfort, H. C. Erik. 1972. *Witch Hunting in Southwestern Germany, 1562–1684.* Stanford: Stanford University Press.

Middleton, John, ed. 1967. *Magic, Witchcraft, and Curing.* New York: Natural History Press.

Miller, Daniel. 1995. *Worlds Apart: Modernity through the Prism of the Local.* New York: Routledge.

Miller, Russell. 1994. "A Leap of Faith." *New York Times,* January 30, p. 8.

Mintz, Sidney W. [1974] 1989. *Caribbean Transformations.* New York: Columbia University Press.

Mintz, Sidney, and Richard Price. 1976. *An Anthropological Approach to the Afro-American Past: A Caribbean Perspective.* Philadelphia: Institute for the Study of Human Issues.

Mintz, Sidney, and Michel-Rolph Trouillot. 1995. "The Social History of Haitian Vodou." In Donald J. Consentino (ed.), *Sacred Arts of Haitian Vodou.* Exhibition catalog. Los Angeles: UCLA Fowler Museum of Cultural History, pp. 123–147.

Miyares González, Fernando. [1775] 1954. *Apuntes particulares de la isla y plaza de San Juan Bautista de Puerto Rico.* Compiled and with an introduction by Eugenio Fernández Méndez. Río Piedras: Universidad de Puerto Rico.

Monter, E. William. 1976. *Witchcraft in France and Switzerland.* Ithaca: Cornell University Press.

———. 1983. *Ritual, Myth and Magic in Early Modern Europe.* Brighton, Sussex: Harverster Press.

Moore, Robin 1997. *Nationalizing Blackness: Afrocubanismo and Artistic Revolution in Havana 1920–1940.* University Park: University of Pittsburgh Press.

Morales Carrión, Arturo, ed. 1974. *El proceso abolicionista en Puerto Rico: Documen-*

tos para su estudio, la institución de la esclavitud y su crisis: 1823–1873. Vol. 1. San Juan: Centro de Investigaciones Históricas de la Universidad de Puerto Rico.

———. 1983. *Puerto Rico: A Political and Cultural History.* New York: W. W. Norton.

Morris, Nancy. 1995. *Puerto Rico: Culture, Politics, and Identity.* Westport, Conn.: Praeger.

Murga, Vicente, and Álvaro Huerga, comps. 1989. *Episcopologio de Puerto Rico III de Francisco de Cabrera a Francisco de Padilla (1611–1695).* Ponce: Universidad Católica de Puerto Rico.

———. 1990. *Episcopologio de Puerto Rico IV de Pedro de la C. Urtiaga a Juan B. Zengotita (1706–1802).* Ponce: Universidad Católica de Puerto Rico.

Murphy, Joseph M. 1988. *Santería: An African Religion in America.* Boston: Beacon Press.

———. [1988] 1993. *African Spirits in America* (with a new preface). Boston: Beacon Press.

———. 1994. *Working the Spirit: Ceremonies of the African Diaspora.* Boston: Beacon Press.

Negrón-Muntaner, Frances, and Ramón Grosfoguel, eds. 1997. *Puerto Rican Jam: Essays on Culture and Politics.* Minneapolis: University of Minnesota Press.

Negrón Portillo, Mariano, and Raúl Mayo Santana. 1992. *La esclavitud urbana en San Juan.* Centro de Investigaciones Sociales Universidad de Puerto Rico. Río Piedras: Ediciones Huracán.

Nevárez Nieves, Rafael. 1994. "El origen y trascendencia de las promesas de Reyes en Puerto Rico." *El Pilató* 1(6):7–9.

Núñez Meléndez, Esteban. 1982. *Plantas medicinales de Puerto Rico, folklore y fundamentos científicos.* Río Piedras: Editorial de la Universidad de Puerto Rico.

Núñez Molina, Mario A. 1987. "Desarrollo del medium: The Process of Becoming a Healer in Puerto Rican *Espiritismo.*" Ph.D. dissertation, Harvard University.

O'Connor, James. 1973. *The Fiscal Crisis of the State.* New York: St. Martin's Press.

Orsi, Robert A., ed. 1999. *Gods of the City: Religion and the American Urban Landscape.* Bloomington: Indiana University Press.

Ortiz, Fernando. 1906. *La hampa afrocubana: Los negros brujos.* Miami: Ediciones Universal.

———. [1940] 1947. *Cuban Counterpoint, Tobacco and Sugar.* Trans. Harriet de Onis, introd. Bronislaw Malinowski, prologue Herminio Portell Vila. New York: Alfred A. Knopf.

———. 1975. *Historia de una pelea contra los demonios.* Havana: Editorial de Ciencias Sociales.

Partsch MacMillan, Jaime. 1994. "La crisis de 1898 y sus impactos sobre las instituciones de la vida religiosa en Puerto Rico." M.A. thesis, Centro de Estudios Avanzados del Caribe y Puerto Rico, San Juan.

Perea, Salvador. 1972. *Historia de Puerto Rico.* San Juan: Instituto de Cultura y la Universidad Católica de Puerto Rico.

Pérez, Louis A. 1988. *Cuba: Between Reform and Revolution.* New York: Oxford University Press.

Pérez y Mena, Andrés Isidoro. 1991. *Speaking with the Dead: The Development of Afro-Latin Religion among Puerto Ricans in the United States: A Study of the Interpenetration of Civilizations in the New World.* New York: AMS Press.

Perry, Mary Elizabeth, and Anne J. Cruz, eds. 1991. *Cultural Encounters: The Impact of the Inquisition in Spain and the New World.* Berkeley: University of California Press.

Picó, Fernando. 1988. *Historia general de Puerto Rico.* Río Piedras, Puerto Rico: Ediciones Huracán.

Pieterse, Jan Nederveen. 1995. "Globalization as Hybridization." In Mike Featherstone, Scott Lash, and Roland Robertson (eds.), *Global Modernities.* London: Sage, pp. 45–68.

Poulantzas, Nicos. 1972. "The Problem of the Capitalist State." In Robin Blackburn (ed.), *Ideology in Social Science: Readings in Critical Social Theory.* New York: Vintage Books, pp. 238–253.

Price, Richard, ed. 1979. *Maroon Societies: Rebel Slave Communities in the Americas.* Baltimore: Johns Hopkins University Press.

Quezada, Noemí. 1991. "The Inquisition's Repression of *Curanderos.*" In Mary Elizabeth Perry and Anne J. Cruz (eds.), *Cultural Encounters: The Impact of the Inquisition in Spain and the New World.* Berkeley: University of California Press, pp. 37–57.

Quintero Rivera, Ángel. 1995. Personal communication. Universidad de Puerto Rico, Río Piedras.

———, ed. 1998. *Vírgenes, magos y escapularios: Imaginería, etnicidad y religiosidad popular en Puerto Rico.* San Juan: Centro de Investigaciones Sociales de la Universidad de Puerto Rico.

Rand, Ayn. 1964. *The Virtue of Selfishness: A New Concept of Egoism.* With additional articles by Nathaniel Branden. New York: New American Library.

Redmayne, Alison. 1970. "Chiganga: An African Diviner with an International Reputation." In Mary Douglas (ed.), *Witchcraft, Confessions and Accusations.* Toronto: Tavistock.

Rodríguez Escudero, Néstor A. 1991. *Historia del espiritismo en Puerto Rico.* Quebradillas, Puerto Rico: N.p.

Rodríguez Pastor, J. 1954. *Males del medio ambiente.* San Juan: Editorial del Departamento de Instrucción Pública.

Rogler, Lloyd H., and August B. Hollingshead. 1961. "The Puerto Rican Spiritualist as a Psychiatrist." *American Journal of Sociology* 67(1):17–21.

Romberg, Raquel. 1993. "Authenticity in the Discourses of Folklore and the Avant-Garde: A Dialogical Account of Modernism." Paper presented at the annual meeting of the American Folklore Society, Eugene, Oregon.

———. 1996a. "The Pragmatics of Nationhood, Migration, Citizenship, and Cultural Identity." Paper presented at the annual meeting of the American Ethnological Society, San Juan.

———. 1996b. "Saints in the Barrio: Shifting, Hybrid and Bicultural Practices in a Puerto Rican Community." *Multicultural Review* 5(2):16–25.

———. 1998. "Whose Spirits Are They? The Political Economy of Syncretism and Authenticity." *Journal of Folklore Research* 35(1):69–82.

———. 1999a. "A Flight Perfected at Death: Mimetic Memories of Witchcraft in Puerto Rico." Paper presented at the 34th World Congress of the International Institute of Sociology, Tel Aviv.

———. 1999b. "Spiritual Time: A Discourse Approach to Divination and Magic."

Paper presented at the annual meeting of the American Anthropological Association, Chicago.

————. 1999c. "Symbolic Piracy: Puerto Rican Witchcraft from Heresy to Entrepreneurship." Paper presented at the Spring Seminar of the Institute of Global Studies in Culture, Power and History, Johns Hopkins University.

————. 2000. "Hoy, Changó es Changó, Or How Africanness Becomes a Ritual Commodity for Puerto Rican Brujos." Paper presented at the annual meeting of the Latin American Studies Association, Miami, Florida.

————. N.d. "From Charlatans to Saviors: Espiritistas, Curanderos, and Brujos Inscribed in Discourses of Progress and Heritage." Forthcoming, *Centro Journal*.

Rosaldo, Renato. 1988. "Ideology, Place, and People without Culture." *Cultural Anthropology* 3(1):77-87.

Roseberry, William. 1989. *Anthropologies and Histories: Essays in Culture, History and Political Economy*. New Brunswick, N.J.: Rutgers University Press.

Rostas, Susanna, and André Droogers, eds. 1993. *The Popular Use of Popular Religion in Latin America*. Amsterdam: Center for Latin American Research and Documentation (CEDLA).

Rowe, William, and Vivian Schelling. 1991. *Memory and Modernity: Popular Culture and Modernity in Latin America*. London: Verso.

Ryle, John. 1987. "Miracles of the People: Attitudes to Catholicism in an Afro-Brazilian Religious Center in Salvador, Bahia." In Wendy James and Douglas H. Johnson (eds.), *Essays in the Social Anthropology of Religion*. New York: Lilian Barber Press, pp. 40-50.

Saavedra de Roca, Angelina. 1969. "El espiritismo como religión: Observaciones sociológicas de un grupo religioso en Puerto Rico." In *Primer Ciclo de Conferencias Publicas sobre Temas de Investigación Social*. Río Piedras: Centro de Investigaciones Sociales, Universidad de Puerto Rico, pp. 106-290.

Sacred Rhythms of Santeria. 1995. CD. Produced by the Centro de Desarrollo de la Música Cubana, and annotated by Dr. Olavo Alén Rodríguez. Washington, D.C.: Smithsonian Folkways Records.

Salvatore, Ricardo D., and Carlos Aguirre, eds. 2001. *Crime and Punishment in Latin America: Law and Society since Late Colonial Times*. Durham: Duke University Press.

Santiago, Juan José. 1983. "The Spiritistic Doctrine of Allan Kardec: A Phenomenological Study." Ph.D. dissertation, Gregorian University, Rome.

Scarano, Francisco A. 1984. *Sugar and Slavery in Puerto Rico: The Plantation Economy of Ponce, 1800-1850*. Madison: University of Wisconsin Press.

Scott, David. 1991. "That Event, This Memory: Notes on the Anthropology of African Diasporas in the New World." *Diaspora* 1(3):261-284.

Silva Gotay, Samuel. 1985. "Social History of the Churches in Puerto Rico, Preliminary Notes." In Lucas Vischer (ed.), *Towards a History of the Church in the Third World*. Papers and Reports about the Issue of Periodization, presented at the Ecumenical Association of Third World Theologians, Geneva, July 17-21, 1983.

————. 1997. *Protestantismo y política en Puerto Rico, 1898-1930*. Río Piedras: Editorial de la Universidad de Puerto Rico.

Singer, Merrill, and Roberto García. 1989. "Becoming a Puerto Rican Espiritista: Life History of a Female Healer." In McClain Carol Shepherd (ed.), *Women as Healers: Cross Cultural Perspectives.* New Brunswick, N.J.: Rutgers University Press, pp. 157–185.

Skocpol, Theda. 1980. "Political Response to Capitalist Crisis: New Marxist Theories of the State and the Case of the New Deal," *Politics and Society* 10:155–201.

Smith, Anthony D. 1990. "Towards a Global Culture?" In Mike Featherstone (ed.), *Global Culture, Nationalism, Globalization and Modernity.* London: Sage, pp. 171–191.

Spyer, Patricia, ed. 1998. *Border Fetishisms: Material Objects in Unstable Spaces.* New York: Routledge.

Stanford, Ron. 1997. *Yo soy hechicero/I Am a Sorcerer.* Videorecording. Produced by Ivan Drufovka. Narberth, Penn.: Ron Stanford.

Starrett, Gregory. 1995. "The Political Economy of Religious Commodities in Cairo." *American Anthropologist* 97(1):51–68.

Stewart, Charles. 1995. "Relocating Syncretism in Social Science Discourse." In Göran Aijmer (ed.), *Syncretism and the Commerce of Symbols.* Göteborg, Sweden: Institute for Advanced Studies in Social Anthropology (IASSA) at Göteborg University, pp. 13–37.

Stewart, Charles, and Rosalind Shaw, eds. 1994. *Syncretism/Anti-Syncretism: The Politics of Religious Synthesis.* London: Routledge.

Stoller, Paul. 1997. *Sensuous Scholarship.* Philadelphia: University of Pennsylvania Press.

Suárez Rosado, Ángel. 1992. "Ese constante sabor por comunicarnos con el más allá." In *La tercera raíz: La presencia africana en Puerto Rico.* San Juan: Centro de Estudios de la Realidad Puertorriqueña (CEREP), Instituto de Cultura Puertorriqueña, pp. 123–128.

Sued Badillo, Jalil, and Ángel López Cantos. 1986. *Puerto Rico negro.* Río Piedras, Puerto Rico: Editorial Cultural.

Tambiah, Stanley J. 1968. "The Magical Power of Words." *Man* 3:175–208.

———. 1970. *Buddhism and the Spirit Cults in North-East Thailand.* Cambridge: Cambridge University Press.

———. 1985. *Culture, Thought, and Social Action: An Anthropological Perspective.* Cambridge, Mass.: Harvard University Press.

———. 1990. *Magic, Science, Religion, and the Scope of Rationality.* Cambridge: Cambridge University Press.

Taussig, Michael. 1987. *Shamanism, Colonialism and the Wild Man: A Study of Terror and Healing.* Chicago: University of Chicago Press.

———. 1992. *The Nervous System.* New York: Routledge.

———. 1993a. "Maleficium: State Fetishism." In Emily Apter and William Pietz (eds.), *Fetishism as Cultural Discourse.* Ithaca: Cornell University Press, pp. 217–247.

———. 1993b. *Mimesis and Alterity: A Particular History of the Senses.* London: Routledge.

———. 1997. *Magic of the State.* New York: Routledge.

———. 1999. *Defacement: Public Secrecy and the Labor of the Negative.* Stanford: Stanford University Press.

Taylor, Charles. 1991. *The Ethics of Authenticity*. Cambridge, Mass.: Harvard University Press.

————. 1994. *Multiculturalism, Examining the Politics of Recognition*. Ed. and introd. Amy Gutmann. Princeton: Princeton University Press [expanded from 1992 ed.].

Thomas, Keith. 1971. *Religion and the Decline of Magic: Studies in Popular Beliefs in Sixteenth- and Seventeenth-Century England*. London: Weidenfeld and Nicolson.

Toro-Sugrañes, José A. 1991. "El Maunabo conocido y vivido por José Gumersindo Sugrañes, boticario de Aldea: Un estudio de micro-historia social, 1895–1945." M.A. thesis, Centro de Estudios Avanzados del Caribe y Puerto Rico, San Juan.

Touraine, Alain. 1995. *Critique of Modernity*. Oxford: Blackwell.

Towler, R. [1968] 1969. "The Social Status of the Anglican Minister." In Roland Robertson (ed.), *Sociology of Religion*. Harmondsworth: Penguin, pp. 443–450.

Trouillot, Michel-Rolph. 1995. *Silencing the Past: Power and the Production of History*. Boston: Beacon Press.

Turner, Edith. 1992. *Experiencing Ritual: A New Interpretation of African Healing*. Philadelphia: University of Pennsylvania Press.

Tweed, Thomas A. 1999. "Diasporic Nationalism and Urban Landscape: Cuban Immigrants at a Catholic Shrine in Miami." In Robert A. Orsi (ed.), *Gods of the City: Religion and the American Urban Landscape*. Bloomington: Indiana University Press, pp. 131–154.

Urban, Greg. 1993. "Culture's Public Face." *Public Culture* 5:213–238.

Valle Ferrer, Norma. 1985. Fiestas de Cruz: Tradición y devoción en la comunidad Puertorriqueña. San Juan: Instituto de Cultura Puertorriqueña.

Veray, Francisco X. 1970. "Buhiti." *Buhiti* 1(1):3.

Vidal, Jaime R. 1994. "Citizens Yet Strangers: The Puerto Rican Experience." In Jay P. Dolan and Jaime R. Vidal (eds.), *Puerto Rican and Cuban Catholics in the U.S., 1900–1965*. Notre Dame, Ind.: University of Notre Dame Press.

Vidal, Teodoro. 1986. *San Blas en la tradición puertorriqueña*. San Juan: Ediciones Alba.

————. 1989. *Tradiciones en la brujería puertorriqueña*. San Juan: Ediciones Alba.

Vrijhof, Pieter Hendrik, and Jacques Waardenburg, eds. 1981. *Official and Popular Religion: Analysis of a Theme for Religious Studies*. The Hague: Mouton.

Wagenheim, Karl, and Olga Jiménez de Wagenheim, eds. [1994] 1996. *The Puerto Ricans: A Documentary History*. Updated ed. Princeton: Markus Wiener.

Walters, Jonathan S. 1995. "Multireligion on the Bus: Beyond 'Influence' and 'Syncretism' in the Study of Religious Meetings." In Pradeep Jeganathan and Quadri Ismail (eds.), *Unmaking the Nation: The Politics of Identity and History in Sri Lanka*. Colombo, Sri Lanka: Social Scientist Association.

Weber, Max. 1958. *The Protestant Ethic and the Spirit of Capitalism*. Trans. Talcott Parsons, foreword R. H. Tawney. New York: Charles Scribner's Sons.

————. [1915] 1969a. "Gods, Magicians and Priests." In Roland Robertson (ed.), *Sociology of Religion*. Harmondsworth: Penguin, pp. 407–418.

————. [1915] 1969b. "Major Features of World Religions." In Roland Robertson (ed.), *Sociology of Religion*. Harmondsworth: Penguin, pp. 19–41.

———. 1983. *Capitalism, Bureaucracy, and Religion.* A selection of texts edited and in part newly translated by Stanislav Andreski. London: Allen & Unwin.

Williams, Raymond. 1980. "Base and Superstructure in Marxist Theory." In *Problems in Materialism: Selected Readings.* London: Verso, pp. 31–49.

———. [1976] 1983. *Key Words: A Vocabulary of Culture and Society.* Rev. ed. New York: Oxford University Press.

Wolf, Eric. 1982. *Europe and the People without History.* Berkeley: University of California Press.

Yañez, Teresa Vda. de Otero. 1963. *El espiritismo en Puerto Rico.* San Juan: Federación de Espiritistas.

Zeitlin, Maurice. 1974. "Corporate Ownership and Control: The Large Corporation and the Capitalist Class." *American Journal of Sociology* 79(5):1073–1119.

Zeno, F. M. N.d. *Historia de la capital de Puerto Rico.* Vol. 1. San Juan: Publicación Oficial del Gobierno de la Capital.

Zenón Cruz, Isabelo. 1974. *Narciso descubre su trasero: El negro en la cultura Puertorriqueña.* Vol. 1. Humacao, Puerto Rico: Editorial Furidi.

phernalia and herbs), 51, 54; blessings of, 89–91; books at, 81, 83, 94; and commodification, 81–83, 84–88; consultations at, 83, 89, 151; fresh plants and herbs in, 88; as gift shops, 88; and globalization, 18, 81–88; and immigrants, 88; legal aspects of, 94–95; levantar (raise up), 90; location of, 88; manufacturers and suppliers for, 91–93; in the media, 101; as a mission, 89; as multireligious fields, 83, 86; networking at, 93–94, 143–144; New Age in, 88; novelty in, 89, 92 fig. 3.5, 204–205; offerings at, 88–89, 90 fig. 3.4; owners of, 88–91, 265; prosperity of, 89–91; registration of, 94–95; syncretism in, 83 (*see also* syncretism); and transnationalism, 81–83, 85–86; under commonwealth, 94–95 (*see also* commonwealth); under laissez-faire, 95; and witchcraft, 90. *See also* boticarios; boticas; yerbateros

boticarios (traditional pharmacists), 83–84. *See also* botánicas

boticas (traditional pharmacies), 83, 88, 95. *See also* botánicas

Bourdieu, Pierre, 6, 273n. 7

Bram, Joseph, 272n. 4

Brandon, George, 285n. 3, 287n. 24, 287n. 2

Brown, David, 272n. 5

Brown, Karen McCarthy, 11

brujería (witch-healing), x, 271n. 5, 271n. 7, 286n. 9; and African religions, 2, 140, 269, 274n. 9; and Americanization, 17; and American Protestantism, 19, 24 (*see also* Protestantism); as "calling," 2; and Catholicism, 16, 19, 24, 140, 172–174, 188–198, 269 (*see also* escapularios; resguardos); Catholic perceptions of, 1; commodification of, 209, 264, 266, 268–269; and commodities, 86, 140; eclecticism of, 208, 266; efficacy of, 3; and euphemisms, xi; and European witchcraft, xi; faith in, 3; fear of, 5–6; and fees, 112; and folk Catholicism, 2; as heritage, 96–102; individualism in, 14, 19, 140, 183–184; innovation in, 23, 208, 257, 266, 269; and Kardecean Spiritism, 2, 17; legal aspects of, 94, 95–96; and legal case, 96; and mainstream, 22, 140, 269; media against, 69–71, 72–74, 267; media celebrates, 78, 96, 98–100, 267, 282–282n. 11; and migration, 86; and modernity, 1–3, 10–13, 140, 266; and moral civility, 13–14, 24; and nation-building,

17, 24, 140; and New Age, 174–176; and novelty, 104 (*see also* novelty); as opposed to modernity, 67, 69; persecution history of, xi, 1–2; and pride, x, xi; and progress, 25; and prosperity, 25; as "residual," 6; and Santería, 172–174, 175, 176–182, 173 fig. 6.1, 182, 267; secrecy of, 3, 208–209; and secular ideology, 1; and self-identity, *see* self-identity; shifting histories of, 22, 23–25; and spiritualized materialism, *see* spiritualized materialism; and slavery, 17; state programs against, 69–72; and success, 2, 14, 25, 135; as "superstition," 1; types of, 138; under Catholic rule, 139 (*see also* Catholic rule); under commonwealth, 2, 94, 95–96, 234; under consumerism, xiv, xv, 2, 3, 10–13, 16, 22, 139–140, 163, 217, 269; under globalization, 11–14, 16–19, 23, 206–208, 209, 264–265, 266, 267 (*see also* globalization); under laissez-faire, 2, 19, 25, 82, 104–105, 139, 208; under postcapitalism, xi, 3, 10–11, 210–214; under state-building, 1, 69–74; under transnationalism, 10–11, 18–19, 22, 24–25, 179, 202–203, 204, 206, 207, 265, 266; under welfare, xv, 2–3, 10–11, 22, 212, 217, 235, 269; unorthodoxy of, 2, 14, 22, 23, 208; vs. Enlightenment, 1–2; as white or positive, 138

brujos, 271n. 5, 271n. 6, 271n. 8; as advocates, 230–231; and African deities, 22, 131–132; against animal sacrifice, 267 (*see also* espiritistas); against churches, 14, 52–53, 184–187; and American corporations and federal systems, 22–23; appropriation of Catholic signs and gestures by, 16, 30, 188–198, 190 fig. 6.5, 257 (*see also* novenas; spiritual: weddings, spiritual: exorcisms); assertiveness of, 135; and author, ix–xiii, 134; and bible, xiii (*see also* bible); blessings of, *see* blessings; as brokers, 140, 212, 235; calling of, 2, 130; and Catholicism, 22, 29–30, 122, 123 fig. 4.4, 124 fig. 4.5, 160–161, 166, 181, 283n. 8 (*see also* escapularios; resguardos; novenas); charity of, 25; as charlatans, *see* charlatanism; cleansing of, xiii, 164; collaborating with santeros, 176, 180–182; as commercial agents, 14, 211–212, 217, 220–221; and consumption, 132, 267; and daily news, *see* trabajos; as docents, 217; during elections, *see* trabajos; empowerment of, 5,

20, 25, 98; and espiritismo, 22, 54–57 (*see also* espiritismo; Spiritism); as espiritistas, x; fame of, xi–xiv, 30, 102, 112, 132–134, 137, 139, 207, 265, 284n. 21; fear of, 139; foul language of, 135–136, 231, 284n. 5; gifts of, xi, 78, 116, 120; and God, 129–131; and Halloween, 22, 255–257, 256 fig. E.1, 258–259 fig. E.2, 262, 264–265, 267–268; as heretics, *see* heresy; and holism, 22, 25, 139, 141, 216, 228; house of, 5, 162–163 (*see also* La Caridad); imitating Jesus, 111, 116, 120–124, 129–130 (*see also* mimesis); imitating priests, 16, 30 (*see also* mimesis); innovation among, 265 (*see also* botánicas); invocations of, 15; as lawyers and judges, 236, 237, 240–241, 243, 245–248; legal advice by, 227, 228–229; limited liability of, 137–138, 171; mainstream, 11, 14–15, 25, 235; mission of, xv, 25, 110–111, 115, 118, 120, 128–130, 132 (*see also* spiritual; spiritual work); and modernity, 25; moral charter of, 212, 218–220, 226–228, 240, 248–249; and New Age, 22; as poets, 265; positive work of, xiv; prayers improvised by, 109–110, 189 fig. 6.4, 282n. 3; pride of, xi, xv, 30, 179; professional, 145, 204, 209; prosperity of, 116, 134, 162–163, 264; as protectors of the law, 238, 243; and Protestantism, 283n. 8; revelations and apparitions of, 29, 130–132, 184; revival of, *see* folklorization; sacrifice of, xii–xiii, xiv, 25, 110, 130, 132 (*see also* pruebas); as saints, 140; and Santería, *see* brujería, Santería; as saviors of tradition, 100, 267; and self-identity, *see* self-identity; specialization of, 138–139; Spiritist ethos of, 14, 218, 235; as spiritual consultants, *see* spiritual; as spiritual entrepreneurs, *see* spiritual entrepreneurs; as state agents, 14, 22, 25, 212–213, 214, 215–216, 217–219, 220–226, 225 fig. 7.2, 257; and technology, *see* technology; under commonwealth, *see* commonwealth; visions of, 142

Bruner, Edward M., and Barbara Kirshenblatt-Gimblett, 257

Buddha, 19, 20 fig. I.1; trabajos entrusted to, 157 fig. 5.6 (*see also* mimesis; trabajos), 225, 237

Cabrera, Lydia, 93, 175, 274n. 9, 282n. 4

Candomblé, 3, 279n. 20, 287–288n. 3

Canino, Marcelino, 281n. 9

Caridad del Cobre. *See* La Caridad del Cobre

Caro Costas, Aida R., 274n. 15

Carr, Raymond, 279n. 25

cartas (Spanish cards), reading, 77–78, 138, 145, 231, 252

Catholicism: anticlerical, ix, 57, 58, 59, 62, 275n. 20; antiecclesiastical, 48–53; and brujos, 52–53 (*see also* brujos); and civility, 16; and espiritistas, 52 (*see also* espiritistas); folk or popular, 50–51, 201 (*see also* vernacular religions); and mediums, 51–52; and santeros, x; and slavery, 275n. 22

Catholic mimesis. *See* mimesis

Catholic rule, 24; and Alfonso X, 36, 37; and attacks on brujería, 2; civil control of population during, 37–38, 42–43; control of devotions during, 43–45; control of ritual objects during, 45–47, 48–50; and edicts, 41–42; and ermitas (country chapels), 39; evangelization during, 40–41, 42, 275n. 24, 275n. 27; hacendados during, 40–42; heresy during, *see* heresy; and Inquisition, *see* Inquisition; and medieval divination, 31, 36–37; miracles during, 47–48; and persistence of popular devotions, 50–53; prohibition of bomba dances and drumming, 41, 276n. 30, 276n. 31, 276n. 36; regulation of cofradías (fraternities) during, 44–45; and rezadoras and mantenedoras (female devotees in charge of liturgy and ritual objects), 40; and "royal patronage," 31, 37; sacred space of, 31–32, 36; sanctification of, 30–31, 37; slave restrictions during, 40–42, 275n. 25, 276n. 31; and superstition, 37 (*see also* superstition)

catolicismo popular (folk Catholicism), ix. *See also* Catholicism

causas (curses, misfortune), 55, 155–156, 277n. 1; born with, 153–154; lifting, 158–161 (*see also* muertos; ritual: exorcism); motives for, 136. *See also* espíritus de existencia; muertos

Chambers, Iain, 18

Changó (Shango), 86 fig. 3.2, 99, 173, 181, 282n. 14

charlatanism: and brujos, 22, 24, 96; folk or popular, 50–51 (*see also* vernacular religions); and heretics, 69; and media, 69; and medical establishment, 24, 69; and state-building, 69

Chinese deities, figurines of, 81, 83
círculos de oración (prayer circles), 174, 205, 275n. 21
clave (code), 145, 158–159, 233, 284n. 4
Clifford, James, 16
Club Amor y Ciencia, 65
cofradías (fraternities). *See* Catholic rule
coger muertos (grab the dead in trance). *See* muertos
collares (color beaded necklaces), 88, 267
Coll y Toste, Cayetano, 33, 34, 40, 41, 42, 43, 62, 275nn. 23, 25, 26, 276n. 31
Comaroff, Jean and John, 10, 12, 15, 261, 265–266
commodification: of ritual objects, 82–83, 84–88; spiritual, 24–25, 105; and transnationalism, 20, 24–25, 82–83, 84–87, 105; and unorthodoxy, of faith, 82
commonwealth, 25. *See also* brujería
Congos, 149, 176; attributes, 150
consultations. *See* spiritual work
Cornelius, Steven, 18, 179
Creole: culture, 281–282n. 11; as empowerment, 10; elites, 17–18; and slavery, 9–10
Creolization, historical roots of, 79
Cruz Monclova, Lidio, 57, 61, 62, 63, 278n. 11
Csordas, Thomas J., 283n. 14, 287n. 3
cuadros (spiritual power), xi, xiii, 142–149, 155, 284n. 1, 285n. 11; advanced or God-given, 147; against evil, 137, 169; beautiful, clean, clear, or precious, xi, 143, 144; definition of, 142; development of, 142–143, 144–145, 147, 147 fig. 5.2, 148 fig. 5.3, 172 (*see also* mediumship; pruebas; spiritual); enhancement, 144; open to the light, enlightened, or of light, 144–145; passing on, transferring, or sharing, 143, 143 fig. 5.1, 145–146, 147, 284n. 2; as protecciones, 149, 152; rewards of, 143–144; work and travel of, 147–149. *See also* spiritual
cultural nationalism, 97, 266, 267
curanderismo. See curanderos
curanderos, 271n. 5, 279n. 17, 289n. 30; attacked in media, 69–71; celebrated in media, 78; and heritage, 97; medical establishment attack on, 71–72; state programs attacks on, 69
Curbelo de Díaz, Irene, 25n. 20

Dávila, Arlene, 69, 97, 279n. 26
Dayan, Joan, 9
"dead, the." *See* muertos

de Certeau, Michel, 6
Departamento de Instrucción, 71
desenredar (disentangle), 158
Desmangles, Leslie G., 281n. 4
despojos (spiritual cleansings), 66, 190–191, 195 fig. 6.7, 196, 239, 257
De Todo, 103–104
Díaz Quiñónez, Arcadio, 64
Díaz Soler, Luis M., 39, 42, 45, 275n. 27
Dietz, James, 59
divination, x, xiii, xiv, 25, 31, 77, 138, 141, 144, 152, 155, 159, 166, 176, 179, 181, 183, 189, 191, 238, 284n. 6; medieval, 35–37, 43, 30; messages during, 125, 135, 154, 157, 158, 164, 165, 168–169, 170, 187–180, 194–195, 201–202, 252, 267, 283n. 7; performative aspects of, 216–217, 225–226, 231, 233–234, 249–251, 284n. 14, 287n. 4 (Chap. 7); Yoruba, 93. *See also* spiritual work
Don Gregorio, 85, 86 fig. 3.2
Douglas, Mary, 7, 284n. 23
Duany, Jorge, 97, 179, 214, 234, 272n. 3, 272–273n. 10, 273n. 15, 277n. 5, 282n. 15

Ekeko, 85, 92
Eleggua, 88, 176, 181, 286n. 18
El Indio, 20–21 fig. I.1, 85, 88, 160, 181, 256; Armando as, 180, 181; attributes of, 151; smoke for, 120, 121 fig. 4.2, 151, 173, 174 fig. 6.2. *See also* Indios
El Mundo, 32, 50, 69, 70–71, 72, 73–74, 182, 283n. 11
El Niño de Atocha, 19, 197, 202, 202 fig. 6.12; prayer to, 56, 237 fig. 8.1
El Reportero, 100–102, 182, 282n. 16
El Santo de Atocha. *See* El Niño de Atocha
El Vocero, 96, 102–103
Enlightenment. *See* brujería; superstition; witchcraft and magic
envidia (envy), 163, 268; and causas, 136, 161; intrigues of, 169–171; over involvement as sign of, 164, 285n. 14; pick up (recoger), 164; in speech, 162, 164; in thoughts, 162, 164–165, 285n. 15 (*see also* trabajos malos)
ermitas (country chapels), 39
Errington, Shelly, 207, 261
escapularios (scapulars): empowered, 237 fig. 8.1; as spiritual insurance policy, 189
esoteric schools. *See* Freemasonry; Scientific Spiritism; Spiritism
espiriteros (derogatory term for espiritistas), 72, 75, 280n. 30

espiritismo (Spiritism), xiii, 271n. 2, 271n. 4, 281n. 4; authentic, 105 (*see also* authenticity); as calling, *see* brujería, brujos; as euphemism, ix; true, *see* Scientific Spiritism; vs. black magic, 105. *See also* Spiritism

espiritismo folklórico (folkloric Spiritism). *See* Spiritism

espiritistas, 271n. 2, 271n. 6, 278n. 11; against animal sacrifice, 173–174, 267; and Catholicism, 51–53; and environmentalism, 174–176; godly gifts of, 128; mission of, 128; and New Age, 174 (*see also* New Age); and Santería, x, 153, 204 (*see also* Santería); and santeros, 285n. 5. *See also* Spiritism

espíritus atrasados (undeveloped spirits). *See* spirits

espíritus de existencia (evil spirits). *See* causas; muertos; spirits

espíritus de luz (spirits of light or enlightened spirits). *See* spirits

espíritus intranquilos. *See* spirits

Estado Libre Asociado (ELA). *See* commonwealth

Evans-Pritchard, E. E., 7–9

exorcism. *See* ritual

Fabian, Johannes, 261–262

facultades (spiritual powers). *See* spiritual

Favret-Saada, Jeanne, 7, 8

Featherstone, Mike, 16

Featherstone, Mike, Scott Lash, and Roland Robertson, 16, 207

Ferguson, James, and Akhil Gupta, 206, 261–262

Fernández Méndez, Eugenio, 32, 33, 37, 47, 48, 274n. 9, 274n. 12

Fernández Olmos, M., and L. Paravisini-Gebert, 10, 281n. 4

Ferré, Rosario, 281–282n. 11

fiesta espiritual (spiritual festivity), 54, 55, 116–117, 132, 134–135, 172, 178, 256–257; as investment, 137 (*see also* spiritual capital)

Firpi, José, 275n. 20

Flores, Juan, 17

fluídos (mediumistic powers), 115, 131, 217

folk Catholicism. *See* Catholicism

folklore, 24, 280n. 35; as negative, 78, 273n. 4, 279–280n. 27; as opposed to the market, 264; as superstition, 74–75, 77 (*see also* superstition)

folklorization: of brujería, 99, 182, 207, 260–261, 266–267; of Candomblé, 258; of curanderismo, 99; of espiritismo, 174–176; of Santería, 258–260; of vernacular religions, 182 (*see also* vernacular religions)

Foster, Robert J., 261

Foucault, Michel, 1–2

Frazer, Sir James George, 15, 208

Freedom of Worship Decree, 60

Freemasonry, Theosophy, and Rosicrucianism, 61, 277n. 4, 277n. 5, 278n. 11

fuente (lit. fountain, a spherical, transparent bowl filled with water), 135, 283n. 13; reading, 138, 145

Ganesh, 85, 86

Garrido, Pablo, 273n. 4

Garrison, Vivian, 272n. 4

Geschiere, Peter, 10, 274n. 9

Giddens, Anthony, 2, 12, 13, 236

Gitana. *See* La Gitana

Glazier, Stephen D., 16

globalization: academic and lay interest in, 16; and Americanization, 17–18; and Catholicism, 16–17, 23; and the circulation of ritual commodities and experts, 18; and consumerism, 16; as hybridization, 17–18; and identity politics, 78; and modernity, 23, and modernization, 17–18; and nationalism, 17, 23; and slavery, 16–17; and transnationalism, 18–19; vernacular, 17; waves of, 16–19

Gluckman, Max, 7

Gold, Ann, 281n. 2

Gort, Jerald, Hendrik Vroom, Rein Fernhout, and Anton Wessels, 280n. 35

Greenleaf, Richard, 277n. 4

Grosfoguel, Ramón, 68, 99, 211, 214, 272–273n. 10, 287n. 1

Grosfoguel, Ramón, Frances Negrón-Muntaner, and Chloe Georas, 17, 97

Guerra, Lillian, 64

Gupta, Akhil, and James Ferguson, 261–262

Habermas, Jürgen, 77

Hagedorn, Katherine J., 258–260, 287n. 2

Hajosy Benedetti, María Dolores, 174–176

Hall, Stuart, and Paul du Gay, 16

Handler, Richard, and Jocelyn Linnekin, 257, 261

Hannerz, Ulf, 78, 281n. 37

Hanson, Allan, 257

Harwood, Alan, 272n. 4
healing plants: miracles with, 198–199; power of, 199–200, 199 fig. 6.9, 200 fig. 6.10
heresy, 97; accusations of, at official levels, 34–35; among priests, 31, 34–35; and brujos, 22, 24, 30, 96 (*see also* brujos; brujería; Catholic rule; Inquisition); and malleability of accusations, 35–36; misrecognitions of, 32–33; social production of, 36
Hess, David J., 74, 278n. 10, 279n. 16
Hindu deities, 82, 83. *See also* Ganesh
Hinkson, John, 16
Hirschman, Albert O., 1, 11
Hobsbawm, Eric, and Terence Ranger, 260
Hubbard, L. Ron, 272n. 2
Huerga, Álvaro, 43, 44, 276n. 34

icons. *See* santos
imitation. *See* mimesis
Indio. *See* El Indio
Indios, 87 fig. 3.3, 149, 286n. 20; attributes of, 150. *See also* El Indio
Inquisition, 24, 30, 31–32, 273n. 3, 273n. 6; among public officials and priests, 34 (*see also* heresy); and auto de fé (act of faith or burning at the stake), 33; and confessions behementi, 34; discursive misrecognitions of, 32–33; and estampas (engravings related to heretics), 32; legacy of, xi; proceedings of, 32–34; and public flagellations, 34; and quemadero (place of burning), 32; and sambenitos (penitential garments), 32

jaibería (astuteness), 17. *See also* sociedad cimarrona
Japanese deities, figurines of, 81, 85
Jesus. *See* Papá Dios

Kardec, Allan, 24, 280n. 33, 281n. 3; books by, 54, 57, 58, 64; views of, on Spiritism, 58
Kelly, John D., and Martha Kaplan, 15
Kendall, Laurel, 261, 284n. 23
Knight, Franklin W., 39, 274n. 16, 274n. 17
Koss, Joan D., 271n. 6, 272n. 4, 285n. 18
Kwan Yin, 85

La Caridad del Cobre, 52, 54, 87 fig. 3.3; attributes of, 150–151; invocation of,

181; miracle of, 123–124, 277n. 40; new altar for, 117–118, 119, 162, 162 fig. 5.9; as Ochún, La Madama, and Cachita, 285n. 1; as patron saint, 55, 109, 110–111, 114, 179, 256, 277n. 40; shrine for, 162–163, 163 fig. 5.10; veneration of, 188; yearly fiesta for, 134–135 (*see also* fiesta espiritual)
Laderman, Carol, 206, 207, 262–263, 265, 284n. 23
Laguerre, Michel S., 18, 263
La Gitana (gypsy), 81; attributes of, 150; cuadro of, xiii, 149; summoning, 151
La Madama, 19, 85, 86 fig. 3.2, 149, 160, 256; attributes of, 150; cleansing spray of, 174 fig. 6.1, 178–179
La Mano Poderosa, 19, 21 fig. I.1
Lange, Yvonne, 275n. 20
Larner, Christina, 272n. 8, 272n. 9
Las Casas, Bartolomé de, 273n. 2
Law of Cause and Effect, 58, 212, 236, 238
Law of Love, 58, 143, 236, 238, 251, 253
Law of Reincarnation, 236
levantamiento de causas (lifting of curses). *See* causas; muertos
levantar (lift curses; i.e., improve) botánicas, 90
Lévi-Strauss, Claude, 3–4, 283n. 14
Lewis-Fernández, Roberto, 9, 284n. 22
Leyes de Puerto Rico Anotadas, 96
Lionnet, Françoise, 273n. 12
López Cantos, Ángel, 274n. 18
los muertos. See muertos

Macfarlane, Alan, 272n. 9
Machuca, Julio, 78, 277n. 2
Madama. *See* La Madama
magic, xv; African, 2; black, 105; as label, 24; nature of, 26, 264–265; and ritual mimesis, 15; technologies of, 15; vs. religion, 6–7. *See also* trabajos; trabajos malos; witchcraft and magic
Mair, Lucy, 284n. 23
Malinowski, Bronislaw, 7
Mano Poderosa. *See* La Mano Poderosa
maroon society: origins, 38–39; and vernacular religions, 17 (*see also* Catholic rule)
Marta la Dominadora, 19, 20–21 fig. I.1, 158, 227
Marwick, Max, 282n. 6, 283–284n. 19
Masquelier, Adeline, 10
matas (plants). *See* healing

santos (Catholic saints and their figurines), 65, 82, 275n. 20, 279n. 18; as folk art, 97, 281n. 8; personal relationship with, 20; as spiritual entities, 20, 149

Scarano, Francisco A., 59

Scientific Spiritism, 271n. 2, 278n. 15, 279n. 16, 279n. 21, 289n. 32; appeal of, among elites, 17; appeal of, among lower classes, 64; appeal of, among revolutionary liberals, 57–59, 61–64; antiecclesiastical nature, 58; anticlerical nature, 57–59, 62; attacks on African influences, 74–78; attacks on syncretism, 74–75 (*see also* syncretism); canon of, 105; Catholic church attacks on, 62–63; European heritage of, 98; and extraterrestrials, 58, 75; and independence, 59; and Kardec, *see* Kardec; messages in books of, 65; and modernization, 64; and nation-building, 59; and New Age, 98 (*see also* New Age); orthodox, 66; as a philosophy, 58; and reincarnation, *see* reincarnation; role of, 65; trance in, 136 (*see also* trance); unorthodox forms of, 65–66 (*see also* Spiritism); vs. popular Spiritism, 72–73, 74, 77–78, 279n. 22, 280n. 30; of the White Table, 18

Scientific Spiritism centers, x; attacks on popular Spiritism, 74–75, 77–78, 279–280n. 27, 280n. 30; classes and lectures at, 75, 113, 125–126; founding of, 62, 65, 278n. 13; government surveillance of, 63–64; moral and civic agenda, 64–65; redefinition of *veladas* at, 75. *See also* Scientific Spiritism

Scott, David, 267

secular ideology: and transcendental practices, 2; vs. *brujería*, 1

self-identity, 11–13; and blessings, 12 (*see also* blessings); and *brujería*, 11–13, 139–140, 269 (*see also* *brujería*); and *brujos*, 140, 268–269 (*see also* *brujos*); and novelty, 22 (*see also* *brujería*)

Silva Gotay, Samuel, 37, 60, 61, 62, 63, 67, 278n. 6, 278n. 9, 278n. 12, 278n. 14

Singer, Merrill, and Roberto García, 284n. 22

Smith, Anthony D., 273n. 13

sociedad cimarrona (maroon society). *See* maroon society

Spiritism: African elements in, 99, 173; and Americanization, 66; books, 56, 81; entities of, 20; "folkloric," 74–75; Kardecean,

see Scientific Spiritism; in media, 99–102, 285n. 7; *metafísica* classes or workshops of, 75, 88, 136, 205, 280n. 33, 281n. 3; and nationalism, 105; as opposed to rationality and modernity, 77; popular appeal of, 64; and Santería, 181, 279n. 20; scholarship, 8–9; "true" vs. "false," 72, 74, 77–78, 280n. 30; unorthodox, 9; and yuppies, 87–88. *See also* Scientific Spiritism

Spiritists. *See* *espiritistas*

spirits, 283n. 7; belief in, 13; "blessed" by, 2; communication of, 145; cosmopolitan, 84, 90–91 fig. 3.4; "to educate," 75–77; "enlightened" or of light, x, 55, 77, 78, 121; "evil," x, 153–154, 285n. 11; guardian, 135; speaking bad and clear, 136, 284n. 5; transactions with, 12–13; transnational, 202, 204; troubled, 169, 196–197; "undeveloped," 75; "wild," x, 75

spiritual: affinity, 176, 180; apprenticeship of author, xiii; assets, *see* spiritual capital; battle during trance, 127, 198; blessings, *see* blessings, *cuadros*; bread, xiii, 54, 55, 109; calling, 2; choices, 19, 102; clash, 126–127; cleansing, 78, 141, 172 (*see also* *despojos*); commodities, 20, 25, 85, 105; consultants and astrologers, 86, 180, 182, 215; dancing, 177, 181; debts, 124–125, 168, 236; development, 55, 126, 136, 146, 161, 163, 179, 281 (*see also* *cuadros*; mediumship; *pruebas*); diet, 103; drainage, 118–119, 132, 148–149; duels among *brujos*, 94, 179–180; eclecticism, 183–184; entities, 20, 83, 131, 149–153, 251 (*see also* *protecciones*); exorcism, 161, 197–198, 264; feasts, *see* *fiestas espirituales*; gifts, 51, 112, 120, 131, 132; godly duty, 2; healing, 2, 3, 43, 72, 101, 116, 141, 183, 198, 205, 206, 264 (*see also* *santiguos*; herbal healing); individualism, 14, 19; innovations, 80; justice, 167, 212, 238; laissez-faire, 2, 25, 104; laws, 14, 238, 243, 253; leaders, xiv; maelstrom, 13; mission, 129, 130; music, 54; power, 12, 13, 20, 22, 51–52, 98, 112, 116, 120, 127, 130, 131, 132, 133, 135, 136, 140, 142, 147, 154, 180, 188, 189, 202, 204, 205, 208, 212, 222, 223, 239, 240, 264, 268, 284n. 3 (*see also* blessings; *cuadros*); power of *botánicas*, 91; power of objects, 46; progress, 2; prosperity, 228; protection and royal patronage, 31; recipes, 56, 93, 182; responsibility, 14; success, 25; voyages, 148;

unorthodoxy, 14; weddings, 191, 192–193 fig. 6.6; well-being, 13, 219

spiritual capital, 25, 137, 153, 171, 265

spiritual entrepreneurs, 14, 22, 25, 102–104, 217, 235. *See also* brujos

spiritual entrepreneurship, 25, 26, 85, 102–105, 209, 266; of botánicas, 85, 91, 93, 265 (*see also* botánicas)

spiritualized materialism, 2, 3, 25, 105, 137, 139, 163, 269

spiritual pharmacies. *See* botánicas

spiritual work: beginnings, 29, 101, 130, 181, 205; documentation of, xiii; as euphemism, 77; experiential aspects of, 4; goals of, 146; innovations in, 205; liability limits of, 137; miraculous, 124; mission of, 109, 112; nationalist, 105; over the phone and by mail, 203–204; performance of, 216–217, 225–226, 229–230, 231–232, 233–234, 245, 247, 283n. 14, 287n. 4 (Chap. 7); positive, xiv; pruebas of, 113; rewards of, 221; risks of, xii; sacrifices of, 109, 118–119; shared by bruja and santero, 179; transnational nature of, 202–203, 205, types of, x. *See also* brujos; brujería; despojos; divination; espiritistas; ritual; trabajos; trance

Stanford, Ron, 285n. 3

Starrett, Gregory, 273n. 14

Stewart, Charles, 79, 80; and Rosalind Shaw, 79

Stoller, Paul, 4, 15

Suárez Rosado, Ángel, 97, 285n. 3

Sued Badillo, Jalil, and Ángel López Cantos, 275n. 22

superstition, 96, 97; as administrative rubric, 69, 72–73; battle against, 69; brujería as, xi, 273n. 6; medical establishment vs., 69; as negative label, 2; religion vs., 2; science vs., 71; secular ideology vs., 1. *See also* Catholic rule; Scientific Spiritism

Spyer, Patricia, 288n. 5

syncretism, xv, 18, 22, 32, 280n. 35; in botánicas, 83, 85; commodity-based transnational, 85; as "cross-fertilization," 18, 264; emergent aspects of, 180–181; and globalization, 79–80, 260–261 (*see also* brujería); historical roots of, 79; and nation-building, 79 (*see also* Scientific Spiritism); as negative, 74, 78, 264; politics of, 78–80; as positive, 78, 260–261. *See also* ritual; vernacular religions

Taíno legacy, 97, 100

Tambiah, Stanley J., 15, 272n. 1, 283n. 14

tape recording: and author, xiii–xiv; and ethnography, xiii–xiv, 29–30, 55; and fame, xiv

Taussig, Michael, xiii–xiv, 9, 10, 12, 13, 14–15, 16, 32, 261, 268–269

Taylor, Charles, 97, 257, 281n. 10

technology and brujos, 19, 21 fig. I.1. *See also* brujos

Thomas, Keith, 272n. 9, 273n. 5, 283n. 9

Toro-Sugrañes, José A., 83–84

Touraine, Alain, 272n. 1

trabajo espiritual (spiritual work). *See* spiritual work; trabajos

trabajos (healing, cleansing, and magic works), 273n. 1, 283–284n. 19; for atonement, 168–169, 168 fig. 5.12 (*see also* spirits: troubled); and daily news, 215; during elections, 215; effectiveness of, 286n. 22; expansion of, 207; failure of, 111, 171; fees for, 132, 143, 273n. 1; free of charge, 127, 128–129 fig. 4.7, 132, 230, 273n. 1; good, clean, or white, 138; mailing, 203; making of, 29, 138–139, 157, 226; material evidence of, 222; and mimesis (*see* mimesis); in the monte, 111, 181, 220, 220 fig. 7.1; and muertos, 153 (*see also* muertos); placed in the altar, 227–228; purpose of, 241; recipes for, 219, 222–223, 229; success of, 111; types, 156–157

trabajos buenos. See trabajos

trabajos malos (black magic), 158, 282n. 6, 286n. 22; caught in the middle of, 125; in the cemetery, 220 fig. 7.1, 253; empowerment via, 139, 237 fig. 8.1; envy as cause of, 136; failure of, 171; good motives for, 139; making of, 226–227, 241–242, 242 fig. 8.2, 244–245, 244 fig. 8.3, 252–253; and mimesis, *see* mimesis; and muertos, 153, 155, 166 (*see also* muertos); placed in altar, 253; with psalms, 187–188, 286n. 12; as retaliation, 138, 152, 167; revocation of, *see* revocar; success of, 115; types of, 156

trance: cleansing during, 151; "educate," 75–77; as learned, x; material protected during, 76, 76 fig. 2.3; messages during, 145, 146, 216–217, 224, 230, 231–232, 235, 247, 249–251, 252, 256–257, 287n3; and muertos, 280n. 34 (*see also* muertos); rulings emerge during, 236; signs of, 145–146;